Divine Wrath in Paul

Divine Wrath in Paul

An Exegetical Study

Gerald L. Stevens

PICKWICK *Publications* • Eugene, Oregon

DIVINE WRATH IN PAUL
An Exegetical Study

Copyright © 2020 Gerald L. Stevens. All rights reserved. Except for brief quotations in critical publications or reviews, no part of this book may be reproduced in any manner without prior written permission from the publisher. Write: Permissions, Wipf and Stock Publishers, 199 W. 8th Ave., Suite 3, Eugene, OR 97401.

Pickwick Publications
An Imprint of Wipf and Stock Publishers
199 W. 8th Ave., Suite 3
Eugene, OR 97401

www.wipfandstock.com

PAPERBACK ISBN: 978-1-7252-9094-5
HARDCOVER ISBN: 978-1-7252-9095-2
EBOOK ISBN: 978-1-7252-9096-9

Cataloguing-in-Publication data:

Names: Stevens, Gerald L.

Divine wrath in Paul : an exegetical study / Gerald L. Stevens.

Description: Eugene, OR: Pickwick Publications, 2020 | Includes bibliographical references.

Identifiers: ISBN 978-1-7252-9094-5 (paperback) | ISBN 978-1-7252-9095-2 (hardcover) | ISBN 978-1-7252-9096-9 (ebook)

Subjects: LCSH: Bible | N.T. | Pauline Epistles

CLASSIFICATION: BS2625.53 S75 2020 (PRINT) | BS2625.53 (EBOOK)

Manufactured in the U.S.A.   11/05/20

Dedicated to my students
past, present, and future

Credits and Permissions

I am indebted to the extensive tradition on Pauline studies, which I have been pursuing for quite some time. This volume is the result of a combination of research activity accomplished in two distinct stages, earlier and later, separated significantly in time. I tried to document from where ideas derived. At the same time, some ideas I came to independently. Most of this present publication came from my own original research. I do readily confess, however, that at times in my career, what I considered a novel thought of my own, I discovered only at some later point that somewhere, someone had said something similar without my awareness. I still want to regard those ideas as my own, because that is how they came to me.

As always, especially assisting the production of this volume has been my wife, Jean M. Stevens. She is extraordinary for her patience, support, and continual contributions. My career is not mine. All my accomplishments represent a team effort in ways not even countable.

All photographs and illustrations, unless indicated otherwise, are by Gerald L. Stevens, Copyright © 2020 Gerald L. Stevens, 3777 Mimosa Ct., New Orleans, Louisiana. All rights reserved.

Photographs by Jean M. Stevens, Copyright © 2020 Jean M. Stevens, 3777 Mimosa Court, New Orleans, Louisiana. Used by permission. All rights reserved.

Cartography images are generated and processed from Accordance, ver. 13.1.2, OakTree Software, Inc., 498 Palm Springs Drive, Suite 100, Altamonte, FL. Used by permission. All rights reserved.

Wipf and Stock kindly have given permission for the reuse of images, illustrations, and descriptions taken from the prior publications *Revelation: The Past and Future of John's Apocalypse* and *Acts: A New Vision of the People of God*.

Scripture quotations unless marked otherwise are the author's own translation.

Scripture quotations marked (NRSV) are taken from the *New Revised Standard Version* (NRSV) Copyright © 1989 by the Division of Christian Education of the National Council of the Churches of Christ in the USA.

Contents

List of Figures • x
Preface • xiii
Abbreviations • xxiii

1 Introduction • 1

2 Greco-Roman Background • 13

3 Jewish Background • 53

4 New Testament Background • 87

5 Pauline: 1 Thessalonians • 109

6 Pauline: Romans • 137

7 Pauline: Other Contexts • 195

8 Conclusion • 217

Bibliography • 225
Scripture Index • 241
Ancient Documents Index • 253
Modern Authors Index • 259
Subject Index • 261

Figures

Figure 1.1 Via Egnatia Milestone • 8
Figure 1.2 Augustus Cameo • 10
Figure 2.1 *Iliad* Sarcophagus • 14
Figure 2.2 Defeat of Hector • 14
Figure 2.3 Hector's Burial Preparation • 15
Figure 2.4 Hector's Wake • 15
Figure 2.5 Hector's Funeral Procession • 15
Figure 2.6 Ruins of Ancient Troy • 16
Figure 2.7 Walls of Ancient Troy • 16
Figure 2.8 Zeus: The Artemision Bronze • 17
Figure 2.9 Pergamum: The Great Altar of Zeus • 17
Figure 2.10 Gathering of the Gods • 18
Figure 2.11 Minerva Holding Owl • 19
Figure 2.12 Athena of Velletri • 20
Figure 2.13 Parthenon of Athens • 21
Figure 2.14 Gold Stater of Alexander • 21
Figure 2.15 Apollo Ritual Procession • 22
Figure 2.16 Helios Rising • 22
Figure 2.17 Apollo Playing Cithara • 23
Figure 2.18 Asklepios • 23
Figure 2.19 Asklepios and Hygieia • 23
Figure 2.20 Poseidon • 24
Figure 2.21 Poseidon and Demeter • 25
Figure 2.22 Alexander Coin • 25
Figure 2.23 Poseidon with Sea Horses • 26
Figure 2.24 Demeter and Persephone • 26

Figure	2.25	Syncretistic Religion • 27
Figure	2.26	Dionysius Mosaic • 28
Figure	2.27	Sarcophagus Theater Masks • 30
Figure	2.28	Theater Mask Copy • 31
Figure	2.29	Muse with Mask • 31
Figure	2.30	Ostia Antica Theater Road • 32
Figure	2.31	Pergamum "Z" House Mosaic • 32
Figure	2.32	Syracuse Theater • 33
Figure	2.33	Aspendos Theater • 33
Figure	2.34	Sepphoris Theater Model • 34
Figure	2.35	Comic Actor as Slave • 34
Figure	2.36	Euripides Relief • 35
Figure	2.37	Athenian Actor Ikairos • 35
Figure	2.38	Sarcophagus Relief: Medea Saga • 36
Figure	2.39	Actor Dressed as Papposilenus • 36
Figure	2.40	Raphael's School of Athens • 40
Figure	2.41	Socrates • 41
Figure	2.42	Epicurus • 41
Figure	2.43	Philosopher • 42
Figure	2.44	Ancient Corinth • 48
Figure	3.1	Ghiberti's Moses Receiving the Law • 56
Figure	3.2	Altar at Dan • 63
Figure	3.3	Panias • 63
Figure	3.4	Grotto of Pan • 64
Figure	3.5	Jerusalem Temple Model • 64
Figure	3.6	Jerusalem: Valley of Hinnom • 78
Figure	3.7	Qumran Scroll Replica • 80
Figure	4.1	Pieratti's St. John the Baptist • 91
Figure	4.2	Lead Oracle Tablet • 97
Figure	4.3	The Dragon Cycle • 100
Figure	4.4	Bowl Judgments—Perspectives • 100
Figure	5.1	Thessaloniki Inscription • 112
Figure	5.2	Galerius Arch • 112
Figure	5.3	Aerial of Thessalonica Roman Forum • 112
Figure	5.4	Thessalonica Forum Shops • 113
Figure	5.5	Thessalonica Forum Shops Detail • 113
Figure	5.6	Thessalonica Forum Odeon • 114
Figure	5.7	Bust of Livia • 114

Figure 5.8   Emperor Augustus • 114
Figure 5.9   Forum Deity • 115
Figure 5.10   Statue of Dionysus • 115
Figure 5.11   Forum Deity (Zeus) • 115
Figure 5.12   L. Titonus Primus • 116
Figure 5.13   Aretalogy Stele • 116
Figure 5.14   Aretalogy Stele Translation • 116
Figure 5.15   Bust of Honorable Citizen • 117
Figure 5.16   Thessalonica Patroness • 117
Figure 5.17   Relief Illustrating Social Hierarchy • 118
Figure 5.18   Hagios Demetrios • 118
Figure 5.19   Tombstone • 129
Figure 5.20   Praetorian Guard • 132
Figure 5.21   Roman Helmet • 133
Figure 6.1   "God Delivered Them Over" Triad • 145
Figure 6.2   Pauline Perspectives on Revealed Wrath • 167
Figure 6.3   Parallel Expressions in Rom 5:8–10 • 172
Figure 6.4   Roman Potter's Wheel • 176
Figure 6.5   Roman Pottery Drinking Cup • 177
Figure 6.6   Roman Pottery Storage Vessel • 177
Figure 6.7   Denarius of Tiberius • 185
Figure 6.8   Bust of Nero • 186
Figure 6.9   Roman Swords • 187
Figure 6.10   Nero Coin with Fasces Symbol • 187
Figure 7.1   Map of Ancient Colossae • 198
Figure 7.2   Colossae Tel • 198
Figure 7.3   Signorelli's Judgment Angels • 202
Figure 7.4   Ancient Olive Tree • 213

Preface

LIKE SO MANY ISSUES WITH PAUL, the language of divine wrath is not a popular subject in church or out of church. As with so many of the other issues surrounding his life and letters, Paul by the very force of his personality and words acts like a social lightning rod attracting the flash points of contemporary discussion. He may be appreciated and depreciated, but he is hard to ignore. He stands there, pointing to the heavens, just tempting the next bolt to ground itself on him.

Even trying to set Paul into his own context can attract the criticism of ignoring one's own. Studying Paul sometimes leaves one with the decided impression the whole matter is a lose, lose proposition. Paul is the posterchild for the truism that you can please some of the people some of the time, but you most certainly cannot please all the people all the time. Yet, I simply refuse to capitulate and walk away. I have been following in Paul's footsteps, both literarily and geographically for decades. I have walked the ancient Roman roads he traveled in Israel, Turkey, Cyprus, Crete, Rhodes, Macedonian, Greece, Malta, Sicily, and Italy and visited museums all over the world trying to get a sense of the ancient world in which he lived so that I have something to say in my contemporary context vivified by personal experience.

I have been fascinated with Paul's language of divine wrath for quite some time, mostly because I easily could see that Paul definitely had something to say on the subject, but I noticed how little was said by preachers or in Bible studies in my youth and young adult life. Curiosity killed this cat. When I arrived at seminary, I continued my study of Paul and suddenly found that I had a dissertation awaiting me on this very topic of the literary background and theological significance of the wrath of God in the Pauline epistles. So, I was off and running on a scholarly journey to explore this topic that rewarded me richly both then and in my later ministry.

In my teaching career, I have written numerous textbooks for the seminary classroom on subjects of great love, including Greek grammar, apocalyptic, including the book of Revelation, and, of course, the book of Acts, because Paul was the main character of the second half of the narrative. I even have facilitated numerous doctoral students in getting their own dissertations published. Yet, in all this publishing activity over a lifetime, I never once thought to publish my own original research into the area of the language of the wrath of God in Paul, which I now find quite strange. So, I wanted to try to remedy the lacuna in my publishing career. Nothing fancy is contained herein. This work is just normal historical-critical exegesis and close reading of the text.

I had a problem trying to decide which way to go in terms of audience. The original was purely for the scholar, but the information could be so helpful to the general reader too. Thus, I confess I tried to straddle the fence. For this reason, I have offered English translations for the original language material with transliterations of the Hebrew and Greek, as well as English for what originally was German. I hope in this way that non-scholars might be able to access and benefit from the study, which I think is as timely today as forty years ago. We still have a hard time getting a handle on Paul's distinctive take on his theology of divine wrath. I think a deeper appreciation for God's amazing grace would be one benefit.

Gerald L. Stevens
New Orleans, Louisiana
Yom Kippur 2020

Abbreviations

AB	Anchor Bible
ANET	*Ancient Near Eastern Texts*
ASOR	American Schools of Oriental Research
AV	Authorized Version
AYDB	*Anchor Yale Dictionary of the Bible*
BBC	Broadman Bible Commentary
BDAG	*A Greek-English Lexicon of the New Testament*
BECNT	Baker Exegetical Commentary on the New Testament
BET	Beiträge zur evangelischen Theologie
BNTC	Black's New Testament Commentaries (Harper's)
BS	Bibliotheca Sacra
CBQ	Catholic Biblical Quarterly
CBSC	Cambridge Bible for Schools and Colleges
CECNT	Critical and Exegetical Commentary on the New Testament
CGTC	Cambridge Greek Testament Commentary
CJ	The Classical Journal
CRINT	Compendia Rerum Iudaicarum ad Novum Testamentum
ET	Expository Times
IB	Interpreter's Bible
ICC	International Critical Commentary
IDB	*Interpreter's Dictionary of the Bible*
IVP NTC	InterVarsity Press New Testament Commentary
JBL	*Journal of Biblical Literature*
JBLMS	Journal of Biblical Literature Monograph Series
JJS	Journal of Jewish Studies
JQRMS	Jewish Quarterly Review Monograph Series
JSNT	Journal for the Study of the New Testament
JSNTSup	Journal for the Study of the New Testament Supplement

JSPSS	Journal for the Study of the Pseudepigrapha Supplement Series
JTC	Journal for Theology and the Church
JTS	Journal of Theological Studies
LBS	Library of Biblical Studies
LCL	Loeb Classical Library
MNTC	Moffatt New Testament Commentary
NA^{28}	*Novum Testamentum Graece*, Nestle-Aland, 28th ed.
NAC	New American Commentary
NASB	New American Standard Bible
NCB	New Clarendon Bible
NICNT	New International Commentary on the New Testament
NIGTC	New International Greek Testament Commentary
NIV	New International Version
NIDNTT	New International Dictionary of New Testament Theology
NRSV	New Revised Standard Version
NT	Novum Testamentum
NTA	*New Testament Apocrypha* (Hennecke, Schneemelcher)
NTL	New Testament Library
NTS	New Testament Studies
OGIS	*Orientis Graecae Inscriptiones Selectae*
OTL	Old Testament Library
PNTC	Pillar New Testament Commentary
SBLDS	Society of Biblical Literature Dissertation Series
SIG	*Sylloge Inscriptionum Graecarum*
SJT	Scottish Journal of Theology
SNTS	Society for New Testament Studies
SNTSMS	Society for New Testament Studies Monograph Series
Str-B	Hermann Strack and Paul Billerbeck, *Kommentar*
StudBib	Studia Biblica
TBC	Torch Bible Commentaries
TDNT	Theological Dictionary of the New Testament
TDOT	Theological Dictionary of the Old Testament
TNTC	Tyndale New Testament Commentary
TS	Theological Studies
UBS^{5}	*The Greek New Testament*, United Bible Societies, 5th ed.
USQR	Union Seminary Quarterly Review
WBC	Word Biblical Commentary
WGRWSS	Writings from the Greco-Roman World Supplement Series
WTJ	Westminster Theological Journal

SCRIPTURE

Old Testament

Gen	Genesis	Song	Song of Solomon
Exod	Exodus	Isa	Isaiah
Lev	Leviticus	Jer	Jeremiah
Num	Numbers	Lam	Lamentations
Deut	Deuteronomy	Ezek	Ezekiel
Josh	Joshua	Dan	Daniel
Judg	Judges	Hos	Hosea
Ruth	Ruth	Joel	Joel
1–2 Sam	1–2 Samuel	Amos	Amos
1–2 Kgs	1–2 Kings	Obad	Obadiah
1–2 Chr	1–2 Chronicles	Jonah	Jonah
Ezra	Ezra	Mic	Micah
Neh	Nehemiah	Nah	Nahum
Esth	Esther	Hab	Habakkuk
Job	Job	Zeph	Zephaniah
Ps (*pl.* Pss)	Psalm (Psalms)	Hag	Haggai
Prov	Proverbs	Zech	Zechariah
Eccl	Ecclesiastes	Mal	Malachi

New Testament

Matt	Matthew	1–2 Thess	1–2 Thessalonians
Mark	Mark	1–2 Tim	1–2 Timothy
Luke	Luke	Titus	Titus
John	John	Phlm	Philemon
Acts	Acts	Heb	Hebrews
Rom	Romans	Jas	James
1–2 Cor	1–2 Corinthians	1–2 Pet	1–2 Peter
Gal	Galatians	1–2–3 John	1–2–3 John
Eph	Ephesians	Jude	Jude
Phil	Philippians	Rev	Revelation
Col	Colossians		

Apocrypha

Tob	Tobit

Jdt	Judith
Wis	Wisdom of Solomon
Sir	Sirach (Ecclesiasticus)
Bar	Baruch
1–2 Macc	1–2 Maccabees
1 Esd	1 Esdras
Pr Man	Prayer of Manasseh
3 Macc	3 Maccabees
2 Esd	2 Esdras
4 Macc	4 Maccabees

PSEUDEPIGRAPHA

Gk. Apoc. Ezra	Greek Apocalypse of Ezra
Apoc. Mos.	Apocalypse of Moses
As. Mos.	Assumption of Moses
2 Bar.	2 Baruch (Syriac Apocalypse)
1 En.	1 Enoch (Ethiopic Apocalypse)
2 En.	2 Enoch (Slavonic Apocalypse)
4 Ezra	4 Ezra (= 2 Esdras)
LAE	Life of Adam and Eve
Let. Aris.	Letter of Aristeas
Pss. Sol.	Psalms of Solomon
Sib. Or.	Sibylline Oracles
T. Benj.	Testament of Benjamin
T. Levi	Testament of Levi
T. Naph.	Testament of Naphtali
T. Reu.	Testament of Reuben
Jub.	Jubilees

OTHER ANCIENT SOURCES

Aeschylus

Ag.	*Agamemnon*
Prom.	*Prometheus vinctus*

Aristotle

Eth. nic. *Ethica nicomachea (Nicomechean Ethics)*
Rhet. *Rhetorica (Rhetoric)*

Aurelius Victor

Caes. *De Caearibus (The Caesars)*

Cassius Dio

Hist. *Historia Romana (Roman History)*

Chrysippus

Min. Frag. *Minor Fragments*

Cicero

Mur. *Pro Murena*
Nat. d. *De natura deorum (On the Nature of the Gods)*
Off. *De officiis (On Duties)*
Tusc. *Tusculanae disputationes (Tusculan Disputations)*

Dead Sea Scrolls (Gaster)

ET   Epochs of Time
Ex   Exhortation (Weal and Woe)
H   The Book of Hymns
HabC Habakkuk Commentary
HosC Hosea Commentary
L   Lamentation for Zion
LJ   Last Jubilee (Melchizedek Texts)
M   Manual of Discipline
PI   Prayer for Intercession
RB   The Rout of Belial
W   The War of the Sons of Light and the Sons of Darkness
Z   The Zadokite Document

DEMOSTHENES

Chers.	De Chersoneso (On the Chersonese)
Fals. leg.	De falsa legatione (False Embassy)
Halon.	De Halonesso (On the Halonnesus)
Meg.	Pro Megalopolitanis (For the Megalopolitans)
Mid.	In Midiam (Against Meidias)
1–3 Philip.	Philippica i–iii (1–3 Philippic)
Rhod. lib.	De Rhodiorum libertate (On the Liberty of the Rhodians)
Timocr.	In Timocratem (Against Timocrates)

DIO CHRYSOSTOM

1 Tars.	Tarsica Prior (First Tarsic Discourse, Or. 33)

DIOGENES LAERTIUS

Lives	Lives of Eminent Philosophers

EPICTETUS

Disc.	The Discourses
Frag.	Fragments

EPICURUS

Let. Men.	Letter to Menoeceus

EURIPIDES

Med.	Medea
Hipp.	Hippolytus
Bacch.	Bacchae (Bacchanals)

HESIOD

Op.	Opera et dies (Works and Days)

HOMER

Il.	Ilias (Iliad)
Od.	Odyssea (Odyssey)

Josephus

Ant.	*Jewish Antiquities*
Apion	*Against Apion*
J.W.	*The Jewish War*
Life	*The Life of Josephus*

Livy

Ab urbe cond.   *Ab urbe condita (History of Rome)*

Lucretius

Rer. n.   *De rerum natura (On the Nature of Things)*

Lycurgus

Ag. Leoc.   *Against Leocrates*

Marcus Aurelius

Com.   *The Communings with Himself (Meditations)*

Marcus Minucius Felix

Oct.   *Octavius*

Menander

Epitrep.	*Epitrepontes (The Arbitrants)*
Eun.	*Eunuchus (The Eunuch)*
Her.	*Heros (The Hero)*
Min. Frag.	*Minor Fragments*
Sam.	*Samia (The Girl from Samos)*

Pausanias

Descr.   *Graeciae descriptio (Description of Greece)*

Petronius

Satyr.   *Satyricon*

Philo

Abraham	*On the Life of Abraham*
Dreams 1, 2	*On Dreams 1, 2*
Heir	*Who Is the Heir?*
Moses 1, 2	*On the Life of Moses 1, 2*
Sacrifices	*On the Sacrifices of Cain and Abel*
Unchangeable	*That God Is Unchangeable*

Plato

Leg.	*Leges (Laws)*

Plutarch

Caes.	*Caesar*
Cic.	*Cicero*
Mor.	*Moralia (On Moral Virtue)*
Per.	*Pericles*

Polybius

Hist.	*Histories*

Seneca

Ep.	*Epistulae morales ad Lucilim (Moral Epistles to Lucilius)*

Sophocles

Aj.	*Ajax*
Ant.	*Antigone*
Oed. tyr.	*Oedipus tyrannus (Oedipus the King)*

Suetonius

Aug.	*Divus Augustus*
Claud.	*Divus Claudius*
Galb.	*Galba*

Tacitus

Ann.	Annales (The Annals of Tacitus)
Hist.	Historiae (The Histories of Tacitus)

Talmud (Babylonian)

'Abod. Zar.	'Abodah Zarah (Avodah Zarah)
Ned.	Nedarim
Šabb.	Šabbat (Shabbat)
Sanh.	Sanhedrin
Zebaḥ.	Zebaḥim (Zevahim)

Thucydides

War	History of the Peloponnesian War

Virgil (Vergil)

Aen.	Aeneid

MUSEUMS

AM	Acropolis Museum, Athens, Greece
AMA	Aphrodisias Müzesi, Aphrodisias, Turkey
AMAC	Archeological Museum of Ancient Corinth, Greece
BMB	Bergama Müzesi, Bergama, Turkey
BML	British Museum, London, England
EMS	Ephesos Müzesi, Selçuk, Turkey
HMM	History Museum of Mobile, Alabama
HAMC	Heraklion Archeological Museum of Crete
IAM	Istanbul Archeoloji Müzerleri, Istanbul, Turkey
IHAM	Izmir History and Art Museum, Turkey
IMJ	Israel Museum, Jerusalem, Israel
LP	The Louvre, Paris, France
NAMA	National Archeological Museum of Athens, Greece
NMB	National Museum of Bargello, Florence, Italy
NNAM	Naples National Archeological Museum, Italy
OAM	Ostia Antica Museum, Ostia Antica, Italy
PMB	Pergamon Museum, Berlin, Germany

QNPM	Qumran National Park Museum, Qumran, Israel
TAM	Thessaloniki Archeological Museum, Greece

1

Introduction

The Language of Divine Wrath

Paul begins his discussion of the good news in Romans with bad news of the wrath of God (1:18–32). To many this introduction has seemed rather out of place. The gospel is about love, and wrath has no place in that conversation would be the immediate assertion. However, whether love and wrath are mutually incompatible is a matter of definitions and philosophical presumptions. We might ignore him, but Paul speaks of divine wrath more than any other New Testament writer.

BASIC PROBLEM

The question before us is, how do we understand Paul's language of divine wrath exegetically? Five terms for "wrath" or "anger" are used in ancient Greek literature. The minor players were κότος, *kotos*, μῆνις, *mēnis*, and χόλος, *cholos*. Θυμός, *thumos*, and ὀργή, *orgē* were the two major players. Of these two, *thumos* is the oldest term, so gets the lion's share of usage. The New Testament uses *thumos* and *orgē* almost exclusively. Paul provides most occurrences of *orgē*.[1]

Understanding Paul, therefore, requires understanding how he defined and applied the terms. Coming to terms with the language of divine wrath is imperative for understanding the gospel Paul preached.

---

[1] The one exception for the minor players is a cognate verb of χόλος (*cholos*) in John 7:23. Half of all occurrences of the primary terms are in Paul (26/52). Almost two-thirds of occurrences of ὀργή (*orgē*) are in Paul (21/34). Paul clearly dominates New Testament usage.

The present study intends to assist in that journey of understanding. The study of Paul can be delimited to those contexts where divine wrath is explicit or implicit.[2]

C. H. Dodd's approach to God's wrath in his 1932 commentary on Romans in the Moffatt series defined for generations the basic idea that divine wrath was impersonal. Wrath language in Paul was simply a way of describing this impersonal nexus of sin and retribution. The advantage of Dodd's approach was to insulate any concept of human emotion from the character of God. The character of God was freed from any reproach of unjust anger or fit of emotion later regretted, as with humans. Uncontrolled emotion was unbecoming to divinity, so, beneath God. As we shall see, this concept of the gods as like humans in their anger with uncontrolled fits of capricious rage was the classic Homeric understanding of the gods in Greek mythology. Ancient Greek philosophers already were working on the problem before Dodd, but they were laboring with similar presuppositions about the necessary immutability of divinity so that gods were not subject to emotion. The behavior and character of the gods could not be impugned with wrath.

The impact of Dodd can be seen in T. C. Smith's 1944 thesis, "The Meaning of Ὀργὴ Θεοῦ in the Pauline Epistles." Smith simply reiterated Dodd's impersonal nexus of sin and retribution.[3] Smith also followed closely the philosophical treatment of the idea of the holy of Rudolf Otto.[4] Smith's exegetical treatment also was lacking. For example, Smith declared that in 1 Thess 1:10, the "coming wrath" was "not to be viewed as eschatological but rather as a present progressive reality."[5] That is, Paul is describing how Jesus rescues sinners out of their present darkness into the light. This interpretation is highly unlikely for ignoring entirely the apocalyptic tenor of the context. The coming wrath of which Paul warned the Thessalonians in context is eschatological. This focus is clear in both letters Paul wrote to these new

---

[2] Matt 3:7 (Luke 3:7); 18:34; 22:7 (Luke 14:21); Mark 1:41 (variant); 3:5; Luke 21:23; John 3:36; Rom 1:18; 2:5 (twice); 2:8 (twice); 3:5; 4:15; 5:9; 9:22 (twice); 12:19; 13:4, 5; Eph 2:3; 5:6 (Col 3:6); 1 Thess 1:10; 2:16; 5:9; Heb 3:11; 4:3; Rev 6:16, 17; 11:18; 14:10 (twice); 14:19; 15:1, 7; 16:1, 19 (twice); 19:15 (twice).

[3] Cf. Smith, 87, 101.

[4] In terms of the mystery and mystic of the numinous in the human mind, Otto, *The Idea of the Holy*. Cf. Smith, 21–22.

[5] Smith, 90.

believers. Aus demonstrated clearly this overall eschatological focus of Paul in the Thessalonian material.[6]

Even today Dodd's approach continues to have its impact. This impact is subtle, but is reflected in the casual dismissal of any idea of a God of wrath heard often in sermons, Bible lessons, YouTube videos, and social media posts. At least the solution is not that of the ancient philosophers that God is immutable. Popular philosophy seems much more amenable to the idea that God can express love. So, the message of 1 John 4:8 is to be heard in these theological constructs, but that of Rom 1:18 is to be ignored. Popular messages thus invent their own canon within the canon to meet the political correctness of theological presumptions. One also has the tendency in some Pauline scholarship to misconstrue Romans 1–4 as a picture of a forensically retributive judge, coercive in relationship, prone to violence when not happy, which, in a massive monograph on Paul, Campbell criticized harshly.[7]

By focusing in on the key words, a basic historical-critical investigation illuminates the New Testament usage. Passages of explicit and implicit divine wrath in the New Testament contextualize the study of Paul's use of the language of divine wrath. The literary background for this study is in Greek and Roman literature, Hebrew and Samaritan literature, and the general New Testament literature. While primary passages are those in which the terms for divine wrath are explicit, implicit contexts can complement the discussion.

BASIC ETYMOLOGY

Greek Literature

Five terms for "wrath" or "anger" are used in ancient Greek literature. The minor players were κότος, *kotos*, μῆνις, *mēnis*, and χόλος, *cholos*. Θυμός, *thumos*, and ὀργή, *orgē* were the two major players.

BDAG defined θυμός (*thumos*) sometimes as "passion" (e.g., Rev 14:8; 16:19) but much more frequently as "anger," "wrath," or "rage."[8] Büchsel said that all New Testament occurrences meant "wrath."[9] The

---

[6] Aus, "Comfort in Judgment."
[7] Campbell, *The Deliverance of God*.
[8] BDAG, s.v. "θυμός."
[9] Büchsel, "θυμός," *TDNT* 3:167.

turbulence of air or water, the shaking of the earth, and the riotous movement of animals or men could be described with the root θύω (*thuō*), and from the derivative sense "to well up," "to boil up," developed the meaning "to smoke," "to cause to go up in smoke," "to sacrifice."[10] For the root meaning, Thayer also listed "to rush along," "be in a heat," "breathe violently."[11] The term *thumos* acquired various meanings in Homer and the Greek tragedies, including those of impulse, spirit, anger, sensibility, and disposition. This multiplicity of meaning was lost in the prose writers for whom *thumos* was reduced to mean spirit, anger, rage, or agitation.[12] Various passages in the Septuagint, Philo, and Josephus show that the sense of the inner passion of anger, rage, or agitation became the common use of *thumos*.

The other primary term, ὀργή (*orgē*), developed after *thumos*.[13] Definitions of *orgē* include "anger," "indignation," or "wrath."[14] Also, the root may be related to ὀργάω (*orgaō*), which means "to teem," "to swell lavishly with sap and vigor," "thrusting and upsurging."[15] Less probable is ὀρέγω (*oregō*), which means "upward striving," "impulse," "prominent desire."[16] Impulsive human disposition actively breaking forth was an evident derivative sense of *orgē*. The inner passion of *thumos* became the outward expression of *orgē*. Such a semantic distinction is a fine line of comparison and should not be pressed, due to later usage. Later in the history of the two terms, their meanings began to coalesce so that they regularly could be used almost synonymously. However, if a given writer differentiated between the two terms, generally *thumos* was contextualized as the surge of emotion momentarily experienced and immediately expressed, whereas *orgē* was that anger representing an abiding disposition of mind.[17]

[10] Ibid.

[11] Thayer, *Lexicon*, 293.

[12] Büchsel, "θυμός," *TDNT* 3:167.

[13] First occurring in Hesiod, *Op.* 302.

[14] BDAG, s.v. "ὀργή."

[15] The Sanskrit root, ūrg, ūrga, ūrgas ("fullness of sap. power, energy") has been proposed often. See Curtius, *Principles of Greek Etymology*, 1:216; Wharton, *Etymological Lexicon*, 96; Kleinknecht, *TDNT*, s.v. "ὀργή," 5:383, n1; Hofmann, *Etymologisches Worterbuch des Griechischen*, 236.

[16] Donaldson, *The New Cratylus*, 718–22.

[17] Diogenes Laertius, *Lives* 7.114. Cf. Trench, *Synonyms*, 130–34.

Other terms for wrath include κότος, *kotos*, μῆνις, *mēnis*, and χόλος, *cholos*. Frequent in classical poetry, these Homeric terms do not occur in the New Testament, with the singular exception of a cognate verb in John 7:23. They are not considered in this etymological review.

Hebrew Terms

In Hebrew, a wealth of terms for wrath illustrates a broad diversification of the language. Only a representative presentation of the linguistic usage will be offered. Some basic terms follow:[18]

- אף (*'p*), meaning "nostril," "nose," "face," "anger," from אנף (*'np*), "to be angry," translated "anger" (Exod 32:12); verb always used of God

- חמה (*ḥmh*), meaning "heat," "rage," from יחם (*yḥm*), "to be hot," "to conceive" (piel), translated "wrath" (Isa 27:4)

- קצף, (*qṣp*), meaning "wrath," from קצף (*qṣp*), "to be wroth," translated "wrath" (Isa 60:10)

- חרון (*ḥrwn*), meaning "(burning of) anger," from חרה (*ḥrh*) "to burn," "to be kindled"; noun used always of God's anger, mostly with אף (*'p*); חרון אף (*ḥrwn 'p*) in thirty-three of thirty-nine occurrences

- עברה (*'brh*), meaning "overflow," arrogance," "fury," from עבר (*'br*), "to be arrogant," "to infuriate oneself" (hithpael only), translated "wrath" (Zeph 1:18)

- זעם (*z'm*), meaning "indignation," from זעם (*z'm*), "to be indignant"; used mainly for divine wrath; cf. Isa 26:20; Dan 8:19; 11:36

- זעף (*z'p*), meaning "storming," "raging, "rage," from זעף (*z'p*), "to be enraged"; postexilic, except for Gen 40:6

- כעס (*k's*), meaning "vexation," "anger," from כעס (*k's*), "to be vexed," "to be angry" (1 Kgs 15:30)

- רגז (*rgz*), meaning "agitation," "excitement," "raging," from רגז (*rgz*), "to be agitated," "to quiver," "to quake," "to be excited," "to be perturbed"; the noun for God's wrath only in Hab 3:2

---

[18] Cf. Brown, Driver, Briggs, *A Hebrew and English Lexicon*. Also, Bergman and Johnson, *TDOT*, s.v. "אנף," 1:348–60. Details pertinent to New Testament usage are in Grether and Fichtner, *TDNT* s.v. "ὀργή," 5:392–94.

The language of wrath in Hebrew is particularly theological.[19] The words חרון (ḥrwn), חרון אף (ḥrwn 'p), זעם (z'm), and the verb אנף ('np) were used regularly with God; קצף (qṣp) and עברה ('brh) were used a majority of times with God. When terms for wrath were united linguistically, they referred exclusively to God's wrath. Combinations served to strengthen the thought and to emphasize the dual aspects of power and dissimilarity—the awesome, irresistible power of God's wrath and its great dissimilarity to the anger of man.[20] The covenant name Yahweh (יהוה, yhwh) regularly was joined to nouns of wrath; thus, divine wrath and the covenant relationship were associated closely.[21]

The language of divine wrath in Hebrew is graphic. The language could refer to an emotion and to an act. God's wrath was a fire that was kindled, so that fire and smoke came forth from his nostrils, and even his breath was as a stream of brimstone. God's wrath was a storm that brewed until the anger broke forth in devastating fury. God's wrath was a liquid filling the cup of wrath, to be drunk to the very dregs of the bottom, or to be poured out, mainly upon Israel, but also upon the heathen. The "winepress of wrath" was another vivid picture of judgment. Conflation of images occurred when God's wrath was said to be a fire pouring forth.[22]

Postexilic literature reflects the proclivity of writers to disassociate God from expressions of wrath. This interpretation is based upon the linguistic evidence of the nouns of wrath in placed in absolute constructions.[23] This effect may be the result of the impact of Hellenistic philosophy on postexilic Jewish thought. Another example of dissociation of wrath from the character of God is a modification made by

---

[19] Of 455 times, nouns of wrath are used 375 times for the wrath of God (Fichtner, *TDNT* s.v. "ὀργή," 5:397, n92). Wrath of another deity is possible in 2 Kgs 3:27, unique in Hebrew Scripture if so. Fichtner (*TDNT* s.v. "ὀργή," 5:396, n101) said no term for divine wrath occurs in Genesis. However, note חרה (ḥrh) in Gen 18:30, 32.

[20] Cf. Ps 59:11-13; 76:7; 90:11; Nah 1:6.

[21] Mainly, אף ('p), חמה (ḥmh), עברה ('brh), and קצף (qṣp), with exceptions in Ps 78:31; Num 22:22; Ezra 10:14; Job 21:20.

[22] Cf. Nah 1:6; Lam 2:4. For the above paragraph, cf. Num 11:10; Deut 6:15; Josh 7:1; 1 Sam 28:18; 2 Sam 6:7; 22:8-9; 2 Kgs 13:3; 1 Chr 13:10; 2 Chr 36:16; Job 20:23; 21:20; 42:7; Ps 106:40; 89:46; 69:24; 78:49; Isa 5:25; 30:27-30, 33; 50:11; 51:17, 22; 63:1-6; Jer 10:25; 15:14; 23:19-20; 25:15; 30:23-24; Ezek 5:13; 6:12; 7:8; 14:19; 20:8; Hos 5:10; 8:5; 11:9.

[23] Cf. Fichtner, *TDNT* s.v. "ὀργή," 5:396.

the Chronicler. The source of David's temptation no longer was the wrath of Yahweh, but the Satan.[24]

New Testament Terms

New Testament writers used ὀργή, *orgē*, and θυμός, *thumos*, rather than κότος, *kotos*, μῆνις, *mēnis*, and χόλος, *cholos* to refer to the wrath of God. With the exception of Rom 2:8, use of *thumos* for divine wrath in the New Testament is exclusive to Revelation. The term is translated "wrath" or "anger," except when coordinated with *orgē*[25] and translated "fierceness," "fury," "fierce," or "passion." This doubling of synonyms was an obvious strengthening of the thought for dramatic emphasis.

The use of *orgē* for divine wrath in the New Testament is predominantly Pauline. Major New Testament categories are as follows:

- with the qualifying genitive "of God" (τοῦ θεοῦ, *tou theou*)[26]
- when "of God" is unexpressed but implicit[27]
- with the qualifying genitive "of the Lamb" (τοῦ ἀρνίου, *tou arniou*)[28]
- when "of the Lamb" is unexpressed but implicit[29]
- in reference to Jesus[30]

The cognate verb ὀργίζομαι may have been used for divine wrath three times in the New Testament. In two parables, divine wrath possibly can be understood.[31] The only other possible occurrence of the verb in relation to divine wrath is in a variant reading in the story of the Cleansing of the Leper in Mark.[32]

---

[24] 2 Sam 24:1; 1 Chr 21:1.

[25] Rev 16:19; 19:15.

[26] John 3:36; Rom 1:18; Eph 5:6; Col 3:6; Rev 14:10; 16:19; 19:15.

[27] Matt 3:7; Luke 3:7; 21:23; Rom 2:5 (2x), 8; 3:5; 4:15; 5:9; 9:22 (2x); 12:19; 13:4, 5; Eph 2:3; 1 Thess 1:10; 2:16; 5:9; Heb 3:11; 4:3; Rev 11:18.

[28] Rev 6:16.

[29] Rev 6:17 (and the variant).

[30] Mark 3:5.

[31] The Unmerciful Servant (Matt 18:23-34) and The Marriage Feast (Matt 22:1-14; cf. Luke 14:16-24).

[32] Mark 1:40–45 (1:41 in the variant).

Historical Settings

Because of the importance of material in both Thessalonians and Romans for this study on the wrath of God, brief comments on the historical settings for these two letters in particular will be helpful. The focus is upon the influence of the historical context upon the language of divine wrath.

Thessalonians

Paul arrived in Thessalonica by traveling the famous Via Egnatia Roman road from Philippi. His missionary activity in Macedonia met stiff opposition. He suffered and was mistreated in Philippi and faced hostility in Thessalonica. He instructed his converts in a typical Pauline parenesis including Jewish eschatological traditions. Paul's ministry was interrupted prematurely when he was forced out of the city. Paul sent Timothy back to Thessalonica to discover how the young church was bearing up under persecution. Timothy brought good news of an enduring faith (1 Thess 3:1–7). Paul later wrote a letter (1 Thess) to indicate his earnest desire to return to Thessalonica (2:17–18; 3:11), to defend his behavior and missionary activity (2:3–12), to give exhortation on believers' conduct, and to clear up confusion over eschatological teachings. The first letter probably was written in early spring of AD 50 at the beginning of Paul's stay in Corinth.[33] A second letter was necessary.

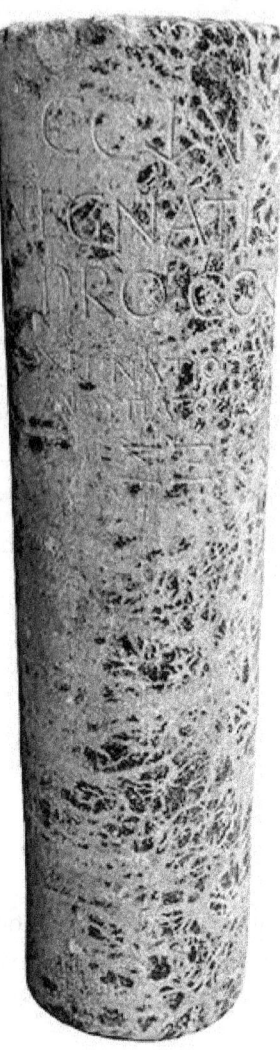

FIGURE 1.1. Via Egnatia Milestone. Bilingual inscription mentions the governor of Macedonia, Gnaius Egnatius, responsible for contruction of the road. The CCLX measures 260 miles from Dyrrachium on the Adriatic coast to the Gallikos River of the stone find, 150–100 BC (TAM).

[33] On the complexity of Pauline chronology, cf. Jewett, *A Chronology of Paul's Life*.

Paul's eschatological parenesis at Thessalonica was preoccupied with the parousia of Jesus. In his brief letter of 1 Thessalonians, Paul six times either referred or alluded to the coming of Jesus.[34] Paul was certain he would live to see that parousia. In 4:15 he says, "We who are alive and remain." The emphatic position of "we" underscores Paul's attitude.[35] Paul was eager for the parousia, one reason being a desire for the public vindication of his work among the Gentiles (2:19-20). The imminence of the parousia governed Paul's teaching at Thessalonica and provided the occasion for misunderstanding after his abrupt departure.

Another feature of the eschatological language in 1 Thessalonians is the presence of technical terminology.[36] Such a list of eschatological terms in Thessalonians could be lengthened.[37] Thus, the use of the term *orgē*, besides having an eschatological endowment from previous use in the Hebrew Scripture and the intertestamental period, also is found woven into the Pauline complex of eschatological ideas. In 1 Thessalonians, the technical terms of the Pauline parenesis probably reflect aspects of the mission work itself and the preaching of the gospel at Thessalonica.

[34] 1 Thess 1:10; 2:19; 3:13; 4:15; 5:2, 23. Cf. Davies, "Genesis of Belief in an Imminent Parousia," 104-07.

[35] Cf. Lake, *Earlier Epistles of St. Paul,* 92-93. For a summary of theories of evolution of eschatological ideas in Pauline thought, cf. Sanders, *Paul and Palestinian Judaism,* 432, n9. On the coherence of Paul's future expectations, cf. Davies, *Paul and Rabbinic Judaism,* 311-18; Sanders, *Paul and Palestinian Judaism,* 447-48. Moule argued that Paul's use of eschatological terms was tailored to each individual occasion and varying need, so that one cannot outline a supposed "development" in Paul's eschatology, "The Influence of Circumstances on the Use of Eschatological Terms."

[36] E.g., "tribulation" in 1 Thess 1:6; cf. Strack and Billerbeck (Str-B), 2:274-77; Schilier, *TDNT,* s.v. "θλίβω," 3:139-48; Mattill, "The Way of Tribulation," 535-39. For "in Christ," cf. Bultmann, *Theology of the New Testament,* 1:311. Note the fixed content of "parousia" in 1 Thess 2:19; 3:13; 4:15; 5:23; as a technical term, cf. Deissmann, *Light from the Ancient East,* 369-73. On the use of "day of the Lord" and "the times and the seasons," cf. Jer 25:11; 36:10; Dan 9:24-27; 2 Esd 6:59; 2 Bar. 24:4. Pseudepigraphal works will be referred to according to the scheme of Charles, except that 4 Ezra will be referred to as 2 Esdras. For "birth-throes" in 5:3, cf. Str-B 1:950 on the "woes of the messiah"; Mark 13:8; Matt 24:8; cf. Acts 2:24.

[37] Cf. "kingdom" and "glory" in 2:12 and "salvation" in 5:8-9. Peculiar to Paul is ὄλεθρος (*olethros*) in 5:3, which possesses a common setting with *orgē*; cf. Vos, *The Pauline Eschatology,* 262-63. This association will be discussed later in the section, "Eschatological Destruction" in chapter 7.

The element of divine wrath in Paul's understanding of the gospel was part of the larger context of divine judgment. Implicated in the preaching of the resurrection of Jesus is lordship, return, and a judgment that would issue in the final salvation of believers and the destruction of unbelievers (cf. Phil 3:18-21). The triad of death, resurrection, and return is apparent in 1 Thess 4:14: "For if we believe that Jesus died, and rose again, even so also God will bring with him." In Acts, judgment appears in missionary preaching as a datum of faith.[38] Paul's use of the language of the wrath of God a priori does not have to be considered incongruous with the early church traditions concerning judgment.[39]

Romans

At the time of the writing of Romans, Paul considered his mission to the East complete (15:23). Romans was a self-introduction to enlist Roman support for Paul's future missionary enterprise (15:24). The desire to have the support of Rome for the work in Spain necessitated a formal presentation to the church of the essence of the gospel he preached in his mission. The letter to the Romans was a deliberate theological formulation of the gospel Paul preached (1:16). While Romans does not have a one-to-one correspondence to Paul's missionary sermons, Romans does contain the condensate of

FIGURE 1.2. Augustus Cameo. This three-layered sardonyx cameo depicts Augustus wearing the Aegis (shield) of Minerva and a sword belt (20–14 BC). The gem-bedecked headband evokes the Greek laurel wreath of victory, and became iconic on later imperial coins (BML).

---

[38] E.g., Acts 10:42; 17:30-31. Cf. Dodd, *The Apostolic Preaching and Its Developments*.

[39] Cf. Moule, "The Judgment Theme in the Sacraments," 464–81. On the continuity between Paul's teaching and the early church traditions, see Schoeps, *Paul*, 62; Hunter, *Paul and His Predecessors*, 106.

Paul's thought about his apostleship when exposed to his own Jewish background. Paul's comments were motivated by the issue of Israel's eschatological destiny to lead the nations to the worship of God, allied with the impending visit to Jerusalem. In Romans, Paul demonstrated the legitimacy of his diaspora mission, not only by giving that mission theological foundation in the grace of God, but also by tying that mission to the eschatological salvation of Israel. Paul is aware his audience is more Roman in cultural context than the Jewish pigeonhole category of "gentile" allows, so he will use *ethnē* as much with the meaning of "nations" as "gentiles" to counter Roman imperial propaganda about Rome's right to rule the nations of the world. This use will conform to his understanding of his fulfillment of the vision of Isaiah about Israel and the nations in Isa 11:10 (Rom 15:12).

In his introduction to his letter to the Romans, Paul revealed that he was convicted of a consecration to the gospel and of a call to apostleship (1:5). The gospel was about Jesus Christ "through whom we have received grace." The apostleship was "to bring about the obedience of faith among all the nations."[40] This divine grace and the obedience of faith are two key elements in Paul's presentation in Romans. In the integration of these two key elements, Paul made the gospel universal. First, Paul showed human guilt to be axiomatic. Human guilt fundamentally was disobedience to God. Second, Paul showed how the grace of God was extended to all the guilty ones through the obedience of faith unto righteousness, Jesus Christ.[41] Paul grounded the gospel within the will of God by using the Abrahamic traditions he inherited as a Jew. The promise to Abraham was for Paul the basis for interpreting the grace revealed in Jesus Christ.[42]

---

[40] Rejecting *ethnē* here as "among all the gentiles." The choice between "gentiles" or "nations" actually is significant. That Paul means "nations" in Rom 1:5 easily is seen by Paul's later concluding quote of Isa 11:10 in Rom 15:12. In the LXX, Isa 11:10 has two occurrences of *ethnē*, both translated "nations" in most English translations. Isaiah's vision is for the nations. Paul is not focused on gentiles as much as on Israel's eschatological destiny for the nations, inspired by Isaiah's vision. "Gentile" comes into play when circumcision is explicit. Circumcision is unmentioned in all of Romans 1. Translating Rom 1:5 as "among all the gentiles" misses this prophecy fulfillment motif driving Paul from Isaiah. Nations drive Paul's mission, just as they did Augustus's Rome.

[41] Rom 5:15–19.

[42] On the promise to Abraham motif in Pauline thought, cf. Barrett, *From First Adam to Last*, 34–39; Käsemann, "The Faith of Abraham in Romans 4," 79–101; Sten-

The salvation history stemming from the promise to Abraham had its sharpest focus in God's dealings with Israel, the sons of Abraham in the flesh. Romans 9–11 represents the climax of Paul's discussion, as the high emotive content of this section of the letter makes transparent. In this section, Paul discussed the fullness of the meaning of the promise to Abraham. The analytical basis for an outline of Romans is the summary statement in 11:32 that occurs just before Paul's concluding doxology. Three phrases in this statement functionally provide the three parts of the discussion of Romans 1–11. The first phrase is, "For God has shut up all in disobedience," which is the development of Romans 1–4. The second phrase is, "in order that he might show mercy," which is the development of Romans 5–8. The last phrase is "to all," which is the development of Romans 9–11.

dahl, *Paul among Jews and Gentile*, 1–4. Cf. Munck, *Paul and the Salvation of Mankind*, 42–49; VanHorn, "Arguing from Abraham."

2

Greco-Roman Background

Divine Wrath in Athens and Rome

ANCIENT WRITERS MOST CERTAINLY had a lot to say about divine wrath. The wrath of the gods universally was understood to be constitutive of their lives, fortunes, fates, and destinies. We examine this background literature concerning divine wrath to discover ideas that are expressed about the nature of that wrath. This material provides comparisons and contrasts helpful for understanding Pauline ideas.

GREEK LITERATURE

Classical Period

A study of divine wrath in Greek literature is incomplete without briefly considering the alternate terms κότος, *kotos*, μῆνις, *mēnis*, and χόλος, *cholos* and their cognates. These ancient terms for wrath occur in Greek literature before the use of ὀργή, *orgē*.

Mythology

In Homeric literature, wrath was expressed among the gods themselves. Divine wrath could be aroused by provocation, arrogance, fraud, jealousy, bitterness, favoritism, interference, or impudence.[1] Wrath among the gods was a reaction against any perceived transgression of acceptable behavior. The wrathful behavior among gods was a normal oc-

---

[1] Homer, *Il.* 4.23–24; 5.34, 762; 8.1–27, 397, 407, 421, 430, 449, 460–61; 15.119–41, 184–99, 212–17; 19.112–34; 24.55, 479. Homer, *Od.* 5.146.

currence. Once, Homer said that Zeus himself laughed for joy as he observed all the inhabitants of Mount Olympus embroiled in strife.[2]

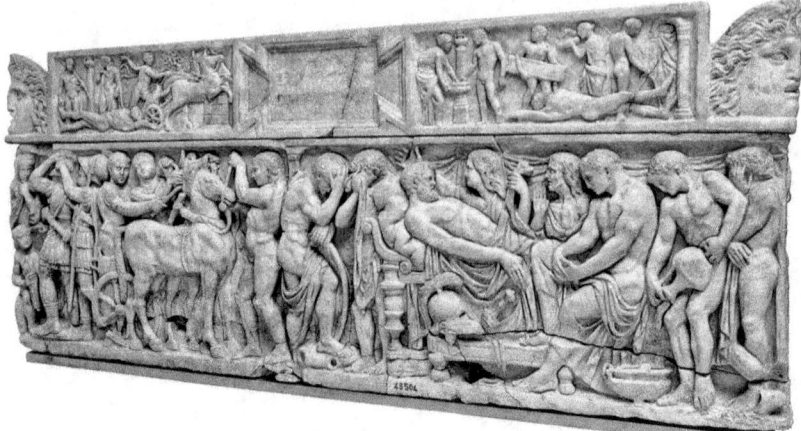

Figure 2.1. *Iliad* Sarcophagus. Homer's lyrical poems had incalculable impact upon Greek society, thought, and religion for centuries. *Iliad* and *Odyssey* images are pervasive throughout the Greek and Hellenistic world, inspiring scenes in mosaics, frescoes, statuary, friezes, jewelry, and numismatics into the Roman Empire. This sarcophagus portrays one of the most famous scenes from Homer's *Iliad*, the death of the Trojan hero, Hector, at the hands of the legendary Greek warrior, Achilles. The Roman sarcophagus, dating to AD 160, was found in the necropolis of Pianabella outside Ostia Antica, the port city of Rome, in 1976. (OAM).

Figure 2.2. Defeat of Hector. Achilles, finest of all Greek warriors, was merciless after his duel with the champion of the Trojans, Hector, outside the city walls of Troy to avenge the death of his friend, Patroclus, at the hands of the Trojans, for which he blames Hector. Olympian gods intervene, Apollo (favoring the Trojans), Athena (favoring the Greeks), and Zeus (striving for neutrality) all playing a role. In the end, Achilles kills Hector. In the rage of his wrath, Achilles desecrates Hector's body by tying the corpse to his chariot and dragging the body in front of the city walls for all the defenders of Troy to witness, including king Priam, Hector's father. (OAM).

[2] Homer, *Il.* 21.388–90.

2—Greco-Roman Background   15

Figure 2.3. Hector's Burial Preparation. The Trojans retrieve the body of Hector and prepare for burial by washing the mangled corpse. (OAM).

Figure 2.4. Hector's Wake. Trojans mourn the death of their champion, including his wife, Andromache, and mother, Hecuba, queen of Troy. (OAM).

Figure 2.5. Hector's Funeral Procession. Trojan warriors prepare a chariot for Hector's funeral procession and public lament. (OAM).

Figure 2.6. Ruins of Ancient Troy. Troy and its "high walls" was the epicenter of the Trojan War, abruptly concluded with the sack of Troy and slaughter of its inhabitants through a Greek ruse of a wooden horse. Greeks and Romans never doubted its historicity. However, in modern critical history, the city was presumed a mythological fabrication of poetic imagination by Homer. The search for ancient Troy was not dissuaded by these doubts. The location of the ancient city finally was identified in the early 1800s and confirmed by later archeologists. The topography of the immediate area perfectly matches the details as given by Homer, including the location of the Greek camp near the mouth of the River Scamander (modern Karamenderes), with the city across a plain from the river on a hill. Alluvial flooding over the centuries filled in and obscured the ancient bay, but geological findings have identified the ancient coastline, with the details aligning closely with Homeric descriptions. The site has many occupation levels and times of abandonment, but Troy VI is associated with Homeric Troy. The image above is part of the wall foundations for Homer's Troy.

Figure 2.7. Walls of Ancient Troy. Artistic imagination in an on-site illustration of one stage of the walls of ancient Troy. Troy had multiple levels of occupation over a millennium. Her famous history relates to Homer's Trojan War epic and destruction of the Trojan city state by the Greeks, likely Troy VI level (c. 1750–1300 BC), the level accessible today at the site.

Figure 2.8. Zeus: The Artemision Bronze. The seven-foot tall "Artemision Bronze" (found off Cape Artemision in north Euboea) likely is Zeus in Greek heroic style (nude). He is portrayed in action, frozen in time in extended stride throwing a great thunderbolt (or trident, if Poseidon). A prime example of the "Severe" style, the statue probably was a votive for a Zeus temple. In his speech on the Areopagus, Paul reminded the Athenians that the God who made heaven and earth, "does not live in shrines made by human hands" (Acts 17:29), echoing the words of Stephen in Acts 7:48, "Yet the Most High does not dwell in houses made with human hands" (NAMA).

Figure 2.9. Pergamum: The Great Altar of Zeus. This altar was built by king Eumenes II two centuries before Christ and was situated on the foremost promontory of the acropolis of Pergamum in Asia Minor. The altar is the apex of Pergamum's famous art and architecture and a masterpiece of Hellenistic art. Restored here is the west façade. The base displays in high relief a frieze of the famous Gigantomachy, or cosmic battle of the Olympian gods against the Giants, children of primordial goddess Gaia (Earth). Perched at the peak on the edge of the acropolis, the altar was visible for miles from both major roads coming into Pergamum. The Zeus altar may be the reference point of Rev 2:13, "I know where you live, where Satan's throne is" (PMB).

Figure 2.10. Gathering of the Gods. Hydria vessel, c. 510 BC, depicting a gathering of the gods on Olympus. Bearded Zeus is seated in the center with thunderbolts clasped in his left hand. Beside him is daughter Athena with spear in the right hand. Athena's left hand is outstretched in the common ancient gesture to signal making a speech (cf. Paul to king Agrippa, Acts 26:1). Hermes stands behind in traveling clothes at the ready to deliver any message from Olympus to humans. Behind Hermes is Dionysus with his main attribute symbol, a kantharos drinking vessel, usually for holding wine at banquets, but also used for rituals and offerings. The two women to the right of Zeus cannot be identified because their depicted attributes are too indistinct (PMB).

Figure 2.11. Minerva Holding Owl. This 2nd cent. AD restoration of an onyx statue as Minerva includes holding an owl. Minerva is the Roman equivalent of Athena. The owl is a symbol of knowledge, wisdom, and erudition (LP).

Figure 2.12. Athena of Velletri. First-century AD Roman copy of a lost Greek bronze of c. 430 BC by Kresilas found in the ruins of a Roman villa in Velletri. Athena was goddess of wisdom, war, and crafts, and favorite daughter of Zeus (LP).

Figure 2.13. Parthenon of Athens. The Athenian acropolis was crowned with the most significant artifice of the ancient world, which has become the paradigmatic symbol of Greece, democracy, and Western civilization. Built from 447–438 BC by Pericles to celebrate the stunning Hellenic victory over the Persian Empire's advance westward, the monument also celebrates the golden age of the Athenian Empire. Dedicated as a temple to Athena, whom the Athenians considered their patron goddess, the colossal statue of Athena inside was lost to history. The building is designed as a peripteral octastyle Doric temple garnished with Ionic architecture and is legendary as one of the most perfect buildings ever constructed. The sophisticated parabolic upward curvature of the platform (stylobate) allowed both gentle water drainage and extra strength to resist earthquakes; the slight taper of the interior walls matched the exterior curves; the slight swelling of the columns (*entasis*) by a mere 1.6 inches made them look straight at a distance; they also had a minor inward lean such that, if extended, they all would converge at a point one and a half miles above the exact center of the building. All these architectural elements and more demonstrate extraordinary attention to visual optics. Regrettably, during a siege of Athens in 1687 against Ottoman occupiers who used the Parthenon as an ammunition dump, Venetian bombing ignited the munitions stored inside and the resulting catastrophic explosion heavily damaged the structure. Large-scale restoration finally began in 1975 and has continued in multiple campaigns. Paul acknowledged to the Athenians, "I see how extremely religious you are in every way" because he found an altar dedicated to an unknown god in the city (Acts 17:22–23).

Figure 2.14. Gold Stater of Alexander. Alexander the Great coin, dated before 281 BC. Pictured is the obverse side depicting the head of Athena, legendary goddess of Athens in traditional Corinthian war helmet. As Athena fought for Achilles at Troy, the goddess fights for Alexander, explaining the outstanding success of his military campaigns. Use of gold staters—in contrast to the silver stater—was Macedonian in origin (NAMA).

Figure 2.15. Apollo Ritual Procession. Marble relief, 30–10 BC. Apollo walks solemnly with sister Dianna and mother Latona to an altar where goddess Victory is performing a libation with bowl and vessel, sacred temple in background (PMB).

Figure 2.16. Helios Rising. This terracotta bowl, dated to c. 470 BC, shows Helios rising for the day to drive his horse-drawn chariot across the sky. He regularly is depicted with sunrays over his head, which in this artifact have deteriorated over the passage of time. The Romans transformed this minor Greek god into a major force by identification with Roman solar divinities, such as Apollo and Sol. Emperor Domitian associated his person with Apollo, giving rise to John's play on words in his title for the king of the abyss, "Apollyon," in Rev 9:11 (AM).

Figure 2.17. Apollo Playing Cithara. This 2nd cent. AD statue was found in Miletus where Paul preached to the Ephesian elders in Acts 20:17–35 (IAM).

Figure 2.18. Asklepios. AD 160 copy of the original features Asklepios, god of healing. Pergamum boasted a major *asklepion*, healing center (NAMA).

Figure 2.19. Asklepios and Hygieia. Found near Thessalonica, this 5th cent. BC relief depicts Asklepios, son of Zeus, and one of his five daughters, Hygieia, goddess of health, cleanliness, and sanitation (cf. "hygiene"). Her sisters were Panacea (universal remedy), Iaso (recuperation), Aceso (healing process), and Aegle (beauty, splendor, adornment). The snake-entwined staff of Asklepios is the symbol of modern medicine. The most famous *asklepion* healing center was adjacent to Pergamum, where the famous physician Galen worked (IAM).

Figure 2.20. Poseidon. Classic deity nude pose wearing himitaion, Poseidon's right hand held a trident, left leg supported by dolphin, c. 125–100 BC (AM).

Figure 2.21. Poseidon and Demeter. High relief of Poseidon and Demeter from the Antonine Period found in the agora of Smyrna. Goddess of harvest and agriculture, Demeter presided over grains and earth's productivity. Along with her daughter, Persephone, Demeter was central to the Eleusinian Mysteries (IHAM).

Figure 2.22. Alexander Coin. Silver tetradrachm of Alexander the Great (336–323 BC). The obverse depicts Alexander as Hercules in lion skin headdress; the reverse shows Zeus enthroned holding eagle and scepter, inscription ALEXANDROU, indicating the approval of Olympus of Alexander's rule. Rulers used the myth of divine right to rule to legitimate their dynasties, which continued into the Roman Empire (IHAM).

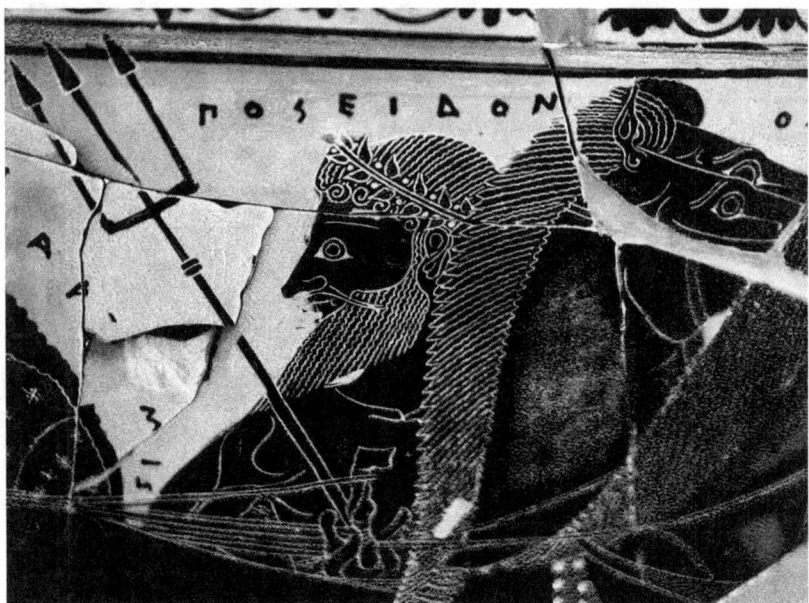

Figure 2.23. Poseidon with Sea Horses. Earliest known calyx krater by Exekias, c. 530 BC, the only one of its shape, pictures various Greek scenes around its central side. In this scene, Poseidon with his trident drives his sea horses (AM).

Figure 2.24. Demeter and Persephone. Terracotta votive of the 4th cent. BC by Ninion portraying Demeter, goddess of harvest and agricultural fertility, and Persephone, her daughter, who was the goddess of vegetation and grain. As wife of Hades, Persephone also was co-ruler of the Underworld and prominent in the Eleusinian Mysteries (LP).

Figure 2.25. Syncretistic Religion. This statue group is a premier example of religious syncretism, or mingling and integration of beliefs from different religions during Hellenistic and Roman times. The dog is Cerberus, the multi-headed dog guarding the gates of the Underworld to prevent those in the afterlife from leaving. Cerberus defines the two gods as Pluto and Persephone, god and goddess of Hades. Note carefully, however, that their images have been subtly merged into Egyptian religion by using elements to represent another god and goddess pair, Serapis and Isis of Egypt. The transformed combination Pluto-Serapis is deftly accomplished by the addition of an Egyptian *modius* on the head, a grain-measuring instrument. Again, Persephone-Isis is created by adding the crescent moon, solar disk, and snake (Uraeus) on the forehead. Her right hand holds a *sistrum*, an Egyptian musical instrument, but her left hand holds a leash restraining Cerberus—two religions in two hands. The worship of Serapis and Isis was very popular throughout the Greco-Roman world. Rome itself had a double temple to both deities near the Campus Martius, and temples to one or the other or both could be found throughout the empire, but especially in Asia Minor where Paul traveled extensively (HAMC).

Figure 2.26. Dionysus Mosaic. The rarely visited site of ancient Metropolis, twenty-one miles north of Ephesus, has this beautiful floor mosaic of the god Dionysus, son of Zeus, god of wine, grape cultivation, fertility, religious ecstasy, and theater. Most plays and dramatic presentations in ancient theaters began with ritual libations to Dionysus. Some cities even erected temples to Dionysus adjacent to their theater complexes, as did the theater at Pergamum in Asia Minor.

Humans were subject to the wrath of the gods of Olympus. Lycurgus was blinded and soon died for fighting against the gods. Failure to offer the first fruits of harvest brought upon Oeneus the anger of Artemis. The men of Odysseus knowingly butchered the prize cattle of the Sun for meat and were drowned in the sea. The insolence of humans always should be requited, Zeus assured Poseidon. The Cyclops Polyphemus did great harm to Odysseus and his company. Through subterfuge, Odysseus blinded the Cyclops and escaped his captivity. The god Poseidon, enraged because the injured Polyphemus was his offspring, tormented Odysseus and obstructed his return home to Ithaca. Ruthless behavior more than once provoked the divine anger upon Achilles. Once aroused, the wrath of the gods was difficult to assuage.[3]

Gods guided human destiny. Divine wrath was an instrument to secure a person's destiny. The god Apollo prevented Patroclus from taking Troy just when matters seemed that Patroclus was near to accomplishing this feat—sacking the city was not the divinely intended destiny for Patroclus.[4] Balancing of the golden scales consigned a person's destiny.[5] Some god or goddess specifically secured that destiny personally. For example, through Athene's duplicity, Hector was lured to his destruction.[6] The meaning of the name "Odysseus" may have been a word play implying "man of wrath."[7] The name may have been intended to be indicative of the destiny of treacherous voyages through which Odysseus suffered much evil by the anger of the gods (and men).

In the closing lines of the *Odyssey*, Zeus became exasperated with Odysseus. That exasperation resulted from the interminable strife among the men of Ithaca.[8] In wrath, Zeus intervened to check the spread of the conflict on Ithaca. Thus, divine wrath set the limits of human actions. These limits could not be resisted with impunity. Humans had to accommodate to the boundaries externally imposed by the gods or else suffer the consequences of trespassing those boundaries. The vicissitudes of life could be construed as the result of the wrath of the gods for trespassing divine boundaries set for human behavior. However, these divinely set boundaries could change. Inconstant fortunes often were interpreted to be the result of a capricious Zeus.[9]

---

[3] Cf. Homer, *Il.* 1.92–100; 5.177–78; 9.534–40. Contrast the usage in *Il.* 5.34 versus *Od.* 5.145–47. For the above paragraph, cf. *Il.* 2.66–67; 5.177–78, 440–44; 6.138–43; 9.534–40; 18.367; 21.136–47; 24.134–37, 606; *Od.* 1.66–79; 3.134–36, 141–47; 11.71–73; 12.376–83, 415–19; 13.139–45; 14.283–84.

[4] Homer, *Il.* 16.707–11.

[5] Ibid., 22.208–13.

[6] Ibid., 22.297–305.

[7] Cf. Homer, *Od.* 1.60–62 and 19.409–10.

[8] Ibid., 24.539–44.

[9] Homer, *Il.* 17.546, 626–27.

Drama

The term ὀργή (*orgē*) began to be used for the wrath of the gods in Attic tragedy. Divine wrath in Attic tragedy retained the powerful and invidious nature that the concept had in Homeric literature. In the plays of Aeschylus, Zeus bound Prometheus on a forsaken rock to force divulgence of the knowledge of the fall of his power; Artemis stirred a contrary wind against the ships of Agamemnon, requiring sacrifice of his virgin daughter, Iphigenia; and Zeus struck out at Paris for neglecting religious sacrifices.[10] In the plays of Sophocles, the conceit of Ajax invoked the wrath of Athena; as dogs ate Polynices, he prayed that Proserpine and Pluto would restrain their anger.[11] In the plays of Euripides, hidden poison given to Creon's daughter caused the princess to foam at the mouth and convinced her attendant the wrath of Pan or some other god had fallen; Phaedra's inordinate desire for her stepson was blamed on the wrath of Venus; and Orestes endured torture from the gods.[12] Euripides's general advice was that a humble life avoided the more dangerous road of a proud life, which could incur the wrath of a god.[13] Thus, in the Greek dramatists, any offense by humans incurred stiff anger, and even graceless words could win a deity's wrath. Generally, though, divine wrath on most occasions was provoked by some misstep of humans.[14] Thus, Greek playwrights perpetuated and propagated Homeric ideas of divine wrath to later generations for centuries through the institution of the Greek theater. Widely disseminated, Homeric ideas of the wrath of the gods impacted the early church.

Figure 2.27. Sarcophagus Theater Masks. One of the main features of ancient Greek theater was the theater mask. These masks became a *topos* of Hellenistic art from sarcophagi to floor mosaics. Here in a sarcophagus dated AD 120–130 are two Hellenistic masks of tragedy displaying high hairstyle, representing Heracles and a woman. Masks usually had a large "funnel" mouth to allow voice projection (PMB).

[10] *Prom.* 190; *Ag.* 221; 70.

[11] *Aj.* 776; *Ant.* 1200.

[12] *Med.* 1172; *Hipp.* 43; *Iph. taur.* 987.

[13] *Med.* 130.

[14] Aeschylus, *Ag.* 70, 215; Sophocles, *Aj.* 776; Euripides, *Med.* 1172; *Hipp.* 438.

Figure 2.28. Theater Mask Copy. This marble copy of a theater mask, dated AD 100–150, is depicted with a hand and garment folds on the side showing that the mask was held on stage by an actor, poet, or muse. The mask has the characteristic wide-open mouth, holes for the eyes, and exaggerated features (PMB).

Figure 2.29. Muse with Mask. This late 1st cent. AD marble statue from the theater at Aphrodisias near Hierapolis depicts a muse with a theater mask. According to Greek mythology, the nine Muses were the daughters of Zeus and Mnemosyne (Titan goddess of memory) according to Diodorus Siculus 4.7.1–2. The Muses presided over literature, arts, and sciences and were considered the source for the great forms of poetry, songs, and myths, such as the Homeric sagas, passed on orally for centuries before being written down. Their number, names, and functions, however, vary in our ancient sources. The Greek Muses are the basis of the contemporary concept of a force in human experience that inspires creative artists of all types (AMA).

Figure 2.30. Ostia Antica Theater Road. The road to the theater at Ostia Antica, Rome's ancient port city at the mouth of the Tiber River, has these columns capped with images of various theater masks lining the way.

Figure 2.31. Pergamum "Z" House Mosaic. In the middle acropolis area of Pergamum is a Roman-era house, called "Bau Z," or "Z House," with beautiful mosaic floors that rival the Hatay Mosaics Museum in Antakya, Turkey. Geometric boundaries are executed beautifully. An octagonal variation on the roundel motif houses two sets of images showcasing society's two main venues of entertainment. The outer twelve set has stereotypical theater masks. The inner quad set depicts a leopard, a lion, and two fighting cocks, stereotypical symbols of gladiator contests in the amphitheater.

Figure 2.32. Syracuse Theater. The theater at ancient Syracuse in Sicily had a dramatic vista overviewing the Syracuse bay and harbor. This huge theater dates back to the 5th cent. BC. Some of the original plays of Aeschylus were produced in this theater.

Figure 2.33. Aspendos Theater. One of the most complete theaters in the ancient world, the theater at Aspendos is not far from Perge of Pamphylia, the port city where Paul and Barnabas disembarked after leaving Cyprus on the 1MJ (Acts 13:13). The theater had a sloping wooden ceiling for shade. The ceiling did not survive the ravages of time, but the postholes that used to hold the fifty-eight masts supporting the awning (*valerium*) that could be pulled out over the seated crowd for shade still remain in the upper level. This theater with a capacity for 12,000 people has an intact *skene* (*scaenae frons*), or back wall structure, enclosing the theater. Originally a temporary structure as simple as a cloth hanging from a rope, the Romans developed the Greek *skene* into a massive, permanent part of theater architecture, sometimes including a front platform raised above the orchestra for scenery (*proskenion*), as well as multiple floors with rooms for costume storage, stairs to entryways for actors to use as balconies for speeches, and niches to display honorary local civic and imperial statues. The statuary reinforced local civic honor codes in an honor-shame society, as well as patron-client relationships of the citizenry to the provincial elite, and the provincial elite to imperial Rome.

Figure 2.34. Sepphoris Theater Model. Sepphoris (Hebrew, Zippori) was rebuilt by Herod Antipas as his capital city on a hilltop in Galilee just three miles from the small village of Nazareth where Jesus grew up. The theater seated about four thousand. This model shows how the *skene* was a permanent part of the overall construction. A common theater term, "hypocrite" (ὑποκριτής, hypokritēs), meant "stage actor," or one who played a role on stage wearing a mask to emulate a character and emotion in a tragedy or comedy. Jesus alone uses this term in the New Testament, often for his religious opponents (never in John, and mostly in Matt; cf. Matt 6:2, 5, 16; 7:5; 15:7; 22:18; 23:13, 15, 23, 25, 27, 29; 24:51; cf. Mark 7:6; Luke 6:42; 12:56; 13:15). The words of Jesus in the Sermon on the Mount, "a city set on a hill cannot be hidden" (Matt 5:14), may be a reference to king Antipas's capital city of Sepphoris.

FIGURE 2.35. Comic Actor as Slave. First to second century AD bronze statue of a comedian *hypokritēs*, from Egypt. This *hypokritēs* is playing the role of a slave in a comedy. As did all actors on the ancient stage, he wears a mask suited to the role played, with the typical funnel-shaped mouth. This actor also is wearing a chiton tunic high-girdled at the chest with a belt, along with a close-fitting theater costume (PMB).

Figure 2.36. Euripides Relief. Found in Smyrna and dated 1st cent. BC to 1st cent. AD, this relief honors Euripides, famous writer of Greek tragedies. Euripides is seated in an honorary chair; a basket behind holds a tragedy theater mask. Dionysus, elevated behind and above symbolizing divine status, pours a wine libation in the playwright's honor. Melpomene, muse of tragedy, offers a symbolic gift of inspiration (IAM).

Figure 2.37. Athenian Actor Ikairos. This relief found at Ephesus depicts Dionysus visiting famous Athenian actor, Ikairos. Slaves, pigmy sized to emphasize the god's divinity, attend to Dionysus. The god Pan playing the pipes behind Dionysus is the god of theatrical criticism. Ikairos reclines with a female companion on a couch with raised hand as if to give a speech. Theater masks are stored under the couch. (IAM).

Figure 2.38. Sarcophagus Relief: Medea Saga. This mid-2nd cent. AD marble sarcophagus relief depicts scenes of the Medea saga, the famous tragedy of Euripides, first produced in 431 BC. Unfaithful husband, Jason, violates marriage vows to his wife, Medea, to marry Creusa, daughter of Creon, king of Corinth. From left: (1) Medea's two young sons innocently offer wedding gift cursed by Medea to Creusa; (2) Creusa's cursed dress bursts into flames, killing her, along with her father, King Creon, who also burns to death trying to save her; (3) Medea just prior to murdering her own sons to prevent them from being enslaved as a result of her actions; (4) Medea kidnaps her children's bodies. Discovered in 1887 in front of Porta San Lorenzo in Rome (PMB).

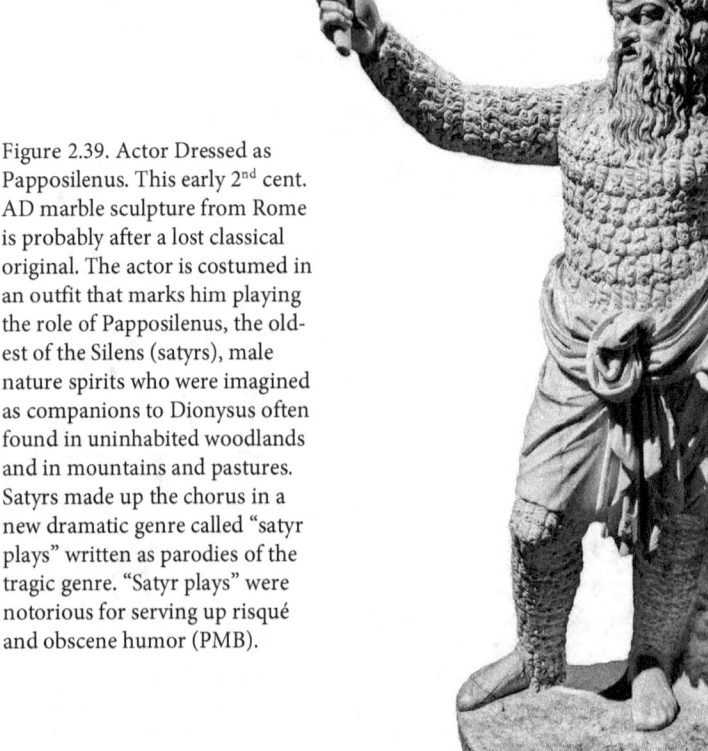

Figure 2.39. Actor Dressed as Papposilenus. This early 2nd cent. AD marble sculpture from Rome is probably after a lost classical original. The actor is costumed in an outfit that marks him playing the role of Papposilenus, the oldest of the Silens (satyrs), male nature spirits who were imagined as companions to Dionysus often found in uninhabited woodlands and in mountains and pastures. Satyrs made up the chorus in a new dramatic genre called "satyr plays" written as parodies of the tragic genre. "Satyr plays" were notorious for serving up risqué and obscene humor (PMB).

A significant development on the nature of divine wrath involved the incipient forms of myth criticism found in fuller form in Greek philosophy. This criticism involved a distinction between divine and human anger: that the wrath of the gods be of the same nature as the anger of men was not proper.[15] Philosophers would work on solving this conceptual dilemma.

In a further use of the word, *orgē* was an important ingredient in Attic tragedy. Humans, moved by wrath, determined their fate through the consequence of their own actions.[16] An ill-considered action could result from unthinking rage.[17] Anger caused bad choices. Irrational action so conceived could bring only misfortune and evil. The fate of Creon and his royal family in *Antigone* is a case in point. Because such evil, as in the case of Creon, was incumbent upon the expression of *orgē*, the term increasingly acquired negative connotations in Greek literature.[18]

In Attic tragedy, divine wrath could be used concerning preservation of established world order. Also, a manifestation of wrath defended those who were treated unjustly. The philosopher Aristotle once said, "And the gods are supposed to assist those who are wronged."[19] Creon's refusal to give Polyneices proper burial brought ruin to the state because such abomination caused the gods to refuse all sacrifice.[20] Often, the only prayer was one for mercy: "We offered first a prayer / To Pluto and the goddess of cross-ways, / With contrite hearts, to deprecate their ire [*orgas*]."[21]

Government

The idea that through wrath the gods preserved the established order, noted in Greek tragedy, was paralleled in ideas about Greek government. For those who ruled, wrath became the "characteristic and legiti-

---

[15] Euripides, *Bacch.* 1348.

[16] Sophocles, *Ant.* 870–80.

[17] Ibid., 280, 766; Sophocles, *Oed. tyr.* 523–24.

[18] Cf. Sophocles, *Oed. tyr.* 404–07; "irrational" here not in a philosophical sense.

[19] Aristotle, *Rhet.* 2.2.1 [Freese]. Aristotle made no attempt to distinguish *orgē* from *thumos* and reflected use in Homer's *Iliad*. See *Rhet.* 2.2.2. (*Il.* 18.109); *Rhet.* 2.2.6 (*Il.* 1.356); *Rhet.* 2.2.7 (*Il.* 1.82; 2.196); *Rhet.* 2.3.16 (*Il.* 24.54).

[20] Sophocles, *Ant.* 999–1033.

[21] Ibid., 1199–1200 [Storr].

mate attitude of the ruler who has to avenge injustice."[22] Kleinknecht noted that "worthy of terror and wrath" (δεινὸν καὶ ὀργῆς ἄξιον, *deinon kai orgēs axion*) was a fixed formula in rendering a judgment.[23] In civil cases, *orgē* came to mean "punishment."[24] The function for wrath was to guard against evil in order to secure the right. The expression of wrath could be considered just. The orator Demosthenes reckoned that to do what was just was to preserve the peace, but to insist on fighting was to act unjustly. For Demosthenes, the men of Athens always purposed to save the victims of injustice; for certain cases, wrath was the preeminent expression of justice: "The more justly would these very speakers incur your anger [*orgēs*]."[25] In a letter of Claudius (ca. A.D. 41), the citizens of Alexandria were urged to put an end to the enmity with the Jewish population or, Claudius warned, "I shall be driven to show what a benevolent prince can be when turned to righteous indignation [ὀρὴν δικαίαvl."[26] The historian Cassius Dio also evidences the explicit association of wrath and justice. The Roman senate had given Pompey the consulship, which was a novel action. Cassius Dio said Pompey realized that his rival Caesar would feel neglected and would show thereby "some righteous anger [τινὰ ὀργὴν δικαίαν, *tina orgēn dikaian*]."[27] Such use by Cassius Dio approached Aristotle's definition of *orgē* as that emotion aroused by some perceived slight or injury thought to be undeserved.[28]

Showing wrath could be an expression of just retribution. However, this positive evaluation of wrath gave way at times to a repudiation of wrath as an undesirable emotion. Human wrath could be associated with irrational behavior, the iconic problem for understanding divine wrath.[29] Because wrath led to other evils, its expression was to be subjected and censured. Wrath was considered immoral. Therefore, if the

---

[22] Kleinknecht, *TDNT* s.v. "ὀργή," 5:384; cf. Demosthenes, *Timocr.* 118; Homer, *Il.* 9.98–99; Homer, *Od.* 5.7–20.

[23] Kleinknecht, *TDNT* s.v. "ὀργή," 5:384; cf. Demosthenes, *3 Philip.* 31; *Fals. leg.* 7.

[24] Demosthenes, *Mid.* 147.

[25] Demosthenes, *Meg.* 19 [Vince]. For the above, cf. Demosthenes, *Meg.* 6; *Halon.* 1; *Chers.* 1; *Rhod.* lib. 1.

[26] "Letter of Claudius to the Alexandrians," *Select Papyri* 212 [Hunt].

[27] Cassius Dio, *Hist.* 40.51.2 [Carey].

[28] Aristotle, *Rhet.* 2.5.21.

[29] Sophocles, *Oed. tyr.* 523–24, but also note Homer, *Od.* 7.308–10.

gods were moral, they could not be angry like mortals.[30] Judging wrath an emotion to be avoided was taken up as a moral demand in Greek philosophy and developed into a dogma by the Stoics.[31]

Hellenistic Period

Introduction

In classical literature, wrath was understood as the loss of rationality.[32] By the later Hellenistic period, the irrationality of wrath was a predominant characteristic idea. Divine wrath operated within a person's mind (νοῦς, *nous*). Invading the mind, the alien force of the "anger of the spirits" (ὀργὴ δαιμόνων, *orgē daimonōn*) purloined intelligence, created deficient judgment, and thereby generated the errors of unreasonable behavior. The wise person held sway over irrational wrath. For a human, wrath could lead to nothing but harm.[33]

In popular belief, one should not fight against the gods; the gods parcelled out circumstances as they willed; to neglect the gods would be senseless.[34] Yet Menander, the acknowledged master of Attic comedy, aimed his satire at just such popular notions. In a soliloquy by the character Niceratus, the making of sacrifice is ridiculed.[35] The notion that the gods busied themselves daily with dispensing good and ill to every individual person meant that the gods lived a life of incessant toil.[36]

Hellenistic Philosophy

Both Plato and Aristotle were cautious about expressing anger. Plato warned, "But in dealing with the man who is totally and obstinately perverse and wicked one must give free course to wrath [τὴν ὀργήν, *tēn orgēn*]."[37] Aristotle rode the fence: "The middle disposition is praise-

---

[30] Euripides, *Bacch.* 1348.

[31] Diogenes Laertius, *Lives* 10.139.

[32] Meleager was angered "as even a wise man can be" (Homer, *Od.* 9.553 [Murray]). Cf. Sophocles, *Ant.* 280, 766; *Oed. tyr.* 523–24.

[33] For the above, see Lycurgus, *Ag. Leoc.* 159.22; Menander, *Sam.* 155; *Min. Frag.* 574K, 629K; "irrational" not philosophically, but as *moved* by "spirits" or alien forces.

[34] Menander, *Eun.* Frag 187K, Frag 190K; *Her.* 29–51.

[35] Menander, *Sam.* 187–89.

[36] So Onesimus explained to Smicrines in Menander, *Epitrep.* 872–79.

[37] Plato, *Leg.* 731D [Bury].

worthy, which leads us to be angry [ὀργιζόμεθα, *orgizometha*] with the right people for the right things in the right manner and so on."[38] Thus, from the beginning, we see Greek philosophers wrestling with divine wrath, uncomfortable with Homer's poetic notions about how Olympus operated. These early philosophical cautions gave way to the judgment by Epicurus that surrendering to the expression of *orgē* as an emotion was a weakness that eroded attainment of virtue. If so, the implication was obvious: *orgē* was a passion to which divinity inherently must be impervious by nature, since the divine to be truly divine had to be pure virtue. Therefore, no wrath allowed.[39] Epicurus in particular opposed the popular supposition that the gods sent great evils to the wicked.[40] Evils humans endured in the main were the result of bad choices.

Philosophers may have been unaware of the full force and future impact of these thoughts. They brought down Homer. Quite the feat.

Figure 2.40. Raphael's School of Athens. Italian Renaissance artist Raphael painted this famous scene of the "School of Athens" representing philosophy as part of the decoration of the Stanze di Raffaello in the Apostolic Palace in the Vatican. The work is considered his masterpiece with perspective a key feature. Plato is in the center left, but represented by the face of Raphael's master, Leonardo da Vinci, because Leonardo led the way in the European rediscovery of ancient Greek culture.

---

[38] Aristotle, *Eth. nic.* 4.5.14 [Freese].

[39] According to Diogenes Laertius, *Lives* 10.139.

[40] Epicurus, *Let. Men.* 123–24(a).

Figure 2.41. Socrates. Considered along with his famous student Plato as the founder of Western philosophy, Socrates was the first in a long line of moral philosophers. Similar to Jesus, Socrates left no writings, so is known only through secondary sources, such as Plato's dialogues. How much these secondary sources accurately reflect his thought is argued. His trial by Athens for "impiety" and forced suicide put an end to his 4th cent. BC career (EMS).

Figure 2.42. Epicurus. After Socrates and Plato, the 3rd cent. BC brought another philosopher who would have a profound impact on Western thought. Epicurus was founder of Epicureanism, striving for the virtue of a happy, tranquil life. Two freedoms defined this life: freedom from fear, and the absence of pain. Epicurus created a new school in Athens against Plato. He taught no life after death, so death was not to be feared. Fear of death was the source of most pain in life; so, overcoming this fear had the greatest impact on reducing a sense of pain. Epicurus was notable in his day in Athens for allowing women to join his school (NNAM).

The Stoic, as the Epicurean, renounced *orgē*.[41] Stoic philosophers classified emotions into four major categories of grief, fear, desire (passion), and pleasure. Chrysippus, in his work *On the Passions*, explained that the passions were considered as judgments made by reason.[42] For a Stoic, then, passion essentially was not to be distinguished from reason, simply just a conversion of one and the same reason into two aspects; in fact, passion was simply a vicious and intemperate reason formed from an evil and perverse judgment.[43] Unlike Plato, who subdivided the soul into two parts of the rational and the irrational, the Stoic maintained that the soul was one entity; passion was the unnatural and irrational movement of that soul.[44] Anger (*orgē*) was classified as a passion, defined as lust to punish someone thought to have caused injury.[45] In his book *On the Failure to Lead a Consistent Life*, Chrysippus is reported by Plutarch to have said, "Anger is a blind thing: often it prevents our seeing obvious matters, and often it obscures matters which are already apprehended."[46] Chrysippus then quoted the lines of Menander, "Ah woe, alas for me! Where ever were / my wits awandering in my body then / When I made choice to do not this, but

Figure 2.43. Philosopher. Representation of a philosopher as a mature, bearded man with a staff and books beside his leg. The head is rendered as Roman iconography for philosophers, but the body follows 5th cent. BC prototypes. Probably portrays Apollonious of Tyana, Neopythagorean philosopher, teacher, healer, magician, and mystic, who visited Knossos on the island of Crete with his students and taught at Gortna and Lebena on the island. He later died at the sanctuary of Diktynna in west Crete. Late 2nd, early 3rd cent. BC statue (HAMC).

---

[41] A primary source book on the Stoics is Hans F. A. von Arnim, ed., *Stoicorum Veterum Fragmenta*. Zeno's doctrine also is outlined in Cicero, *Mur.* 29 [Rackham].

[42] Diogenes Laertius, *Lives* 7.111.

[43] Plutarch, *Mor.* 441D, 446F.

[44] Cicero, *Tusc.* 4.10, 23; Plutarch, *Mor.* 441C; Diogenes Laertius, *Lives* 7.110.

[45] Diogenes Laertius, *Lives* 7.113; Cicero, *Tusc.* 4.21.

[46] Plutarch, *Mor.* 450C [Babbitt].

that?"⁴⁷ Stoics urged cultivation of sound judgment to oppose the poor judgment of anger. Sound judgment would make the soul firm, i.e., difficult for passions to attack.⁴⁸ For this reason, when Cleanthes once was reproached for cowardice, he quickly responded, "That is why I so seldom go wrong."⁴⁹ Wise control of human passions was applied subsequently to an understanding of the nature of divinity. The perfection of deity was understood as the maturity of immutability. Unaffected by the instability of passion, deity experienced no anger. Humans who mastered the emotion of anger were godlike, attaining something of the divine nature within themselves.⁵⁰

Hellenistic History

Polybius used *orgē* and *thumos*, but most commonly in reference to mortals, not gods. Sometimes the two terms occurred together with apparently little or no distinction in meaning.⁵¹ The writings of Polybius exhibit a studied absence of the language of divine wrath to explain historical events. Polybius preferred to call Fortune into account for the changing tide of events.⁵² For occasions that would seem to induce the language of divine wrath, Polybius refrained from any such suggestion.⁵³ Polybius said his reason for restraint was because divine action should be assigned only when the cause of an event could not be deciphered by other rationale (*Hist.* 36.17). Polybius used the example of Hannibal's crossing of the Alps to score other historians on this matter. He concluded with the following observation:

> The natural consequence is that they get into the same difficulties as tragic dramatists, all of whom, to bring their dramas to a close, require a *deus ex machina*, as the data they choose on which to found their plots are false and contrary to reasonable probability. These writers [the historians] are necessarily in the same strait and invent apparitions of heroes and gods, since the beginnings on which they build are false and improbable; for how is

---

⁴⁷ Chrysippus, *Min. Frag.* 567 [von Arnim].
⁴⁸ Plutarch, *Mor.* 454B–D ("On the Control of Anger").
⁴⁹ Diogenes Laertius, *Lives* 7.171; cf. 7.173 [Hicks].
⁵⁰ Ibid., 7.119.
⁵¹ Polybius, *Hist.* 2.58.15; 3.3.3, 7.2; 4.29.7, 4.7; 15. 5.11, 33.10; 16.1.2; 38.18.10.
⁵² Ibid., 1.4; 1.35.2; 1.58.1; 2.7.1–2; 2.35.5–6; 2.27.6; 3.118.6; 15.9.4; 23.10.2; 30.6.6.
⁵³ E.g., *Hist.* 1.48; 2.70.4–8.

it possible to finish conformably to reason what has been begun in defiance of it?[154]

According to Polybius, people could fail in most enterprises by their own fault. What most writers would attribute to the favor of the gods was no more than straightforward mental ability and sound judgment. The greatest reason for Rome's success he ascribed to that state's constitution, not the help of the gods. Thus, Polybius opposed irrational historical claims. However, irrational claims in the case of religious marvels (if not excessive) might be excused at least because they served to inculcate a sense of piety among the common people![55]

Polybius was not beyond a judicious reference to divine intervention into human affairs. Sacrilege could be compared to making war on the gods. Wrath (μῆνις, *mēnis*) seemed to visit Prusias instantly for his impiety. The historian Timaeus justly would receive divine wrath for his vicious lies.[56] A clear case was evident, in Polybius's words, when "wrath [μῆνιν, *mēnin*] from the gods fell against all the Macedonians."[57]

However, Polybius was not the voice of popular belief. The aristocratic historian held himself aloof. His literary expression did not represent the life experience of the common people. His own writing is evidence that the beliefs he sought to counter were pervasive. In popular belief, the will of the gods was important to life's successes, so that prayer to the gods for help and propitiation of the gods against harm were important. In the swearing of a treaty, the presence of the gods was invoked. Only by suing the Romans for peace could the Macedonians avoid incurring the just divine wrath of heaven, his court advisers warned Perseus. An inscription preserved the testimony that righteous doom would fall on an unrighteous king.[58]

Hellenistic Inscriptions

Greek inscriptions yield examples in which *orgē* was used in cultic contexts. In an effort to secure the eternal sanctity of a cultic ordinance issued by King Antiochus of Commagene (first century BC), the "wrath

---

[54] *Hist.* 3.4.8–9 [Paton].

[55] Cf. *Hist.* 3.118.8–9; 6.1.9–10; 9.16.2–4; 10.2.7; 16.2.5, 9.

[56] Ibid., 4.62.3–4; 11.23.8; 12.23.3; 18.54.11; 32.15.14.

[57] Ibid., 36.17.15.

[58] Ibid., 3.62.8; 3.111.10–11; 3.112.8–9; 4.33.3; 7.9.1–3; 27.8.4.

[*orgē*] of the powers and all gods" was invoked.[59] Similarly, for anyone who committed sacrilege against a particular burial, "He will be seized by the great wrath [*orgēn*] of the mighty Zeus."[60]

Another example from the inscriptions illustrates *orgē* as a righteous act in the human sphere. In an epistle of Augustus to Cnidios, the emperor said that to kill in a certain case would be to act "as perhaps someone who by wrath [*orgēs*] not unrighteously was overcome."[61]

Later Hellenistic Writers

Motifs already developed continued in the popular imagination. In spite of criticisms by philosophers, historians, and playwrights, popular mythological traditions and cultic ideas prevailed in common parlance. However, these popular traditions also continued to be opposed.

Plutarch argued against the idea that, after a time of concealment, *orgē* mysteriously would break forth without hope of atonement. For Plutarch, the poets misconstrued the nature of divinity by representing the gods as full of malice and *orgē*. Thus, Plutarch gave expression to Stoic thinking on the nature of divinity, although he disagreed with Zeno on the nature of the soul of man.[62] Likewise, the Stoic Epictetus argued that divinity must be free from passions such as *orgē*. Wrath for Epictetus was a weakness to overcome.[63]

In contrast, in his *Description of Greece*, Pausanias stated that he adopted the "received tradition" in matters of divinity. Thus, Pausanias used the older term μῆνις (*mēnis*) in its cultic setting. In earlier times, the unjust were visited openly with "the wrath" (ἡ ὀργή, *hē orgē*); in Pausanias's day, the wrath of the gods (μήνιμα, *mēnima*) was reserved for the unjust until they had entered the next world.[64] Pausanias shows coalescence of meaning for *orgē* and *mēnis* within the sacral sphere.[65]

---

[59] *OGIS*, 383.210 [Dittenberger].

[60] *SIG* 1237.5 [Dittenberger].

[61] *SIG* 780.20 [Dittenberger].

[62] Cf. Plutarch, *Mor.* 447B; *Per.* 39; *Mor.* 12.20, 25 ("Delay of the Deity in the Punishment of the Wicked").

[63] Epictetus, *Frag.* 363, 365, 366.

[64] Pausanias, *Descr.* (*Arcadia*) 2.4; 2.5; 7.6; 8.3–4; *Descr.* (*Laconia*) 4.6; *Descr.* (*Messenia*) 24.6; *Descr.* (*Elis*) 1.1.7.

[65] Pausanias, *Descr.* (*Arcadia*) 8.25.6; 10.32.10–11. Cf. coalescence with χόλος (*cholos*) in Dio Chrysostom, *1 Tars.* 33.50.

Hellenistic Papyri

Mentioned previously was the copy of the letter Claudius sent to the Alexandrians (A.D. 41).[66] In another document, questions and answers on antiquarian subjects contain a use of *orgē* in a legend about Hermes.[67] In an apparent glossary to the first chapter of Homer's *Iliad*, *orgē* is used as a synonym for μένος (*menos*, "rage") at *Il.* 1.103.[68] The cognate verbal form ὀργίζω (*orgizō*) is used of human anger. The expression of human anger can be tied with having just cause for anger.[69] These papyri examples serve to confirm uses of *orgē* already encountered.

ROMAN LITERATURE

Roman Myth and Philosophy

Roman writers adopted and adapted the heritage of Greek thought.[70] The mythological background of divine wrath was similar.[71] For some, Rome achieved greatness through the early favor granted by the gods.[72]

Roman writers rehearsed Greek philosophical criticism of divine wrath. In the time of Nero, Petronius composed his pungent satire on the wrath of the Homeric gods through a parody involving the wrath of the phallic god Priapus.[73] Cicero's Epicurean spokesman, Velleius, reviewed the theology of the poets, in which the gods were represented as "inflamed by anger and maddened by lust," and proclaimed, "Anyone pondering on the baseless and irrational character of these doctrines ought to regard Epicurus with reverence, and to rank him as one

---

[66] *Select Papyri* 212.

[67] P.Oxy. 2688.14–20 (perhaps third century AD, edited reconstruction).

[68] P.Oxy. 2405.117 (second to third century AD).

[69] P.Oxy. 1606.118–19 (copy of Lysias, *Orations*, second to third century AD).

[70] Cicero, *Tusc.* 4.1. In the following discussion, *ira deum* is associated with ὀργὴ θεοῦ, (*orgē theou*); see Buck, *A Dictionary of Selected Synonyms in the Principal Indo-European Languages*, 1134-37.

[71] Virgil, *Aen.* 7.285–316. Cf. Tacitus, *Ann.* 3.61; Lucretius, *Rer. n.* 5.399–401; Cicero, *Tusc.* 4.9. Native Italian myths succumbed to Greek legends, but Roman mythology is more than a simple extension of Greek mythology, having deep roots in pre-Roman Italic tribes such as the Sabines and the Etruscans; cf. Morford and Lenardon, *Classical Mythology*, 395-96.

[72] Livy, *Ab urbe cond.* 1.9.

[73] Petronius, *Satyr.* 126–41.

of the very gods about whom we are inquiring."[74] Lucretius also diligently espoused Epicurean philosophy.[75]

Stoicism had its vigorous exponents. The second book of Cicero's *De Natura Deorum* has the main doctrines of Stoicism, a philosophy Cicero championed.[76] Other notable proponents of Stoicism included Seneca,[77] and later, Marcus Aurelius, who counseled even in practical matters to have no need of anger.[78] Such Roman writers reflected the reservations of Stoic philosophers in ascribing passions such as wrath to deity.

Roman History

The evidence from Roman writers is that the roots of Roman attitudes toward divine wrath resided in the ancestral Roman religion.[79] *Ira deum* was integral to this ancient Roman cultus. The expiatory rites of Roman religion were necessary to avert the wrath of the gods.[80] Cultic legends preserved by the historians manifest this relationship between *ira deum* and the ancient cult.[81] The very welfare of both the state and the government was grounded in the *religio* of the ancient cultus and disrupted by the associated *ira deum*. The wrath of the gods was responsible for the mutinous behavior of soldiers (Tacitus *Ann.* 1.39); the force impelling factions into civil war (Tacitus *Hist.* 2.38); the expanding evils of Nero's reign (*Ann.* 16.16); the destruction of Corinth and Carthage (Cicero *Nat. d.* 3.38); the successes of Hannibal (Livy, *Ab urbe*

---

[74] Cicero, *Nat. d.* 1.16 [Rackham]. Cicero himself adamantly was against Epicurean philosophy; cf. *Tusc.* 5.27.78; 4.3.6; *Off.* 3.116-20.

[75] Lucretius, *Rer. n.* 1.58-89; 2.645-46, 651; 5.1194-96; 6.51-53, 70-72, 753-54.

[76] Cicero, *Nat. d.* 3.40; *Off.* 3.102.

[77] Seneca, *Ep.* 10-12 (Epistle 107, *On Obedience to the Universal Will*); 6-8 (Epistle 116, *On Self Control*).

[78] Marcus Aurelius, *Com.* 5.27-28; 10.30; 11.8.

[79] Cicero, *Nat. d.* 3.2, said the elements of this religion were: (1) rituals—ceremonies traditionally tied to the ancient Roman cultus, (2) auspices—protection secured by patronage of certain deities, and (3) auguries—prophetic warnings from oracles, omens, dreams, prodigies, and the *haruspex*. Cf. Marcus Minucius Felix, *Oct.* 7. Kleinknecht's presentation on Roman historians (*TDNT* s.v. "ὀργή," 5:389-92) has been verified as substantially sound and is followed.

[80] Livy, *Ab urbe cond.* 5.14; 8.8; 9.29; 22.9; 27.23.

[81] E.g., Tacitus, *Ann.* 14.22; Livy, *Ab urbe cond.* 2.36.

cond. 22.9); the rise of Sejanus (*Ann.* 4.1); the Roman carnage at Cannae (*Ab urbe cond.* 25.6); the defeat of the legions of Quintilius Varus by the Germans (Cassius Dio, *Hist.* 56.23.1; 24.1–5); and the reduction of the Capitol to ruins (Tacitus, *Hist.* 4.54).

Figure 2.50. Ancient Corinth. Corinth revolted against Rome as part of the Achaean League but was defeated and razed to the ground by the Roman general Lucius Mummius in 146 BC. Roman historians interpreted this disaster the wrath of the gods for the impiety of revolt. The city lay in ruins for a century, but Julius Caesar refounded Corinth as a Roman colony in 44 BC, repopulated with Romans, becoming capital of the province of Achaia (Greece) in 27 BC with a large immigrant population. This culturally mixed city had strong Greek heritage but dominantly Roman society by the time Paul encountered the Roman proconsul, Gallio, during the 2MJ (Acts 18:12).

The most potent expiation of divine wrath was the cultic-military rite of "devotion" to death, a drastic action to vitiate impending divine wrath. In 340 BC, the consul Decius so devoted himself to divert divine wrath from his legions to his own person and to the enemy troops whom he had dedicated along with himself. Legionnaires, witnessing their comrade expiating the divine wrath, renewed the attack with fresh vigor, their spirits relieved of religious fears.[82]

---

[82] Livy, *Ab urbe cond.* 8.9.

Roman historians amplified the role of divine wrath in destiny already present in Greek literature. Divine wrath constituted one of the forces of destiny (*fatum*), both *ira deum* and *fatum* linked together in mutual operations.[83] The lives of humans were fitted into patterns with intended goals, and to resist the destiny expressed through the wrath of the gods was futile. The very existence of the Roman state was tied to the destiny produced by divine wrath.[84] Even acts of insanity did not lie outside the bounds of destiny, being identified with the wrath from heaven. A wise person heeded the direction of divine wrath. For this reason, Rome avoided provoking the wrath of any deity.[85] According to Minucius Felix, Roman attitude toward *ira deum* produced acceptance of numerous cults throughout their history.[86]

Destiny was revealed through the prodigies. Prodigies were strange or abnormal events in nature, such as the birth of a two-headed snake or the flight path of birds, or natural disasters, such as flooding of the Tiber, destructive fires, deadly plagues, or lightning strikes, interpreted as signs of the anger of the gods that required expiation. Prodigies could be ignored, but not falsified. Various marvels pointing to inevitable fate were prelude to major upcoming events, such as the death of an emperor or the defeat of a general. Access to the Sibylline Oracles helped one to ascertain the future irrevocably decreed by this divine *fatum*. This access was given by the office of the *pontifex maximus* of Rome, so emperors sought this office to control the interpretation of their reign and consolidate political power. Apparently, people inclined toward considering *every* abnormal occurrence a prodigy of *ira deum* and *fatum*. Against Livy's complaint of not enough prodigies, later Roman historians sought to check popular but ill-advised designations of events as prodigies.[87] Otherwise, Roman historians systematically used *ira deum* as a literary construct for historical interpretation.

---

[83] Livy, *Ab urbe cond.* 25.6; Tacitus, *Hist.* 4.26.

[84] Tacitus, *Ann.* 16.16. Cf. Polybius, *Hist.* 1.4; Virgil, *Aen.* 1.2–4; 5.784; 8.50–58.

[85] Cf. Tacitus, *Hist.* 2.38; Livy, *Ab urbe cond.* 2.36; Suetonius, *Aug.* 93.

[86] Marcus Minucius Felix, *Oct.* 7.2. Cf. Josephus, *Ant.* 14.4.4; 16.2.3.

[87] Livy, *Ab urbe cond.* 43.13.1–2. Cf. Suetonius, *Galb.* 18 (Plutarch, *Cic.* 1.2); Suetonius, *Claud.* 46; Tacitus, *Ann.* 12.43 (Plutarch, *Caes.* 69.3); Suetonius, *Aug.* 92; Tacitus, *Ann.* 13.17; Polybius, *Hist.* 4.26. Some prodigies were taken as positive; cf. Polybius, *Hist.* 4.81. Omens, however, much more were a matter of personal interpretation; cf. the omens that Augustus regarded as infallible in Suetonius, *Aug.* 92.

SUMMARY

Greek Literature

Five terms for "wrath" or "anger" are used in ancient Greek literature. The minor players were κότος, *kotos*, μῆνις, *mēnis*, and χόλος, *cholos*.[88] Θυμός, *thumos*, and ὀργή, *orgē* were the two major players. Of these two, *thumos* was the oldest term, so gets the lion's share of usage. Almost exclusively, the New Testament uses only *thumos* and *orgē*, with Paul providing most of the occurrences of *orgē*.

Classical Period

Traditions about the nature of divine wrath already were developed in Homeric literature by the time *orgē* appeared for the first time in Hesiod. The term *thumos* already was used in Homer variously, including impulse, spirit, disposition, and anger. The basic meaning of *orgē* as a "swelling up" pictures the surge of emotion that preceded an outburst of anger. As far back as Aristotle, no distinction was made between *orgē* and *thumos*, and Aristotle also provides evidence that *orgē* could be used for the Homeric terms for divine wrath. Coalescence of meaning also can be exampled in the writings of Pausanias. A connection between *orgē* and *asebeia* ("ungodliness") normally was made.

Divine wrath was expressed against humans and among the gods themselves. Divine wrath in Homeric literature was powerful, but invidious. Zeus could be capricious in his wrath. At the same time, divine wrath could be described along rational lines as the divine reaction against a perceived transgression of acceptable behavior. The idea that the gods guided a person's destiny meant that divine wrath could function as an instrument through which a person's destiny was secured. Divine wrath set the limits of human actions, limits that could not be resisted with impunity.

As a tragic element in Greek drama, *orgē* on the human level came to be associated with a fate-determining action bringing only misfortune. The idea that wrath brought evil could generate a corresponding devaluation of the emotion of anger. However, on the divine level, the expression of wrath preserved the order of state and religion and defended justice. This idea of the preservation of the proper world order

---

[88] The New Testament has one occurrence of a cognate verb in John 7:23.

was paralleled in ideas about Greek government. In civil cases, *orgē* came to mean "punishment," proper for rulers avenging all injustice.

Hellenistic Period

By the Hellenistic period, the ideas about human anger shifted to an emphasis on the irrationality of the emotion. The philosophers criticized the traditions about divine wrath inspired by Homeric literature. From the philosophical schools of the Epicureans and the Stoics came traditions about wrath as a weakness of the soul to be overcome. The idea that a person's anger should be controlled or eliminated was applied to an understanding of the nature of deity. The gods were immutable. The gods did not express wrath.

The works of Polybius show a rational approach to the writing of history. Polybius resisted the fabrication of an element of divine wrath to explain certain momentous events. However, popular notions about the nature of divine wrath are revealed in Polybius's writings and are evidence that Homeric types of understanding of divine wrath were prevalent in Polybius's day. These popular ideas also reflect the importance that was attached to prayers to the gods for help and propitiation of the gods against harm. Inscriptions show that the term *orgē* could be used in this cultic context.

The traditions about the nature of divine wrath continued into the later Hellenistic period with few alterations. Papyri documents show uses of *orgē* already encountered in earlier Greek literature.

Roman Literature

Roman writers developed their own traditions about divine wrath, but they incorporated much from Greek thought. Greek myths and criticisms of myth were absorbed. However, a significant development in Roman writers took place among the historians. Roman attitude toward divine wrath derived from traditions of the ancestral Roman religion. In Roman thought, the welfare of state and government was grounded in the *religio* of the ancient cultus and disrupted by the associated *ira deum*. Because Romans emphasized the idea of *fatum*, religion and divine wrath were linked inseparably to state and destiny. For this reason, Roman historians systematically could use *ira deum* as a vehicle for historical interpretation.

3

Jewish Background

Divine Wrath in Jerusalem and Samaria

FROM THE WRITING OF RELIGIOUS HISTORY to their calendrical observances, the language of divine wrath was central to Hebrew expressions of faith. The exodus and the exile were two great moments of Hebrew history, as interpreted in the traditions of Israel. The language of divine wrath found its path along the ellipse determined by these two foci: the exodus revealed God's righteous salvation; the exile revealed God's awesome wrath. God's power and God's sovereignty were key elements of each revelation, which provides two of the main motifs of this material.[1] While salvation was understood as the gift of a promised land, judgment was the loss of that land.[2] The language of divine wrath could be used as a key to narrative development. For example, in the programmatic history of the Deuteronomist, the language of divine wrath provided a structural function that helped to create an ominous atmosphere from the beginning of the story, as well as pointing forward to the final catastrophe. Such a narrative technique alerts the reader to how crucial to Jewish thought was reflection on the wrath of God.[3]

---

[1] Central to the exodus story is the theme of Yahweh's power and the revelation that Yahweh is Lord; in 2 Kgs 17:36, Yahweh's nature is interpreted on the prior assumption of his power; cf. Rylaarsdam, "Exodus," IB 1:846. In other texts provided by Pritchard, ed., *ANET*, compare the motifs reflected in The Gilgamesh Epic, Tablet 5, lines 79-80; Tablet 11, lines 170-74; The Akkadian Creation Epic, Tablet 1, lines 41-43.

[2] Deut 4:26; 29:28; 1 Kgs 14:15.

[3] McCarthy, "The Wrath of Yahweh," 106.

The language of wrath became part of calendrical observances of the Jewish year. The three great pilgrim feasts became associated with the exodus of the children of Israel from Egypt on the historical plane: Passover—release from bondage; Pentecost—events at Mount Sinai; Succoth—the wilderness sojourn. Thus, the annual feasts pointed to the salvation provided by God's providence. In contradistinction, the annual fasts, which developed later in Jewish observance, pointed to the wrath that was executed in God's judgment. Each fast was associated with a stage in the catastrophe of the Jerusalem temple's destruction: the tenth of Tebet—the commencement of Nebuchadnezzar's seige of Jerusalem; the seventeenth of Tammuz—the first breach of city walls; the ninth of Ab—the traditional date when both the first and second temples were destroyed (586 BC and AD 70); the third of Tishri—the assassination of Nebuchadnezzar's Judean viceroy Gedaliah. The Jewish calendar also was punctuated with the two most solemn days of Rosh Hashanah and Yom Kippur. These austere seasons of introspection, confession, and repentance eventually led to the activities of the lenten season serving in part as a time of warning.[4] The historical realization of divine wrath in the past variously was relived, and the memory of the past served as a warning for the future. The thought can be analyzed along the lines of the motives provoking divine wrath and the meaning of this part of the character of God and the covenant.

JEWISH LITERATURE

Hebrew Scripture

Motives for Scriptural Wrath

Motives for Yahweh's wrath in Hebrew Scripture are explained from within an ancient worldview. One explanation is the irrational, an alien operation begging for comprehension in a non-scientific approach to knowledge. Examples are uncommon. The other explanation is rational. Most of expressions of wrath are comprehended and explained, often in some way upon the basis of Yahweh's covenant with Israel.

The "irrational" side of the wrath of Yahweh was grounded in the mystery of the person of Yahweh himself. Seemingly fortuitous events

---

[4] Gaster, *Festivals of the Jewish Year*, 110.

characterized this aspect of wrath. In some cases, the terms for wrath may not appear, but the essential content of a mysterious threat to existence is present. The wrestling of Jacob with the angel, the surprise attack at night upon Moses by God himself, the opposition of the angel of the Lord to Balaam's journey, the divine anger that stirred David to number the people, and the complaint of Job are all examples of what could be interpreted as "irrational" wrath.[5] Direct contact with holiness could produce death without any reason specifically outlined.[6]

This restricted sense of the "irrational" wrath of Yahweh was not a demonic element attributed to Yahweh, as was the case in other ancient religions.[7] Rather, these cases involved the intimate complexities of the personality of Yahweh who was at once known and unknown. Even if inexplicable, divine wrath still was not considered as impersonal. The action of Yahweh in wrath simply was mysterious.[8] Ultimately, Yahweh's actions could defy analysis.[9] Yahweh's wrath was experienced as mysterious in certain cases: (1) when people encountered Yahweh personally, (2) in Yahweh's warfare with his enemies, (3) when holiness had been violated, (4) when wrath was hypostatized, and (5) in the operation of what could be termed "secondary cause" factors, such as in curse, bloodshed, and wickedness.[10] The sheer incomprehensibility of wrath could elicit charges of injustice or pleas that wrath be stayed by mercy.[11] But this mysterious wrath cannot be described adequately as simply an ancient's encounter with a vaguely defined divine *tremendum*.[12] Hebrew religion was not a "numinous state of mind" but submission to a personal will.[13] Wrath was experienced as the exercise of the personal zeal of Yahweh.[14]

---

[5] Gen 32; Exod 4:24; Num 22:22; 2 Sam 24:1; Job 14:1-4.

[6] Exod 19:9-25; 33:20; Judg 13:22; 1 Sam 6:19; 2 Sam 6:7.

[7] Cf. Eichrodt, *Theology of the Old Testament*, 1:261.

[8] Gen 32:30; Exod 4:24-25; 19:9-25; 20:18-21; 33:20; Num 1:52-53; Judg 13:22; 1 Sam 6:19; 26:19; 2 Sam 6:7; 21:14; 24:1; 1 Kgs 22:20-21.

[9] Isa 55:8-9; Job 40-41. Obscuring the irrational character of Yahweh's wrath is a problem in the study of Haney, *The Wrath of God in the Former Prophets*.

[10] Saphir, "The Mysterious Wrath of Yahweh."

[11] E.g., Exod 32:9-14; Job 16:9; 29:11; Ps 6:1; 38:11; 77:9; 88:15; Jer 10:24; Hab 3:2.

[12] *Contra* Otto, *Idea of the Holy*, 21, 97. See Saphir, "Mysterious Wrath," 123-29.

[13] Agreeing with Saphir, "Mysterious Wrath," 126.

[14] Num 25:11; Ps 79:5; Zeph 1:18; Nah 1:2. Cf. Eichrodt, *Theology* 1:211, 258.

Figure 3.1. Ghiberti's Moses Receiving the Law. The seventh panel in the East doors of the Florence Baptistery in Florence, Italy, depicting Old Testament scenes. This scene is Moses receiving the tablets of the Law as the children of Israel wait below. Executed by the famed artist, Lorenzo Ghiberti, in gilded bronze in the early 1400s.

The rational side of the wrath of Yahweh basically derived from the covenant. Through corporate personality and collective solidarity in the covenant, destinies of individual and the community mutually were tied to the operation of divine wrath.[15] Divine wrath also was a function of the law.[16] In contexts of personal relationships, "It is noticeable that the wrath of God never acquires the characteristics of μῆνις [menis] that malicious hatred and envy which bulks so large in the implacability of the Greek and also of the Babylonian deities."[17] Often

---

[15] E.g., Num 25:1–11; Josh 7:5–15; Lev 10:1–6 (contrast Num 16:22).

[16] Exod 22:24 (cf. Lev 10:1–2).

[17] Eichrodt, *Theology*, 1:261.

the judgment of Yahweh was announced beforehand so that his sovereignty could be understood correctly.[18]

Basically, the revelation of Yahweh's wrath revealed the character of sin, the character of Yahweh, and the character of the covenant. First, the wrath of Yahweh on behalf of the covenant was a manifestation of the character of sin. Sin destroyed the life-sustaining relationship to Yahweh and resulted in death. Covenant wrath preserved the life of the covenant community by extirpating the sin that destroyed life. The cult of the covenant in part served to illustrate the seriousness of sin and to provide a sense of restored relationship through the reconciliation provided by Yahweh. Also operative in this understanding of the character of sin was a perceived act-consequence relationship.[19] Any particular deed was thought to release a force that eventually would return to the author with disastrous consequences. The cause-effect relationship of the sin-consequence cycle was the basis of the objective character of sin and incumbent guilt.[20] Guilt was a person's liability to contract the disastrous consequences of sin. Atonement was a covering of guilt so that the inevitable consequences of sin could be circumvented. For example, in Deut 21:1-9, provision was made to circumvent the guilt of the shedding of innocent blood. Through atonement, the connection between sin and calamity was broken.[21] Without atonement, guilt remained to run its course.

Second, the wrath of Yahweh on behalf of the covenant was a manifestation of the character of Yahweh. In the relationship of a person to God, the presence of sin emphasized the vast qualitative difference between God and humans, theologically codified in the concept of God's holiness. The holiness of God was not a passive characteristic. Anything brought into the presence of Yahweh was affected by the action of his holiness.[22] Holiness was that aggressiveness of Yahweh that preserved the integrity of his person. Yahweh's holiness annihilates sin.

---

[18] Cf. Num 16:28-35; 2 Sam 12:1-14; 1 Kgs 21:17-22.

[19] See von Rad, *Wisdom in Israel*, 128-30; 195-96.

[20] Exod 34:7; 20:5; Lam 5:7. See Ringgren, *Sacrifice in the Bible*, 33-38.

[21] von Rad, *Old Testament Theology*, 1:271. Eichrodt, *Theology*, 2:508, presumed the Servant endured Yahweh's wrath, but see Westermann, *Isaiah 40-66*, 262-63.

[22] E.g., Exod 3:5; 19:10-13, 21-25; 34:29-35; 39:30; Deut 7:6; Ps 68:2; 97:5; 114:7; Isa 57:15; Nah 1:5.

As in Exod 33:22, the very presence of a holy Yahweh could become a dangerous threat to one's existence. Such a threat had nothing to do with emotion. This threat had everything to do with pure difference. This threat of Yahweh's holiness was a quality unlike any conceptualization of deity in a pagan, polytheistic, Greco-Roman world of Homeric lineage. Because of the sinful behavior at Sinai, the presence of God had to be forfeited as an act of divine grace simply to preserve the very existence of Israel, as in Exod 33:7 and Num 17:13. The Tent of Meeting had to be moved outside the camp. In Num 1:53, Yahweh charged that the Levites were to be established as a mediating institution around the tabernacle of testimony, "That there may be no wrath [קֶצֶף, *qsp*] on the congregation of the sons of Israel." Likewise in Num 18:5, the charge of the altar was given strictly to Aaron and his sons after the Korah rebellion, "That there may no longer be wrath [קֶצֶף, *qsp*] on the sons of Israel." But while the presence of God could threaten one's very existence, to be cut off from God was to be cut off from life.[23] In Jer 52:3, wrath explicitly is associated with being cast out from Yahweh's presence. His character presents a conundrum: simultaneously salvation and judgment. Relationship with God is no easy task.

Because of the premier association of this peculiar quality of holiness with Yahweh, wrath was not conceived in Hebrew thought as contrary to Yahweh's character; in fact, wrath was imperative to preserve his character. The more the quality of Yahweh's holiness was meditated upon, the more the realization surfaced of how incredibly slow Yahweh was to express his anger. Understanding Yahweh's wrath as core to his holiness meant celebrating Yahweh's patience with the unholy.[24] In Ps 30:5, the thought of Yahweh's reticence to express wrath is complemented with meditation upon the short time of wrath: "For His anger [אַף, *'p*] is but for a moment [רֶגַע, *rgʿ*]."[25] Trouble could produce the question whether Yahweh would be angry forever.[26] But according to Exod 34:4–7, Yahweh fundamentally always was merciful and gracious, longsuffering, and abundant in goodness and truth. In Isa 54:7–8, the

---

[23] Exod 33:14; Lev 22:3; Num 6:25; Deut 31:17–18; 32:20; Ps 16:11; 51:11; Jer 23:39; Mic 3:4.

[24] Neh 9:17; Ps 103:8; 145:8; Joel 2:13; Jonah 4:2; Lam 3:33; Nah 1:3.

[25] Ps 30:6 in the Masoretic text. Cf. Isa 57:16; 64:9; Jer 3:12; Mic 7:18; Lam 3:31.

[26] Ps 79:5; 80:4; 85:5; Lam 5:20.

moment of wrath only set into sharp relief assurance of Yahweh's everlasting lovingkindness:

> "For a brief moment I forsook you,
> But with great compassion I will gather you.
> "In an outburst of anger [קֶצֶף, *qṣp*]
> I hid my face from you for a moment;
> But with everlasting lovingkindness I will have compassion on you,"
> Says the Lord your Redeemer.

From Isaiah's perspective on the horizon of sacred history, the years of exile could be resolved into a single point.

Third, the wrath of Yahweh on behalf of the covenant was a manifestation of the personal character of Yahweh's covenant. Yahweh was zealous to preserve the integrity of his relationship to his people and their relationship to him. Single-minded devotion to Yahweh was the essence of the first commandment. While sin impaired the relationship to Yahweh, apostasy was the absolute failure of that relationship. In Ps 106:43–45, the psalmist captured the poignancy of Yahweh's consistent faithfulness to the covenant in spite of Israel's continual unfaithfulness. The theme of apostasy became a capsule statement of the history of Israel and of Judah. According to Judg 2:12, wrath had fallen from Yahweh because his covenant people deserted Yahweh and bowed their knees to other gods. The incident of the golden calf at the foot of Sinai (Exod 32) was prophetic of the subsequent history of the people.[27] Often, divine wrath was understood as effected through foreign oppression.[28] If the king abandoned Yahweh, the whole nation was implicated in divine wrath; reform was a return to the covenant, as under Hezekiah and Josiah.[29]

In Deut 11:26, 29, and 30:1, the covenant was understood as the instrument of both Yahweh's blessing and Yahweh's curse. Saphir noted how a Hebrew term such as זַעַם (*z'm*) could serve both for "curse"

---

[27] Cf. Deut 29:24–28; 2 Kgs 17; 2 Chr 24:18; Ezra 9:14; Ps 95:10–11.

[28] E.g., Judg 3:8; 10:7; Isa 9:12; 10:5–6; 2 Chr 12:2–7. Cf. 2 Chr 28:9–11.

[29] 1 Kgs 11:9; 14:9; 16:2; 2 Kgs 13:3; 21:6; 18:4–6; 22:13; 2 Chr 29:10; 30:8; 34:21. Cf. Hos 13:9–11. However, the political dimension cannot be separated from the context of religious reform.

and for "wrath"; other passages demonstrate parallel usage.[30] Through the curse, divine wrath and the covenant integrally were associated. From generation to generation, the story of apostasy could be retold. Out of continuing trouble came the reflection in Ps 90:9, "all our days have declined in your fury [בעברתך, b 'brtk]."

This rational side of Yahweh's wrath also included individual cases of wrath not tied necessarily to abject apostasy from the covenant.[31] As well, wrath received a rational and individualistic interpretation in the varied meditations in the psalms.[32] Prophets considered that heathens though outside the covenant yet were subject to Yahweh's wrath.[33] The psalmist also frequently invoked Yahweh's wrath upon the heathen.[34]

In sum, the motives for wrath most often relate to the covenant. The vast majority of texts on wrath in Hebrew Scripture focus on the historical outworking of Yahweh's covenant blessings and curses.

Meaning of Scriptural Wrath

Like the motive for wrath most often turns on the covenant, the meaning of Yahweh's wrath in Hebrew Scripture inevitably turns on interpreting the experience of exile and its aftermath. The sad story of wrath through exile is interpreted as Yahweh expressing ultimate sovereignty and power. All the stories of destruction preserved from the past were told as lenses through which to focus an explanation of the exile. Catastrophic disasters such as Noah and the flood, the destruction of Sodom and Gomorrah, Mount Perazim, and the Valley of Gibeon were understood to be manifestations of divine wrath. From the stories of the past, the divine wrath that fell was used to exemplify the wrath of the exile upon the covenant people of Yahweh.[35]

---

[30] Saphir, "Mysterious Wrath," 214–19. Also, note Deut 29:19–20, 26–27; 2 Kgs 22:13; Num 23:7-8; Prov 24:24; Isa 10:5; Nah 1:6; Jer 10:10; Ps 38:4.

[31] E.g., Exod 4:14; Num 12:1–15; 22:22; 1 Sam 28:18; 2 Chr 19:2; 32:24–25 (but cf. 32:26); Job 42:7; Eccl 5:6.

[32] E.g., Ps 38:1; 88:7; 102:10.

[33] Jonah 3:9; Jer 50:13; Hab 3:12; Mic 5:15.

[34] Ps 2:5; 21:9; 79:6; 110:5.

[35] As in Noah and the flood (Genesis 6–9): Isa 54:9; Sodom and Gomorrah (Gen 18:20—19:29): Deut 29:23; 32:32; Isa 1:9–10; 3:9; 13:19; Jer 23:14; 49:18; 50:40; Lam 4:6; Ezek 16:46-56; Hos 11:8; Amos 4:11; Zeph 2:9; Mount Perazim and the Valley of Gibeon, (Josh 10:6–14; 2 Sam 5:17-25): Isa 28:21 and Ezek 13:13.

Yahweh's wrath during the wilderness wanderings were intimations of Yahweh's wrath of the exile. The children of Israel were afflicted by a chronic disenchantment with Yahweh. His gracious provisions were spurned continually as inadequate, a disaffection summarized in the words, "so the people grumbled at Moses."[36] Ten times Yahweh declared he had been put to the test; the last time, when the report of the spies just returned from Canaan was rejected, Yahweh condemned that generation to die in the wilderness.[37] The Korah rebellion and the bronze serpent episode manifested the persistence of the problem of departing from Yahweh.[38] Wilderness experiences of wrath, then, could be understood as early warnings of exile.[39] In the end, the exile became the preeminent historical paradigm for the wrath of Yahweh.[40]

Yahweh's Sovereignty. The exile revealed Yahweh's sovereignty to judge as necessary, regardless his longsuffering patience. The exile was understood as the instrument through which Yahweh vindicated his sovereignty against the wickedness of a wayward nation. Preexilic prophets of woe prepared the way for this interpretation.[41] An inflated sense of confidence in election had produced a false sense of security against judgment among the people of Israel.[42] Sin and ignorance had caused the word of salvation to be misunderstood and rejected, turning into an instrument of judgment and condemnation.[43]

The prophet Jeremiah is representative of the preexilic proclamation of doom and the vindication of Yahweh's sovereignty.[44] Infused with the empathy of divine wrath, Jeremiah gave powerful expression

---

[36] E.g., Exod 15:24; 16:2; 17:2-3; cf. Exod 5:21; 14:11; 32:1; Num 11:1, 4; 12:1; 14:2.

[37] Num 14:22-23, 26-38; cf. 14:11-12.

[38] Num 16; 21:4-9.

[39] Cf. Deut 31:25-29.

[40] 2 Chr 36:13-21 (cf. Ps 78:38); Zech 1:2, 12; 7:8-14; Ezra 5:12; Ps 85:1-4; Jer 32:37; Lam 2:1-3; 5:22; Isa 42:25; 47:6; 51:17; 54:8; 60:10.

[41] Including Amos and Micah, implicitly following understandings in Isaiah and Hosea; cf. Simpson, "Divine Wrath in the Eighth-Century Prophets," 103.

[42] Cf. Amos 3:2; 5:18; Hos 13:9-11; Isa 5:18-19; 28:14-22; Mic 3:11; Zeph 2:2; Jer 7:4; 28:1-17; Ezek 5:13; 16:38.

[43] Isa 28:13; Jer 23:29. Cf. Isa 28:21.

[44] For the following discussion, see Jer 2:1-3, 13, 31-32; 3:1-2, 19-20; 4:4, 22; 5:7-9; 6:11, 22, 26; 7:20, 29; 8:26; 13:25; 15:17; 17:4, 13; 18:15; 19:4; 20:9; 23:9, 19-20; 31:2-3, 9; 32:31; 36:7.

to the wrath of God. Jeremiah still proclaimed great assurance of Yahweh's profound love for his people. Yahweh continued his faithfulness in everlasting love. Jeremiah idealized the wilderness time, referring to Israel's devotion of her youth. As a tender, loving father to Israel, he had given a pleasant land as an inheritance among the nations. The intimate nature of marriage was used as a pattern for the relationship of God and Israel. Nuptial imagery gave forceful expression to the adultery and harlotry of Israel's unfaithfulness to Yahweh. In the prophetic conscience, Israel's desertion caused Yahweh anguish. In this way, wrath could be understood as the expected counterpart to wounded love.[45] In the words of Jer 14:17,

> "And you will say this word to them,
> 'Let my eyes flow down with tears night and day,
> And let them not cease;
> For the virgin daughter of my people has been crushed with a mighty blow,
> With a sorely infected wound.'"

Judgment was understood in the context of love, the threat of exile in the context of the promise of restoration.[46]

Other prophets used the theme of harlotry to exemplify Israel's apostasy.[47] Ezekiel frequently referred to the divine wrath. Ezekiel told the story of two sisters, Oholah and Oholibah, representing Samaria and Jerusalem. They became wives of Yahweh but were unfaithful harlots.[48]

Yahweh's Power. Another message of the exile was Yahweh's power. Righteousness in daily affairs was a basic demand of the covenant relationship increasingly ignored by the people of Israel. In prophetic accusations, because the nation obeyed not the voice of the Lord their God, Israel was rejected and forsaken, having become the generation of his wrath. God's power in his wrath inevitably could overcome the nation's rebellion. The people sorely miscalculated both God's intent and ability to enforce the judgment of covenant curse.

---

[45] Fichtner, *TDNT* s.v. "ὀργή," 5:403.

[46] Jer 12:7–13; 31:15–17. On wrath as part of the divine *pathos*, see Heschel, *The Prophets*, 279-98.

[47] E.g., Hos 3:1; 4:7–19; 5:1–7, 10; 9:1; Ezek 16:42. Cf. Ps 106:39–40.

[48] Ezek 23:1–35. Ezekiel was quite vocal about the wrath of Yahweh; e.g., Ezek 5:15; 6:12; 7:8; 8:18; 14:19; 16:38; 20:8.

Figure 3.2. Altar at Dan. Israel divided into northern and southern kingdoms after king Solomon. King Jeroboam built a high place at Dan as a competitive cultus to Jerusalem in 920 BC with a golden calf idol (1 Kgs 12:26–30). King Ahab (c. 874–853 BC) enlarged the altar area and devoted activities to the worship of Baal. Finally, king Jeroboam II remodeled the area again (c. 760 BC). The modern iron frame outlines Jeroboam II's remodeled stone altar, with some of the original steps leading up to the altar still remaining. Amos warned Israel of Yahweh's wrath, which fell in 722 BC.

Figure 3.3. Panias. Jordan headwaters flow from Panias, where the Greek god Pan was worshipped. Herod the Great built a temple to Caesar here, and Herod Philip remodeled as Caesarea Philippi. Jesus asked his disciples about his identity here (Mark 8:27).

Figure 3.4. Grotto of Pan. An artist's conception of the Grotto of Pan at Caesarea Philippi. The natural cave in which welled up the headwaters of the Jordan River was sanctified by the Greeks and dedicated to the worship of Pan, god of the forest and shepherds. Herod the Great received the area from Augustus and dedicated a temple to honor the emperor near the Grotto. Rock-carved niches in the hillside held statues dedicated to the worship of other gods, including Zeus, Asklepios, Athena, Hera, Aphrodite, Artemis, Dionysus, and Aris. The history of Panias reveals how idolatrous northern territory surrounding Galilee continued to be even centuries after the exile.

Figure 3.5. Jerusalem Temple Model. This model of the city of Jerusalem just prior to the First Jewish War is about 22,000 square feet, based on reconstructions from the Mishnah, Josephus, and archeology, now part of the Israel Museum. The architecture is thoroughly Greco-Roman, but Jewish emphases are also dominant, such as no statuary or images in the streets, and only one temple complex. In Matt 23:37–39, the city's recalcitrant rejection of her prophets forebodes God's future wrath (IMJ).

Even in the midst of this proclamation of judgment, the promise was given that if Israel would return to the Lord, God would heal their apostasy, would love them freely, and would turn away his anger from them—even at the last moment.[49] However, the warnings from Yahweh by the prophets were ignored as having no substance. Thus, the people's obdurate contemning of the covenant through flagrant violation of its laws and precepts irrevocably provoked the power of God's wrath as expressed through the exile. The spread of wickedness had caused an illusion: evil was called good; good called evil; and the belief was that Yahweh would not be angry.[50] The crisis eminently was summarized and immortalized in the words of 2 Chr 36:16, "But they *continually* mocked the messengers of God, despised his words and scoffed at his prophets, until the wrath of the Lord [חמת יהוה, *ḥmt yhwh*] arose against his people, until there was no remedy."

Postexilic Reflections

Mixed messages about the results of the exile present a puzzle to try to decipher. On the one hand, as a result of the experience of exile, the feeling within some prophetic circles was that Israel was requited of the injured relationship with Yahweh. One premier example is how the immediate prospect of return from exile inspired words of comfort in Isa 40:1–2,

> "Comfort, O comfort my people," says your God.
> "Speak kindly to Jerusalem;
> And call out to her, that her warfare has ended,
> That her iniquity has been removed,
> That she has received of the Lord's hand
> Double for all her sins."

A double payment was considered a payment in full. "My people, . . . your God" were covenant words that reaffirmed a fundamental datum of the faith of Israel.[51] These expectations are so full of hope for a bright future. Nothing remains for which Israel needs to atone.

Exilic Enigma. Yet, problems crop up right away. The story has the look and feel of the exodus redemption from Egypt that inexplicably

---

[49] Cf. Isa 10:1–6; Jer 7:28–29; 32:29–32; 44:8; cf. Zech 7:12; Hos 14:1–4.

[50] Zeph 1:12; Amos 9:10; Isa 5:16–25.

[51] Scott, *Isaiah*, IB, 5:424.

was followed by Aaron's golden calf incident at Sinai. The problems are apparent in the postexilic writings of Ezra and Nehemiah. After the exile, Ezra felt the need to guard against apostasy through marital exclusiveness in Ezra 10:14. In a similar fashion, Nehemiah had to harp on Sabbath observance as a means to avoid divine wrath in Neh 13:8.

Why is such an irreligious attitude surfacing in postexilic Israel? The strong impression from Jewish lament rhetoric in the face of exile is of a hard lesson learned, as in Ps 44:14–15,

> You have made us a byword among the nations,
>   a laughingstock among the peoples.
> All day long my disgrace is before me,
>   and shame has covered my face
> at the words of the taunters and revilers,
>   at the sight of the enemy and the avenger. (NRSV)

Again, Lamentations is full of remorse, as in Lam 2:11,

> My eyes are spent with weeping;
>   my stomach churns;
> my bile is poured out on the ground
>   because of the destruction of my people,
> because infants and babes faint
>   in the streets of the city. (NRSV)

After the punishment of the exile and the lessons that should have been learned, the developing situation in Jerusalem truly is an enigma. In spite of a feeling among some returning Israelites of a restored relationship to God, the bleak situation in Jerusalem upon the return from Babylon encouraged a feeling that the wrath of God somehow was still on Israel even after the bitter experience of the exile.[52] For inhabitants of Jerusalem, the question was whether a one-to-one correspondence of desert and punishment existed after the exile. In such a climate of thought, theodicy defending the ways of God became a problem that needed to be solved in late wisdom material.[53]

Power and Sovereignty. Other messages about divine wrath after the exile included God's power and sovereignty. In a typical way, wrath expressed God's power. Attention, however often turned to the heathen nations. After the exile, wrath turns back onto the heathen nations for

---

[52] Cf. Hag 1:5–11; Zech 1:3, 19; Isa 64:9. Cf. Ps 74:1–8; 85:4–6.
[53] Cf. Hengel, *Judaism and Hellenism*, 250.

their own hubris and idolatry. After the exile, the nations were seen as the objects of God's wrath.[54] Overwhelmed by its enemies, the feeble Jerusalem community felt itself in a precarious position; their survival depended on the direct aid of God.[55] Yahweh's power would protect Israel. A standard theme developed in the literature: against the raging of the nations, God would save Israel from her enemies.[56] This theme could be augmented until the wrath of God against other nations was declared eternal.[57] Such an attitude, however, would present a problem for postexilic Israel in defining her relationship and obligation to the nations of the world in terms of Israel's divinely intended destiny.

Again, in a typical way, God's sovereignty was another postexilic motif about wrath. Wrath on Israel and the nations expressed God's dominion over all human arrogance. Humans had limits beyond which they were not allowed. Transgression of those limits drew divine response, an idea common in Greek literature. Assyria, the rod of Yahweh's anger, arrogantly looked upon success as from the strength of its own hand, and for that, Yahweh turned his wrath upon Assyria itself, and the same was true for Moab.[58] Ezekiel warned Israel's neighbors that gloating over Jerusalem's desolation drew divine indignation; further, the unwarranted pride of Tyre and of Egypt had provoked Yahweh.[59] In Zech 1:15, heathen nations that had aggravated Israel's disaster more than God had intended had aroused Yahweh to great wrath against them; they inordinately had interfered with Yahweh's Israel. Without divine sanction, such interference with Israel infringed upon Yahweh's sovereignty and would not be tolerated. At stake was the inalienable prerogative of Yahweh's sovereignty. In the "Song of Moses" in Deut 32:1–43, the wrath that fell upon Israel would boomerang onto the heathen, lest they misinterpret Israel's misfortunes and not perceive the true origins of that calamity. Vengeance belonged to God alone. In Ezra 7:23, Artaxerxes commanded the restoration of Yahweh's house in deference to the divine wrath that otherwise might be provoked.

[54] Cf. Isa 59:18; 63:3–6; 66:14.
[55] Zech 1:14; 2:1–5; 8:2, 7.
[56] Isa 42:13; 48:9–11; 59:17; 63:15; Zech 1:16–21.
[57] Mal 1:4; cf. Nah 1:9; 3:19.
[58] Isa 10:5–15 (cf. 14:4–6); 16:6–7.
[59] Ezek 25:1–7; 28:2; 29:3.

Divine Name. Yahweh expressed his power in order to reveal his Name to all the inhabited earth.[60] Therefore, offering blind, lame, and sick animals as sacrifices profaned the Name of Yahweh in Malachi's postexilic community, a serious offense (Mal 1:7–12). Yahweh was displeased because he was intent that his Name should be great among the nations (Mal 1:11). Malachi made clear that Yahweh's dealings with Israel interpenetrated his purposes among the heathen. Just as the forgiveness of sins of the individual and the community was for his namesake, Yahweh's pity on Israel also was meant to sanctify his great Name that the heathen should know him as God.[61] Thus, even the exile was not the full venting of Yahweh's wrath, even with the assurance of Isa 40:1–3, which must be interpreted in a relative sense in the strict terms of divine holiness. For his own praise, Yahweh deferred his full wrath, because such wrath would destroy Israel utterly.[62] Yahweh would reveal his judgments so that all of the inhabitants of the world would learn righteousness.[63] That goal always was the point of Israel: "the earth is the Lord's and the fullness thereof" (Ps 24:1). Yahweh as the only God was to be known among the nations, not just in Israel.

Eschatological Wrath. Postexilic reflections on Yahweh's wrath took on eschatological dimensions. The Day of the Lord of which one reads in Amos was used subsequently in oracles of judgment upon Israel and upon the world.[64] The judgment of Babylon became particularly significant.[65] In Zeph 1:14–18, the Day of the Lord would be the day of Yahweh's wrath. In Isa 26:20–21, eschatological wrath would take its course, and the people of Yahweh would have to be preserved from this ineluctable process.[66] As the time of the end was appointed, so the

---

[60] As through Pharaoh in Exod 9:16; cf. Ezek 20:9, 14, 22, 44. See Josh 7:9; 1 Kgs 8:42–43; 9:3 (cf. Jer 7:14–15); Ps 8:1, 9; 106:8.

[61] Ps 25:11 (cf. 109:21); 79:7; Ezek 36:21–22. Cf. 1 Sam 12:22; Num 14:13–21.

[62] Isa 48:9; cf. Deut 6:15.

[63] Cf. Isa 5:16; 10:22; 26:9; Zeph 3:4; Ps 9:8; 96:13; 98:9. Contrast Ps 69:22–28 with Dan 9:16. Wrath and righteousness are not explicitly linked in Scripture (Fichtner, *TDNT* s.v. "ὀργή," 5:408), but note Vriezen, *An Outline of Old Testament Theology*, 159–60.

[64] Amos 5:18–20; cf. Joel 2:1–11, 28–32; 3:9–16; Zeph 3:8; Isa 2:12; 13:9–11, 13; 24:1–23; 26:19–21; 34:1–10.

[65] Kaiser, *Isaiah 13–39*, 12–13.

[66] Compare this thought with the last plague's passing over of the death angel in Exod 12:23–32.

divine indignation obtained an element of determination. Such an appointed time for the season of eschatological wrath was immutable. The divine wrath would be accomplished inexorably.[67]

Greek Septuagint

The linguistic phenomenon on divine wrath in the Greek translation of the Hebrew Scripture has several striking features. First, one immediately is confronted with the virtual absence of the old Homeric terms κότος, *kotos*, μῆνις, *mēnis*, and χόλος, *cholos*. On rare occasions, these Homeric terms were used for human anger, as in Gen 49:7 and Eccl 5:16. The terms κότος, *kotos*, and χόλος, *cholos*, are missing altogether in noun or verb form in relation to divine wrath. The noun μῆνις, *mēnis*, does not appear at all for divine wrath, and its cognate verbal form appears only twice in Ps 102:9 and Jer 3:12. The quick result is, of the five Greek words for wrath, the translators used almost exclusively the terms θυμός, *thumos*, and ὀργή, *orgē*, for divine wrath.

Second, any distinction between the use of θυμός, *thumos*, and ὀργή, *orgē* in the Septuagint is imperceptible. Translation evidence indicates indiscriminate substitution of one term for the other, both in noun and verb forms.[68] Frequently found are constructions of the verbal form of one term with the noun form in the instrumental case of the other, i.e., as ὀργίζεται θυμῷ (*orgizetai thumōi*)[69] or θυμοῦσθαι ὀργῇ (*thumousthai orgēi*).[70] The nouns occur in reversible roles in genitival constructions, i.e., as ὀργὴ θυμοῦ (*orgē thumou*), or θυμὸς ὀργῆς (*thumos orgēs*).[71] Synonymity is illustrated further in the use of the terms

---

[67] Dan 8:19; 11:36; Young (*Daniel*, 177; cf. 15–17) designated הזעם (*hz'm*) as a technical term for the wrath of God, specifically of the Babylonian exile as "the Wrath"; thus, the appearance of Antiochus IV Epiphanes marks the last portion of this period of wrath. For זעם (*z'm*) as a technical term, see chapter 1, p.5.

[68] Of nouns, cf. Judg 9:30; 14:19; Isa 5:25; 10:4; Jer 10:25; Lam 4:11; 2 Chr 29:8. Of verbs, cf. Deut 11:17; Judg 9:30; 10:7; 14:19; Isa 5:25.

[69] E.g., Exod 22:24; Num 22:22; 25:3; 32:10, 13; Deut 6:15; 7:4; 29:27; 31:17; Judg 2:14, 20; 3:8; 10:7; 2 Kgs 13:3; 2 Chr 35:19; Ps 105:40. Frequently used for the expression חרה אף (*ḥrh 'p*).

[70] E.g, Exod 4:14; 32:10, 11; Num 11:1, 10; Deut 11:17; Josh 7:1; 2 Sam 6:7; 2 Kgs 1:18; 1 Chr 13:10; Isa 5:25. Frequently used for חרה אף (*ḥrh 'p*).

[71] E.g., Exod 32:12; Num 12:9; 14:34; 25:4; 32:14; Deut 13:17; 29:24; 1 Sam 28:18; 2 Kgs 23:26; 2 Chr 28:11, 13; 29:10; 30:8; 35:19; Ezra 10:14; Ps 68:25; 77:49; 84:3; 89:7;

either directly together[72] or in parallel constructions.[73] The adjectival form ὀργίλος (*orgilos*) is not used of God, and the form θυμώδης (*thumōdēs*) is used only once of God (Jer 37:23). The passive forms of ὀργίζω (*orgizō*)[74] and θυμόω (*thumoō*)[75] are used of God meaning "to become angry" or "to be angry." The compound verb παροργίζω (*parorgizō*), meaning "to provoke" or "to provoke to anger," is used of God, frequently in the Kings material.[76] The associated nouns παρόργισμα (*parorgisma*) and παροργισμός (*parorgismos*) also are used of God.[77]

Third, the translation at times appears to have been mechanical. The Hebrew term חמה (*ḥmh*), often meaning wrath, also could mean the poison of serpents or arrows. The translators of the Septuagint made no distinction and used *thumos* in cases where "poison" was the obvious meaning.[78] Similarly, the term אף (*ʾp*), "nose," was translated with *orgē* when the anatomical "nose" was appropriate, as in Ps 17:8, 15. Besides these obvious denotational mistakes, deliberate alterations in the meaning are made. References to God's wrath were eliminated by reference to human sin instead.[79] Other innovative alterations also helped reduce the association of wrath with God, a move clearly influenced by Greek philosophical considerations.[80]

105:23; Isa 7:4; 9:19; 13:13; 30:27; 42:25; Jer 4:26; 37:24; Lam 1:12; 2:3; 4:11; Ezek 23:25; Hos 11:9; Jonah 3:9; Nah 1:6; Zeph 3:8. Frequently used for חרון אף (*ḥrwn ʾp*).

[72] E.g., Deut 9:19; 29:23, 28; Josh 17:26; Ps 101:10; Isa 5:25; 10:5; 13:19; 30:30; 59:19; Jer 7:20; 21:5; 43:7; Ezek 5:13; Dan 9:16; Mic 5:15.

[73] E.g., Ps 2:5; 6:1; 37:1; 77:38, 49; 89:11–12; Prov 15:1; 21:14; 27:4; Isa 34:2; Jer 39:31, 37; 45:5; 51:6; Lam 2:2; Ezek 7:8; 13:13; 20:8, 21; 22:31; 25:14; Hos 13:11; Nah 1:6; Zeph 2:2.

[74] See note 69 above; also 1 Kgs 11:9; Ps 2:12; 17:7; 59:1; 78:5; 79:4; 84:5; 102:9; Eccl 5:5; Isa 12:1; 28:28; 57:6, 16; 64:5, 9; Lam 5:22; Hab 3:8; Zech 1:2, 15.

[75] See note 70 above; also, Deut 1:37; 4:21; 9:8; 2 Sam 22:8; 2 Kgs 17:18; Isa 37:29; 54:9; Hos 11:7.

[76] Deut 4:25; 31:29; Judg 2:13; 1 Kgs 15:30; 16:2, 7, 13, 26, 33; 20:20, 22; 22:54; 2 Kgs 17:11, 17; 2 Chr 28:25; Ezra 5:12; Ps 77:40; Job 12:6; Isa 1:4; Jer 7:18; Ezek 16:26; Mic 2:7; Zech 8:14.

[77] 1 Kgs 16:33; 20:22; 2 Chr 35:19; 1 Kgs 15:30; 2 Kgs 23:26.

[78] Deut 32:24; Ps 58:4; Job 6:4.

[79] E.g., Job 42:7; Num 1:53; Isa 57:17.

[80] Mal 1:4; Isa 66:14; Zech 1:12. Already noted by Fichtner, *TDNT* s.v. "ὀργή," 5:411–12. Cf. Fritsch, *The Anti-Anthropomorphisms of the Greek Pentateuch*.

Apocrypha, Pseudepigrapha

In terms of material in Hebrew, Sirach[81] reveals the continuing use of various Hebrew terms already investigated, e.g., אף (᾿p), חמה (ḥmh), זעם (z῾m), רגז (rgz), and חרון אף (ḥrwn ᾿p).[82] In terms of material in Greek, the synonymous terms *orgē* and *thumos* were dominant (though other terms were used), while the use of *orgē* appears to have been more frequent.[83]

The wrath of God was understood to be an experience of individuals.[84] In one classic example, the Prayer of Manasseh, a short work of only fifteen verses,[85] reveals the wrath of God was considered a serious threat to the individual's life (5, 10, 13). The author felt he had no recourse against divine wrath other than to entrust himself to the great mercy of God to respond to a contrite, repentant heart.

The wrath of God also was understood as a corporate experience. Divine wrath was understood to have fallen upon multiple groups, whether the exiled Jews, the Jews under Antiochus IV Epiphanes, or the two and a half tribes of the northern kingdom. Above all, however, divine wrath especially was upon heathens and all sinners.[86]

---

[81] Or, Wisdom of Jesus the Son of Sirach (Latin: Ecclesiasticus). From the third to second cent. BC, Sirach is a prototypical example of Jewish wisdom genre. Though in the Septuagint, therefore the Roman Catholic canon, Jewish authorities rejected the book as apocryphal, so not in the Masoretic text behind the Protestant canon.

[82] Sir 5:6, 7; 16:11; 36:7; 39:23; 45:19. Cf. Levi, *The Hebrew Text of the Book of Ecclesiasticus*.

[83] E.g., Jdt 8:14; 9:8, 9; Wis 5:18; 16:5; 18:20, 21; 19:1; Bar 1:13; 2:13, 20; 4:6, 9, 25; 1 Macc 1:64; 2:49; 3:8; Letter of Aristeas 254 (in Hadas, *Aristeas to Philocrates*); T. Levi 3:10; 6:11 and T. Reu. 4:4 (in De Jonge; *Testamenta*); 1 En. 10:22; 13:8; 99:16; 101:3; 106:15; (in Black, *Apocalypsis Henochi Graece*,); 3 Bar. 4:8, 13; 9:7; 16:2, 3 (in Brock, *Testamentum Iobi*); Apocalypse of Moses 8, 14, 16, 18, 21 and Apocalypse of Esdras 15 (in Tischendorf, *Apocalypses Apocryphae*) For other terms, cf. Bar 4:7; Wis 18:22.

[84] Cf. Apoc. of Moses 3, 16, 18, 21; T. Reu. 4:4; 4 Macc 9:32; Jub. 3:23.

[85] Manasseh was the most idolatrous king of Judah. His supposed repentance from idolatry, recorded only in 2 Chr 33:15–17 but never mentioned in 2 Kings, is an obvious attempt to rehabilitate his image. His prayer is mentioned but not given in 2 Chr 33:19, so some Greek writer in the second or first century BC supplied the prayer. Universally rejected as apocryphal, the text still made some editions of the LXX, the Vulgate, the AV, and a few early English translations.

[86] 2 Esd 8:30, 34–35; Sir 5:6, 7; 6:6; 16:6; 18:24; 36:7, 23, 39; Bar 1:13; 2:13, 20; 4:6, 9, 25; Wis 19:1; Jdt 8:18–19; 9:8–9; 1 Macc 1:64; 2:49; 3:8; 2 Macc 5:17–20; 7:33, 38; 2 Bar. 48:14–15, 17; 64:3; 3 Bar. 16:2; Pss. Sol. 4:25; 7:4; 8:7–9; Jub. 15:34; 24:30; 36:10; As. Mos.

Themes from Hebrew Scripture on the wrath of God continued to be developed in the literature of this later period.[87] For example, the tension of understanding the interoperation of wrath and mercy was given expression, while divine wrath continued to be understood as God in his love remonstrating with Israel over her sin. Again, the short time of wrath could be emphasized. Writers recalled past deeds of salvation to persuade God to remove his present wrath. Apostasy was understood as a basic cause for wrath, and the motif entered into the eschatological perspective. As in the Hebrew Scripture, divine wrath could be viewed as a strange work; in such cases, the confession was a straightforward admission that fundamentally the ways of God were inscrutable. The experience of divine wrath could be understood as being forsaken by God. Another idea was that the impious would be destroyed.[88] The manifestation of divine wrath could be described as "from heaven," and those upon whom wrath fell "children of wrath."[89]

Divine wrath currently operative in history was proleptic of the final day of wrath.[90] Eschatological perspectives were augmented into apocalyptic speculations.[91] In an apocalyptic work such as 1 Enoch,

> Injustice was the salient fact of life.... The author reveals, first of all, an imminent future in which the present injustices will be reversed and the tensions which they have created will be alleviated.[92]

8:1; 10:3; 4 Macc 4:21; 1 En. 10:22; 62:12; 90:15, 18; 91:7, 9; 99:16; 101:3; Sib. Or. 3:51–56; 4:159–60; 5:508; T. Levi 3:10.

[87] E.g., the Flood in Sir 44:17; Sib. Or. 4:51–53; 1 En. 106:15; Sodom in Jub. 36:10; the Wilderness in Wis 16:5; men of Shechem in T. Levi 6:11; Korah's rebellion in Sir 45:19; upon Solomon's children in Sir 47:20.

[88] For the above statements, see Jdt 8:14, 18–19; Wis 11:9; 16:5–6; 19:1; Sir 5:6; 16:11; 2 Bar. 2:13; 4:9; 1 Macc 3:8 (note here the association of *orgē* with ungodliness, *asebeis*); 2 Macc 5:17, 20; 7:33; Sib. Or. 4:159–60; Pss. Sol. 7:4; 2 Bar. 59:6; Apoc. Ezra 15; 1 En. 5:9; 91:7; Jub. 15:34.

[89] Sib. Or. 3:309; 5:298.

[90] Jub. 24:28–33; 36:10.

[91] Cf. Wis 5:17–23; Sir 36:8–9; 39:23–30; 48:10; Sib. Or. 3:545–61, 796–812; 4:160–61; 5:298–305, 344–60, 508; As. Mos. 10:3–10; 1 En. 10:22; 55:3; 62:10–12; 90:15, 18; 91:7–9; 99:16.

[92] Nickelsburg, "The Apocalyptic Message of 1 Enoch 92–105," 325.

The end time doom could be considered eternal.[93] One function assigned to the eschatological prophet Elijah was the reconciliation and restoration of all the tribes of Jacob before the onslaught of the eschatological wrath.[94]

New features appeared in apocryphal and pseudepigraphical literature. The novel motif of the Watchers developed. The fall of Azazel and his cohorts was used to explain the origins of evil and the presence of divine wrath.[95] The quest for theodicy that already had taken root in Hebrew Scripture was extended with a new attitude about mankind revealed in the questions asked. How could God turn in wrath against those who were no better than beasts and lacked any understanding? How could God express wrath toward a race doomed to sin because of prevailing corruption and inherent weakness?[96] The assumption of prevailing corruption among humans also was expressed in 2 Esd. 8:30–35; not one person existed who had not sinned. In T. Levi 3:10, a general ignorance was blamed for the problem of sin. The justification for God's wrath offered in 2 Esd. 8:59–60 was that the Most High willed no one be destroyed, but his Name was defiled through the ungratefulness of people who rejected life. Another idea occurring in the Pseudepigrapha concerned an attitude toward physical death. Death explicitly was identified as the instrument of the wrath of God in Apoc. of Moses 14.

Divine righteousness and wrath were associated together as part of the armor of God in Wis 5:18. Compare Pss. Sol. 8:7–9 [Charles]:

> I thought upon the judgments of God since the creation of heaven and earth;
> I held God righteous in his judgments which have been from of old.
> God laid bare their sins in the full light of day;
> All the earth came to know the righteous judgments of God.
> In secret places underground their iniquities (were committed) to provoke (him) to anger.

---

[93] E.g., 1 En. 91:7–9. Cf. Jub. 15:34; 36:10.

[94] Sir 48:10; cf. 36:11.

[95] Almost exclusively in the Enochean material, as in 1 En. 13:8; 18:16; 55:3; 68:4; 84:4–6; as auxiliaries of divine punishment, cf. 53:3–5. Cf. 3 Bar. 4:8; Jub. 5:1–7; 7:21. Cf. Thompson, *Responsibility for Evil in the Theodicy of IV Ezra*, 37–49.

[96] 2 Esd 8:30–35; 2 Bar. 48:14–17; Gk. Apoc. Ezra 15.

The use of divine wrath in 4 Macc 4:21 and 9:32 is after a Hellenic pattern. That is, the divine δίκη (*dikē*, "righteousness") functioned to preserve proper social–political–religious order. The idea was noneschatological. According to the legend recorded in 4 Maccabees, when Apollonius and his armed hosts marched into the Jerusalem temple to seize its monetary treasures, the wrath of a host of heavenly angels was stayed only by the prayer of the high priest. Onias made intercession, "Lest the king Seleucus possibly should consider that Apollonius had been overthrown by a human device and not by divine justice [θείας δίκης, *theias dikēs*]" (4:13). Similarly, Jason, the high priest, enforced Hellenization on Jerusalem. "For this reason the divine justice [ἡ θεία δίκη, *hē theia dikē*] becoming indignant brought Antiochus himself against us" (4:21). Divine righteous anger perhaps is to be understood as having its counterpart in the action of Mattathias, who slew a Jew in "righteous anger," as recorded in 1 Macc 2:24. Actions of wrath on both levels of the human and the divine could be described as righteous.

The treatment of the eruption of Mount Vesuvius in Sib. Or. 4:130–39 is similar to the historical interpretations of extraordinary events as manifestations of divine wrath that are found in the Roman historians. However, the martyrdom of the seven brothers and their mother in 2 Macc 7:1–42 as an act of expiation of divine wrath has little resemblance to the Roman cultic rite of "devotion." The deaths of the Jewish brothers might bring to an end the wrath of the Almighty upon the Jewish nation (7:38), but this action taken in context was not the vicarious suffering of the innocent (cf. 7:32). On the question of martyrdom, the figure of Taxo in the Assumption of Moses may have been a new development in eschatological discourse. Jacob Licht concluded that "the *Assumption of Moses* is unique in teaching that the End will come *because* vengeance shall finally be provoked [i.e., through martyrdom]."[97] Finally, Stoic attitude is reflected in the Letter of Aristeas 253–54 [Charles], in which the concluding charge is given, "'It is necessary to recognize that God rules the whole world in the spirit of kindness and without wrath at all, and you,' said he, 'O king, must of necessity copy his example.'"

---

[97] Licht, "Taxo," 97. The Assumption of Moses might be evidence of the practical ideology for those submitting to martyrdom (Licht, "Taxo," 100).

Methods of alleviating the divine wrath were not worked out systematically in the Apocrypha and Pseudepigrapha. The intercession of Moses (Wis 18:20–25) established the pattern appointed to the eschatological Elijah (Sir 48:9–10). Noah's righteousness secured his own passage through the time of wrath in the Flood (Sir 44:17). Martyrdom could expiate the demands of divine wrath (2 Macc 7:38). The Prayer of Manasseh reveals a release sought through repentance and confessional prayer. In Manasseh's prayer, God alone could allay the divine wrath through his great mercy. This motif of the saving advocacy of God himself appeared in the retelling of the wilderness experience of the stinging serpents in Wis 16:5–7. God provided the bronze serpent to save the people. The author concluded with the thought, "For he who turned toward it was saved, not by what he saw, but by you, the Savior of all" (Wis 16:7 RSV).

Josephus

Josephus used the terms μῆνις, *mēnis*, (*Ant.* 15.243, 299) and χόλος, *cholos* (*J.W.* 7.34, 332), but mainly he used *orgē*.[98] He did not use the term *thumos* and its cognates. With a view to the forthcoming story of the Jews, Josephus set out his programmatic history with the thematic observation that "God, as the universal Father and Lord who beholds all things, grants to such as follow him a life of bliss, but involves in dire calamities those who step outside the path of virtue" (*Ant.* 1.20). As in Greek literature, the human manifestation of wrath could have bad consequences. Divine wrath was a forensic process, punishment meted out as justice against transgressors. Though God's wrath might delay, eventually that wrath would overtake the offender. Impiety was particularly odious to God and could bring immediate retribution. Josephus frequently incorporated the language of divine wrath in discussion of Herod and his house.[99]

Josephus incorporated judgment motifs from Hebrew Scripture. These motifs were part of his literary style and conveyed the degree of gravity attached to the event being reported. This degree of gravity especially was true for the Zealot factions whom Josephus blamed almost

---

[98] E.g., *Ant.* 3.321; 4.130; 11.127, 141; 12.221; 16.222, 263; 19.19.

[99] *Life* 266; *J.W.* 7.34; *Ant.* 1.20, 194–95; 3.321; 11.127, 141; 13.294; 15.243, 299, 376; 17.168. Note Whiston's translations at *Ant.* 14.2.2; 15.7.7; 16.7.2; 17.5.2.

exclusively for the destruction of Jerusalem. In one passage alone, Josephus piled on the Korah rebellion, the Flood, and the Sodom and Gomorrah traditions (*J.W.* 5.13.6).

Josephus concluded his *Jewish War* chronicle on a note about the divine wrath. Josephus related a personal experience of calumny by one Catullus, governor of Pentapolis. Catullus had captured a Jewish insurgent leader named Jonathan. In collusion with Jonathan, Catullus began accusing wealthy Jews of insurrection activity. Josephus himself was included, even in Rome under the patronage of the emperor. Vespasian, fortunately, understood the falsehood, because he had come to know Josephus during the war and fully was aware of how Josephus tried to dissuade Jerusalem inhabitants against resistance to the Roman legions who had arrived at the gates of Jerusalem, including Josephus's own family. Vespasian summarily cleared Josephus, but surprisingly did not condemn Catullus. Josephus interpreted as divine providence the distemper that soon thereafter seized Catullus and killed him. "Thus he became as great an instance of divine providence as ever was, and demonstrated that God punishes wicked men" (*J.W.* 7.11.4). With this parting word incorporating the motif of divine wrath, Josephus concluded his *Jewish War* on a note similar to how he began *Antiquities*.

Philo

In his effort to accommodate Hebrew thought to Greek philosophy, Philo is representative of a mediating position between Hebrew Scripture and Greek Stoicism. A point of stress in Philo's accommodation concerned the wrath of God. Though God could be said to be angry, or unusual events interpreted as the result of divine anger, Philo felt obliged to assert that such descriptions were only anthropopathisms. In reality, God was above passion. The language of divine wrath was a literary contrivance intended simply to meet the needs of those who were ignorant of a higher knowledge of God. This philosophical position at times would give way to moral reason, and Philo unwittingly would relapse into an admission using the language of divine wrath, as in *Dreams* 2.179. Philo evidences a distinct preference for *orgē* to express the divine wrath over the use of *thumos*.[100]

---

[100] For the above paragraph, cf. Philo, *Dreams* 1.235; 2.177–79; *Moses* 1.6, 119; *Sacrifices* 95–96; *Abraham* 202; *Unchangeable* 52–54, 59–60.

Rabbinic Literature

In terms of anger and wrath, rabbinic literature reflected attitudes in evidence in wisdom literature. As human anger generally was condemned in the wisdom movement, such expressions of anger also were condemned by the rabbis.[101] At the same time, God could be described as angry without any apparent inhibition.[102] That divine anger at times was quite arbitrary seemed to pose no special problem to be solved.[103] However, even if the expression of divine wrath was absent a rational explanation on rare occasion, the rabbis expressed abiding confidence in the mercy of God even in his wrath. Thought about divine wrath regularly was coordinated with meditations on divine mercy. For example, Deut 32:19 dealt with God's spurning of Israel. Yet this passage evoked the thought that if God could be merciful to pagan sinners, even more so could mercy be extended to his own people. In this way, the rabbis expressed confidence that a time of mercy would follow wrath. This association was not axiomatic, though, since divine wrath not always was linked to mercy. In fact, discussion even might gravitate to the question whether divine wrath produced a lasting effect.[104] The certain truth was that "as long as the wicked exist in the world, there is fierce anger in the world; when the wicked perish from the world, fierce anger disappears from the world."[105]

Attempts were made to absolve God of expressions of wrath as on the pattern of human anger. Philo already was making attempts to rationalize these anthropomorphisms of Scripture on this very same issue. Philosophical considerations had their impact among the rabbis as well. One rabbinic technique was to invoke a mediating agent. This agent could be used to place God one step away from the expression of divine wrath. One such mediating agent, for example, used to mitigate anthropomorphisms was the Angel of Destruction.[106]

---

[101] Str-B 1:276–78; cf. Prov 19:11; Eccl 7:9.

[102] E.g., Sanh. 105b (2:718), quoting Ps 7:12; cf. ʿAbod. Zar. 4b (pp. 15–16). Epstein, *The Babylonian Talmud*. Page numbers refer to the Soncino edition.

[103] Cf. Str-B 3:409, 685, 687.

[104] Zebaḥ. 102a (pp. 490–91).

[105] Sanh. 111b (2:768). Similarly, Sanh. 113b (2:781).

[106] Cf. Str-B 3:30–31; Šhab. 55a (1:254); Ned. 32a (p. 95).

The concept of divine wrath intersects with the Jewish imagery of Gehenna. Gehenna is translated literally as the "Valley of Hinnom" a small valley immediately south of Jerusalem that merges with the eastern Kidron valley at the city's southeastern corner. History rendered the valley synonymous with idolatry, since propitiatory sacrifices were offered here to the god Molech by burning children in fire.[107] This abomination rendered the place cursed and used as a metaphor for the destination of the wicked. Gehenna could be considered equivalent thematically to the concept of divine wrath in rabbinic thought. The Talmud index records only four references to divine wrath, but seventy-seven references to Gehenna.[108] The impetus for this rabbinic trajectory could have been the development of the idea of Topeth (Valley of Hinnom) as a place of divine judgment particularly by Jeremiah just prior to the wrath of exile.[109]

Figure 3.6. Jerusalem: Valley of Hinnom. Mount of Olives view of the Valley of Hinnom intersecting with the Kidron Valley at the southwest corner of the city wall.

---

[107] LXX as "Molech"; cf. Lev 18:21; 20:2, 3, 4, 5; 1 Kgs11:7; 2 Kgs 23:10 (implicitly, 16:3; 21:6); Jer 32:35. Cf. Stephen, Acts 7:43. Cf. Heider, "Molech," *AYDB* 4:897–98.

[108] Slotki, *Index Volume*, 21, 157. Roetzel, *Judgment in the Community*, 64, for example, equated Gehenna with the language of divine wrath in the rabbis.

[109] Jer 7:32; 19:6; 32:35.

The name of Gehenna came to be associated with the eschatological fire of punishment in the afterlife.¹¹⁰ In rabbinic literature, thought of God's final judgment introducing the future eon generated thought of a final Gehenna. God's final judgment would be the eradication of the enemies of God from the world; however, if the mode of judgment were understood as total annihilation, Gehenna no longer would be necessary. Punishment could conceive bodily suffering; in contrast, the idea that Gehenna involved a disembodied state was rare. Though praise to God was possible from Gehenna, nowhere does the salvation of the condemned take place on the basis of this praise. Very rarely expressed is the thought of possible salvation for those in Gehenna.¹¹¹ By the first century AD, Gehenna was conceived as a place of punishment in an intermediate state for the ungodly.¹¹²

Dead Sea Scrolls

Determinism underlay the religious language of the Dead Sea Scrolls.¹¹³ God had predetermined all the epochs of time, and all events strictly conformed to the divine plan.¹¹⁴ Two eras divided history. The present era was the Era of Wrath (or Wickedness), and the coming era was the era of Divine Favor.¹¹⁵ The doctrine of fixed epochs was explained in the work The Epochs of Time.

The language of divine wrath took its shape under the rubric of this determination. "But the wicked hast Thou created / for the time of Thy [wr]ath, / reserving them from the womb / for the day of slaughter."¹¹⁶ The theme of humanity as a shape molded of clay underscored the sovereignty of God. Divine actions might illustrate a deterministic path for humans, but never could impugn God's righteousness.¹¹⁷ Final destruction would serve only to reveal God's righteousness. "Thou wilt

---

[110] E.g., 2 Esd 7:36; 1 En. 27:1–3; 90:26; 2 Bar. 59:10; 85:13.

[111] For the above, cf. Str-B 4:1093; 4:1100–02.

[112] Jeremias, *TDNT*, s.v. "γέεννα," 1:658; Gaster, IDB, s.v. "Gehenna," 2:361–62.

[113] Gaster, *The Dead Sea Scriptures*, is one of the best available for non-scholars.

[114] M 3:13—4:26; Z 2:2–13; H 15:15–20; ET 2 (reference scheme: Gaster, 547–48).

[115] Z 1:1—2:12; 4:6–12; 5:17—7:6a; 13:20; 14:18; 15:1—16:20; HosC 2:8; HabC 1:12–13; H 15:15.

[116] H 15:15–20.

[117] H 12:25–32; cf. H 1:5–9.

bring eternal doom / on all frowardness and transgression, / and Thy righteousness will stand revealed / in the sight of all Thou hast made."[118]

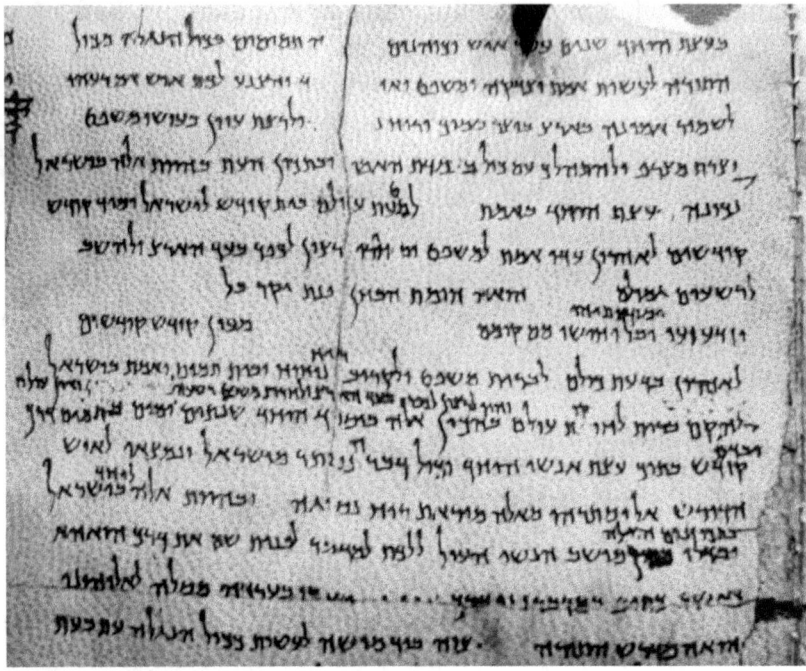

Figure 3.7. Qumran Scroll Replica. The museum at the Qumran archeological site has on display this replica of a Qumran scroll (QNPM).

The people of the Dead Sea community used and interpreted Hebrew Scripture.[119] Further, they incorporated standard judgment motifs of the period into the language of wrath, including the Watchers of heaven, Noah and the Flood, Sodom and Gomorrah, the Wilderness murmurings, and royal apostasy.[120] Review of chronic human wickedness concluded with the summary observation, "throughout antiquity, however, God has always taken note of the deeds of such men, and his anger has always been kindled against their acts."[121] Especially serious was the highhandedness that could characterize an attitude toward things patently revealed in God's ordinances. In M 5:7–20, such action incurred God's angry judgment, which would not be exhausted

[118] H 14:16.

[119] Z 2:14—3:12; 7:9—8:21; 9:2–8. Cf. RB 5–6; L 1:2:1.

[120] Z 2:14—3:12; 16:11—17:15; PI 2; ET 3:4–8.

[121] Z 4:12—5:17.

until the offenders were destroyed without remnant. In ZD 2:13, this destruction could be a passive action; i.e., God would leave the wicked alone to wander astray. In HabC 2:16, the cup of God's wrath would confound the wicked, and the theme of wrath and power is manifested in ZD 2:2–13.

In light of the determinism, humans were faced with the choice of following either of two spirits, according to M 3:13—4:26. One was the spirit of truth and the other the spirit of perversity. All actions, all afflictions, and all periods of well-being could be explained by the two spirits within each person. Individual behavior testified to which spirit was followed. The one practicing righteousness was under the domination of the Prince of Lights; the one practicing perversity was under the domination of the Angel of Darkness. A list of characteristic actions typified each category. The horrible fate of those who followed the spirit of perversity was described in part as "everlasting perdition through the angry wrath of an avenging God" (M 4:12).

The language of wrath was integral to the work Prayer for Intercession. Enduring continual provocation, God yet refused to reject the seed of Jacob in the history of Israel. Recalling such mercies of the past, the supplicant beseeched God with the refrain, "So now let Thine anger and Thy wrath be turned away from us" (PI 2, 6).

An apocalyptic perspective dominated the thought of the community of the Scrolls. Interpretation of Scripture and present experience reflected the well-entrenched belief that the end was imminent.[122] The coming doom would realize the eternal wrath of God.[123] The final fate of the wicked would be annihilation.[124] In W 3:1—6:6, the accoutrements of the eschatological war included instruments and vessels upon which were inscribed the language of divine wrath and vengeance upon Belial and his hosts. In W 6:4, for example, on the second dart of the squadron throwing javelins was to be written: "Spurtings of blood, causing men to fall slain through the anger of God."

Finally, mention should be made of a quite curious interpretation witnessed in the Code for the Urban Communities section of the Za-

---

[122] M 1:16—2:18; 3:13-4:26; Z 7:9—8:21; H 3:25-29; 14:15-20; 15:15-20; HabC 2:20; W 3:1—6:6; RB 5–6; ET 2.

[123] M 1:16—2:18; 3:13—4:26; H 3:25-29; 14:15-20; ET 2.

[124] M 1:16—2:18; 3:13—4:26; Z 2:2-13; 7:9—8:21; W 3:12—4:2; 15:1-2; HabC 2:20.

dokite Document (10:4–10). Here, the loss of mental acumen in old age was attributed to an ancient decree by God given in the heat of his anger against the inhabitants of the earth. This interpretation is quite distinctive, perhaps unique.

SAMARITAN LITERATURE

Samaritan life and community evocatively echo ancient Judaism. Their traditions offer promise for understanding New Testament texts, most particularly in John 4 and Acts 8, but also in Paul, but their religious materials are late, about the fourth century AD on, which renders study of the first-century context difficult. The Samaritan Pentateuch, dating back to the second century BC, offers an alternative resource for a study of the ancient Hebrew text, with some readings likely original.[125]

An important feature of Samaritan theology is to be discerned in their liturgy. The last tenet of their creedal affirmation is belief in what they called the Day of Vengeance and Recompense. This doctrine was derived from Deut 32:35, in which the Masoretic text was altered to read "on the day of vengeance and recompense."[126] This eschatological day was the consummation of the Age of Disfavor.

According to Samaritan history,[127] Eli coveted the high priesthood for himself. Eli established a rival and illegitimate cultus at Shiloh in competition with the ancient sanctuary at Shechem. Eli opposed the legitimate priest Uzzi, whose family line traced back through Phinehas to Aaron. Eli's unsanctioned act thus introduced the Age of Disfavor.

> There was considerable animosity among the Israelites, for the community of Eli presumed to take their offerings to Shiloh. The Lord's wrath [אף, 'p] waxed against Israel and the angels of the Lord departed from them. The Lord was angry [ויקצף, wyqṣp]

---

[125] For a review of Samaritan history and its impact on the New Testament, see Stevens, *Acts*, 233–35. Another brief summary with bibliography is Ferguson, *Backgrounds*, 534–36. An excellent resource for their history, beliefs, and way of life up to the present is Pummer, *The Samaritans: A Profile*. Also, note additional resources in Barton, *The Samaritan Pentateuch*; Bowman, *The Samaritan Problem*; Macdonald, *The Theology of the Samaritans*; Montgomery, *The Samaritans: The Earliest Jewish Sect*; Purvis, *The Samaritan Pentateuch and the Origin of the Samaritan Sect*.

[126] Agreeing with the LXX. Cf. Macdonald, *Theology*, 381–82.

[127] See Macdonald, *The Samaritan Chronicle No. II*. References follow Macdonald's scheme. For this paragraph, cf. 1 Samuel, Section B, vv. 0*–V*.

at them and he withdrew his regard for them; the light departed from the sanctuary, and the fires of the Lord which were upon the altar of stones and on the altar of bronze were withdrawn.[128]

In his wrath, God hid the tabernacle and its furnishings. The tabernacle and its furnishings God caused to be swallowed up in a cave on Mount Gerizim, hidden till the coming of the Taheb (*ta'eb*, "the one who restores"). The Taheb would reveal the ancient sanctuary.

The Taheb was the expected eschatological prophet to come at the end of days. This prophet would be Moses *redivivus*, someone "like unto Moses." This understanding arose from interpretations of Deut 18:18.[129] Thus, to be able to reveal the tabernacle or its furnishings was an eschatological sign.[130] The coming of the Taheb would conclude the Age of Disfavor and usher in the Day of Vengeance, after which the primeval Age of Favor would be restored, on the pattern of back to the Garden of Eden.[131] Resurrection occurred on the Day of Vengeance for the purpose of judgment. Preparation for this Day of Vengeance was essential.

> It behoves you to understand about the last day and to do action that will give you rest then. Woe to any man whom no [good] action precedes [i.e., in the Day of Vengeance]! It will be stored for him there![132]

Every minute detail of life would be examined on that fateful day. Marqah described that eschatological day as

> the Day of Reckoning for all things done, the Day of Recompense for the good and the evil, the Day of Interrogation about all things done by all creatures, the Day of Trembling for all feet, the Day of Terror for all limbs, the Day of Reckoning for all actions, a day in which every person receives recompense, the Day of Judgment.[133]

---

[128] *Samaritan Chronicle No. II*, 1 Samuel, Section B, vv. G*–I*.

[129] Cf. Teeple, *The Mosaic Eschatological Prophet*.

[130] Pilate dealt harshly with a Samaritan agitator who claimed to know where the holy vessels were hidden (Josephus, *Ant.* 18.85–87). Cf. John 4:25.

[131] Cf. Purvis, *Samaritan Pentateuch*, 88, n1; Bowman, *Samaritan Problem*, 41–42; 126, n17; Macdonald, *Theology*, 15–21.

[132] Marqah *Memar* 4.5 (2:152) in Macdonald, *Memar Marqah*.

[133] Marqah *Memar* 4.12 (2:182).

For Marqah, a Samaritan's belief in Moses was equated with belief in the Lord. This belief would preserve one from the future divine wrath. "His [Moses] words were from the words of his Lord. Believe in him— and you will be safe from all wrath [רגז, *rgz*]."[134] Similarly, Marqah warned, "Do not be an enemy to your Lord, or you will be in judgment. You will have no control over it and you will have no deliverer."[135]

SUMMARY

Jewish Literature

Hebrew Scripture

Both in Jewish literature and in Jewish observance, divine wrath was the language of the judgment of Yahweh. While the wrath of Yahweh could be irrational, his wrath was not considered impersonal. The experience of the irrational wrath of Yahweh was still an experience of his personal zeal. The rational side of the wrath of Yahweh basically derived form ideas about the covenant. Through the covenant concept, the Hebraic understanding of the wrath of Yahweh can be distinguished from the Homeric understanding of the wrath of the gods. The covenant was a revelation from Yahweh. The covenant revealed the character of sin, the character of Yahweh, and the character of the personal relationship between Yahweh and his people. However, Yahweh's people continually spurned him both in the wilderness and in the promised land. In the end, the exile became the preeminent historical paradigm for the wrath of Yahweh. Through the exile, Yahweh vindicated both his sovereignty over Israel and his power to judge. Yet the exile did not exhaust the wrath of Yahweh. His wrath was subordinated to the proclamation of the divine Name. Israel was preserved to proclaim the divine Name among all the inhabitants of the earth. However, according to Malachi, the people of Yahweh continued to subvert his purposes even after the exile. Eschatological use of the language of divine wrath was a later development. Eschatological traditions were grounded in traditions about the "day of the Lord." The day of the Lord would be the day of Yahweh's wrath.

---
[134] Ibid., 4.7 (2:160).
[135] Ibid., 4.5 (2:152).

Greek Septuagint

The Septuagint provides important evidence for the absence of certain Homeric terms for divine wrath in the translation of the Hebrew Scripture into the Greek language. The Septuagint shows virtually exclusive use of *orgē* and *thumos* for divine wrath. Since the translators knew the Homeric terms for wrath, the disuse of the Homeric terms for divine wrath is significant. Linguistic features of the translation of the Septuagint show that *orgē* and *thumos* were used synonymously.

Other Jewish Literature

Various themes on divine judgment from the Hebrew Scripture were reapplied in the Apocrypha and Pseudepigrapha. These themes included the Flood, Sodom and Gomorrah, and the Wilderness. Regularly, thought about God's wrath was coupled to emphasis upon God's righteousness. However, the problem of theodicy also developed. Eschatological perspectives on divine wrath were augmented into apocalyptic speculations. The figure of Taxo in the Assumption of Moses may reflect the thought that martyrdom could provoke the divine vengeance. Literature such as the Letter of Aristeas and 4 Macabees are evidence for the influence of Greek ideas on Hebrew thought. The retribution of divine justice in the case of Apollonius in 4 Maccabees is evidence for the Greek idea that divine wrath was a preservation of proper social-political-religious order. The Letter of Aristeas provides evidence for Stoic thought about the immutability of the divine nature.

Josephus provides further evidence for the non-eschatological use of divine vengeance as a penal retribution effected in human affairs. As with other Jewish writers, Josephus used judgment themes from the Hebrew Scripture. These included the Flood, Sodom and Gomorrah, and the Wilderness. Josephus did not use *thumos* for divine wrath. Although he used other terms, Josephus mainly used the term *orgē* for divine wrath.

Philo's philosophical position led him to explain instances of the wrath of God as anthropopathisms. At times, though, Philo was inconsistent. The wrath of God could be presented as a reality of God's nature. Philo used the terms *orgē* and *thumos*, but he seems to have preferred *orgē* for divine wrath.

That God could express anger was accepted in rabbinic thought. Normally, discussion of God's wrath would involve emphasis on God's mercy. In contrast, figures such as the Angel of Destruction show attempts to dissociate wrath from God. If the concept of Gehenna is to be associated with the language of divine wrath in rabbinic thought, the language of wrath is pervasive in the literature. By the first century AD, Gehenna was conceived as a place of punishment of the ungodly.

The Dead Sea community interpreted their existence and their writings from an apocalyptic perspective. Determinism underlay this perspective. History was divided into the Era of Wrath and the Era of Divine Favor. The language of divine wrath took its shape in the mold of such apocalyptic and deterministic thought forms. Judgment themes from Hebrew Scripture were used to enhance pictures of apocalyptic judgment.

Samaritan Literature

The idea of the Day of Vengeance, derived from Deut. 32:35, was determinative for Samaritan theology of divine wrath. Eli's defection to Shiloh instigated the Age of Disfavor and caused the Gerizim tabernacle and furnishings to be engulfed in a cave, hidden in God's wrath until the coming of Taheb. The Taheb was the eschatological prophet "like unto Moses" who would reveal once again the tabernacle on Gerizim and usher in the Day of Vengeance of divine judgment. After this divine retribution for the minute details of life, the primeval Era of Favor would be restored. For Marqah, a Samaritan's belief in Moses would preserve one from the divine wrath when the prophet "like unto Moses" appeared.

4

New Testament Background

Divine Wrath in the New Testament

NEW TESTAMENT WRITERS IN GENERAL did not incorporate the language of divine wrath as extensively as one might imagine. In truth, Paul is the reason this topic gets any traction in the New Testament and in theological discussion in the first place. Therefore, the objective for this chapter is not to do exhaustive exegesis of the passages considered. Rather, we seek to draw the general profile of divine wrath language. This profile will generate a general canonical feel for the topic in its New Testament context. This New Testament context will set in sharp relief the distinctiveness of the Pauline language of divine wrath.

EXPLICIT CONTEXTS

Examining the language of divine wrath in the New Testament reflects the background of ideas current in New Testament times for canonical writers. All of the documents considered are within fifty years of the time of Paul, though the genre of the material represented in these writers does vary. Our primary target will be contexts in which divine wrath is explicit. We then briefly will consider sample contexts in which divine wrath seems to be implicit as a secondary target, suspecting conformity to the main ideas in the explicit contexts.

Unmerciful Servant Parable

The parable of the Unmerciful Servant (Matt 18:23–34) obviously was illustration of forgiveness. When the lord in the parable discovered the unmerciful behavior of the slave who had received mercy, he was moved with anger [ὀργισθείς, *orgistheis*] and proceeded to exact payment of the forgiven debt (18:34). This parable in 18:35 is applied directly to the interaction of God and humans. The question for scholars is originality of the application. While the originality can be questioned, scholars generally have understood the application to God to be original to the parable.[1] With a note of caution, even Bultmann said the application "could very well be original."[2] If so, the teaching here is that human relationships should reflect divine values. Lack of commensurability of human values with those of the divine offends the divine and draws attention and response. This concept immediately is compatible with ideas from the general Greco-Roman world. Deity protects and secures justice (however conceived within the prevailing social construct). The parable calls upon general social conventions, so does not offer anything at the surface radically distinctive.

At the same time, how those divine values are conceived radically changes how the parable is applied. Divine values reflect divine character. If we are talking petulant Zeus, that is one matter. If we are talking the God revealed in Jewish Scripture who works on the basis of an established covenant relationship with fully known expectations, that is another matter altogether. The Jewish God has well-known, covenant-revealed character. This God is holy, just, and merciful. While this triad creates a complex and multidimensional deity, sometimes mysterious and difficult to ponder on occasion, this profile is set far apart from concepts of deity in Greece or Rome. What makes this God angry has nothing to do with Zeus or Jupiter, so the anger of the landowner has a decidedly Jewish context to consider since this landowner stands for the Jewish God. This is not your human father's anger, nor that of Olympus.

King's Invitation Parable

Matthew and Luke record the parable of the King's Banquet Invitation (Matt 22:1–14; Luke 14:16–24) in which the king becomes enraged at

---

[1] E.g., Jeremias, *The Parables of Jesus*, 179, 211; Hunter, *Interpreting the Parables* 23, 56–57; Tasker, *The Biblical Doctrine of the Wrath of God*, 28–29. Contrast Hanson, *The Wrath of the Lamb*, 121–23.

[2] Bultmann, *History of the Synoptic Tradition*, 184.

the murder of his messengers who were sent out to offer an invitation to his wedding banquet. This parable inclines scholars to a different interpretive approach in contrast to the parable of the Unmerciful Servant. In Matthew's version, this king behaves in a predictably human manner by an immediate honor-shame riposte, a power play of sending troops to destroy the murderers in his summary royal punishment. The audience instantly would have grasped the relevant social dimensions of this interaction, but the behavior of the king is not at the center of the parable, as in the Unmerciful Servant. The center of this parable is the insistence upon pushing out an invitation to a celebratory banquet even to those one naturally would not assume to be socially deserving. Notice that Luke compresses the story details by suppressing the king's reaction in Matthew's version. Luke in this way focuses more directly and effectively upon the parable's central point of the extension of the banquet invitation to the unexpected—specifically, the undeserving.

In each of these versions of this parable by Matthew and Luke, the anger of the king probably does not represent a reference to God. The king's reaction is simply superfluous detail that does not reinforce the main point, as Luke's version makes clear.

Cleansing of the Leper

In the events narrated in Mark's first chapter, a leper beseeched Jesus for healing (Mark 1:40–45). The Greek manuscripts vary in the verb of Jesus's response to the leper's request for healing.[3] One reading describes Jesus as "moved with compassion" (σπλαγχνισθείς, *splanchnistheis*). The other reading describes Jesus much differently as "moved by anger" (ὀργισθείς, *orgistheis*). The second variant of the Western text clearly is the more difficult reading; some scholars will opt for this reading accordingly as a principle of textual criticism.[4] If this reading is original, Jesus would be described as angered. If so, one immediately would presume some righteous indignation, but the exegetical question would

---

[3] Cf. Metzger, *Commentary*, 65. The best attested reading is "compassion." The suggestion of scribal correction of Jesus being angry does not coordinate with other indications of Jesus's anger that go uncorrected (Mark 3:5; 10:14). Though speculation, a possibility is sound confusion in the original Aramaic of two verbs for compassion and anger.

[4] Lane, *Mark*, 86–87; Guelich, *Mark*, 74; France, *Mark*, 117.

be, angered at what, exactly? The leper for his (in some way) impertinent request? Sin's tragic consequences ravaging the human condition so obvious in the leper's situation and reflective of the larger cosmic struggle with evil? This second option at least contextually would flow congruently with the on-going literary development in the first chapter of a cosmic struggle theme.[5] The leprous disease was contrary to God's order of creation. The anger of Jesus revealed the intensity of the cosmic struggle. The authority of Jesus was challenged by forces of evil, and the challenge from the Pharisees in this story was a silhouette of a supernatural struggle that would climax in the cross and resurrection.

This interpretive scheme for this incident in Mark would speak to the ancient world as consistent with the typical Greco-Roman understanding of the divine as appropriately angered by that which is opposed to divine intentions. In this case, again, however, one would see those intentions as finding their distinctive definition in biblical context vis-à-vis the Greco-Roman world in the God revealed in Scripture. To draw the profile for this God, as opposed to Olympus, one would have to begin with a doctrine of creation and a revealed creator God who is the only God, who is holy, and whose holy will in and for creation relates to humans through a covenant clearly defining expected behavior within the covenant relationship. In this reading, the anger of Jesus, if read at Mark 1:41, is biblical and revelatory of a creator God.

Pharisees' Hardness of Heart

In Mark 3:5, Jesus was grieved at the Pharisaic hardness of heart. He looked on them with anger (*orgē*). This pericope is part of the theme of the questioning of the authority of Jesus and the persistent stubbornness of the Pharisees to accede to Jesus's authority as from God. Mark's plotline has Jesus engaged in a supernatural struggle with the forces of evil, and the Pharisees unwittingly are playing right into that struggle. Once again for Mark, as with the cleansing of the leper (if the variant reading is adopted), the anger of Jesus is righteous indignation and appropriate in the context of the spiritual struggle taking place.

---

[5] Mark's preemptively announced Son of God is heralded by a divinely appointed forerunner, is confirmed by a heavenly voice at his baptism; engages in supernatural struggle with Satan in the wilderness; and pursues this continued wrestling with forces of evil in healing diseases, curing sicknesses, and exorcizing demons.

John the Baptist

Matthew 3:7

The prophetic preaching of John the Baptist included the language of divine wrath, as he called people to prepare for God's kingdom and flee "from the coming wrath" (μελλούσης ὀργῆς, *mellousēs orgēs*, Matt 3:7; Luke 3:7). Both Matthew and Luke incorporate this call and message into their Gospels from their common source besides Mark. In both Gospels, John's "coming wrath" has an eschatological overtone. John's baptizing ministry gives expression to this coming judgment, exhorting repentance as preparation. This judgment ministry is juxtaposed with the judgment ministry to be executed by the Coming One, an agent who will realize this coming kingdom (Matt 3:11–12).

Figure 4.1. Pieratti's St. John the Baptist. Domenico Pieratti captured this portrayal of John the Baptist about 1620, originally standing in the courtyard of the Palazzo del Bargello in Florence, Italy (NMB).

In 3:13, Matthew structurally reinforced this thematic connection by abruptly moving in his narrative on John the Baptist immediately into a pericope on the baptism of Jesus: "Then Jesus arrived from Galilee at the Jordan to John in order to be baptized by him." John's anticipated future judgment suddenly had confronted Israel in the person of Jesus of Nazareth. Matthew associated John's "coming wrath" with a divine judgment to be actualized in the person of Jesus.[6]

---

[6] Davies's (*The Sermon of the Mount*, 106) original framing of the crisis character of this John the Baptist tradition combining the twin elements of future judgment and wrath of the coming kingdom set the pace for interpreting the text; e.g., Morris, *Matthew*, 58.

Jeremias equated the "sentence of Gehenna" spoken against the Pharisees later in Matt 23:33 with the "sentence of death" in Matt 3:7.[7] Jeremias's identification of *gehenna* and *orgē* in Matthew probably is correct. Further, since both *gehenna* and *orgē* appear as eschatological terms in Matthew, *gehenna* may be Matthew's rabbinic equivalent to Paul's "wrath of God" (ὀργὴ θεοῦ, *orgē theou*). This approach is in concord with our previous study of rabbinic literature.

Luke 3:7

How the judgment preached by John the Baptist was understood by Luke can be perceived through the manner in which Luke treated two traditions: the sermon at Nazareth by Jesus and the later prediction of the destruction of the Jerusalem temple. The two redactional keys are the manner of Luke's citation of Isa 61:1–2a (and 58:6) by Jesus in the inaugural sermon at Nazareth that only Luke includes among the Gospels (Luke 4:18–19) and the only other occurrence of *orgē* in his gospel in Luke 21:23, which, like the use in Luke 3:7, is in a context with eschatological overtones.

In Jesus's synagogue sermon, the future year of the Lord that had been announced in ancient prophecy in Isa 61:1–2 Jesus declared fulfilled in his own preaching and healing ministry.

> "The Spirit of the Lord is upon me, for the sake of which
>   he has anointed me
>   to bring good news to the poor.
>   He has sent me
>   to proclaim release to the captives
>   and recovery of sight to the blind,
>   to let the oppressed go free,
>   to proclaim the acceptable year[8] of the Lord."

Note carefully, though, Luke omitted from the last half of the tail end of this prophetic citation the following phrase from Isaiah, "and the day of vengeance [ἐκδικήσις, *ekdikēsis*] of our God." Apparently for Luke, the ministry of Jesus could not be characterized by such words. Yet, at the conclusion of Jesus's ministry in Jesus's prophetic address to Jerusalem, Luke introduced a significant collocation of terms. Luke reported that

---

[7] Jeremias, *TDNT* s.v. "γέεννα," 1:658.

[8] Or, "year of the Lord's favor."

John the Baptist announced a "coming wrath [*orgē*]." Yet, surprisingly, for the duration of his Gospel, Luke lets this eschatologically freighted term *orgē* ("wrath") simply disappear from the text. Luke thereby infers that Isaiah's "day of vengeance" is inappropriate for characterizing the ministry of Jesus. This inappropriateness sets up a narrative tension for interpreting the imminent eschatological divine wrath as preached by John. Luke clearly does not try to avoid this element in John's preaching. How does he conceive of John's imminent eschatological wrath?

Luke's narrative tension is not resolved until Jesus's eschatological discourse on Jerusalem in Luke 21:20–24. In this eschatological section, Luke said that when armies surrounded Jerusalem, the inhabitants of the city would have to flee to the mountains. This "flight" is a carefully designed intratextual echo of the question of the Baptist to the Pharisees who had showed up to do surveillance at his baptism: "Who has warned you to flee from the coming wrath?" Isaiah's "year of the Lord's favor" Luke interpreted as the ministry of Jesus. Rejection of the Messiah, however, eventually would have a day of reckoning that would alter the year of the Lord's favor into the self-inflicted day of vengeance (ἐκδικήσεως, *ekdikēseōs*, 21:22). Luke is saying that the Baptist's ominous warning would discover an ironic fulfillment in Jerusalem's desolation in the siege conditions of war. In those circumstances of siege, the divine judgment of which John the Baptist warned finally would be realized (21:20). At last would come "wrath [*orgē*] to this people" (21:23). Thus, for Luke, rejection of Jesus during his ministry ("the acceptable year of the Lord") would actuate the latent wrath of God against Israel ("the day of vengeance of our God"). In this way, Luke historicized the future but imminent judgment of God in the preaching of John the Baptist as Jerusalem's destruction by the armies of Rome.

We should not fail to note how similar is Luke's literary scheme for using divine wrath for interpreting historical events to that of the Roman historians with their religious use of *ira deum* as a vehicle for historical interpretation. For the Roman historians, the very existence of the Roman state was tied to the destiny produced by divine wrath. Luke's application of *orgē* offers a close literary parallel. He also tied the existence of the Jewish state to the destiny produced by divine wrath. In this way, the language of the wrath of God, admittedly infrequent in Luke, still has significant theological value, since this *orgē* language appears to have the form of a *terminus technicus* of Lukan eschatology.

A close reading shows his redactional activity is very precise in order to achieve this objective.

Nicodemus Discourse

John 3:36 has two bounding narratives[9] on either side that help to interpret John's language of divine wrath in this focal verse. One bounding story is the Cleansing of the Temple (John 2). The other bounding story is the Samaritan Woman (John 4). In both bounding narratives, Jewish and Samaritan eschatological expectations are confronted and challenged. These eschatological expectations relate to temple worship, which becomes an issue in each narrative.

In the front bounding story of the cleansing of the temple, an acted judgment parable is performed. Now that Messiah has arrived suddenly, Jewish postexilic institutions stand under imminent judgment based upon response to God's appointed eschatological agent of the end time. Cleansing of the temple in Jerusalem had clear prophetic and messianic overtones (cf. Mal 3:1–4). Note that in Malachi, the temple would be defended, not destroyed (cf. Zechariah 14). In John, Jesus declared that God's true temple was his body, not the temple in Jerusalem. Parallel to Malachi's expectation, the temple of Jesus's body ultimately would be defended, not destroyed (alluding to resurrection).

The back bounding story is about the Samaritan temple. In fact, the Samaritans had no temple, because the Jewish Hasmonean king, John Hyrcannus I, destroyed the Samaritan temple on Mount Gerizim in 128 BC. The Samaritans never had the means to rebuild, but they still fervently worshipped on their mountain of Gerizim, as did southern Jews on their mountain of Zion. For this reason, the Samaritans developed a tradition of a coming eschatological temple to appear on their mountain where they would worship once again. This new temple would be revealed miraculously by the future Taheb to come.

Samaritan teaching also labeled that future day revealing the new temple a Day of Vengeance—for all, themselves included, not just for their enemies. They expected a retribution for every minute detail of life, a day of reckoning for all individual actions.[10] For this reason, when Jesus revealed knowledge of the Samaritan woman's past, he revealed

---

[9] For "bounding stories" as narrative technique, see Stevens, *Acts*, 244–45, 276.

[10] As expressed in Marqah *Memar* 4.12.

himself to be a prophet. Her attention was pricked (John 4:19). The question was whether Jesus might be *the* Prophet, the Taheb. If he was, then the Samaritan Day of Vengeance was at hand, and the Samaritan woman had obvious cause for concern because of her lifestyle.

To pursue the matter, the Samaritan woman brought up Samaritan eschatological expectations. Jewish claims about worship centered on Jerusalem, while Samaritan claims centered on Gerizim. The Taheb in Samaritan teaching, naturally, would settle the issue in favor of the Samaritans (John 4:20). Jesus responded to this pointed probe about the significance of his person that true worship of God was in Spirit and truth (John 4:21–24). Now confused about her traditional eschatological expectations about the Taheb, the Samaritan woman fell back on the revelatory function of that figure (John 4:25). The Samaritan woman is following the Samaritan eschatological script point by point. Jesus offers her receptivity a rare revelation of his identity (John 4:26).

Notice how in both bounding stories to divine wrath language in John 3:36 (Cleansing of the Temple, Samaritan Woman), eschatological expectations of both Jews and Samaritans are challenged and transcended. John made the center of that challenge the person of Jesus. Key to the effectiveness of this literary design is how the language of divine wrath was integral to both Jewish and Samaritan eschatology. For the evangelist, response to Jesus was the paramount issue, not any expected temple of worship, regardless of location. Worship in "Spirit and truth" transcended place and ethnicity.

John set in classic formulation the crucial question of response to Jesus in John 3:16. In this verse, two eschatological destinies are set before every human: destruction (μὴ ἀπόληται, *mē apolētai*) and eternal life (ζωὴν αἰώνιον, *zōēn aiōnion*). Present response to Jesus actuates this future final judgment, the heart of eschatology (3:18).

Thus, we arrive at the focal verse of divine wrath in John 3:36. The thought of a future judgment realized in the present has its climatic summary in John 3:36. This verse is repeated below in three elements to emphasize its inherent structure:

- "the one who believes in the Son has eternal life"

- "the one who disbelieves in the Son will not see life"

- "but the wrath of God [ἡ ὀργὴ θεοῦ, *hē orgē theou*] abides on him"

The expression "eternal life" marks the context as eschatological. John then marks the verb in the first element of this eschatological summary with present tense (ἔκει, *ekei*). Present tense transcends any single action. The present tense speaks to a pattern of behavior and supports the realized eschatology of the evangelist.

The second element sets up antithetical contrast to the first, which is disbelief. This disbelief is active, an on-going disobedience, since, again, the repeated present tense in this second verb relates to a pattern of behavior as in the first element. Unbelief is manifest in continual disobedience. Also, the thematic variation on "having" life in element one is not "seeing" life in element two. Eternal life is impossible for the one who continues in a state of disobeying the Son. As long as one rejects Jesus, the wrath of God abides on that person. Future judgment does not involve a delayed decision that is pending adjudication. That is, the heart of eschatology is decided already through self-condemnation in the present (cf. 3:18). The present tense of the verb "abides" (μένει, *menei*) emphasizes continuing action. The eschatological wrath of God is a self-imposed condition resulting from one's own rejection of Jesus. With the Samaritan woman episode adjacent in context, one may compare Samaritan theology in which belief in Moses would provide safety from all wrath, as in Marqah *Memar* 4.8.

"Abiding" is a characteristic and core Johannine thought.[11] This distinctive, if not unique, combination of eschatological language with typically Johannine thought of present tense "abiding" demonstrates how thoroughly the evangelist has transformed the typical language of the wrath of God from his general culture. The singular occurrence of "the wrath of God" (ἡ ὀργὴ θεοῦ, *hē orgē theou*) in the Gospel of John gives cogency to Johannine realized eschatology.

Wilderness Wrath

Hebrews has two explicit occurrences of divine wrath in Heb 3:11 and 4:3 in the form of the noun *orgē*. Both passages involve citation from Ps 95:11 (LXX) related to the wilderness experience of the Israelites. In the Psalm quoted, the psalmist recalled the grumbling of the children of Israel that prevented that generation from entering the promised land after escaping Egypt (narrated in Num 21). The language of divine

---

[11] John 5:38; 6:56; 8:35; 12:46; 14:10; 15:4–7, 9–10. Cf. Sir 5:6.

wrath implicit in the Numbers account is explicit in Deut 1:34–35. As for the Deuteronomist, the language of wilderness wrath is explicit in Ps 95:11 as well. In Ps 95:6–8, the psalmist extended a call for the worship of Yahweh lest the people harden their hearts as in days of old.

The author of Hebrews, like the psalmist, was exhorting his readers not to fail to move on into the "rest" of God. For this author, the language of divine wrath is a viable part of his exhortation to the people of God. The overarching context, of course, in all of the Pentateuch is the covenant and the God of the covenant. His character and expectations are no secret to divine as if seeking to consult an oracle on the "maybe" chance of hearing from a god or goddess, and even then, in cryptic phrasing that could be interpreted multiple ways with positive or negative spin. As in the wilderness traditions, the language of wrath in Hebrews occurs in the context of judgment. The assumption is that the God of this judgment and his expectations are well known to all (Heb 4:11–13). This covenant frame is inherent in how the author synthesizes past faith and its cultus with present faith and its Christ.

Figure 4.2. Lead Oracle Tablet. Lead tablet dated 450 BC from the sanctuary in Dodona, Epirus, in northwestern Greece, the oldest Hellenic oracle. Inscribed is the oracle's response to the devotee's question about trade in Epidamnos, a colony on the Illyrian coast. The answer on the reverse side is positive (TAM).

Apocalyptic Wrath

The question of God's sovereignty during persecution of believers is a key issue facing John in writing his apocalypse. His answer takes seventeen chapters to work out in a long narrative unit that runs from the Vision of Heaven (Revelation 4–5) through a triadic judgment cycle of judgment heptads. The passion of Christ releases God's judgment upon the world (Revelation 6–16). Four perspectives interpret these judgments (Revelation 17–20). The Vision of Heaven's theology of sovereignty and salvation provides the foundation for this judgment cycle.[12]

[12] See Stevens, *Revelation*, 377–79.

The vision of heaven in Revelation 4–5 affirms the sovereignty of God and the salvation of his Christ. The visions of Revelation 6–16 affirm the final and complete victory of God over all opposition. Within such a structure, the language of God's wrath is to be understood. That language of wrath is especially related to persecution of followers of the Lamb.

Sixth Seal (Revelation 6:16, 17)

The seal judgments are built on the eschatological woe traditions of the Synoptic Gospels. Mark 13 is particularly relevant. The application is upon the destruction of Jerusalem. Thus, John writes of events that fulfill God's sovereignty within history. This historical paradigm sets up the pattern for understanding the dynamics of the end.[13]

The events John narrated in apocalyptic fashion in Rev 6:12–17 (the opening of the sixth seal) included the desperate plea to be hidden from the presence of the one seated on the throne "and from the wrath [*orgēs*] of the Lamb" (Rev 6:16). At that time, all would seek security "because the day of their great wrath [*orgēs*] has come" (Rev 6:17). Joel's eschatological "Day of the Lord" with God leading his avenging army and Joel's astronomical disturbances in sun and moon on that terrible day provide an allusive background (Joel 2:11, 31). The call for mountains and rocks to fall to provide hiding places is similar to Jesus's prediction in Luke 23:28–30. A similar thought appeared in the prophets Isa 2:19 and Hos 10:8. In the Lukan context, the saying was not applied to the crucifixion but to a future experience. Concerning John's picture of the Day of Judgment, one may compare Zeph 1:14a (LXX) and 1:15a (LXX) on the day of the Lord as a day of wrath.

Wrath in Revelation 6 is about eschatological judgment. This conclusion is supported by consideration of the prayer of the martyrs in the fifth seal. The implication of the question "how long?" in Rev 6:10 shows that wrath against the persecutors of believers not yet was consummated. Avenging the blood of the Lamb's martyrs would have to await the completion of the full number of martyrs (6:11). To answer the question asked in the prayer of the martyrs, the author in his sixth-seal vision utilized a composite picture of the great day of judgment anticipated by ancient prophets. In that judgment, wrath fully would

---

[13] Ibid., 402.

be effected: "And who is able to stand?" The same question was asked in Nah 1:6 (LXX). Those guilty of the blood of martyrs would fall under divine judgment. Martyrdom that provokes divine vengeance may be compared to the figure of Taxo in the *Assumption of Moses*. Use of an apocalyptic oracle of judgment in Rev 6:9–17 to comfort persecuted believers also is similar to the context of 2 Thess 1:6–10 with its use of a judgment oracle to comfort afflicted believers.

The elephant in the room is the discordant tying of "lamb" with "wrath." Few would find that imagery meaningful, a rhetorical non-sequitur. The Lamb, however, is the one who opens the Seals (Rev 6:1). Thus, the Lamb releases these forces into history, which is through the cross (Rev 1:5; 5:6; 12:11). The dramatic imagery in Revelation has obfuscated John's Christology. Whatever divine wrath is for John, that wrath is the "wrath of the Lamb" and has the shape of a cross. Often forgotten is that a slaughtered Lamb begins all the subsequent visions of judgment by opening the first seal in Rev 6:1.

Other passages on divine wrath that rehearse the basic approach John takes in Rev 6:16 with variations on the theme are:

- Rev 11:17, the twenty-four elders sing praise at the end of the trumpet heptad of judgments because the nations raged but God's wrath (*orgē*) came; the nations raging is that royal enthronement imagery of Ps 2:1 of God's anointed king who would subdue the heathen nations threatening Jerusalem that was interpreted messianically in later Jewish tradition and that the Jesus movement applied to Jesus (Acts 4:25–28)

- Rev 15:1, introduction of the seven angels with the seven bowls of plagues, which are the last, because "in them the wrath [*thumos*] of God is ended"; the triadic series of judgment heptads is being drawn to a close, and the purposes of God's wrath in history as the outworking of the cross of Christ are finalized

- Rev 15:7, after an interlude of the singing of "the song of Moses, the servant of God, and of the Lamb," the opening in heaven of the temple's tent of witness reveals the seven angels with the seven bowls "full of the wrath [*thumos*] of God"; interpretation of this wrath John has sublimated entirely to his Christology

- Rev 16:1, the command to the seven angels with the seven bowls of the wrath (*thumos*) of God to commence pouring out their bowls
- Rev 16:19, the seventh bowl brings from heaven the declaration "It is done!" with cosmic disturbances, and an earthquake splitting "the great city" three ways, the fall of the cities of the nations, and a concluding summary to transition to the next chapter's Babylon image, the great whore: "God remembered great Babylon and gave her the wine cup of the fury [*thumou*] of his wrath [*orgēs*]"; clearly, Babylon imagery draws upon the nation historically of God's wrath of exile against Judah, but now the recipient of God's wrath

Angelic Proclamation (Rev 14:8)

We must be careful to note that by jumping to this passage, we have passed into the second half of Revelation. The book of Revelation neatly divides in two on the basis of the main character brought on the stage. The main character in the first half is the Christ. The main character in the second half is the Dragon. The first half is the Christ Cycle portraying the drama of God and his Christ (Revelation 4–11). The second half is the Dragon Cycle portraying the drama of the Dragon and his Beasts (Revelation 12–20). John's purpose in these two halves is to recapitulate the same story, but to shift perspective from portraying God's judgment in Christ from an earthly view to portraying that same judgment from a cosmic perspective as a cosmic battle Christ has engaged through the cross. The second half unpacks the meaning of

Dragon Cycle (12–20)
Red Dragon and His Beasts
Cosmic Conflict (12–13)
• Dragon Attack (12)
• Beast Agents (13)
Messianic Conquest (14–20)
• Bowl Prelude (14)
• Bowl Judgments (15–16)
• Bowl Perspectives (17–20)
Eschatological Climax (20)
• Satan's Defeat (Gog/Magog)
• God's Judgment (White Thr.)

FIGURE 4.3. The Dragon Cycle. This cycle plays out the seventh trumpet's "your wrath came."

Bowl Judgments—Perspectives	
Scene	Perspective
1. Harlot (Rev 17)	Prophet
2. Babylon (Rev 18)	Heaven
3. Rider (Rev 19)	Christ
4. Millennium (Rev 20)	Martyr

FIGURE 4.4. Bowl Judgments—Perspectives. John takes four chapters to continue augmenting the Bowl judgments with four additional perspectives.

the promise in the seventh trumpet that concludes the first half that "your wrath came" (Rev 11:18). Notice that the messianic conquest is a long series of chapters that revolve around dramatizing and bringing out the full significance of the bowl judgments. These bowl judgments have a prelude (Revelation 14) and a postlude (Revelation 17–20) as a part of this interpretive process. This postlude material provides four perspectives on the bowl judgments that will augment an understanding of these judgments. The four perspectives are those of the prophet, heaven, Christ, and the martyrs of the beast. Thus, our first reference to divine wrath is in the prelude material in Revelation 14. Our second reference is in the postlude material in Revelation 17–20.[14]

All of Revelation 14 is prelude to the vision of the bowl judgments anticipating the believer's victory through the Lamb in Messiah's conquest of the Dragon introduced in Revelation 12. The prelude unit has three parts. The first part is the Vision of Zion (Rev 14:1–5). The Lamb is standing on Mount Zion with his victorious followers. They are victorious because they have been true to their confession of Christ ("no lie was found in their mouth," Rev 14:5). The second part is the Vision of the Angels (Rev 14:6–13). These angels make heavenly proclamations that play out the significance more fully of the Vision of Zion.[15] The third part is the Vision of Harvests (14:14–20), a doublet scene.

The second angel proleptically announces the fall of Babylon because Babylon caused "all nations to drink of the wine of the passion [*thumou*] of her fornication" (Rev 14:8).[16] Prophetic and apocalyptic themes are behind the statement that Babylon has fallen.[17] Rome's immorality was considered the natural consequence of idolatry. In Rev 14:18, the worshippers of the beast who had drunk the wine of Babylon's passion would be forced to drink of the wine of the wrath of God (*thumou*) from the cup of his anger (*orgēs*). Thus, "the wine of the passion of her immorality" in 14:8 was paralleled in 14:10 with

---

[14] Cf. Stevens, *Revelation*, 422, 462.

[15] Stevens, *Revelation*, 440–441.

[16] Here, *thumos* could be translated "passion" or "wrath" (*BDAG*, s.v. "θυμός"). In context with "of her fornication" (τῆς πορνείας αὐτῆς, *tēs porneias autēs*), "passion" seems more appropriate.

[17] Jer 25:12–16; 2 Bar. 11:1; Sib. Or. 5:143, 159.

"the wine of the wrath of God." Babylon's wine of passion had its counterpart in God's wine of wrath. Babylon for John is Rome.[18]

God's wine of wrath represented the eschatological consequence of Rome's immorality; this wrath was typified variously as torment, fire and brimstone, a smoke going up forever and ever (cf. Isa 34:8–10), and no rest day or night (Rev 14:10–11). No rest for the condemned contrasted the condition of the believers given in Rev 14:13 (cf. 2 Thess 1:7). Fire and brimstone, along with a fire going up forever, recall the judgment upon Sodom and Gomorrah in Gen 19:24. This intertextual echo enhances translating *thumos* as "passion" in Rev 14:8, since the characteristic sin of Sodom was gross immorality.

Judgment Harvest (Rev 14:19)

In the harvest in view in Rev 14:19, the wicked are cast into "the winepress of the great wrath [*thumou*] of God." Here and in 19:15 are the only occurrences of the winepress metaphor in the New Testament.[19] The combination in Joel 3:13 of harvest and vintage often has been suggested as behind Rev 14:14–20. Without any warrant in the Greek text, Charles tried to explain the double imagery of judgment in this unit by labeling the first scene of Rev 14:15–17 as an interpolation.[20] The later passage using the winepress imagery in Rev 19:15 is a singular judgment executed by the Son of Man, so one might conclude the doublet scenes in which this earlier reference to a winepress of wrath occurs might be multiple perspectives on the same event. However, the New Testament pattern already set up a harvest of the righteous in the Jesus tradition (Luke 10:2; John 4:35–38), so this Jesus tradition may have impacted John's construction here, making the first harvest positive of the righteous and the second negative of the wicked.[21] Similar to the idea in Rev 14:20 is Isa 63:3 and 1 En. 100:3.

---

[18] "Babylon applied to Rome already was a *topos* in Jewish literature after the First Jewish War, because this Rome historically reprised Babylon's destruction of Jerusalem and the temple" (Stevens, *Revelation*, 443). Cf. 2 Bar. 11:1; Sib. Or. 5.143–45.

[19] In Rev 19:15: "the winepress of the wine of the fierce wrath of God Almighty," τὴν ληνὸν τοῦ οἴνου τοῦ θυμοῦ τῆς ὀργῆς τοῦ θεοῦ τοῦ παντοκράτορος, *tēn lēnon tou ooinou tou thumou tēs orgēs tou theou pantokratoros*.

[20] Charles, *Revelation of St. John*, 2:18–19.

[21] Stevens, *Revelation*, 445–46.

The judgment John pictured is the eschatological harvest in which the purposes of God are consummated. Hanson applied "outside the city" to the crucifixion of Jesus.[22] However, the passage could have been another picture of the eschatological consummation outlined in the following chapter. Hanson's presentation of divine wrath as a "process worked out in history"[23] would be foreign to a conviction of a coming catastrophe of eschatological judgment, which seems to have formed a part of John's presentation. One need only to point out that the judgment scenes in the chapters that follow chapter 14 lead directly into the narrative of final victory. In that final victory, the beast and his false prophet, the devil, death and Hades, and those whose names were not written in the book of life are thrown into the lake of fire where "they shall be tormented day and night forever and ever" (20:10).[24] The lake of fire was the "second death" (20:14). Thus, "outside the city" seems to have been an indefinite reference to the place of general judgment; the circle of ideas that surrounded the Valley of Jehoshaphat could have been in mind.[25]

In John's thought, that God would avenge the blood of martyrs transcended any rudimentary vindictiveness; rather, through judgment God restored the integrity of righteousness. For John, the sentence of death pronounced upon the Lamb's followers by idolatrous Rome was not the last word. The fourfold hallelujah from the multitude in heaven (19:1–6) was John's victorious proclamation that God had the last word.

Rider on the White Horse (Rev 19:15)

John has provided multiple perspectives on the bowl judgments to augment their dramatic impact. He gave the perspective of the prophet on the bowl judgments in Revelation 17's harlot image, then heaven's perspective in Revelation 18's catastrophic fall of Babylon image. Now, he gives Messiah's perspective on the bowl judgments in Revelation 19's rider on the white horse image.

---

[22] Hanson, *Wrath of the Lamb*, 175.

[23] Ibid., 174–78.

[24] Rev 19:20; 20:10, 14, 15.

[25] Joel 3:2, 12, 14; 1 En. 53:1. Cf. Barrois, *IDB*, s.v. "Jehoshaphat, Valley of," 2:816. Putting emphasis on the article ("the city"), some think of Jerusalem; cf. Mounce, *Revelation*, 281.

The sword coming out of the mouth of the one riding the white horse is the divine word of judgment. For John, the words of God would be fulfilled (Rev 17:17). Judgment would be actualized. This judgment here is on the "kings of the earth" who participated in the fornication and idolatry of Babylon.

Patterned after the description of the Day of Vengeance in Edom in Isa 63:1–6, the image of the winepress of wrath in Rev 19:15 served to express judicial judgment in divine dealings.[26] The judgment can be interpreted two ways. One would be to consider the judgment yet future. If so the judgment would consist of retribution that remained to be fulfilled. Until such a time as the retribution was fulfilled, the complete purposes of God to establish his righteousness would not be realized.

On the other hand, the judgment could be considered as fulfilled in the cross of Christ. One should note that the heavenly Rider scene of Revelation 19 parallels the slaughtered Lamb scene of Revelation 5. The scene recapitulates the gospel impact of the first coming of Jesus. Jesus has released the power of the gospel into the lives of believers through which they withstand the seduction of the Dragon and his beasts. They conquer through their witness, and their witness destroys the beast (Rev 12:11).[27]

IMPLICIT CONTEXTS

Our primary target has been contexts in which divine wrath is explicit. We still need to give brief attention to sample New Testament contexts in which divine wrath seems to be implicit as a secondary target.

Passages in which divine wrath possibly may be implicit would include a correlative vocabulary and contextual associations. The correlative vocabulary would include the emotions of grief, indignation, and zeal of Jesus.[28] The "cup" figure probably is simply a reference to a

---

[26] Cf. Skinner, *Isaiah*, 215.

[27] Cf. Stevens, *Revelation*, 491–92.

[28] Mark 3:5 (anger is explicit in context) and 10:14, both eliminated by Matthew and Luke (Matt 8:1–4; Luke 5:12–16). John 2:17 (citation of Ps 69:9); cf. 1 Cor 10:22.

destiny of suffering.[29] The so-called "cry of forsakenness" by Jesus on the cross has received varying interpretations.[30]

Contextual associations would include causal relationships assumed between sin and wickedness (or calamity).[31] Such assumptions were rejected by Jesus.[32] Commentary on the actual state of the lost is infrequent, except in Matthew and Revelation.[33] One may contrast the lurid details in non-canonical literature about the state of the lost.[34] Episodes in Acts concerning individuals may be implicit contexts of divine wrath.[35] The call for fire from heaven upon a Samaritan village in Luke 9:51–56 was an allusion to Elijah in 2 Kgs 1:9–16, as clarified in some Greek manuscripts.[36] Scriptural judgment motifs were used, including the Flood,[37] Sodom and Gomorrah,[38] the Wilderness,[39] and the non-canonical motif of the fall of the angels.[40] These judgment

---

[29] Mark 10:38–39; 14:36; Matt 20:22; 26:39; Luke 22:42; John 18:11.

[30] E.g., taken as a supplication in prayer by Bornkamm, *Jesus of Nazareth*, 166–67; taken as genuine God-forsakenness by Cranfield, *Mark*, 459; and so forth.

[31] Cf. the statement by Rabbi Ammi, "There is no suffering without iniquity," Šabb. 55a (1:255).

[32] E.g., John 9:3; with typical Johannine irony, the physical blindness of the man blind from birth was contrasted to the self-induced blindness of the Pharisees (John 9:39–41). See also Luke 13:1–5; for Luke, the calamities referred to were circumstantial, in contrast to the imminent calamity of wrath upon the Jewish nation (cf. the parable of the unfruitful fig tree immediately following Luke 13:1–5).

[33] Matt 13:42; 8:12; 22:13; 24:51; 25:30; 5:22; 18:8–9; 23:32; 25:41. Cf. Luke 13:28; Mark 9:43–49; Jude 7; 2 Pet 3:7.

[34] E.g., Apocalypse of Paul 31–44 (NTA) and Pseudo-Titus Epistle, 2:158 (NTA).

[35] E.g., Judas (Acts 1:15–20); Ananias and Sapphira (Acts 5:1–11); Simon Magus (Acts 8:20); the sorcerer (Acts 13:10–11); Herod Agrippa I (divine punishment is explicit, Acts 12:20–23; cf. Josephus on the death of Catullus (*War* 7.453): "demonstrated that God punishes wicked men"[Whiston]); the high priest Ananias (Acts 23:3).

[36] Jesus rebuked James and John, perhaps because the call for judgment came before the opportunity to respond to the eschatological proclamation of the Mission of the Seventy, which closely follows in the narrative (Luke 10:1–16). In the case of the Mission of the Seventy, judgment for rejection is explicit. Cf. Rom 10:13–16.

[37] Matt 24:37–39; Luke 17:26–27; Heb 11:7; 1 Pet 3:20; 2 Pet 2:5.

[38] Matt 10:15; 11:23–24; Luke 10:12; 17:29; Jude 7; 2 Pet 2:6.

[39] Heb 3:7–11, using Ps 95. In the citation used, God was described as being "provoked" by the Israelites' hardness of heart (Heb 3:8, 15; cf. 3:16). God was "grieved" with that generation (Heb 3:10; cf. 3:17; the verb only here in the New Testament). One is reminded of Mark 3:5.

[40] Jude 6 (cf. 2 Pet 2:4).

motifs received a note of urgency when applied to the church or unbelievers with the supporting thought of the imminence of the end.[41] The only occurrence in the New Testament of the term "grumblers" (γογγυσταὶ, *gongustai*) in Jude 16 may have been a subtle allusion to the pattern of the Israelites in the desert who were condemned to death.[42]

SUMMARY

Explicit Contexts

Gospels

In the New Testament, the language of divine wrath in the Gospels is rare but redactionally significant in specific cases. Occurrences in Luke and John are notable examples (Luke 3:7; 4:18–19; 21:23; John 3:36). Luke connected the divine wrath to the existence of the Jewish nation in a way very similar to the use of *ira deum* (grounded in the *religio* of the ancient cultus) by Roman historians. For Luke, the judgment of a "coming wrath" from the John the Baptist tradition he used to interpret the destruction of Jerusalem.

John's redactional technique concerning the language of divine wrath underscored his realized eschatology. John enhanced his pronouncement about the wrath of God (3:36) by surrounding the third chapter of his Gospel with the specific narratives of the Cleansing of the Temple and the Samaritan Woman. In this way, John provided a hermeneutic on the meaning of the wrath of God in John 3:36 by constructing a challenge to both Jewish and Samaritan eschatological expectations with a central focus upon the person of Jesus. In this way, John radically transformed a concept of a future eschatological judgment into a judgment proleptically realized in personal response to Jesus now. A positive response to Jesus now already predicated the reality of future eternal life. A negative response to Jesus now already

---

[41] E.g., Heb 10:25–39. For Jude, the veracity of a coming retributive judgment was supported in Jude 14 and Jude 15 by a citation from the pseudepigraphical 1 En. 1:9. Jude's own time was interpreted as the last days soon to usher in eschatological judgment (Jude 17, 18). Also, see Jas 4:12 (cf. 5:8–9) and 1 Pet 1:17 (cf. 4:7, 13, 17).

[42] Cf. 1 Cor 10:10.

inaugurated the reality of future divine wrath, uniquely expressed under the Johannine rubric of "abiding."

Other occurrences of divine wrath in the New Testament add nuance but do not change the basic New Testament approach to the concept, which is to adopt but adapt typical Greco-Roman ideas in order to conform the picture to the revelation in Christ. For example, divine wrath possibly can be understood in the background of the parable of the Unmerciful Servant (Matt 18:34). If so, this expression of wrath as framed in the parable conforms to general expectations in the Greco-Roman world, but the profile is changed radically by the profile of the God to whom this wrath relates by inference.

Again, Mark's reference to the anger of Jesus in 1:41 (if the variant is read in the text) would be in line with his cosmic struggle theme in the first chapter of his Gospel. The anger of Jesus in Mark 3:5 resulted from the hardness of heart of the Pharisees that grieved Jesus, and that anger was appropriate in the context of Mark's spiritual struggle motif. Such an expression of anger also conformed to the general idea that the gods should be expected to be offended by that which opposed their will and intentions. Not to be offended is not to care. One clear revelation of God is that as creator, he most certainly cares about his creation and his creatures and has designs for life.

As another example, Matthew's use of the John the Baptist tradition on divine wrath likely should be equated with the rabbinic concept of Gehenna. If so, the context of a prophet warning Israel to get prepared for a coming judgment of God as did the prophets of old would be perfectly understandable. John shows no difference in calling leaders of Israel a brood of vipers in his day than Amos or Jeremiah getting after the religious and royal leaders of their day in the run up to the judgment of exile.

Hebrews

Jewish writers long had used themes of wrath from events in Hebrew Scripture, such as Noah and the flood and Sodom and Gomorrah, to make their points, and the same is true in the New Testament. For example, the author of Hebrews incorporates the theme of wilderness wrath as an illustration and a warning in Heb 3:11 (4:3).

Revelation

One of the problems that developed rather quickly for believing communities, even as far back as the early church in Jerusalem, was persecution. Persecution clearly was the context for the language of divine wrath in Revelation. At the pastoral level, the author wanted to encourage steadfast obedience and faithful witness among followers of the crucified Lamb in trying times. The language of divine retribution for human wickedness in Revelation, then, was not intended so much to explore the gory details of retribution as to comfort afflicted believers. The message was that the death sentence upon believers by idolatrous Rome was not the final word. John's language of wrath declared that God had the last word. God would triumph over evil. Those who gave wrath would get wrath.

Implicit Contexts

Divine wrath in implicit contexts, as expected, conforms to the profile of wrath in explicit contexts. Popular attitudes about divine wrath informed by Homer are on display, as with the sons of Zebedee wanting to call down the wrath of God from heaven. Other instances reinforce the profile of divine wrath in explicit contexts. The key to the difference in how divine wrath is framed in the New Testament is the character of the New Testament God.

5

Pauline: 1 Thessalonians

Deliverance from the Coming Wrath

THE LANGUAGE OF DIVINE WRATH Paul inherited from his world has features that illustrate the ancient mindset upon which Paul had to build his theology of wrath. In doing so, he had to negotiate presuppositions, counteract others, and capitalize on some core ideas. We can see these activities throughout Paul's letters. His comments illustrate from the beginning that what Paul had to say about the wrath of God was not an autonomic cultural reflex without theological reflection. We offer a few preliminary remarks to illustrate.

The term basic to Paul, *orgē*,[1] was basic to Greek usage as well, as was the synonymous use of *thumos*.[2] These two terms actually could be swapped out in translation when the terms occurred together in series.[3] The problem New Testament writers would have with Greek myth was in characterizing divine anger of the gods of Olympus as comparable to human anger. Human anger, of course, often was capricious and irrational. This capricious action when applied to the gods meant one always was in jeopardy of unknowingly offending some god in some obscure way. Prayer petitions to the gods for help and cultic propitiation to ward off harm were features of daily life in the Greco-Roman world of the general populace.

---

[1] Rom 1:18; 2:5 (2x), 8; 3:5; 4:15; 5:9; 9:22 (2x); 12:19; 13:4 (2x); Eph 2:3; 4:31; 5:6; Col 3:6, 8; 1 Thess 1:10; 2:16; 5:9; 1 Tim 2:8.

[2] Rom 2:8; 2 Cor 12:20; Gal 5:20; Eph 4:31; Col 3:8.

[3] Cf. Eph 4:31; Col 3:8.

The irrationality of human anger became a focus and a problem to be solved for the philosophers. They produced various solutions, particularly among Epicureans and Stoics. In general, the answer was simply insisting on the need to control or eliminate anger. Elimination of anger became a philosophical virtue and aspiration. The philosophers insisted that the gods as more than mortals could not possibly express anger. The Olympian gods were immutable. Thoroughly out of sync with this philosophical idea, the Yahweh revealed in Scripture clearly did not come across as immutable.

So, rather than relinquish the idea that God could express wrath, the question for many Jewish writers was nuanced into how to convey in Greek thought that Yahweh had wrath but not irrationality. Thus, the Septuagint, Josephus, and Philo showed a decided trend to deemphasize Homeric terms for wrath by using *orgē* and *thumos* exclusively, with a decided preference for the term *orgē* for divine wrath. The linguistic trend seems to reveal an implicit attempt to suppress Greek associations of irrationality with divine anger. Even the rabbis by inventing figures such as the Angel of Destruction seem to show this trend to dissociate God's wrath from human anger. Paul's usage with its decided preference for *orgē* in contexts of the divine wrath is right in line with this Jewish trend. This usage is clear in Romans 1, for example.

Another Greek idea related to divine wrath was that Olympus used wrath as an instrument to guide human destiny. Divine wrath set limits on human hubris and could not be resisted with impunity. A parallel thought was that divine wrath preserved the state and defended justice. Thus, expression of *orgē* as a function of the state for "punishment" was the proper and expected emotion of an honorable Greco-Roman ruler serious about avenging injustice in the public arena on behalf of the gods. Even in the Hebrew Scripture this idea is witnessed in the description of David's reaction to Nathan's parable—even though David himself was the offender (2 Sam 12:1–6). Paul capitalizes on this standard Greco-Roman concept of divine wrath in Rom 13:1–6.

Another thought to capitalize on was that the Roman historians had a distinctive use of divine wrath as the ground of the welfare of state and government. For the Romans in particular, religion and divine wrath were linked inseparably to state and destiny. Thus, the wrath of the gods was a literary device for historical interpretation of national events related to Rome. This aspect Paul capitalized on in Romans 9–11 in explaining Israel and her historical destiny as supervised by God.

Hebraic understanding of the wrath of Yahweh is distinguished from Homeric thought on the basis of Yahweh's revealed covenant with Israel. The covenant both personalized the divine-human relationship unlike anything that could be conceived by the Greeks and eliminated capriciousness. Wrath was judgment for violation of known covenant stipulations. Another twist in Hebraic thought was the subordination of any expression of divine wrath to the proclamation of the divine Name. Preservation of Israel was not for Israel. Israel did not deserve preservation, as the nation was idolatrous from beginning to end and never held up their side of covenant obligations. Preservation of Israel was for the glory of Yahweh's name among the nations. The expression of God's wrath, no matter how catastrophic, never was the end of the story, not in God's playbook. Here is the core of Pauline thought about divine wrath from his Jewish perspective.

The Dead Sea scrolls and the Samaritan doctrine of the future Taheb redeemer figure show how divine wrath became integrally associated with eschatology. Full reckoning for sin required a final judgment. Paul's eschatology, while not deterministic, was just as emphatic on final judgment (Rom 2:5–11). He, however, integrated this future element of wrath into the present reality of Jesus, as in the Gospel of John and in the Thessalonian material (1 Thess 1:9), to which we now turn our attention in detail.

1 THESSALONIANS 1:10

Immediate Background

When Paul writes to Thessalonian believers that he left behind after a brief stay in Thessalonica, he worried over their congregational stability under persecution. He sent Timothy back to discover the truth of the matter (3:2). Timothy brought good news that they not only were surviving, they were thriving (3:6–10). Their work of faith, labor of love, and endurance of hope stood as testimony to the strength of their life in Christ (1:3), and they had become an example throughout Macedonia and even into Achaia—because Paul likely was bragging on them as he was ministering in Corinth as he wrote this letter (1:7).

Paul's converts in Thessalonica mostly were pagans who came from an idolatrous life (1:9). Their city was heir to Greek and Roman civilization. The transition to following Jesus was difficult. One does not drop on a dime robust religious beliefs and entire ways of life.

FIGURE 5.1. Thessaloniki Inscription. Base of a 2nd cent. AD statue honoring Thessaloniki, wife of king Cassander, who gave her name to the city he founded in 315 BC (TAM).

FIGURE 5.2. Galerius Arch. One of the few Roman remains before the discovery of the Roman forum was this commemorative arch built over the Via Egnatia road leading into Thessalonica celebrating the victory of the Roman general, Galerius, over the Sassanid Persians, constructed AD 299–303.

FIGURE 5.3. Aerial of Thessalonica Roman Forum. Discovered in the 1960s during a downtown construction project, the Roman forum of ancient Thessalonica sits right in the middle of the modern commercial district. The odeon theater is left, with the commercial shop area along the top of the image. The central open square was colonnaded on all sides and had on display honorary statues to the imperial family and prominent civic leaders and benefactors.

FIGURE 5.4. Thessalonica Forum Shops. The Thessalonica forum, like those in other Roman cities such as Smyrna in Asia Minor, was multi-level. These are the second-level shops running along the southern edge, with the colonnaded square above. The excavations revealed active participation in Greco-Roman religions with statues to Greek and Roman gods and goddesses and patronage to the imperial family. One of the well-known statues of Augustus in Greek heroic pose was found here.

FIGURE 5.5. Thessalonica Forum Shops Detail. Detail showing the arched construction of the lower-level shops. The market area of the forum (Greek: agora) in a city would be where Paul would set up business to support himself during his mission endeavors.

FIGURE 5.6. Thessalonica Forum Odeon. An odeon is a smaller theater intended for more intimate venues, such as poetic recitation, musical performances, and speeches.

FIGURE 5.7. Bust of Livia. Imperial family patronage was woven into social fabric and daily life in Thessalonica. This original goddess was converted to portray Livia, wife of Augustus, after AD 42 (TAM).

FIGURE 5.8. Emperor Augustus. Portayed nude in the classic Greek style of a god, this statue of Augustus (27 BC–AD 14) was found within the forum area as part of the imperial statuary of Thessalonica.

FIGURE 5.9. Forum Deity. Unidentified deity found in one of the public buildings in the Thessalonica forum (TAM).

FIGURE 5.10. Statue of Dionysus. Dionysus in this 2nd cent. AD statue leans on a tree trunk with a vine branch around him. Found in the Thessalonica forum (TAM).

FIGURE 5.11. Forum Deity (Zeus). Another unidentified deity found in one of the public buildings in the Thessalonica forum. Likely Zeus or Poseidon (TAM).

FIGURE 5.12. L. Titonus Primus. The inscription on this bust found in the Thessalonica forum names this priest as L. Titonus Primus, dated AD 120–130. Interestingly, we know a priest of Isis of that exact name in the nearby Roman colony of Philippi. If this bust is the same person, which seems possible, this raises the prospect that Italian immigrants like Primus facilitated the spread of the Isis cult from Thessalonica to Philippi (TAM).

FIGURE 5.13. Aretalogy Stele. This stele fragment of the 1st cent. AD preserves part of an aretalogy, a sacred biography listing a deity's attributes or virtuous deeds, found in the Thessalonica forum. The virtues and gifts of this goddess to mankind are lauded in the first person (TAM).

FIGURE 5.14. Aretalogy Stele Translation.
I am the one who discovered wheat for mankind
I am the mother of King Horus
I am the one who rises in the Dog-star
I am the one called Goddess by women / For me was built the city of Bubastis
I separated the earth from the heaven / I showed the paths of the stars
I regulated the course of the sun and moon / I devised the activities of seamanship
I made what is right strong / I brought together woman and man
I assigned to women to bring into light of day their infants in the tenth month
I ordained that children should love parents
I imposed punishment upon those unkindly disposed towards their parents
I with my brother Osiris put an end to cannibalism
I taught men the initiation into mysteries
I instructed them to revere images of the gods
I established the sacred cult places of the gods
I abolished the rules of the tyrants / I put an end to murders
I compelled women to be loved by men
I made the right stronger than gold and silver
I ordained that the true should be considered good / I devised marriage contracts . . .

5–Thessalonians   117

FIGURE 5.15. Bust of Honorable Citizen. The style of clothing and the specific pose all speak to Greek upbringing and education, as well as status as an active citizen and benefactor of Thessalonica. Produced AD 130–140 in the workshop of Veroia (Berea) or Thessalonica (TAM).

FIGURE 5.16. Thessalonica Patroness. Found in the forum of Thessalonica, this 4th cent. AD statue of a woman likely is of a patroness who was a benefactor to some institution, guild, or civic entity in the city. Women had more social freedom in the province of Macedonia than anywhere else in the Roman Empire. One can compare the business activities of Lydia in Philippi, who dealt in the exclusive trade of purple dye, which required an imperial license, and had a home both in Philippi and in her home city of Thyatira (Acts 16:15). This greater status in public space and commercial activity for Macedonian women is a heritage of Macedonian culture. Greek and Roman culture typically greatly restricted the role of women in public space. Paul's churches in this province would reflect this cultural profile, as inferred with Lydia in Acts 16:14–15, 40, along with Euodia and Syntyche in Phil 4:2 (TAM).

FIGURE 5.17. Relief Illustrating Social Hierarchy. This relief illustrates at least three levels of the stratification of Greco-Roman society into rigidly defined roles of aristocrats, freedmen, and slaves. Local aristocrats were landed families with money. If they sought public office, they were obligated to provide expensive city benefaction, which is how temples, public buildings, roads, bridges, monuments, and aqueducts got built. Roman citizenship, if achieved, brought additional political and social advancement and status. Freedmen were former slaves who won their freedom. These individuals could gain the social status of wealth through business, but they never lost the stigma of slavery. Slaves were the lowest level of social structure. They had few rights, and often a harsh existence. This funeral monument relief of about 50 BC shows a family of freedmen, whose poses and attire indicate they had achieved some social status and Roman citizenship. Their slaves are depicted in the background between each figure. Notice the larger size and deeper-cut relief for the freedmen and the smaller size and more shallow relief for the slaves (TAM).

FIGURE 5.18. Hagios Demetrios. Demetrios is the patron saint of Thessaloniki. This church of the 4th cent. AD was built when Thessalonica was the second largest city of the Byzantine Empire. Archeological work revealed the ruins of a Roman bath where Demetrios was thought imprisoned and martyred. A nearby Roman well is conjectured as where the soldiers dumped the body. Where Paul spent at most only a few months still has a church today. Credit: Jean M. Stevens.

Exegesis

Paul opens by commending the Thessalonians' faith and witness. In his concluding remarks he says,

> For they themselves are announcing what kind of entrance we had with you, and how you turned to God away from idols to serve a living and true God and to wait for his Son from the heavens, whom he raised from the dead, Jesus, the one who delivers us from the wrath to come (1 Thess 1:9–10).

Paul probably took the formulation given in 1 Thess 9b–10 from a traditional creed. Words Paul normally did not use can be isolated:[4]

- ἐπεστρέψατε (*epestrepsate*), elsewhere in 2 Cor 3:16 and Gal 4:9

- ἀληθινῷ (*alēthinōi*), only here in Paul

- δουλεύειν (*douleuein*), with God as object, only here

- υἱόν (*huion*), only here in relation to the parousia

- ἐκ τῶν οὐρανῶν (*ek tōn ouranōn*), elsewhere the preposition occurs only with the singular

- ἀναμένειν (*anamenein*), only here

- ῥυόμενον (*hryomenon*), elsewhere with eschatological overtones of salvation, only in Rom 7:24; 11:26 (cf. Col 3:6)

Noticeable in this statement of faith is the absence of any reference to the cross, or of the death of Jesus as "for us," both of which are important ingredients for Paul in giving a summary of faith.[5]

Vocabulary and composition suggest the conclusion that the formula in 1 Thess 1:9b–10 is pre-Pauline. Elimination of the words, "whom he raised from the dead, Jesus," would leave a statement that readily can be interpreted as Jewish preaching to heathens, turning gentiles away from idols to a monotheistic faith, which included a warning of judgment.[6] Paul's messianic addition would be his reference to Jesus

---

[4] Adapted from Best, *Thessalonians*, 81–85.

[5] Rom 5:6, 8; 14:15; 1 Cor 1:13; 8:11; 2 Cor 5:14; Gal 2:20. For a contrary view, see Munck, "I Thess. i.9–10," 95–110. But note Tob 14:6, "Then all the Gentiles will turn [ἐπιστρέψουσιν, *epistrepsousin*] to fear the Lord God in truth [ἀληθινῶς, *alēthinōs*], and will bury their idols."

[6] Neill, *Jesus through Many Eyes*, 47.

and Jesus's resurrection from the dead.[7] As a probable Jewish-believer formula, 1 Thess 1:9b-10 could reflect missionary preaching to the gentiles.[8] After a brief comment on the position of the creedal formula in the letter, several terms in the Greek text are discussed.

The creedal formula concludes a skillfully organized introduction (1 Thess 1:2-10) constructed in the form of a prayer of thanksgiving.[9] Paul reviewed his missionary entrance to the Thessalonians (1 Thess 1:2-5). In the second half of the introduction, Paul moved to the positive response of the Thessalonians to the gospel (1 Thess 1:6-9a). Paul carefully worked in the creedal formula to serve as the conclusion to his introduction (1 Thess 1:9b-10), and to summarize the theme of the epistle.

The use of υἱός (*huios*), "Son," in 1:10 as a title is not as frequent in Paul as the alternate title of "Lord" (κύριος, *kyrios*).[10] But when Paul does use the title, he draws upon the soteriological significance of the term. Three times in the introduction to Romans, the title occurs in connection with the gospel of God (Rom 1:3, 4, 9), and three times in the climactic Romans 8 (8:3, 29, 32).[11] From the position of the title in such contexts in Paul, Hengel concluded that "the form 'Son of God', with its more complicated language, was kept for exceptional usage, at the climax of certain theological statements."[12] Early church tradition may be reflected in the use of this term, especially since only in this context in 1 Thessalonians was υἱός (*huios*) ever used by Paul in relation to the parousia hope.

In 1 Thess 1:10, the verb ῥυόμενον (*hryomenon*) was used in the negative sense of deliverance from danger. Wilhelm Kasch noted that the verb in the New Testament means "to save," a use fully dependent upon the use in the Old Testament, and that eschatologically, the verb

---

[7] Cf. Best, *Thessalonians*, 86.

[8] Neill, *Jesus Through Many Eyes*, 46-47, pointed to parallels in Acts 17.

[9] See Ellingworth and Nida, *Translator's Handbook on Paul's Letters to the Thessalonians*, 5. Formally, 1:2-10 is the thanksgiving period of the letter, but functionally, the introduction "already conveys what is the main purpose of the letter," Boers, "Form Critical Study of Paul's Letters: 1 Thessalonians as a Case Study," 153.

[10] Including Ephesians and Colossians, fifteen times for υἱός (*huios*), compared to almost two hundred for κύριος, *kyrios*.

[11] Cf. 1 Cor 1:9; 15:28; 2 Cor 1:18-19; Gal 2:20.

[12] Hengel, *The Son of God*, 14. Cf. Acts 9:20.

denotes preservation from the sudden loss of eternal salvation in the end as promised by God. Furthermore, Kasch also noted the idea of preservation corresponds closely to that in the Dead Sea Scrolls, where human sinfulness is related not only to humans themselves, but to the eschatological power of evil against which humans are helpless and in the last conflict will plunge them into eternal destruction.[13] Humanity needed a deliverer from eschatological wrath.[14]

The use of ῥυόμενον (*hryomenon*) in 1 Thess 1:10 may reflect early traditions from a cultic setting of worship used by Paul in his eschatological teaching. Besides noting the verb itself, the present tense of the verb indicates that the action of deliverance from future wrath already is being effected. The present tense of the future deliverance occurs in a setting that can be outlined as two three-line stanzas.[15] Aune has noted that ways of conceptualizing realized eschatology among early believers occur with much greater frequency in hymnic material.[16] The material in 1 Thess 1:9b–10 that Paul incorporated into the introduction of his letter may show a flux of traditions. Traditions that were related to missionary activity possibly were integrated into the worship experience of the early church.

The identifying title "Jesus" (Ἰησοῦν, *Iēsoun*), was placed first in the construction of 1:10b. Positioning the term first in Greek signals emphasis in the grammar. Use of the historical name denoted that the issue of eschatology rested with a historical figure and historical events (cf. 1 Thess 4:14). This Pauline feature easily could be missed, but the exegetical point is crucial. The Thessalonian material already provides an early signal that the Christ-event itself is central to Paul's theology of divine wrath. For Paul, Jesus is the hermeneutic of God's wrath.

In 1:10, "the wrath" (ἡ ὀργή, *hē orgē*) connotes an idea familiar to the Thessalonians, because he does not trouble to explain the term. One would be safe to presume, then, that "wrath" was a standard element of

---

[13] Kasch, TDNT, s.v. "ῥύομαι," 6:1002–03.

[14] Cf. Sib. Or. 3:556–61: at the end "when the wrath of the great God shall be upon you," then every soul "shall begin to call to his succour the Mighty king, . . . and to seek who shall come as a deliverer from the mighty wrath." Charles, *Pseudepigrapha*, 372, dated the passage ca. 146 BC; Collins, *The Sibylline Oracles of Egyptian Judaism*, 33, 43–44, dated the work near the time of Ptolemy Philometer VI.

[15] Best, *Thessalonians*, 86.

[16] Aune, *The Cultic Setting of Realized Eschatology in Early Christianity*, 221.

Paul's eschatological preaching and teaching to his newly-minted converts, and particularly pagans.[17] "The wrath" was a technical phrase in Paul's eschatological vocabulary. The paucity of references to God's wrath in rabbinic material suggests that Paul did not derive his ideas on the wrath of God directly from his rabbinic heritage. Rabbinic thought equated the wrath of God with the judgment of Gehenna. Paul never indicated such an equation.[18] Therefore, one may observe right away that Paul's thought about the wrath of God is not rabbinic. The core of his refection is sourced elsewhere, and that observation should punch the pause button before one assumes that when Paul speaks of the "wrath of God" his rhetoric should be thought equivalent to modern rhetoric of the "fires of hell." The term has to be technical for Paul, because Paul is putting a spin on the meaning that is not easily located in existing Jewish or Jesus traditions—particularly, for example, the tradition that obviously impacted Matthew, who provides the lion's share of references to Gehenna in the New Testament. The factor of Paul's own contribution means that an understanding of wrath in Pauline writings should be consistent with the obvious judgment theme in primitive preaching—dominant likely because of the impact of John the Baptist—but that one should be careful exegetically to allow Paul himself to define the nature of wrath in each individual context.[19] When he does so later in Romans, he utilizes the common idea of the wrath of heaven guiding the destiny of humans (Romans 1) and of nations (Romans 9–11). At the same time, he is informed by the distinctive Jewish creation theology and the parameters of a covenant relationship.

The wrath to come in 1 Thess 1:10 is the wrath of eschatological judgment.[20] Ideas that centered on the prophetic Day of the Lord traditions included the thought that the Day of the Lord would be the day

---

[17] A point pretty much totally ignored by the general reader of Paul.

[18] Gehenna is as close as the rabbis ever got to conceptualizing the wrath of God, but the term Gehenna never is mentioned by Paul or even finds a direct allusion. Even the strongly Jewish but short letter of James finds occasion for at least one reference to Gehenna (Jas 3:6). Note Hanson, *Wrath of the Lamb*, 54–55.

[19] Cf. Gager, Jr., "Functional Diversity in Paul's Use of End-Time Language," 325–37; Moule, "Influence of Circumstances," 1–15.

[20] Frame (*Thessalonians*, 89) suggested "is coming" (ἔρχεται, *erchetai*) in 1:10 over μέλλουσα (*mellousa*) emphasized the nearness of the judgment. For repentance turning away wrath, cf. Hos 14:1–4; Sir 5:7, but these lack an eschatological nuance.

of Yahweh's wrath, as in Zeph 1:14–18. From this eschatological wrath the people of Yahweh would have to be preserved (Isa 26:20–21). According to Bornkamm, an eschatological perspective was adopted by the primitive church and applied to the history of Jesus of Nazareth.[21] The idea of preservation from wrath corresponds well with the use of the verb "delivers" (ῥυόμενον, *hryomenon*).

1 THESSALONIANS 2:16

Immediate Background

In the material in 1 Thess 2:3–12, Paul defended his behavior and his missionary activity while in Thessalonica. This material brings in the historical background available from Acts. Regardless estimates of how long Paul stayed in the city, most agree he did not stay long, perhaps a few months at best.[22] His departure also was abrupt, brought about by public disturbance. This departure is problematic in terms of what the action might suggest of his motives, as well as the inadequate time in which to teach the new converts in order to train them fully.

Exegesis

In 1 Thess 2:13, Paul returned to his thought expressed in 1:9, the reception of the divine message among the Thessalonians as a part of Paul's mission. This prior ministry Paul mentions again just prior to a second reference to divine wrath. The passage is disputed, so is quoted in full.

> For you yourselves, brothers and sisters, became imitators of the churches of God in Messiah Jesus which are in Judea, because you yourselves suffered the same things under your own compatriots just as also they under the Jews, who not only killed the Lord Jesus and the prophets, but also drove us out; they are not pleasing unto God and are hostile to all people, hindering us from speaking to the gentiles that they might be saved, so that

---

[21] Bornkamm, *Jesus of Nazareth*, 44–52.

[22] The mention of three Sabbaths in Acts 17:2 is not necessarily the duration of Paul's work in the city. The statement could be read as simply how long Paul was allowed to function in the synagogue before being disinvited to speak again. That he labored with his own hands seems to infer enough time in the market to establish a minimal clientele (cf. 1 Cor 4:12; 1 Thess 4:11; 2 Thess 3:7; Acts 20:33; 18:2).

> they always are filling up the measure of their sins. But the wrath
> has come against them decisively (1 Thess 2:14–16).

In 1 Thess 2:16, Paul states abruptly and without explanation, "But the wrath has come against them decisively" (ἔφθασεν δὲ ἐπ' αὐτοὺς ἡ ὀργὴ εἰς τέλος, *ephthasen de ep autous hē orgē eis telos*).[23] Textual variations in Greek manuscripts imply difficulties with the meaning of the statement from an early time.[24] Even Bruce had his doubts about the integrity of the passage. He does not outright explicitly reject the words as from Paul, but comes just about as close to the insinuation as possible without actually saying "not Paul": "The words of vv 15, 16 are addressed to Gentiles [*sic*] and they have more in common with current Gentile disparagement of Jews than with the positive attitude of affecttion and hope which Paul elsewhere expresses with regard to his 'kinsmen by race' (Rom 9:3)."[25] The balance of textual considerations leans to the words being authentic. We simply have difficulty in exegesis.

What action was in mind in the final statement about wrath having fallen or come? Suggestions for a concrete historical event that could fulfill the aorist sense would include: (1) the expulsion of Jews from Rome by Claudius in AD 49, (2) the sudden and unexpected death of Herod Agrippa I in Caesarea, (3) the insurrection of Theudas, (4) a recent and severe famine, or (5) some unknown event.[26] The im-

---

[23] Paul's statement is paralleled in T. Levi 6:11. A literary relationship sometimes is proposed. Cf. De Jonge, "Die Patriarchentestamente von Roger Bacon bis Richard Simon, mit einen Namenregister," 34; also, De Jonge, "Notes on Testament of Levi II–VII," 260, n49. However, the use in the Testament of Levi is non-eschatological. Paul's use is eschatological, so literary connection, if admitted, would not be conceptual.

[24] The tense varies. An aorist tense is supported by N, A, D1, F, G, with others. The perfect tense is supported by B, D*, 104, with others. The aorist tense could be understood as a specific act of judgment (or a series of acts regarded as one), or as proleptic of judgment to come within a prophetic announcement. The perfect tense would be understood as a judgment already activated but as yet not completed. The extant sentence varies. The entire sentence is missing from one Vulgate manuscript. Finally the source of "the wrath" varies. Divine wrath is made explicit by D, F, G, 629, and a united Latin witness, which seems to infer a question as to the nature of the wrath being clarified.

[25] Bruce, *Thessalonians*, 51.

[26] So Best, *Thessalonians*, 120. The ambiguity has not changed much since Best. Fee, rejecting the scribal notion that the phrase has to mean the wrath *of God*, took the verse as Paul speaking in the vein of a prophet about some concrete event experienced by Judean Jews that is not discernable at this distance in time (*Thessalonians*, 101–02).

mediate context should be recalled. Paul made reference in 2:15 to the specific activity of the Jews in opposing his missionary work, an activity already epitomized in the killing of Jesus. This is the same Jesus earlier described as the deliverer from the coming wrath (1:10). Apart from Jesus, one would be swept away in the swirling vortex of the coming judgment of wrath. All evil would be destroyed; but especially singled out would be direct opposition to God.[27] Direct opposition to God was precisely the kind of activity of the Jews who hindered the mission work of Paul and his cohorts (2:16a). For Paul, such opposition to the gospel could not possibly be pleasing to God and legitimately could be characterized as hostility to everyone (2:15b). If those Jews directly opposed to God by opposing the work of the gospel encountered the final judgment, they would be swept away in the destruction of that eschatological wrath. One may recall Marqah *Memar* 4.6, "Be not an enemy to God, or you will be subject to judgment. You will have no control over it, and you will have no deliverer."

Concerning the creedal formula in 1 Thess 1:10, the centrality of the Christ-event for Paul's language of divine wrath was pointed out. Paul had to consider the possibility that some Jews actually would be caught in judgment, since in the context of his experiences at Philippi, Thessalonica, and Berea, he had little reason to perceive any abating of Jewish opposition to his gospel. The continual opposition by the Jews served to create a standing condition in which the full measure of their sins constantly was being met.[28] The full measure of sins mentioned in 2:16 was a figure for no alternative but devastating judgment.[29] Such an eschatological construct seems to have been grounded in a prior conviction of the imminent parousia. The aorist tense of "has fallen," has arrived" (ἔφθασεν, *ephthasen*) relates to, and complements, the specific

---

[27] From Qumran, cf. M 5:7–20; H 15:20; W 3:1–11; W 3:12—4:2. In such questions, the issue of the sovereignty of God was at stake.

[28] "With the result that they always fill up the measure of their sins," 1 Thess 2:16b, as conceived result, though for Paul, such syntax often indicates purpose (cf. Rom 8:29). Purpose in 2:16 is unlikely in view of "always." For the action here, perhaps the language of Qumran in Z 4:12—5:17 and 7:9—8:21 is comparable; cf. M 5:7–20.

[29] Gen 15:16; 2 Macc 6:12–17. Cf. Wis 19:4. Daniel 12:13 has the noun in an eschatological context. Compare Matt 23:29–35 with the thought in 1 Thess 2:14-16. Romans 11:3 indicates that the Elijah legends probably informed Paul's thinking on persecution (cf. 1 Kgs 19:10); cf. Cooper, "The Intertextual Link."

actions (conceptualized as one of a certain class) in the aorist tenses in "they killed Jesus" and "they drove us out" in 2:15. That class of action was opposition to the gospel of God, which Paul is interpreting as an eschatological sign (cf. Phil 1:28). Paul seems to be operating under the assumption that the final eschatological crisis that would issue in eternal destiny was already in motion through the preaching of the gospel, which seems similar to the sentiment in Rom 13:11. For Paul, the gospel was the eschatological catalyst that differentiated humanity into those "in Christ" and those under the wrath of God. Those "in Christ" were in the sphere of eschatological deliverance: "Jesus, the one who delivers us from the coming wrath" (1 Thess 1:10).

In the Qumran community, a person was understood to exhibit that pattern of behavior of the spirit that dominated the human spirit. These spirits were two, the spirit of truth and the spirit of perversity. One would live in the lifestyle of either spirit until the final inquisition. Each lifestyle had a defining set of characteristics. By these characteristics, the spirit that controlled one's life was discernible. To the one living under the spirit of perversity would come "everlasting perdition through the angry wrath of an avenging God."[30]

Paul did not engage in the strict determinism behind the thought at Qumran.[31] But as at Qumran, Paul believed in an imminent eschatological crisis that would issue in eternal destiny. For Paul, the crux of this issue was Jesus. In Jesus Messiah was salvation; outside of Jesus, the deliverer, was the wrath of God (1 Thess 5:9–10). The chronic enmity displayed by some Jews to the gospel demonstrated a pattern of behavior destined for wrath. Such resistance only could come from perverse and evil persons (2 Thess 2:1–2). The ultimate eschatological sin was opposition to the preaching of the gospel, because the preaching of the gospel presented the opportunity for salvation (2:16).[32]

Paul, convinced of the arrival of the end-time through the eschatological sign of the cross and resurrection, understood that a person's

---

[30] At Qumran, cf. M 3:13—4:26.

[31] One might compare Paul's language of the "children of light" and "children of darkness" in 1 Thess 5:9–10.

[32] Though directed toward heathens, 1 En. 91:6–9 contains the thought of an eschatological consummation of unrighteousness. In Jub. 15:34, a specific category of sin (rejection of circumcision as the covenant sign) was considered so momentous that no more forgiveness was possible, "for all the sin of this eternal error."

current decision about the gospel would effect a discrimination of eschatological destiny in light of an imminent parousia. With Jesus soon to come as Lord, final judgment was at hand. The early church conceived its mission in this final eschatological time as the preaching of the gospel (cf. Mark 13:10). Resisting the gospel was the consummate eschatological sin ("they always fill up the measure of their sins"). For those obstructing the gospel, the final judgment would be one of divine wrath.[33] With a view toward an imminent parousia, Paul's use of the aorist tense of ἔφθασεν, (*ephthasen*, 2:16) represented a foregone conclusion. Paul was struck with the eschatological significance of present antagonism to the gospel of God.[34]

The translation of the difficult phrase, εἰς τέλος, *eis telos*, has been debated. The phrase may be taken qualitatively or quantitatively. The phrase could mean "continually,"[35] "finally,"[36] "forever,"[37] or "fully" (i.e., "decisively").[38] Frame said a temporal meaning would fit well with the structure of parallelism of the clauses. The word "always" (πάντοτε, *pantote*) would be parallel to εἰς τέλος, *eis telos*.[39]

A temporal idea seems to be present, but not without an element of the qualitative idea. Three reasons support this conclusion. First, one may note that, outside of 1 Thess 2:16, Paul used *telos* with an eschatological nuance nine out of ten times. Only in two of these instances is the construction with a preposition, each with ἕως, *heōs*.[40] In these two cases, τέλους, *telous*, refers to "the day of the Lord Jesus," as is ex-

---

[33] Cf. Roetzel, *Judgment*, 93, "Judgment is now beginning on the enemy of the Gospel (1 Thess 2:13–16)."

[34] Ironically, Paul is evaluating his own past as a chief antagonist of the church; cf. Gal 1:13; similarly, note 1 Tim 1:13. Two exegetical elements to note here. First, Paul never tried to hide his past life opposing the gospel. Second, often missed is that Paul's personal involvement in this story of divine wrath in Judea shadows this indictment.

[35] Cf. Arndt-Gingrich, *Lexicon*, 819.

[36] E.g., Frame, *Thessalonians*, 114; Ellingworth and Nida, *Handbook*, 45; Best, *Thessalonians*, 121.

[37] Cf. Arndt-Gingrich, *Lexicon*, 819.

[38] Ibid.; Blass-Debrunner, *Grammar*, 112; Delling, *TDNT*, s.v. "τέλος," 8:56.

[39] Frame, *Thessalonians*, 114.

[40] 1 Cor 1:8; 2 Cor 1:13. For 1 Cor 1:8, D, F and G have ἀχρὶ τέλους, *achri telous* (cf. Heb 6:11; Rev 2:26) and P[46] has τελείους, *teleious*. Cf. μέχρι τέλους, *mechri telous* in Wis 16:5; 19:1 (cf. Heb 3:6, 14) and the statement at Qumran in Z 2:14—3:12, "In the end, his anger was kindled against them."

plicit in the context.⁴¹ But ἕως, *heōs*, with its sense of limited time duration would imply a cessation of the action at a certain point, i.e., "up until," or "up to." Such a temporal meaning apparently did not carry for Paul the essence of what he wanted to say in 1 Thess 2:16.

Second, in 1 Thess 5:9, one may observe the construction, "God has not destined us unto wrath" (ὅτι οὐκ ἔθετο ἡμᾶς ὁ θεὸς εἰς ὀργὴν, *hoti ouk etheto hēmas ho theos eis orgēn*), in a discussion about the Day of the Lord. Here the second aorist verb, "destined" (ἔθετο, *etheto*), is followed by the accusative construction, "unto wrath" (εἰς ὀργὴν, *eis orgēn*), just as the first aorist verb, "has fallen" (ἔφθασεν, *ephthasen*), is followed by the accusative construction, "at last" (εἰς τέλος, *eis telos*) in 2:16. Both contexts carry the eschatological *orgē*. Therefore, it may be possible for εἰς τέλος (*eis telos*) to be the complement of εἰς ὀργήν (*eis orgēn*) in Pauline eschatological language. The phrase εἰς τέλος (*eis telos*) would emphasize the final destruction that results from the operation of the eschatological wrath.⁴² Such an understanding of εἰς τέλος (*eis telos*) would coordinate with the use of τέλος (*telos*) in a predominantly eschatological sense elsewhere in Paul. In other contexts, τέλος (*telos*) was used similarly to emphasize a qualitative result, i.e., the nature of eschatological consummation as death or destruction.⁴³ The contrasting eschatological condition for Paul would be everlasting life or salvation.⁴⁴

Thus, Paul seems to have derived the aorist tenses in both 2:16 and 5:9 from past experiences (cf. "them" and "us") and from his Jewish sense of sovereign design. The eschatological wrath was not an accidental happenstance in the economy of end-time events. God purposed from the beginning to destroy evil from before his presence. In Christ, God had acted decisively for human salvation. However, rejection of Christ would bring just as decisive a condemnation. Whether a person would be caught up in this destruction of the final judgment would be an individual's own choice.

---

⁴¹ D, F, G substitute "appearing" (παρουσία, *parousia*) for "day" (ἡμέρᾳ, *hēmerai*) in 1 Cor 1:8.

⁴² Cf. Thayer, *Lexicon*, 620.

⁴³ E.g., Rom 6:21; Phil 3:19; 2 Cor 11:15. This idea of "destruction" would be compatible with the translation "fully" ("decisively") for εἰς τέλος (*eis telos*) in 2:16.

⁴⁴ E.g., 1 Thess 5:9; Rom 6:22.

1 THESSALONIANS 5:9

Immediate Background

FIGURE 5.19. Tombstone. In this 1st cent. AD tombstone relief from Thessalonica, the military officer L. Cornelius, his horse attended by a slave whose social status is depicted in smaller size, is portrayed in a *dexiosis* scene of farewell to his grieving wife, attended by her slave, with a bilingual inscription underneath the relief. The entwined snake in the tree motif may be of the military hero-horseman theme somewhat particular to Macedonia and surrounding regions (TAM).

We cannot know whether death among believers in Thessalonica was a concern raised only abstractly or was provoked by actual events. If actual events, also unknown would be whether such deaths were from natural causes or the tragic consequence of persecution. The later history of Thessalonica in the case of the martyred saint Demetrios casts a foreboding shadow over the Thessalonian question to Paul, whether in the abstract or in real life. Thoughts about death varied greatly in ancient society, from Epicurus, who denied life after death, to Plato, who argued a soul and body dichotomy, with the soul being eternal. Ancient tomb monuments and funerary memorials testify to the pain and grief of the loss of loved ones. To this ancient world of confusion about death and life after death, the gospel brought an incredible message—not of a *promise* of life after death—but of the *reality* of life after death, because of the resurrection of Jesus. That this risen Jesus would return to claim his own was just icing on the theological cake.

Yet, the good news seemed to have latent bad news. Jesus would return to claim his own. Check. But then, who assuredly belongs to him? How can one know one has not forfeited the privilege? With so much Pauline emphasis on the necessity of sanctification in everyday life (cf. 4:1–8), can lack of satisfactory sanctification at any given moment disqualify a person from this glorious event of the end time, since the timing is unknown, and some might not be putting their best spiritual foot forward at that moment?

Exegesis

In two units in 1 Thess 4:13–5:11, Paul treated two matters related to the parousia of Jesus. In the first unit of 4:13–20, Paul began by attempting to clarify confusion about the status of deceased believers related to the parousia in terms of their participation in the event (4:13–18). Then in 5:1–11, Paul attempted to clarify the status of *living* believers at the parousia related to their *sanctification*. Suggesting pre-Pauline tradition behind the material in 5:1–11 are:

- the impersonal use of "they say" (λέγωσιν, *legōsin*)

- the use of εἰρήνη (*eirēnē*), "peace," as "security"

- the eschatological use of "safety," ἀσφάλεια (*asphaleia*), "sudden," αἰφνίδιος (*aiphnidios*), "comes upon," ἐφιστάναι (*ephistanai*), and "birth pains," ὠδίν (*ōdin*)

Best urged the similarity with Luke 21:34–36.[45] The only two instances of "sudden," αἰφνίδιος (*aiphnidios*), in the New Testament are in Luke and Paul. The rare word "safety," ἀσφάλεια (*asphaleia*, 5:3) nowhere else is used in an eschatological sense or context, bearing only a non-eschatological meaning in non-biblical Greek.[46] A possible scenario could be that Paul used primitive tradition of a proverbial nature, innovating his own eschatological shift, which Luke later modified. Luke's modification could have been induced by the theological stimulus provided in Paul's use of "destruction" (ὄλεθρος, *olethros*) in 5:3.[47] Terms such as "destruction" (ὄλεθρος, *olethros*), "ruin" (ἀπώλεια, *apōleia*), "death" (θάνατος, *thanatos*), "wrath" (ὀργή, *orgē*), and "salvation" (σωτηρία, *sōtēria*) appear as general eschatological categories in Paul's semantic

---

[45] *Thessalonians*, 207.

[46] Cf. Dittenberger, *SIG* 780.20.

[47] The Pauline theological significance of this term is presented in discussion of "Eschatological Destruction" in the section on implicit Pauline use.

universe. The semantic universe exhibited in Luke would be of a type similar to that represented in Ezek 6:12–17 with concrete categories of historical application. Paul's eschatological use of "destruction" (ὄλεθρος, *olethros*) could have triggered Luke's thought against the background of the destruction of Jerusalem.[48]

In 5:1–11, the inescapable destruction that would overtake unbelievers on the Day of the Lord would be a striking feature of the suddenness of the event—as in a thief's unexpected arrival (5:3).[49] However, Paul's emphasis in his review of previous eschatological teaching in 5:1–11 transcended this feature of the suddenness of the Day of the Lord; indeed, the Thessalonians had no need for more instruction (5:1).

Instead, the Thessalonians needed confidence. Two observations point toward a crisis of confidence among some in the community of Thessalonian believers. First, one could assume from Paul's frequent references to the parousia that he had inspired a conviction of the nearness of that event in his missionary exchange at Thessalonica.[50] Second, Paul connected holy and blameless living to appearing holy and blameless before the Lord at the parousia.[51] Any believer who took Paul's teaching to heart could have become obsessed with the fear of lacking the necessary holiness at the parousia, perhaps even with the fear of losing salvation at the last moment. The unexpectedness of the event could have amplified the level of a neophyte believer's worry. One has to remember in the case of such anxieties the pagan world out of which Thessalonian believers came to faith in Jesus. Popular parlance still was quite conversant with the gods of Olympus and the conflicting claims of a polytheistic world to fealty. The first-century stele with an inscribed aretalogy of a goddess making just such claims in Figure 5.14 is illustration. The gods could manifest an inexplicable capriciousness at quite the most inconvenient times.

---

[48] Oral tradition could have been a channel through which Luke encountered such Pauline traditions.

[49] David Daube outlined the development in the New Testament of the "thief" motif in *The Sudden in the Scriptures*, 29, n6; cf. Jeremias, *Parables*, 44–50.

[50] 1 Thess 2:19; 3:13; 4:15; 5:23. Cf. 1:10; 4:16; 5:2, 3.

[51] 1 Thess 2:12; 3:13; 4:3, 6, 7; 5:22, 23. Cf. 1 Cor 1:8. Also, see Donfried, "Justification and Last Judgment in Paul," 147; Moule, "Judgment Theme in the Sacraments," 472.

FIGURE 5.20. Praetorian Guard. Augustus transformed the Praetorians of the Roman Republic who were a security detail for senators and public officials into an elite private bodyguard for the protection of the emperor permanently housed in the Castra Praetoria barracks. For two hundred years, they were the only Roman troops stationed in Italy. They inevitably got involved in imperial politics as audacious as the overthrow of emperors they were sworn to protect. A monumental high relief of the Praetorian Guard reveals their distinctive uniform but typical Roman armor, including the javelin (*pilum*, background), battle sword (*gladius*), helmet, and shield. Paul occasionally used the imagery of military armor, as in 1 Thess 5:8 (LP).

Paul came to his point in 1 Thess 5:4: the Day of the Lord would not overtake believers.[52] The security of the believer at the parousia was guaranteed for two reasons. First, the "light/darkness" motif serves to reinforce that the believer was distinguished from the unbeliever in spiritual origin (5:5).[53] Second, the believer was distinguished from the unbeliever in spiritual equipment; they had the armor necessary for the denouement of judgment (5:8).[54] Therefore, the believer's victory on the Day of the Lord was assured (5:9).[55] Paul clinched his assurance in 5:9 by pointing to the prevenient action of God. The ultimate conse-

---

[52] In Greek, the "you" is in emphatic position.

[53] Light/darkness contrasts were common. Cf. John 3:19–21; at Qumran, M 1:9, 10; 3:13, 24; W 1:1, 3, 7, 10, 16; 3:6, 9; Z 13:12; T. Levi 19:1; T. Naph. 2:7–10; T. Benj. 5:3.

[54] Cf. Isa 59:11; Rom 13:12–14. On the apocalyptic background of military analogies, see Wiens, "Holy War Theology in the New Testament and Its Relationship to the Eschatological Day of the Lord Tradition," 84–88.

[55] Of the items listed by Paul that would not separate the believer from Christ, "things to come" were included in Rom 8:38. Such "things to come" would include the wrath to come (1 Thess 1:9).

quence of the Day of the Lord for the believer would not negate what God already had accomplished for the believer's salvation through the death of Jesus Christ.[56] Whatever the eschatological consequences of the parousia of Jesus, the believer had the assurance of being "with him" (5:10).[57] Grundmann suggestively observed that Paul's "with Christ" idea actually enshrines the Christian hope; he also suggested Paul likely coined the formula.[58]

Paul underscored his pastoral encouragement in 5:1–11 through his embedded epistolary prayers.

FIGURE 5.21. Roman Helmet. Legionnaire helmet with cheek plates (PMB).

Two benedictions conclude the two main divisions of the letter.[59] A part of each benediction is an intercession for complete sanctification of the Thessalonian believers at the parousia of Jesus Christ. The introduction to the letter contains an affirmation of Paul's unceasing prayer vigil for the Thessalonians (1 Thess 1:2). In these prayers, Paul expressed his assurance that the Thessalonians' hope in the Lord Jesus Christ was steadfast (1 Thess 1:3). Their hope was firm because that hope was grounded in the election of God (1 Thess 1:4). Thus, the introduction to the letter seems constructed specifically with 5:8–9 in mind. The last benediction itself concludes with a statement placing emphasis upon God's faithfulness to finish what he had begun (5:24). Paul removed introverted faintheartedness by pointing to the priority and power of God in the business of salvation. Such carefully worded and placed prayers in themselves would serve to encourage the Thessalonians, for as they could hear the letter read aloud (5:27), believers

---

[56] Cf. Gal 3:17.

[57] The aspect of a crisis of confidence among some Thessalonian believers was missed by Kaye, "Eschatology and Ethics in 1 and 2 Thessalonians," 47–57. Cf. Martin, *Thessalonians*, 169.

[58] Grundmann, *TDNT*, s.v. "σύν-μετά with the Genitive," 7:766–97; cf. 7:782.

[59] 1 Thess 3:11–13; 5:23.

could hear Paul's own personal intercession for them. They would be reminded that God was the author of salvation.

To say the Thessalonian believers were flushed with eschatological fever would be a caricature. One should not dissociate the Thessalonian problem from the Pauline mission. Paul was forced to leave his mission in Thessalonica prematurely. Believers in Thessalonica reflected a situation one might expect if new converts had had the conviction of an imminent parousia injected into their hope,[60] but could not benefit from the full complement of his missionary teaching and labor. Indeed, Paul expressed earnest desire to complete his work begun at Thessalonica, a desire that he urgently felt in light of the ensuing problems.[61] In regard to these problems, however, Best noted that

> Paul in no way seeks to decrease, let alone defuse, the eschatological pressure felt by the Thessalonians. He does not suggest that it may be further off than they expect but only reiterates teaching on its unexpectedness and inevitability.

The negative assertion in 5:9a has its positive counterpart in 5:9b. Paul used the verb "destined," ἔθετο (*etheto*), as equivalent in meaning to the Attic ποιῆσαι (*poiēsai*).[62] If so, this equivalency of meaning linguistically ties 5:9a to 5:9b through a word with the same base as the Attic equivalent, περιποίησιν (*peripoiēsin*). The objective genitive that follows this verb confirms a translation in the active sense (rather than the more frequent passive), i.e., "gaining," or "obtaining," salvation.[63]

The thought in 5:9 was an anticipation of that aspect of the believer's salvation yet to be completed. The dual structure of salvation as a present possession and a future consummation was signified in the construction of the theological statements in 5:10. The phrase, "who died for us," reflected the present dimension of salvation. The phrase "that we might live together with him" reflected the future dimension. Both dimensions demonstrated the reality of the assertion in 5:9, "God

---

[60] Cf. the "hope of salvation" in 1 Thess 5:8. The concept of "hope" includes elements not yet completed. This hope anticipates the parousia.

[61] 1 Thess 3:10; cf. 4:13.

[62] Arndt-Gingrich, *Lexicon*, 824, gave the sense as to make, appoint, or destine someone to or for something. This translation is confirmed by the use of the preposition, "unto," εἰς (*eis*), as a logical connection, Oepke, *TDNT*, s.v. "εἰς" 2:428.

[63] Arndt-Gingrich, *Lexicon*, 656. Cf. 2 Thess 2:14.

has not destined us for wrath." The formulation in 5:10 served to highlight why the assertion was true that believers were not destined for wrath. The believer's salvation was grounded in, and governed by, God's action "through our Lord Jesus Christ" (5:9). One might paraphrase Paul's assurance to the Thessalonians in 5:1–11 in the following way:

> God has not designed our eschatological life such that at some unknown future that life suddenly might become subject to his wrath, for what God already has done for us through Jesus Messiah sets the stage for, and signifies the truth of, what he will do for us in the future.

Finally, one must delineate carefully what Paul did *not* say in 5:9 concerning "destined," ἔθετο (*etheto*). Thessalonian believers were addressed in 5:1–11. What was said of unbelievers was incidental to the central issue of encouraging believers. In contradistinction to this purpose, questions about unbelievers cannot be answered from this text. Whether 5:9 relates to the appointment by God of unbelievers to wrath is a moot question. The affirmation about the destiny of believers as secured by God was stated in a negative form. But the obverse of 5:9a does not necessarily follow; Paul did not say that unbelievers were destined by God to wrath. From the text of 5:9, such a statement would be a specious syllogism.[64] Instead, Paul simply said that in a condition of unbelief, one faced the reality of divine wrath in the eschatological dimension. The reality "in Christ" was the difference in destiny. Outside of Christ, eschatological wrath was one's destiny. For Paul, any future destiny, however conceived, would be the result of one's own decision about the gospel, a self-inflicted judgment.

SUMMARY

1 Thessalonians 1:10

In the study of explicit contexts, our key passages are in 1 Thessalonians and Romans. In terms of the 1 Thessalonian material, Paul probably appropriated 1 Thess 1:10 from a traditional creed of the early church. The creed presented Jesus as central to its confession of "deliverance" from "the wrath to come." The creed may offer a glimpse into early Jewish

---

[64] Cf. Whiteley, *Thessalonians*, 18–21.

gospel preaching to gentiles that also was part of worship traditions in the early church. By using this creed to summarize the theme of his epistle, Paul revealed he was comfortable with traditions about divine wrath in part derived from primitive preaching on judgment. Paul never spoke of Gehenna, which is surprising not only given his Pharisaic background, but also because the language of Gehenna figures into Jesus traditions. Paul's conceptual thought world about judgment and the basic operation of divine wrath, both in language and concept, is not rabbinic. His language and concepts show more a reflection on the new messianic age brought about by Messiah. That transformation reconfigured so much he previously had thought, and likely this reconfiguration included his reflection on the wrath of God.

1 Thessalonians 2:16

The Christ-event is central to the creed in 1 Thess 1:10. This centrality is reflected in 1 Thess 2:16. For Paul, opposition to the gospel presented an eschatological sign. Response to Jesus discriminated eschatological destiny. The one who rejected Jesus would realize the eschatological divine wrath. Obstinate opposition to the preaching of the gospel demonstrated a pattern of behavior destined for the divine wrath.

1 Thessalonians 5:9

That Paul had to stress in 1 Thess 5:1–10 that the Day of the Lord would not overtake believers reflects a crisis of confidence among converts in Thessalonica. The confusion concerning one's sanctification at the parousia perhaps stemmed from Paul's premature departure from Thessalonica before he could impart a solid foundation of teaching in which ethics and eschatology properly were related. A believer's imperfect sanctification would not undo salvation at the parousia. Paul insisted that the believer was not destined for wrath. Paul grounded this truth of the believer's security in God's prior activity already accomplished on behalf of salvation. Thus, the parousia would not jeopardize salvation. Instead, the parousia would confirm and consummate what God already had accomplished in Messiah Jesus for salvation. Paul carefully worded and placed his epistolary benedictions to emphasize the security of the believer's hope and the assurance of the believer's sanctification as God's work.

6

Pauline: Romans

A Distinctive Revealed Wrath

THE LANGUAGE OF DIVINE WRATH Paul uses in Romans is so distinctive as almost to beg the claim of being unique in the ancient world. Unfortunately, his subtlety often has been missed and the power of his hermeneutic lost to the detriment of Pauline theology. Yet, Paul also can invoke uses of divine wrath in Romans that are right down the line literary motifs his audience would find familiar.

ROMANS 1:18–32

Immediate Background

As stated in the introductory chapter, the key to the structure of the logic and movement of Romans is in the summary statement in Rom 11:32. The three-part grammar of the summary aligns with the three logical parts of Romans 1–11. Paul summarized his development to this point in Romans by saying, "For God has shut up all in disobedience in order that he might show mercy to all" (11:32). "For God has shut up all in disobedience" summarizes the development of Romans 1–4. "That he might show mercy" summarizes the development of Romans 5–8. Finally, "to all" is that Pauline boomerang using "all" in unexpected ways rhetorically in Romans. Here, "all" is aimed not at the expected pagan nations, but at the nation of Israel, the elect of God, in Romans 9–11, which concludes with the dramatic and exultant declaration, the goal of all of Romans 1–11, "And thus, all Israel will be saved" (11:26).

So the first part of Romans in which our passage is situated is demonstrating that "God has shut all in disobedience." Paul used the introduction to the letter (1:1–7) and the thanksgiving section (1:8–15) to transition smoothly to the theme statement of the letter (1:16–17). Integral to making smooth transition through three opening units is the key word "gospel" that ties all three together (1:1, 15, 16). Paul sets the theological pace for understanding the significance of this gospel with the distinctive phrase, "the gospel of God," in the very first verse. The gospel, that is, fundamentally is not Paul's story. The gospel is God's story. The term "God" straightaway signals this story of Jesus is not a story of just another Greek hero, like Achilles. Admittedly, the story of Achilles also involved heaven, as Athena and other gods and goddesses became embroiled in the Trojan War. But the epic exploits of Achilles (nor Athena for that matter) did not involve a superseding metanarrative that, as a master heuristic device, interpreted not only the entire war, but *predicted its outcome*. Paul's metanarrative is Jewish. This Jewish narrative is not of just another god but of the *only* God. In Paul's Jewish monotheism we already are an order of magnitude beyond Olympus. Further, this God is creator, not accidentally as part of some conflict with other gods by way of vain human imagination, but purposefully for his own intentions. God has purpose in his creation, a design and a goal. The inauguration has a consummation. This God in his sovereignty will achieve all his intentions for everything—seen and unseen. Further, he seems pretty unhurried by any sundial about how much time the process takes. He waits until the right time.

This only creator God claims all creation as his. He will not abide any challenge to his sovereignty. The nations belong to him. No nation absolutely rules the nations, because God does. Rome does not have absolute sovereignty. Further, Rome is only deluded to think of ruling the nations. Rome may have its counterfeit gospel of Roman conquest with gifts of culture and civilization and the *pax Romana*, the Roman peace, to all the barbarian nations in the hinterlands of empire, but only God has a true gospel. God's gospel needs proclamation to counter false gospels such as Rome's supposedly solving the problems of humanity. Ignoring God's gospel brings only the wrath of God. But how is that wrath to be understood, and how is divine wrath experienced? Thus, as Paul begins the body of the letter in earnest in 1:18–32, he moves to establish the reality of a revealed creator and the creator's revealed wrath.

Exegesis

Paul began his statement about the nature of the gospel of God and the basis of his future missionary activity in Romans 1 with a declaration of the revelation of God's wrath against "all human ungodliness and unrighteousness" (1:18).[1] Paul intended to show that God had shut up all humans in their disobedience. By showing that human disobedience was axiomatic, Paul laid the foundation for the need to preach the gospel in territories beyond what he already had covered.

The modern mind might find starting the story of good news with the story of bad news rather incongruous. We must be clear, however, that the ancient mind had no trouble at all. We profitably at this point might remind ourselves that, to the ancients, the most unconscionable sin a human could commit and the most egregious display of human hubris possible in this life was "ungodliness."[2] Notice both the connection between *asebeia* and *orgē* and that Judas Maccabees is lauded because he "went through the cities of Judah; he destroyed the ungodly [*asebeis*] out of the land; thus he turned away wrath [*orgēn*] from Israel" (1 Macc 3:8). A god or goddess who did *not* express wrath at "ungodliness" (in terms of lack of any propriety in consideration of the concerns of Olympus) was a god not worthy of the designation deity, and, more importantly, of no real concern. Our theological quest is to understand Paul's development of divine wrath in contradistinction to his

---

[1] The combination of "unrighteousness" and "ungodliness" in 1:18 is a hendiadys, that is, two words used nearly synonymously. The point is emphasis. Cf. Foerster, *TDNT*, s.v. "σέβομαι," 7:190; Longenecker, *Romans*, 203–04. Note Philo, *Heir* 90. Distinctions between the two words allow incorrect interpretations, one of which is to reduce "godlessness" to the first tablet of the law and "unrighteousness" to the second tablet, as Schlatter, *Gottes Gerechtigkeit*, 49; also Bornkamm, "Die Offenbarung des Zornes Gottes, Röm 1–3," 21, n38. (English in Bornkamm, "The Revelation of God's Wrath (Romans 1–3)," 47–70.) Such an interpretation fails because Paul subsumed both terms under the one governing adjective, "all" (πᾶσαν, *pasan*). In addition, "unrighteousness" was used to cover both terms when Paul charged that all people were suppressing the truth. Human unrighteousness stands opposed to the righteousness of God, and, in association with "godlessness," prevents understanding "godlessness" in a purely cultic way; cf. Käsemann, *Romans*, 38.

[2] Similarly, Jewett, *Romans*, 152.

culture. For this purpose, we have to revision God's holiness. Holiness is what separates God from Olympus, and holiness is what confuses human reflection, since humans have no real clue to the nature and function of this divine quality by their human experience alone. Holiness is alien to humanity. The foreignness of this aspect of God is the result of the fall. A fallen world, therefore, cannot apprehend God's holiness, so finds impossible comprehending what provokes God's wrath. God has to reveal himself in his holiness in order for humans to begin to come to grips with their desperate situation and tragic destiny, and why God, to be God, must express his wrath against sin. In Pauline terms, if God did *not* reveal his wrath, *humans could not be saved*. That is why Paul uses the verb "reveal" in 1:18. He has no case to make if God does not reveal his wrath. God would be unholy and therefore unrighteous to make what effectively would be inordinate demands on human behavior without that revelation.

Notice a peculiar feature of Rom 1:18: *This condemnation is not explicitly directed at gentiles, as often claimed*.[3] In fact, throughout this entire passage, Paul never uses the word gentile once. Who is committing the unrighteousness and ungodliness in this charge? Paul is clear: *human beings* ("man," ἄνθρωπος, *anthrōpos*, here used as synecdoche for "mankind," "humans," "human beings"). This point is important, because Paul will embed a ticking time bomb on this point.

A Revealed Creator (1:18–23)

In the first part of Rom 1:18–23, Paul said that the wrath of God was based on some knowledge of God. The basic charge leveled in 1:18–23 is that the objects of wrath are humans who are suppressing known truth.[4] This truth is the creator's lordship over his creation in two ways: power and deity. Knowledge of the eternal power of the creator should have led to a corresponding dependence upon God by his creatures. Knowledge of the divinity of God should have led to a corresponding attitude of humility on the part of his creatures. But humans

---

[3] Agreeing with Jewett, *Romans*, 152; Käsemann, *Romans*, 33; Longenecker, *Romans*, 196; Fitzmyer, *Romans*, 270. *Contra* Dunn, *Romans 1–8*, 51; Hultgren, *Romans*, 86; Gaston, *Paul and the Torah*, 140; Räisänen, *Paul and the Law*, 97.

[4] Käsemann, *Romans*, 38; Quell, Kittel, and Bultmann, *TDNT*, s.v. "ἀλήθεια," 1:243. For ἐν ἀδικίᾳ ("by unrighteousness") as instrumental, see Meyer, *Romans*, 56. For an adverbial equivalent argument, cf. Godet, *Romans*, 100–101.

suppressed this knowledge of God.⁵ Paul's point in this first part of his accusation against all mankind (1:18—4:25) is that, in spite of the reality of God mediated directly to humans as a natural result of the creator-creature bond (1:20), humans obstinately refused to glorify God or to give him thanks (1:21).⁶ For this refusal, humans are "without excuse" (ἀναπολογήτους, *anapologētous*). This declaration of "without excuse" is the whole burden of Romans 1–4. No human being anywhere has excuse before God in judgment. No one.

Thus, the intent of the "invisible things of him" in 1:20, however they are speculated as known, is to point toward the sovereignty of the creator, and that sovereignty is a known factor.⁷ The proper response of the creature before the sovereign creator should have been to confess the reality of dependency. In the words of Bornkamm,

> For Paul "to give thanks" (and "to glorify") has a different meaning: it is not the final perfection of the "mind' in ecstatic ascent, rather the acceptance of created existence in obedient, grateful submission to the creator, the practical acknowledgement of the

---

⁵ Paul does not explain how humans have this knowledge, other than through the revelatory activity of God, so not the result of human apprehension alone. We are unconvinced, therefore, this passage is a case for "natural" theology, particularly if the phrase means a rudimentary systematic theology (a question in later philosophical reflection among church fathers). The knowledge of God in this passage contextually is simply the reality of God himself provided by divine revelation (1:19b), not the subject of rational apprehension. Cf. Cranfield, *Romans*, 1:116, n3. For an opposite view, cf. O'Rourke, "Romans 1:20 and Natural Revelation," 301–06. Also, note Longenecker, *Romans*, 209 about a revelation "implanted" into creation and the form of Ps 19 evoking a "general" revelation for all and "special" revelation in Torah. Similar to Rom 1:19–20 is Acts 14:17. A kind of comprehension available to pagan nations expressed in Jer 14:22 seems similar; note also Bar 6:53.

⁶ On the human destiny of praise to God, cf. Exod 15:21; Amos 4:13; 5:8; 9:5–6; Isa 12; 38:19; Ps 8:1, 9; 145:5–6; 148; cf. Wolff, *Anthropology*, 228–29. In 2 Esd 8:59–60 is the charge that God did not intend to destroy humans, but God's creatures "have themselves defiled the Name of him that made them, and have proved themselves ungrateful to him who prepared life for them" (Charles's translation). The Stoic philosopher, Epictetus, mused, "Why, if we had sense, ought we to be doing anything else, publicly and privately, than hymning and praising the Deity, and rehearsing His benefits?" *Disc.* 1.16.15–21 [Oldfather]. On gentile failure to praise God in the rabbis, see Str-B 3:43–46. On the possibility of praise even from Gehenna, see Str-B 4:1101–2.

⁷ Deissmann, *Light*, 363, included "power" (δύναμις, *dynamis*) in a list of words belonging to the formulae of the imperial cult functioning to emphasize the imperial sovereignty. The association of "power" with sovereignty, therefore, likely would have been apparent to Roman believers.

recognition of God in the whole person, from the ground up, by decisive recognition of the creator.⁸

In denial of God's rightful claim on his creatures, human worship of the created thing was a direct affront to God and a subtle form of self-worship as an integral part of that creation. Through worship of the created thing, the object of worship and creaturely existence were leveled to one and the same reality. Equal with the created thing, creatures otherwise known as humans became "ungodly." These creatures lost sense of any propriety about the object of worship. They denied the power of the creator who created them and dishonored the deity of the creator who alone was divine. While power and deity belonged to the creator, humans exchanged that truth for a lie. As Paul says in 1:25, "For they exchanged the truth of God for a lie, and worshipped and served the creature rather than the creator, who is blessed forever. Amen."⁹

That the wrath of God is revealed "from heaven" would seem to refer to the cosmic significance and availability of the revelation. This revelation is before all and inescapable to any.¹⁰ Note the distinction between the sphere of the revelation of wrath as "from heaven" versus the revelation of the righteousness of God, which is described as occurring in the gospel ("in it," ἐν αὐτῷ, *en autōi*, 1:17).¹¹ This conclusion is supported by several considerations. First, Paul did not say the revelation of wrath was "in the gospel." Second, the arguments given by

---

⁸ Bornkamm, "Zornes Gottes," 22–23. Original: Für Paulus hat das εὐχαριστεῖν (u. δοξάζειν) einen andern Sinn: es ist nicht die letzte Vollendungsmöglichkeit des νοῦς im ekstatischen Aufstieg, sondern die Übernahme der geschöpflichen Existenz in gehorsamer, dankbarer Unterwerfung unter den Schöpfer, die praktische Bestätigung der Erkenntnis Gottes in der den ganzen Menschen von Grund auf bestimmenden Anerkennung des Schöpfers.

⁹ Cf. 1 En. 99:9, "For they shall have wrought all of their works in a lie, and shall have worshipped a stone." According to T. Naph. 3:3, "The gentiles went astray, and forsook the Lord, and changed their order, and obeyed stocks and stones, spirits of deceit" [De Jonge]. As Barth pointed out, God's wrath fundamentally strikes at human religion, "Speaking of Sin," 288–96. Note Luke's take on the death of Herod in Acts 12:21–23. Cf. Josephus, *Ant.* 14.2.2; 16.7.2; 19.8.2.

¹⁰ Nygren, *Romans*, 100; cf. Calvin, *Romans and Thessalonians*, 30.

¹¹ *Contra* Barth, *Shorter Commentary on Romans*, 26; Schlatter, *Gottes Gerechtigkeit*, 46; Cranfield, *Romans*, 1:109–10. In agreement, cf. Longenecker, *Romans*, 203.

Meyer bear weight.[12] Third, a careful reading of Paul's conjunctions in this section confirms a distinction between the revelation of righteousness in the gospel and the revelation of wrath "from heaven."[13]

In his discussion of 1:18–23, Käsemann called attention to the presence of such abstract terms of popular Hellenistic philosophy as "invisible" (ἀόρατα, *aorata*), "eternal" (ἀΐδιος, *aidios*), "power" (δύναμις, *dynamis*), "deity" (θειότης, *theiotēs*), and "being understood and perceived" (νοούμενα καθορᾶται, *nooumena kathoratai*).[14] Bornkamm illustrated how the language of 1:18–32 paralleled Stoic terminology and was formulated similar to Jewish-Hellenistic apologetics—but the language did not have the same function.[15] For Bornkamm, Paul did not give an apology in 1:18–32, but an accusation; Paul radicalized the language, inverted the point. In Jewish-Hellenistic apologetics, the knowledge of God was the last stage in the upward progression toward true wisdom. By contrast, for Paul the knowledge of God was an inescapable reality thrusting itself upon every human being and issuing in condemnation.[16] The wrath of God followed the knowledge of God, a knowledge that had the power to condemn.

In 1:18–23, Paul's Hebrew heritage is evident too. The very use of "wrath of God" in this context of accusation is reminiscent of the prophets.[17] In that context, divine wrath for the prophets was a function of divine sovereignty and power. In addition, note the use of "heart" for

---

[12] Meyer, *Romans*, 55.

[13] The paragraph notation of the UBS⁵ editors seems to be the correct structure of the text: three compact units of thought in 1:16–17, 1:18–23, and 1:24–32. In each unit, a subject is introduced and then expanded. The "for" at 1:16 introduces the subject of the gospel, which is expanded with each "for" in 1:16b and in 1:17. The "for" at 1:18 introduces the subject of the revelation of the wrath of God, which is expanded with each "because" in 1:19 and 1:21. Finally, the inferential "therefore" at 1:24 introduces the subject of the nature and function of the wrath of God, which is tied together carefully with a literary *inclusio*, that is, a beginning and concluding "which ones" in 1:25 and 1:32. Though distinct, the subjects are integrated into a composite whole.

[14] Käsemann, *Romans*, 39. Note also the rare terms "the things made" (τοῖς ποιήμασιν, *tois poiēmasin*), "without excuse" (ἀναπολόγητος, *anapologētos*), "make futile" (ματαιόω, *mataioō*), and "claim" (φάσκω, *phaskō*).

[15] Bornkamm, "Zornes Gottes," 12–18.

[16] Ibid., 19. Cf. Meyer, *Romans*, 61.

[17] Cf. Roetzel, "The Judgment Form in Paul's Letters." Roetzel included 1:18–32, but the form is a weak one, as pointed out by Doty, *Letters in Primitive Christianity*, 67.

"mind" in 1:21, "creator" not "artificer" (as in Wis 13:1), and allusions to Jer 2:5 (in 1:21) and Ps 105:20 (in 1:23).[18] Countering the thought of the blasphemous action mentioned in 1:25 with a doxology also is a typical Jewish response.

Perhaps the most extensive Jewish feature of the material is its close similarity to Wisdom of Solomon, a mid-first century BC sapiential work. Paul's analysis of sin, even wording, in 1:19–32 is very close to Wis 13:1—14:31, within material lauding Jews and castigating gentiles. The question is whether Paul knew this document (likely) and whether his presentation reflects the same approach (unlikely).[19] Paul was plenty competent to develop his own thoughts. If intentional, his allusion to Wisdom of Solomon was subversive, since his employment of divine wrath theology entirely is rethought and redeployed within a totally different eschatological structure of the new age inaugurated by Christ and with a radically different understanding of God's intentions in regard to the non-Israelite nations so despised in the Wisdom of Solomon.

Finally, one can extend Godet's observation of a parallel between 1:17 and 3:21[20] by pointing out that the discussion of 1:18–32 illumines the statement in 3:23. Briefly, "for all sin" (ἥμαρτον, *hēmarton*) if taken as a gnomic aorist recalls the universal indictment "all human unrighteousness and ungodliness" made against humanity in 1:18. Then, the phrase "and are falling short of the glory of God" in 3:23 recalls "who are suppressing the truth" in 1:18 and "exchanged the glory of the incorruptible God" in 1:23. By denying God his rightful place as sovereign Lord, humans suppress the true glory of God. Thus, the new section beginning at 3:21 seems grounded in and dependent upon the prior discussion of the revelation of God's wrath.

A Revealed Wrath (1:24–32)

Notable immediately in comparison with typical Greco-Roman literature, and even some Jewish literature, is that Paul's language of divine

---

[18] Pointed out by Bornkamm, "Zornes Gottes," 21, n38.

[19] The best general discussion of the issue is Longenecker, *Romans*, 193–95. Note the succinct analysis of Linebaugh, who correctly emphasizes how Paul contradicts Wisdom's assertion of a (fictional) idolatry-free Israel. Paul insists on the opposite, which is more *canonical* ("Wisdom of Solomon and Romans 1:18—2:5," 43).

[20] Godet, *Romans*, 99, 146.

wrath is so specialized and restrained.[21] The crux of Paul's development of divine wrath in 1:18–32 was that God's wrath was a matter of God's revelation. Corresponding to the knowledge of God in 1:19 that was manifested "in them" (ἐν αὐτοῖς, *en autois*),[22] the revelation of wrath in 1:24 equivalently also was "in them" (ἐν αὐτοῖς, *en autois*).[23]

After announcing this revealed wrath, Paul derives an inferential "therefore" in 1:24. This "therefore" inaugurates a three-fold refrain of the repeated "God delivered them over" in 1:24, 26, and 28.[24] Paul used the refrain to interpret "For the wrath of God is being revealed" in 1:18 as the action "God delivered them over." Three human exchanges (1:23, 25, 28) are counteracted by three divine responses (1:24, 26, 28).

"God delivered them over" Triad (Rom 1:24–28)

Human Exchange	*Divine Response*
Glory (1:23)	Uncleanness (1:24)
Truth (1:25)	Passions (1:26)
Knowledge (1:28)	Disapproved Mind (1:28)

FIGURE 6.1. "God Delivered Them Over" Triad.

God remains involved in the process after this "delivering over." Staying involved in the process is precisely how God reveals himself through the process. To exchange the glory of God for a beast is to be become beastly. To exchange the truth about how the creator God has

---

[21] For example, in 1 En. 99:9, the concluding "therefore" was to announce, "in an instant shall they perish." Paul made no similar declaration about the divine wrath.

[22] Or "among them."

[23] Precisely why the revelation of wrath is not in the gospel. This revelation is universal, available to all, and available all the time as creatures of the creator God.

[24] The Greek verb is (παρέδωκεν, *paredōken*), typically translated "gave them up." However, "delivered them over" retains better Paul's idea that divine supervision of the process continues after this divine action, whereas "give up" in colloquial English suggests quitting. The verb *paredōken* does *not* mean God wipes his hands and walks away.

designed creation is to pervert the good elements of creation, such as passion, into enslaving powers. To exchange the knowledge of God is not to know anything, but to live the illusion of thinking one does. Such a mind simply is doomed to make bad life choices that God never could approve. To countermand those choices, God has built the creation in such a way as naturally to work against those choices in a constantly counterproductive, even self-destructive, way. Every step of the way to self-destruction has God's whisper, "I can show you a better way," so represents God's ongoing effort to communicate and to save. God's wrath is in service to God's salvation. God never judges such that he is not trying to save, and that is how God in his wrath is not Zeus in his anger.

Paul's sequence of Greek verb tenses supports this idea of the supervisory and participatory involvement of God throughout the "delivering over" process. In the opening present tense in 1:18 with its aorist counterpart in 1:24, Paul produced a sequence characteristic of the entire passage (1:18–32). Action set forth with a present tense is complemented with an aorist tense counterpart. One can note the variations of the construction: what is manifest (1:19), God manifested (1:21); knowing God, they glorified not nor gave thanks (1:22); professing to be wise, they became fools (1:22); forsaking the natural use of women, they burned in their desires (1:27). This present-past tense sequencing grammatically suggests perfective result. The consequences of a sinful lifestyle today propagate into tomorrow.[25]

The perfective force of the argument in 1:18–32 provides illumination for the perfect passive participle, "being filled" (πεπληρωμένους, *peplērōmenous*), in 1:29. When Paul was ready to introduce a composite list of vices[26] into his argument at 1:29, he did so with a perfect tense. In effect, Paul announced that the vice list was a summary of the phenomena he associated with the wrath of God. Any person's present condition was the consequence of prior decisions. The basis of these prior decisions involved suppressing the truth of God for a lie, that is,

---

[25] Coffey applied the aorist tenses to idolatry of pagans in a "primordial past" ("Natural Knowledge of God," 675–77). However, Coffey totally misses that the past tenses are paired with present tenses. Rom 1:18–32 is not about a "primordial past." Rom 1:18–32 is about *now*, most pointedly, Rome now.

[26] Cf. Gal 5:19–21; 1 Cor 6:9–10; Col 3:5, 8. Cranfield drew attention to other New Testament lists, as well as lists in the Apocrypha and Pseudepigrapha (*Romans*, 1:129, n3).

worship of an idol one's own hands created, so fully known to be a lie. This deceit denied divine dependency in order to live, a fundamental error for a creature that did not cause itself to come into existence. Vice lists, of course, were common in the pagan world, and some have thought the stringent criticism of society reflected in such vice lists in Paul indicated a strain of Stoic influence in Paul's thought.[27] However, Jewish criticism of the pagan world, particularly its idolatry, had no need of Stoicism for its inspiration.[28] Another question is whether the moral scene depicted in 1:24–32 corresponded to actual circumstances, but the answer varies.[29]

In spite of such unanswered questions about this vice list, Paul's point is this. God's wrath is a present experience of human beings. The "delivering over" of God is *deliverance by God into the destiny one has chosen in idolatry with no way out*—life in a sinful world without God to ameliorate the combined consequences of all bad choices. This tsunami of sin no person can abide. Life as God meant life to be lived is wiped out as this catastrophically destructive wave hits humanity's shores. God's wrath is God holding humans fully accountable for rejection of God. So, parallel to the three occurrences of "delivered over" predicated of God are three *prior* occurrences of "exchanged" predicated of humans.[30] Thus, Paul derived aberrations of various kinds in his first-century world from an original spiritual dysfunction. Significantly, though, we should note carefully that in 1:24–31, Paul does *not* describe the wrath of God as simply punitive against human immorality.

---

[27] Stewart, *A Man in Christ*, 59.

[28] Similar to Paul's list here, cf. T. Naph. 3:4, "But ye shall not be so, my children, recognizing in the firmament, in the earth, and in the sea, and in all created things, the Lord who made all things, that ye become not as Sodom, which changed the order of nature" [De Jonge]. The foolishness of idolatry seems to spark Paul's thought in 1:22–23, and in this he followed his Jewish heritage. Cf. the satire of idolatry in Isa 40:18–20; 44:9–20; Wis 13:10; Baruch 6; the story Bel and the Dragon. Also, cf. the Sibylline Oracles.

[29] For an affirmation, cf. Lohse, *The New Testament Environment*, 203. For a caution against the reality of the picture, cf. Deissmann, *Light*, 282–84. Comparing Rom 1:24–32 with Rom 2:14–16, Sevenster noted that 1:24–32 was only one facet of many that made up the gentile world (*Paul and Seneca*, 95). Käsemann labeled the characterization as "in good apocalyptic fashion" (*Romans*, 49), which seems to miss the point.

[30] Cf. Acts 7:39–43. As Schlatter noted, Paul spoke not of an exchange of ideas, but of the relationship of humans to God that determined human existence (*Gottes Gerechtigkeit*, 67).

Rather, God's wrath functions as a *revelation*, because this action by God makes obvious the destructive consequences of human sin. In these terms, one is justified to speak of the "apocalypse of God's wrath" in Paul: For the wrath of God *is being revealed*.

The revelatory function of wrath should temper what is affirmed about the nuance Paul gave to his expression, "disapproved mind," (ἀδόκιμον νοῦν, *adokimon noun*) in 1:28. The idea of the root verb, *dokimazein*, is a testing that results in approval.[31] The converse is a testing that fails. The idea would be like quality assurance controls on a factory assembly line. If the finished product does not meet all designed tests, that item is pulled off the line as "not working as designed." The product works, but not as designed. Thus, a failed test results in disapproval. On this matter, we would have to disagree with Käsemann, who incorrectly said, "He who leaves his Lord loses control over himself together with his sense of the order of being, and can no longer be summoned to responsibility."[32] Numerous commentators agree.[33] However, the logic fails. "No longer be summoned to responsibility" is the exact *opposite* of what Paul said. Paul is insisting on *accountability*; otherwise, his argument completely fails ("without excuse," 1:20).

If Käsemann were correct, that humans "can no longer be summoned to responsibility," then Paul lost his argument at its central issue—the universal guilt of humankind before God. The translation of "disapproved" (ἀδόκιμον, *adokimon*) as "reprobate" is an unfortunate error. The proper nuance is that of a verdict rendered in judgment. Paul's meaning is comparable to that expressed in Jer 11:20 (LXX), which has this same verb for approving: "O Lord, who judges righteously, approving minds and hearts."[34] Further, translating this ἀδόκιμον (*adokimon*) as "disapproved" rather than as "reprobate" is supported by the meaning of δικαίωμα (*dikaiōma*) as "sentence" in 1:32, discussed below. The "disapproved mind" in 1:28 is the verdict rendered upon the disapproved action proscribed in "suppressing the

---

[31] Trench, *Synonyms*, 278–80; Grundmann, *TDNT*, s.v. "δόκιμος," 2:255–60.

[32] Käsemann, *Romans*, 49.

[33] Just to start a list, cf. Cranfield, *Romans*, 1:28; Godet, *Romans*, 109; Murray, *Romans*, 49; Leenhardt, *Romans*, 70; Barrett, *Romans*, 37, 39; Moody, "Romans," BBC, 10:172; Bruce, *Romans*, TNTC, 6:85, and so forth.

[34] κύριε κρίνων δίκαια δοκιμάζων νεφροὺς καὶ καρδίας (*kyrie krinōn dikaia dokimazōn nephrous kai kardias*).

truth in unrighteousness" (1:18). Alternately, this disapproved action has this summary, "as God they glorified not nor gave thanks" (1:21). The term ἀδόκιμον (*adokimon*) represents that which has failed the divine testing, with a verdict of guilty before God. Humans are responsible for that verdict. The point of the epexegetical infinitive, "to do" (ποιεῖν, *poiein*) in 1:28 is that the verdict is accurate.[35]

Further support for understanding δικαίωμα (*dikaiōma*) as "disapproved" and not as "reprobate" is the qualifying phrase, "in the lusts of their hearts" (ἐν ταῖς ἐπιθυμίαις τῶν καρδιῶν αὐτῶν, *en tais epithymiais tōn kardiōn autōn*), which intervenes in the first of three expressions joined to "God delivered them over." Though locative in case, this phrase encroaches upon the instrumental sense.[36] The action of God involved in "delivered them over" from this intervening phrase can be understood as one that capitalized upon a condition of the human heart. God delivered humans over through their own lust. The human "mind" (νοῦς, *nous*), willing to cultivate "passion" (ἐπιθυμία, *epithymia*) into perversion, refused to acknowledge the error of degrading divinely ordained "passion" (ἐπιθυμία, *epithymia*) in this abusive way. God disapproved human approval of passion as lust.

In such an exchange of passion for lust, of the natural for the unnatural, God's wrath was to insure that lust be lust, which means that God allowed lust to mature into a power that controlled life. Instead of God, lust becomes lord. That way, lust will be sure to produce its inevitable destruction. Paul grammatically expressed the lordship of lust in the perfect participle, "being filled" (πεπληρωμένους, *peplērōmenous*), that heads 1:29. Out of this unrighteous lordship comes human responsibility for which God summons human beings. Paul expressed this lordship in typical patterns—the "darkening" of the human "heart" and human reasoning made "futile"[37]—but the original transaction in the exchange of lordship was by human choice. This theological function for divine wrath was Paul's way to describe a God-designed process in

---

[35] Barth, *Shorter Commentary*, 30; Meyer, *Romans*, 68; Grundmann, *TDNT* s.v. "δόκιμος," 2:259.

[36] Cf. "through my falsehood" (ἐν τῷ ἐμῷ ψεύσματι, *en tōi emōi pseusmati*) in 3:7. Several ideas similar to 1:18–32 occur in Isa 64:5b–7 (LXX), including cognate terms. Note especially, "You turned your face from us, and delivered us over [παρέδωκας (*paredōkas*)] through [διά (*dia*)] our sins" (64:7).

[37] Cf. Isa 44:18; Wis 2:21; Ps 93:11 (LXX).

creation used to reveal that this creaturely exchange of lordship was a fate determining deed impacting destiny.

Thus, this explanatory phrase about "lust" (ἐπιθυμία, *epithymia*) in the first construction in 1:24 indicates that the "unto uncleanness" and "unto dishonorable passions" in the first two constructions (1:24; 1:26) are symptomatic of, and resultant from, the radioactive function of "lust" in human experience.[38] As a result, human responsibility is clear. Something similar to Paul's idea is captured in the words of Sir 15:20, "He has not commanded anyone to be ungodly, and he has not given anyone permission to sin."

Paul's third construction in 1:28, "unto a disapproved mind" (εἰς ἀδόκιμον νοῦν (*eis adokimon noun*), represents the divine verdict upon human thinking. Human thoughts are *adokimon*, i.e., unacceptable to God; this verdict is verified in the uncleanness and dishonorable passions expressed in the two prior constructions.[39] God as creator declared that a person could not pervert divinely ordained passion (ἐπιθυμία, *epithymia*) and still preserve the integrity of the creator-creature bond. God would not abide such foolishness.[40] Paul incorporated the vice list in 1:29–31 to illustrate the maturation of the human *epithymia* and the accuracy of God's verdict: the mind that volitionally turned away from God toward perverting passion was "disapproved," that is, rejected.[41] That pattern of thought predicated a destiny of death.

The declaration Paul made in 1:32, as he concluded the vice list, was that the experience of the power of the divine wrath was one that generated a knowledge of "death" (θάνατος, *thanatos*). By the use of *thanatos* in 1:32, Paul did not mean simply physical death, for not all the vices listed would call for a death sentence. Rather, *thanatos* in the present context means spiritual death. The concept is explicit in 6:21,

---

[38] A striking example of lust run wild in a lawless city is given in Thucydides's description of Athens under plague during the Peloponnesian War (*War* 2.8).

[39] According to Sir 10:12–13 (LXX), "The beginning of human conceit is when one departs from the Lord, and when the heart has forsaken its Maker, because the beginning of conceit is sin, and the one taking hold of her [sin] pours out abominations."

[40] The charge in 1:22 does not have to be understood as directed against any particular group, such as Greek philosophers; see Isa 5:21; Jer 10:14 (LXX). On human error, see 1:27; also, cf. 2 Thess 2:11.

[41] Schlatter noted the divine answer was that humans had made themselves useless for fellowship, that humans destroyed all relationships touched, so made from the business of following personal lust this constant destruction (*Gottes Gerechtigkeit*, 69).

"for the end of those things is death."[42] A typical Pauline analysis is given in 6:23, "For the wages of sin is death, but the free gift of God is eternal life in Christ Jesus our Lord." The Pauline use of *thanatos* helps to understand the "decree" (δικαίωμα, *dikaiōma*) to which Paul referred in 1:32 in speaking of death. Paul did not use *dikaiōma* as some written decree or a law of God generally to be perceived through the resources of the human mind.[43] This *dikaiōma*, in context, is known by divine revelation in creation. Note how a creation motif suffuses the passage. The argument starts with creation (1:20), argues about the perversion of creation (1:23), condemns idolatrous worship of creation (1:25), and ends with the death sentence of creation ("you shall surely die," Gen 2:17).[44] The decree is a knowledge that comes as an invasion of divine reality into the human illusion. This knowledge is a function of the revelation of the wrath of God. The wrath of God reveals that the end result of rejection of God is death. Paul rehearses the thought of this *thanatos* decree of 1:32 in 6:23, "For the wages of sin are death." In Rom 2:14–15, Paul basically rehearses his point from Romans 1 that humans inherently know what God requires of them.

Corresponding to this knowledge of death, *dikaiōma* properly should be translated "sentence."[45] In this way, Paul called the wrath of God a present revelation (present tense "is being revealed," ἀποκαλύπτεται, *apokalyptetai*). Divine wrath continuously reveals that denying God is electing death.[46] Thus, 1:32 (that humans possess the knowledge of the "sentence" of death) is a succinct recapitulation 1:24–31 and the crowning conclusion of the opening statement in 1:18, "For the wrath of God is being revealed."

---

[42] The significance of *thanatos* among Pauline eschatological terms is discussed in the section on implicit use under the heading "Eschatological Destruction."

[43] Jewett likely is off target to insist this decree must be a *specific* decree of a death penalty being used to stand for all "such things" (*Romans*, 191). Cf. Fitzmyer, *Romans*, 289–90.

[44] But not accepting Dunn's argument that Romans 1 is a review of Adam's story; cf. Dunn, *Romans 1–8*, 53, 76. The thesis is too specific for Paul's point. See later discussion on "Adam and Israel."

[45] As noted by Quell and Schrenk, *TDNT*, s.v. "δίκη," 2:220–21.

[46] Giving potent expression, for example, to the confession of a drug addict, "You know, this is just killing me." Romans 1:32 as the concluding verse to the unit makes clear that that personal revelation has been divinely superintended. God is trying to save.

The present revelation of the wrath of God for Paul is a measure of the grace of God. God desires human repentance (cf. 2:4). By God's grace, humans are warned about the destiny before them. On the other hand, when spurned, the unequivocal revelation of wrath releases the full force of that destiny of death.[47] Through the revelatory power of wrath, humans gain full cognizance of the consequence of disobedience.[48] Still, humans embraced death; humans embraced their destiny.[49] The dual manifestation of God in creation and the subsequent revelation of divine wrath rendered humans fully culpable for their rejection of God. In 1:18–32, Paul established the universal guilt of creatures in disobedient revolt against the revealed creator upon the ground of the revelatory power of wrath.

C. H. Dodd

In his commentary on Romans, C. H. Dodd noted that Paul never used the verb "I am wrathful" (ὀργίζομαι, *orgizomai*) with God as subject, that the actual phrase "the wrath of God" in Paul was rare, and that no evidence existed that Paul meant wrath of God to portray God as in an angry mood with humans.[50] All these observations are true but entirely misleading, since they in no way support the case Dodd tried to build for banishing the language of the wrath of God from Pauline theology. Dodd in his discussion actually completely missed the point of Rom 1:18–32 that Paul described God's wrath as a revelation whose intent was to try to save. Dodd said the progress of evil in society was "not as the direct act of God," which is stunning, since this claim outright denies what Paul actually said in Rom 1:18–32. Dodd's diluted version of Rom 1:18–32 is this: "The act of God is no more than an abstention

---

[47] Cf. the section headings, for example, on 1:24–32 in Moule, *Romans*.

[48] Stressing the full value of the compounded verb "to know" (ἐπιγινώσκω, *epiginōskō*). Whereas the meaning of the compounded form was washing out in Koine Greek, L. Thomas Strong III has shown that in Paul, the compounded form retains its force ("The Significance of the 'Knowledge of God' in the Epistles of Paul"). On the disobedience motif, cf. 1 En. 99:9; 2 Esd 8:59–60; T. Naph. 3:3; Str-B 3:43–46. Cf. Sir 15:26–28; 1 En. 2:1–5:3; Pss. of Sol. 18:11–14. From Greek literature, disobedience as the crux of evil is reflected in the assertion by Creon, "There is no greater wrong than disobedience" (Sophocles, *Ant.* 672 [Storr]).

[49] Cf. Wis 1:16.

[50] Dodd, *Romans*, 21–23.

from interference with their free choice and its consequences."⁵¹ This "abstention from interference" is opposite the whole point of Paul's "is being revealed." Making matters worse, Dodd impugned the author of Hebrews by asserting Paul theologically had a "finer instinct." Dodd wrote,

> *It is an awful thing*, says the Epistle to the Hebrews (x. 31). [*sic*] *to fall into the hands of the living God*. Paul, with a finer instinct, sees that the really awful thing is to fall out of His hands, and to be left to oneself in a world where the choice of evil brings its own moral retribution. He has therefore succeeded in dissociating the fact of retribution from any idea of an angry God visiting His displeasure upon sinful men, even though he retains the old expression 'the Wrath of God.'⁵²

In this statement, Dodd misrepresented Paul and underrated the author of Hebrews. The verb "delivered over" (παρέδωκεν, *paredōken*) most typically means to transfer to another's authority or put in another's possession, such as in forensic or military settings, as when the tribune, Lysias, delivered over Paul into the custody of the procurator, Felix, in Caesarea (Acts 23:33). Thus, Dodd misread "delivered over" as abandonment (i.e., "abstention from interference"). Paul's meaning, rather, in Rom 1:18–32 is comparable to Rom 4:25, in which Paul said God "delivered over" (*paredōken*) Jesus. God did not abandon Jesus in the passion. God superintended the events of the passion process all the way through the resurrection. In Rom 1:24, *paredōken* is a deliverance, not abandonment, a divinely guided transfer through which God guarantees consummation of the lordship exchange humans have chosen for "lust" (ἐπιθυμία, *epithymia*).⁵³ Humans delivered over into the consuming power of *epithymia* are still humans in the hands of God. The judgment that is a falling into the hands of a living God in Hebrews and the divine wrath that is a delivering over into another lordship superintended by God in Romans are mutually compatible theologies, and the author of Hebrews has just as fine a theological instinct as Paul, *contra* Dodd.

---

⁵¹ Ibid., 29.

⁵² Ibid.

⁵³ For numerous examples of the meaning "to hand over," "to transfer control," as well as meaning "to deliver up" in a more technical and legal sense, see Moulton and Milligan, *The Vocabulary of the Greek Testament*, 482–83.

Dodd's remarks were meant to infer dropping altogether the "old expression of 'the Wrath of God,'" which Paul apparently unnecessarily retained from his culture. Dodd's verdict was that the language of divine wrath was dispensable in a theology of Paul. He could not have been more wrong. Dodd made a category mistake. Like the "lives of Jesus" writers that Schweitzer analyzed in a previous generation of scholarly work in which every "life" simply turned Jesus into the interpreter's own likeness and contemporary cultural sensibilities, Dodd has turned a theology of Paul into his own likeness and the popular contemporary image of God as loving Father minus any consequences of unrighteousness and ungodliness. Strange if so easily discarded as cultural artifact that the astute Paul could not think of any other way to begin his theological masterpiece than with the language of divine wrath.

Paul did say that humans received in themselves the due penalty of their error (1:27). But if Dodd's understanding is followed, he winds up having Paul say little more than Odysseus backhandedly said to the Cyclops, "You might have known your sin would find you out."[54] We do have similar thoughts elsewhere. Polybius spoke of the ulcers of the soul that destroyed a man inwardly and rendered him inhuman.[55] With this one may compare the scorn of Cicero, "Can there be any evil greater than baseness? And if this implies something of disgust in the deformity of person, how much worse should appear the depravity and foulness of a debased mind?"[56] Cicero's "debased mind" indicates a basic human flaw. Background material provided evidence that divine wrath could be perceived as an alien force that invaded the human mind and caused human judgment to err, producing unreasonable behavior. A similar idea is found in the Hebrew prophets in Hos 9:9 (LXX) and in the familiar figure of the stupefying wine of wrath. However, on the basis of wrath as *divine revelation*, the profile of Pauline thought is quite distinguished from such ideas. Dodd misread Paul precisely here: he obfuscated the significance of divine wrath as "revelation."

---

[54] Homer, *Od.* 9.477. Cf. Sophocles, *Ant.* 325–27, "Wicked payments work their own revenge" [Storr]. Menander wrote, "It is impossible to discover anyone whose life is immune from trouble" (*The Necklace* Frag 411K [Allinson]).

[55] *Hist.* 1.81.5–9. Posidonius said the cause of passions was that humans turned to the lower animal principle and let it run away with them, Document 67, lines 1–5, in Barrett, *The New Testament Background*, 65.

[56] *Off.* 3.29.

Dodd's construct of the "nemesis" of sin and retribution can have provisional validity only insofar as this process is not conceived as an "impersonal process" or as a superficial and automatic chain-reaction of cause and effect in the natural world from which God has removed himself. Such an understanding destroys the essence of wrath as a divine "revelation." A principle of sin and retribution in part may have been behind Paul's understanding of divine wrath in 1:18–32, but his emphasis in this section is not on the principle itself, but on the activity of a creator revealing himself and working in everything to save lost human beings. If Paul had written about divine wrath in a way similar to many apocalyptic texts, such as 1 Enoch or those from Qumran, he simply would have said that God in wrath would intervene in human affairs to annihilate iniquity. In such a case, iniquity would be eliminated, but humanity too would be destroyed. Paul indicated that God entered into the human experience ("God delivered them over"), but God's intervention was not a scorched earth policy. Rather, Paul said that God's wrath was a consignment of humans to their immorality. Through this consignment, God's wrath opened up the possibility for human immorality to mature into its deadliest forms. A gardener would capture the Pauline nuance by calling Paul's "delivered over" theology of divine wrath in Romans 1 the "greenhouse of God's wrath." This maturation of immorality God governed in his sovereignty with a purpose: to reveal the end result of rejection of God as death (1:32). The "death" (*thanatos*) of 1:32 can be played either way. Sin pursued *can* cause physical death, but persistent sin *will* cause spiritual death. Thus, in a carefully delimited sense, Paul said matured immorality resulted from divine wrath for the potential that that state could reveal to the human mind about destiny.

In fact, God using sin's maturation process is precisely what Paul will say about the Law and Israel later in Romans. The Law came so that sin could be shown to be exceedingly sinful. That is, Israel experienced the greenhouse effect of God's wrath (Rom 7:11–13). Paul set up that equation here in Romans 1 with his theology of the wrath of God.[57]

---

[57] Also, against Dodd's outline, Paul in 1:18–3:20 did not focus so much upon a nemesis of sin and retribution as he did upon the guilt of all men, "that all the world may become accountable to God" (3:19). Better headings, for example, for 2:1–16 and 2:17–29 than Dodd's are given by Moule, *Romans*, 65, 73.

Adam in Romans 1

Niels Hyldahl argued that the Genesis account of Adam inspired Paul's formulation of 1:18–32, and Morna D. Hooker picked up the theme and provided more discussion.[58] Other scholars are favorable.[59] The idea is immediately reasonable since Adam's story became prominent in Jewish reflection after the judgment of exile.[60] However, the argument that the Adam account was behind Paul's presentation in 1:18–32, making the perspective exclusively past time, does not adequately account for the present tenses that Paul used in this passage.[61] The present-tense context simply receives little attention.

At the same time, Skipper has argued in an intertextual study that *allusive elements* to Eden may be present for strategic *rhetorical purposes*. He noted that an Adam profile in Romans 1 would begin to dismantle social separation of Israel from Hellenists, as well as barbarians, under the same paternal head. Skipper incisively noted how Eden and Sinai are merged in Rom 1:23, since the subtext is idolatry, and that the importance of this connection is shown by reappearing at crucial junctures in the logic in Rom 5:13, 14, 20, as well as in Romans 7, which is about Israel. Thus, even if Romans 1 has echoes of Eden, Israel smartly is caught in the net of this narrative that awaits Paul's fuller development later in the letter.[62]

Israel in Romans 1

Romans is all about Israel. The thesis cannot be pursued presently, but Romans 1 is illustrative of how reframing the target of the rhetoric will redraw the exegetical lines.[63] Calling Paul "apostle to the gentiles" for millennia is a nomenclature that hides Paul's own emphases that come from Isaiah's prophetic vision of eschatological Israel and the nations.

---

[58] Hyldahl, "Reminiscence of the Old Testament at Romans 1:23"; Hooker, "Adam in Romans I"; Hooker, "Further Notes on Romans I."

[59] C. K. Barrett, *From First Adam to Last*, 17–21; Dunn, *Romans 1–8*, 53; Wedderburn, "Adam in Paul's Letter to the Romans," 3.413–30. Garlington, "Obedience of Faith," 51–52.

[60] Cf. Wis 2:23–24; LAE; 2 Esd 4:30; 2 Bar. 54:17–19.

[61] Also, cf. Schlatter, *Gottes Gerechtigkeit*, 61.

[62] Skipper, "Echoes of Eden," 184. Cf. Garlington, "Obedience of Faith," 51–52.

[63] Gerald L. Stevens, *Romans: The Gospel of God* (Eugene, OR: Wipf and Stock), forthcoming.

A case in point is Isa 11:10, quoted by Paul in Rom 15:12. Strangely, almost invariably, English translations will render Isaiah's prophecy of the *ethnē* in the Romans quote as "gentiles." Yet, inconsistently, the same English translations render *ethnē* in the LXX *source text* (Paul's preferred version) as "nations." Why is the text given as "nations" in Isaiah but as "gentiles" in Romans? Because Paul never is conceived as apostle to the nations. He is, of course, instead "apostle to the gentiles." Can *ethnē* mean "gentiles"? Yes. Keep in mind, though, that this Jewish social and religious categorization of humankind is on the basis of the presence or absence of covenant circumcision. Thus, giving *ethnē* as "gentiles" in Paul likely should be reserved for contexts when circumcision is explicit, as in the issue of the circumcision of Titus recounted in Gal 2:1–9. In contradistinction, when Paul is quoting Isaiah, Paul is not referring to circumcision. Paul is referring to the prophet's vision of Israel's eschatological destiny. That destiny is to establish God's sovereignty over the nations. The expression of that sovereignty will have nothing to do with circumcision or uncircumcision (Gal 1:2).[64]

Here is the point for Romans 1. Wrath was part of Israel's story from the beginning. Before Moses could come down from Sinai, the people already had persuaded Aaron to craft a golden calf they could worship (Exod 32:1–5). God's wrath was incited, and he even thought to start over with Moses (Exod 32:6–9). God told Moses to leave him to his fierce wrath.

> "Now let me alone, so that my wrath may burn hot against them and I may consume them; and of you I will make a great nation." But Moses implored the Lord his God, and said, "O Lord, why does your wrath burn hot against your people, whom you brought out of the land of Egypt with great power and with a mighty hand? Why should the Egyptians say, 'It was with evil intent that he brought them out to kill them in the mountains, and to consume them from the face of the earth'? Turn from your fierce wrath. Change your mind and do not bring disaster on you people" (Exod 32:10–12, NRSV).

Notice God's stated goal of calling a people to himself: "and of you I will make a great nation" (Exod 32:10). God's purpose was to make a great nation. The question would be, great for what? Isaiah answered with his

---

[64] Rom 2:26; 3:30; 4:9; 1 Cor 7:18–19.

vision of eschatological Israel in Isaiah 11. Israel's destiny is to facilitate God's sovereignty in the world among all the nations of the world. Isaiah's vision is what drives Paul. Unfortunately, with Israel, divine wrath is like a congenital disease, and that is why the exile was inevitable. So, divine wrath will be integral to the story of Israel as a nation to the very end, as the Chronicler acknowledged in his tragic final summation.

> The Lord, the God of their ancestors, sent presently to them by his messengers, because he had compassion on his people and on his dwelling place; but they kept mocking the messengers of God, despising his words, and scoffing at his prophets, until the wrath of the Lord against his people became so great that there was no remedy (2 Chr 36:15–16, NRSV).

What we need to see in Romans 1 is that Paul has this plight of Israel in mind. Echoes of Sinai clearly are in Rom 1:23. The "exchanging glory" wording deliberately echoes Ps 106:20, *which speaks of Israel at Sinai*: "They exchanged their glory for the image of an ox that eats grass." So-called "gentiles" are not the exclusive focus in Rom 1:23.[65] So, the immediate context of Ps 106 is allusion to Aaron's golden calf incident at the foot of Mount Horeb. The prophet Jeremiah excoriated Israel for still exchanging God's glory in his own day (Jer 2:11), so the Horeb problem never went away. Instead, the golden calf was paradigmatic. Thus, the rhetoric of Rom 1:18–32 is expressed generally as "humans" (ἀνθρώπων, anthrōpōn) specifically not to exclude Jewish humanity. Paul's careful wording reveals that the problem of Israel shadows everything he says, such that the words like 1:23 are even more true of Israel, particularly since Israel had direct access to the divine glory in the holy theophanies experienced at Sinai (Exod 24:15–18). Thus, the past tenses of the triad of exchanges in "God delivered them over" does not at all refer to the "mythological past of Gentiles"[66] One could refer the past tenses to the story of Adam and Eve, but only by way of remembering that this story is told in order to tell the story of Israel.[67]

---

[65] Though wanting to keep the focus on gentiles, commentators are forced to admit this allusion to Israel; for example, Hultgren, *Romans*, 93.

[66] *Contra* Hultgren, *Romans*, 96. Intertextuality in Romans 1 in no way supports that Paul's rhetoric is a vague "mythological" analysis of nothing in particular ("Gentiles").

[67] Postell, *Adam as Israel*.

So, if Israel is under the wrath of God, how will Isaiah's vision of Israel be fulfilled? The problem with Israel, Paul now sees, is that Israel still is in Adam, and this is precisely why Paul expressed himself as the wrath of God being revealed from heaven against *human* (ἀνθρώπων, anthrōpōn) ungodliness. Polytheistic pagans? Of course. Yet, Paul was careful to write not just "against ungodliness" but "against *all* ungodliness." The Pauline "all" boomerang in Romans returns to hit those not seeing the full trajectory of the rhetoric. Israel never was in Moses. Israel was still in Adam. God's solution to this Adamic destiny of death for Israel is Messiah (Rom 5:12–21). In speaking of wrath as present tense, Paul targets not only pagan Rome, but Israel as well. Israel returned from exile but never recovered from exile. So, that divine wrath "is being revealed" against *all* ungodliness is a ticking time bomb rhetorically for Israel, genetically predisposed to provoke God's wrath. Notice that the conclusion to this entire unit of Romans 1–11 begun here in Rom 1:18–32 does not say the Redeemer of Isa 59:20–21 comes *to* Zion in Rom 11:26–27. The Redeemer comes *from* Zion. His purpose is to "turn ungodliness away from Jacob." "Jacob" is synecdoche for the nation of Israel. Romans is all about Israel.

ROMANS 2:5, 8

Following the consequential conjunction, "therefore" (διό, *dio*) at the beginning of Romans 2, a shift occurs from the third person in 1:18–32 to second person. This shift marks a new argumentative approach, the diatribe. However, a deeper shift took place beyond a simple change of style of argument. In the brief Jewish doxology at the end of 1:25, Paul inserted his Jewish *ethos* into the argument. This new section beginning at 2:1 also will show Paul personally involved.[68]

On the basis of the prior discussion of the revealed wrath of God ("therefore"), Paul condemned the one judging as "without excuse" (ἀναπολόγητος, *anapologētos*) which provides an intratextual echo of the crucial idea in judgment and key declaration of the previous 1:18–32 unit, that rebellious humans are "without excuse" in 1:20. This declaration is the whole burden of the development for several chapters.

---

[68] Preconceived notions among scholars of what Paul could or could not have said surface throughout the text of Romans. Käsemann's odd assertion, for example, that 2:1 is an interpolation is simply unnecessary (*Romans*, 54).

Anyone qualifying as *anthrōpos*, "human being," is *anapologētos*, "without excuse." Paul just does not make any exceptions. One can argue or disagree with his logic, but that is his argument in 1:18—3:20 in one word—*anapologētos*. As he says in his closing summary, "that the whole world may be held accountable to God" (3:19).

The arresting rhetoric of the new vocative of address, "O Man" (ὦ ἄνθρωπε, *ō anthrōpe*), is thoroughly consistent with the rhetoric of the wrath of God being revealed against *anthrōpos* in 1:18. In moving from 1:18 to 2:1, the person changes from third person to second person but the focus rhetorically is the same, just a step more personal, from being talked about (third person) to being talked to (second person). Only now, the *anthrōpos* addressed seems to assume God's side, voicing condemnation of the activities in 1:29–31. Paul does not indicate how this condemnation is voiced or in what venue. That the *anthrōpos* judging is broad enough to include the moralizing philosopher, like Socrates, is possible, but not explicit. Without such particularization, anyone in general would qualify as *anthrōpos*. What would not be as clear at this point was whether Jewish humanity could be included in the *anthrōpos* addressed in 2:1, as this inclusion does not become explicit until 2:17. Though who, when, where, and why is unknown, Paul's countercharge is direct and unrelenting: "For you who judge practice the very same (things)." The reference to doing "the very same (things)" is not exactly clear. The nearest reference is to the associated catalogue of vices that illustrate the wrath of God being revealed for suppressing the truth. Yet, the vice list is only symptomatic. The prior action that is more probative is the triadic series of lordship exchanges and divine delivery over. If we take a peek forward to 2:17, from what frame of reference could Paul charge Jews as "suppressing the truth in unrighteousness," as refusing to "give God glory," and behaving "wickedly" and so forth?

The first reminder is such Jew on Jew charges are nothing new in the history of Israel. Note the criticisms in Deut 10:16–17; Jer 4:4; Pss. Sol. 15:8; and Wis 15:1–6. One also has the complaints of the Teacher of Righteousness, whose career is traceable in the Dead Sea Scrolls, against the Hasmonean rulers controlling the priesthood, cultus, and politics of Jerusalem.[69] We also have the complaints of Jesus against

---

[69] Cf. Wise, *The First Messiah*.

the Pharisees (Matt 23:13–39) and a specific example against their oral law interpretations that break the Law, the oral law of "Corban" (Mark 7:9–13, 22).

Galatians 1:16 is apposite. Paul said God was pleased "to reveal his Son in me." In Gal 1:13–14, Paul identified his advancing in Judaism as a zealousness for ancestral traditions, which consequently motivated his desire to destroy the church of God. Paul ceased his efforts against followers of Jesus after a divine revelation to him that Jesus was the Son of God. Paul's response to the divine revelation was to renounce his former actions (Phil 3:6–8). So Paul perhaps writes with some irony in 2:2, "And we know that the judgment of God rightly falls upon those who practice such things," since his self-confession was to be guilty of malice, murder, strife, foolishness, and haughtiness. The first-person plural expresses the general affirmation that would be given to the condemnation behind catalogues of vices. Yet, as Paul wrote Romans, by his own testimony he knew the condemnation of God not only as the theme of a vice list, but as a matter of personal "revelation." When God revealed his Son to Paul, a zealous Jew stood condemned in his very zealousness. Paul could personalize the divine fiat in 1:28, "God delivered them over to a disapproved mind." Perhaps from Paul's own experience came the force of the imperative that believers not conform to this age but be transformed "by the renewing of your mind" (12:2). Just as the divine condemnation had arrested Paul (cf. 11:32, "shut up all in disobedience"), a "model" Jew, Paul with an emphatic "you" (σύ, *sy*) could interrogate, "And do you consider this, O man who judges those who practice such things and yet do them yourself, that *you* will escape the judgment of God?" (2:3).

Paul then highlighted in 2:4 God's present actions as the riches of his kindness, forbearance, and patience. These terms are nearly synonymous. Cranfield outlined background in Jewish literature, pointing out that "patience" (μακροθυμία, *makrothymia*) was used of God's forbearance in holding back his wrath.[70] Such forbearance by God should have led to repentance, but did not because of hard and impenitent hearts

---

[70] Cranfield, *Romans*, 1:144. E.g., with the noun wrath (*orgē*), Ps 7:12 (LXX); with the verb "be wrathful" (*orgizomai*), Ps 102:8–9 (LXX); with the noun anger (*thymos*), Nah 1:2–3; cf. 2 Bar. 59:6.

(2:5, 8).⁷¹ So, instead, rebellious hearts are "storing up wrath [*orgē*] in the day of wrath [*orgē*]." This declaration, once the Jewish audience is engaged in 2:17, functions as Paul's prophetic call to Israel, as did the prophets of old before God's wrath of exile. Amos warned of desiring the day of the Lord as if light when the reality would be darkness (Joel 5:18). Joel pled on behalf of the Lord that the nation return with all their heart, with fasting and weeping and mourning (Joel 2:12).

In 2:5, Paul says this storing up of wrath will burst like a great dam holding back the floodwaters "on the day of wrath [*orgē*], when God's righteous judgment will be revealed." We now are exposed to another aspect of the revelation of divine wrath that is not present tense as in 1:18, but future tense, the divine wrath of a future judgment. This future wrath was Paul's emphasis in 1 Thess 1:10. The two revelations of wrath, present (Rom 1:18) and future (1 Thess 1:10), are integrated in the sovereign purposes of God. God presently is revealing his wrath in the structure of the created world and his involvement with his creation, including humans, trying to save them from sin to avoid the future wrath. The present revelation of wrath is to make sin exceedingly sinful to try to wake up the sinner from the slide to destruction. Almost like a lifeguard having to slap the drowning person flailing their arms to get their attention, God's present revelation of wrath is not easy to receive but has a higher purpose to save. This wrath comes from a holy God making every effort to redeem rebellious creatures bent on self-destruction. Unfortunately, at some point in time, death will have its day ("worthy of death," 1:32). That day is the judgment of God.

Romans 2:4–8 turns to this alternate language of future wrath that is central to eschatological judgment. Illustrating the eschatological nature of the language are terms such as "day of wrath" and "revelation of the righteous judgment of God," along with the binary opposition of "eternal life" in 2:7 and "wrath and indignation" in 2:8. The

---

⁷¹ Cf. Amos 3:10 (LXX): "She knew not the things that would be against her, says the Lord, those who store up wickedness and misery in their countries." Punctuation variations occur both at 2:8 and after "distress" (στενοχωρία, *stenochōria*) in 2:9. The problem of a full stop or minor breaks is estimated variously. A case change from accusative to nominative for "wrath and fury" (ὀργὴ καὶ θυμός, *orgē kai thymos*) would make them grammatically a copulative complement, that is, should require "to be" as the understood copulative verb. The combination "tribulation" (θλῖψις, *thlipsis*) and "distress" (στενοχωρία, *stenochōria*) are understood in the following comments as the resultant effects of "wrath and fury." Consult the UBS⁵ and NA²⁸ Greek texts.

hidden meaning of all history in the making now is revealed only at the end. Every moment of the finite present is a contingent act of God revealing his power moving history unto his purposes.[72] Thus, history gravitates toward a final judgment. In 2:5 Paul shifts to speak of wrath as revelation, not as in 1:18, but as a revelation of that future judgment.

One may compare Targum readings on Deut 32:34 ("vengeance is mine")[73] with the concept of "storing up" wrath against the final day of wrath. These Targum readings illustrate the currency of thought expressed by Paul in Rom 2:5 in the first-century synagogue.[74] *Onkelos* reads, "Are not all their works manifest before Me, laid up in My treasures against the day of judgment? Their punishment is before Me, and I will repay."[75] Similarly, "Are not their secret works all known before Me? Sealed and laid up are they in My treasury! Vengeance lies before Me, and I will recompense them."[76] *Jerusalem* echoes the sentiment, "Is not this the cup of punishment, mixed and ordained for the wicked, sealed in My treasuries for the day of the great judgment? Vengeance is mine: I am he who repayeth."[77]

These same Targum readings provide background for a judgment by deeds anticipated in Rom 2:6. Judgment by works was a thoroughly Jewish idea and found expression elsewhere in the New Testament.[78] The theological statement in 2:6 corresponds to 2 Thess 1:5–7 ("just of God to repay those who afflict you with affliction"), spoken in an eschatological context ("when the Lord Jesus is revealed from heaven," 1:7). In both Rom 2:9 and 2 Thess 1:6, "tribulation" is understood as an expression of the divine wrath. To "obey not the truth" in Rom 2:8 is the opposite of the "obedience of faith" among the nations in Rom 1:5, the gospel to be believed in 1:16. For Paul, the refusal to obey the truth

---

[72] Cf. Pannenberg, *Theology and the Kingdom of God*.

[73] Quoted by Paul in Rom 12:19, but the concept is not exclusive to Deuteronomy; cf. Jer 5:9; 23:2; Hos 4:9; Joel 3:21; Nah 1:2.

[74] Etheridge, *The Targums of Onkelos and Jonathan Ben Uzziel*. Hereinafter referred to as Etheridge. With the idea of "storing up," also compare Marqah *Memar* 4.5.

[75] Etheridge, 2:550–51.

[76] Etheridge, 2:668. The Targum continues, "at the time when their foot shall move to the captivity." Cf. "secrets" with Rom 2:16.

[77] Etheridge, 2:668. The Targum expands with, "the fire of Gehinam is prepared for them."

[78] E.g., 1 Pet 1:17; Rev 2:23. Cf. 1 Cor 3:13; 2 Cor 5:10; Rom 14:12.

(2:8) was in part the disobedience to which God had impounded all rebellious humans (11:32). In context, then, the disobedience featuring in 2:8 is specifically disobedience to the gospel, which mirrors what is said in 2 Thess 1:8. Paul makes future judgment pivot on this one point of the gospel.

This future judgment will apply as much to Jewish humanity as any other humanity, and for similar reasons of offense. One may note that "through the lusts of their hearts," predicated of "humans" in 1:24, has its corollary in the "hardness and unrepentant heart" in 2:5. Compare the anger of Jesus when he was grieved at the Pharisees' hardness of heart in Mark 3:5. This brings up the boomerang effect of the "to the Jew first" motif integral to the theme statement, where the idea when first broached is couched in positive terms (1:16). Now the same idea expresses the dark side of the moon that cannot be seen when the reflection of the good news of the gospel is in view. This deliberate and ironic echo of the theme in 2:10 represents Paul's premonition that if rejection of the gospel continues, the future has dark clouds of wrath on the horizon for the nation.

Meyer pointed out that "futility" (ματαιότης, *mataiotēs*), whose cognate verb appears in 1:21, was a characteristic attribute given by Jews to heathens. Citing passages in the Septuagint such as Jer 2:5, 2 Kgs 17:5, and Ps 104:11, Meyer insisted that 1:21–32 could not apply to the Jew.[79] Meyer was wrong. First, he missed the intertextuality of 1:23, which has the golden calf at Sinai written all over its wording. Second, he missed how 2:17–24 functions rhetorically. Paul's accusation in 2:17–24 is precisely what Meyer denied: Paul now is demonstrating that 1:18–32 *is* about Israel, and was written with Israel in mind. Dunn agreed. Taking the exodus and giving of the law, followed by the golden calf incident, as comparable to a new creation and new fall, he concluded:

> If so, the point is that Paul already had in mind a *twofold* indictment. One draws on the characteristic Jewish condemnation of *Gentile* religion and sexual practice. The other, less overt, contains the reminder that *Israel* itself falls under the same indictment. It is this which makes the indictment truly universal—

---

[79] Meyer, *Romans*, 57, 60.

"on all human impiety and unrighteousness" (Rom. 1.18), "Jew first and Gentile as well" (2.9–10).[80]

The motif of hypocrisy is the conceptual bridge. In 2:17–24, Paul represented present Jewish attitude as hypocrisy. Hypocrisy is simply another way of suppressing the truth. For example, the basic charge in 1:18—that humans suppressed the truth of God—was given its ironic twist in 2:20–22. If truth is revealed in the law, Jews through their disobedience to the law suppressed that truth. If heathens refused to honor God or to give him thanks (1:21), Jews, by breaking the law, also dishonored God; they caused him to be blasphemed (2:23–24). Using the motif of hypocrisy, Paul applied the fundamental truth that characterized humanity in 1:18–32, disobedience to God, to that part of humanity referred to as Jewish in 2:17–24. If pagans were disobedient to a revealed creator, Jews likewise were disobedient to that creator's revealed law. Worse, the law made Jewish culpability more egregious. Culpability is what Paul specifically states in 4:15, "For the law brings about wrath, but where law does not exist, neither does violation." The verses that follow 1:32 and open up Romans 2, then, are a response to the false presuppositions of those Paul encountered who were acting as did Paul in his former life observing Torah. This analysis in Romans 2, then, is the condensate of Pauline thought grounded in the revelation of God's Son to Paul when exposed to Paul's own Jewish background.

So, when Paul frames the law as the focus of knowledge and truth, he simply is revisiting the reality of 1:18, 25, 28. The present situation in synagogue after synagogue of rejecting the gospel for Paul illustrates the lordship exchange profiled in 1:18–32. The power of the Old Aeon remains untouched by the Law. When Paul speaks of blaspheming the Name in Rom 2:24, prophetically he is reflecting Isaiah, who said, "Now therefore what am I doing here, says the Lord, seeing that my people are taken away without cause? Their rulers howl says the Lord, and continually, all day long, my Name is despised" (Isa 52:5).

ROMANS 3:5

In 2:17, Paul addressed explicitly another division of humanity, the Jew. A special covenant expressed in a revealed Law and visibly signified

---

[80] Dunn, *Theology*, 93.

through circumcision distinguished the Jewish nation as a nation. Paul was concerned with boasting in the Law. Boasting manifested a delusion about the Law. Using the Law as the basis of boasting before God displaced its function as a revelation of wrath to the peril of those to whom the oracles were entrusted. The ancient Hebrew idea was that the Law brought those living under its obligations into the sphere of cursing and blessing. Keeping the Law released the power of blessing. Violating the Law released the power of the curse. Evil acts released evil forces that eventually overtook the offender in disastrous consequences. The curse of the Law operated in the nexus of sin and guilt.[81]

Into his discussion of universal disobedience, Paul introduced the question of the Jew in his relationship to the covenant. In 3:3, 5, and 7, Paul coordinated elements of unbelief, unrighteousness, and deceit. These elements represented for Paul the characteristic Jewish response to the covenant. Because of this response, the curse of the Law was invoked. In contrast, the faithfulness of God characterized God's integrity to the covenant.[82]

Paul's diatribe continues in 3:5, "But if our unrighteousness serves to show the righteousness of God, what shall we say? That God, the one inflicting the wrath [*orgē*] is unrighteous?"[83] "The wrath" can be understood to be either eschatological judgment or the present revelation of wrath of chapter 1 (1:18).[84] This wrath is the covenant curse, the

---

[81] Gathercole (*Where Is Boasting?*, 119) provided a double-edged critique of both New Perspective and Lutheran traditions on the functional role of works in Jewish soteriology and eschatology, whether positive or negative. The matter needs revisiting.

[82] Ljungmen demonstrated that covenant terminology in this section has a background in synagogue benedictions (*Pistis: A Study of Its Presuppositions and Its Meaning in Pauline Use*, 13–19). Cf. Liao, "The Place of Covenant in the Theology of the Apostle Paul." Wright, *Paul and the Faithfulness of God*, 800–01.

[83] Taking the participle as attributive in 3:5, "the one who inflicts" (ὁ ἐπιφέρων, *ho epipherpōn*) results from the diatribe context. Otherwise, the participle might be taken as temporal ("while inflicting") or causal ("because he inflicts"). Either would be consistent with Paul's other statements about God.

[84] For eschatological, cf. Sanday and Headlam, *Romans*, 73; Käsemann, *Romans*, 83; Bultmann, *Theology*, 1:288–89. For present wrath, cf. Dodd, *Romans*, 45; Hanson, *Wrath*, 88; Smith, "ὀργὴ θεοῦ" 91–92. Jewett (*Romans*, 247–48) and Dunn (*Romans 1–8*, 135) opt for both. Neither Fitzmyer (*Romans*, 329) nor Longenecker (*Romans*, 349–50) even raise the question. Dunn accused Paul of getting off track and becoming self-contradictory: "The trouble is that Paul's argument now seems to be going in two contradictory directions. The powerful exposition of God's wrath in chaps. 1–2 has

nexus of sin and guilt in the law of the covenant. This wrath, that is, is the historical manifestation of divine wrath Israel has experienced and to which Israel can testify as to exactly how righteous and just was this expression of wrath. That Paul immediately says, "Otherwise, how will God judge the world?" in 3:6 does *not* demand the wrath spoken of here must be eschatological. Actually, Paul's point is the opposite: God is righteous and just to inflict wrath at whatever point in time he chooses to do so, and Israel is first on the witness stand to testify to this truth. Paul's logic is straightforward and simple: If God cannot express wrath justly *in* history, how could humans expect God to express his wrath justly *at the end* of history? But God *does* express his wrath justly in history, and postexilic Israel should be able to testify to all human beings of this truth. When God expresses his wrath, in history or at the end of history, God is just. That is ground zero of a theology of divine wrath for Paul. God is absolutely just whenever he inflicts wrath.

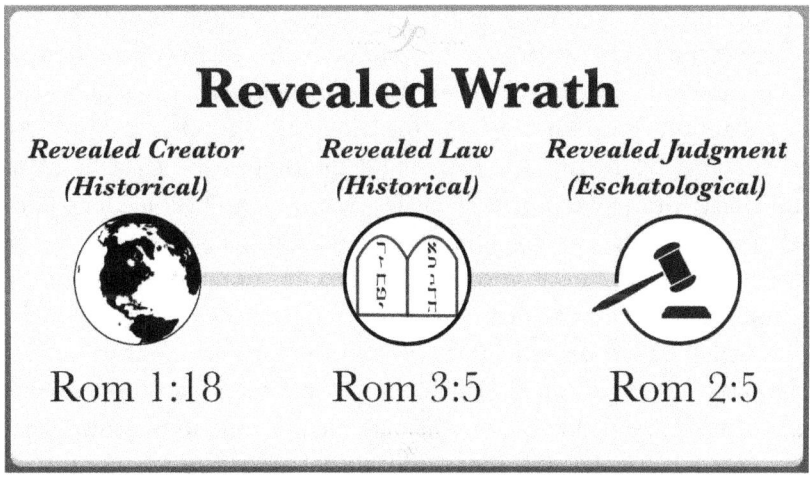

FIGURE 6.2. Pauline Perspectives on Revealed Wrath.

Paul affirmed that the righteousness of God was sufficient and necessary to establish human unrighteousness, but he did not say the converse. If human unrighteousness were necessary to establish the righteousness of God, the sinner justly could not be condemned for doing what was necessary. Inflicting the wrath of the curse on Israel

been thrown completely off course by the gratuitous assertion that God nevertheless remains faithful to faithless Israel" (*Romans 1-8*, 141). Dunn misses Paul's actual point about revelatory wrath in history and its connections with the end of history.

would be unjust, and God rightly could not judge the world for sin. Further, if human unrighteousness were necessary to establish the righteousness of God, human unrighteousness not only could be tolerated, but actually logically should be promoted to achieve this end. Apparently, some had charged Paul with this very error of promoting unrighteousness (3:8). By so doing, his point had been misconstrued and the integrity of his missionary labor undercut.

Paul's maxim that human unrighteousness (of the Jew) revealed the righteousness of God was subtle allusion back to 1:28. In that verse, the "disapproved mind" was the divine verdict upon human "lust" (*epithymia*). Paul insisted in that context that the accuracy of the divine "disapproval" verdict was verifiable in the unrighteousness with which humans visibly were filled (1:29). In this sense, human unrighteousness confirmed God's righteous judgment, because the "greenhouse of wrath" effect demonstrated conclusively where all this rebellion ended up and why God could not "just let it go" (cf. 2:2). Conditions that characterized humanity at large were conditions that characterized Jewish failure in light of the covenant—unbelief, unrighteousness, and deceit.

Paul's inclusion of Jews into the "humanity" condemned in 1:18–32 becomes explicit in 3:9. Here the dichotomous Jewish division of humanity into Jew and gentile is shown to be an illusion. In spite of Abraham or Moses or any other storyline that situates Israel among the nations, humanity never escapes parentage in Adam by reason of the ubiquitous "missing the mark," or "sin" (ἁμαρτία, *hamartia*) for everyone, which Paul soon will charge (Rom 3:23). Sin is not a problem. Sin is a power. The solution is a greater power that can destroy sin's power, and history already has proven through the exile and its aftermath that that solution is not Torah. The disobedience inherent in the gentile response to the revealed knowledge of God in creation also is inherent in the Jewish response to the revealed knowledge of God in Torah. Jewish humanity, particularly with its more culpable knowledge of Torah, fundamentally is revealed as the *anthrōpos* characterized in 1:18–32. If the parameters of the vice list look more pagan than Jewish, that would be the problem, Paul would insist.

The universal disobedience inherent to the human situation underscored both for Jew and gentile unwillingness to acknowledge the divine verdict of the "disapproved mind." This divine verdict judged perversion of *epithymia*. Human refusal to accept the divine verdict revealed the most basic ungodliness. This ungodliness perverted divinely created *epithymia* into uncontrollable lust that produced all kind of unrighteousness.[85] For this disobedience, all humans became accountable to God. Paul then proceeded to demonstrate scriptural warrant for his argument with a catena of quotations from the Psalms and Isaiah in the following verses (3:10–18).

ROMANS 4:15

Paul has been arguing that all humans are shut up in disobedience. In 3:21–26, he anticipates what he will develop more fully in Romans 5–8, similar to 3:1–8 anticipating fuller development in Romans 9–11. While God has impounded all humans in their disobedience, God still is able to show mercy because of the New Aeon inaugurated by the Messiah (3:21). God's action was according to grace. Otherwise, human beings had no security. Inevitably, they would be swept up in that tsunami of wrath against all human ungodliness and unrighteousness at the final judgment. Jesus Messiah is God's offer of grace. Jesus's righteousness of faith holds back the entire tsunami wave of eschatological judgment through the obedience of the One (5:19). In Romans 4, the new hermeneutical motif, already embedded intratextually earlier in Romans 2, is the Abraham tradition. That motif was the promise to Abraham that he would be heir of the world.[86]

The promise to Abraham could not possibly be fulfilled through the law. Paul insisted in 4:14–15 that the promise must be through the righteousness of faith, "For if those who are of the law are heirs, faith

---

[85] Cf. Marcus Aurelius, *Com.* 9.1: "The one who does wickedly is ungodly" (ὁ ἀδικῶν ἀσεβεῖ, *ho adikōn asebei*).

[86] Philo philosophically allegorized Abraham's promise, turning "heir" into the "wise man" and "land" into the "wisdom of God" (*Heir* 313–16). Käsemann noted "heir," "promise," and "law" all can be eschatological (*Romans*, 118–19). Yet, wrath also has a historical component in Paul, such as the wrath of the exile, so enters into Paul's discussion as a development of the law's curse triggered by transgression. Cf. Cranfield, *Romans*, 1:238, for and against non-eschatological wrath here. For "law" in Paul, cf. Campenhausen, *The Formation of the Christian Bible*, 24–37; Dunn, *Theology*, 128–59; Sanders, *Paul and Palestinian Judaism*; Westerholm, *Israel's Law and the Church's Faith*; *Perspectives Old and New on Paul*; Wright, *The Climax of the Covenant*; Räisänen, *Paul and the Law*; Schreiner, *The Law and Its Fulfillment*; Thielman, *Paul and the Law*. For Paul's take on the rich Jewish tradition on Abraham as behind all of Romans 1–4, including elements of Romans 2, cf. VanHorn, "Arguing from Abraham."

has been made futile and the promise nullified, for the law works wrath, and where no law is, neither (is there) transgression." Paul appealed to the historical consciousness of the Jew. Under the law, Israel was under the powerful nexus of sin and guilt. That Israel could not survive under the law was the preeminent lesson of the exile. The exile became the historical paradigm of the wrath of Yahweh. Even with renewed emphasis upon keeping the law after the exile, some had the sense that the curse still remained, as real life did not seem to correlate with prophetic anticipation.[87]

One presumption prior to the exile by the people of Israel that agitated the prophets was the inflated sense of confidence in election. This overconfidence had produced a false sense of security against judgment.[88] An echo of this preexilic prophetic warning may be heard in Romans in Paul's denunciation of boasting in the law. If the promise really did come through law, the gospel was an exercise in futility. But the law in truth was a destructive force in Israel's experience. This force was the inevitable and inescapable result of transgression.[89] More significantly, the law through transgression threatened the fulfillment of the promise. The law worked wrath, not blessing. This observation was not hidden under a basket. This observation was no brilliant insight on Paul's part. This observation was a historical lesson available to all in Israel. Paul charged current boasters in the law with ignoring the lesson.

In contrast to the law, the gospel obviated transgression. Faith disqualified the lordship of *epithymia*. Outside the righteousness of faith realized in the gospel, the promise to Abraham that he would be heir of the world had no possible means of fulfillment. The gospel, grounded in the security of God's grace, guaranteed the fulfillment of the promise (4:16). This gracious act by God was Paul's good news.

Paul had warned his Corinthian congregation similarly with an example of historical wrath. Paul in 1 Cor 10:1–12 used the theme of

---

[87] Ps 90:9; 74:1–8; 85:4–6; Hag 1:5–11; Zech 1:3, 12; Isa 64:9. From the Dead Sea Scrolls, cf. PI 2, 6.

[88] Amos 3:2; 5:18; Hos 13:9–11; Isa 5:18–19; 28:14–22; Mic 3:11; Zeph 2:2; Jer 7:4; 28:1–17; Ezek 5:13; 16:38.

[89] Cf. Menander, *Min. Frag.* 700K [Allinson], "A law observed is nothing more than merely Law; when broken it is law and executioner." Paul's concept of sin and incumbent guilt was drawing upon a familiar relationship to Jews under the law that could be extended to extremes of application, as in John 9:1–2 and Luke 13:1–5.

wilderness wrath to warn the Corinthians about participation in pagan sacrificial meals. In the Corinthian passage, history was used with allusion to the language of divine wrath. Here in Rom 4:15, Paul also used the language of divine wrath with an allusion to history.

ROMANS 5:9

Romans 5:1–11 is transitional to the theme of the reign of grace in Jesus Christ. Evidence of this reign of grace is the peace of reconciliation. The mark of the eschatological now of this peace is the Holy Spirit, who communicates to the believer the love of God (5:5). Peace is the sign that the lordship of *epithymia* that reigns in the ungodly and creates enmity with God has been exchanged. The exchange of lordship is the work of Jesus Christ who alone procures this help for the weak. He died for the ungodly (5:6). The literary construction of 5:8–10 reveals how what is *not* said about divine wrath also can be important. Note the parallel phrase construction and the obvious missing element.[90]
The "much more" is reminiscent of rabbinic argumentation *a minori ad maius*.[91] This argument is grounded much like the one in 1 Thess 5:1–11. In that passage Paul says (in paraphrase):

> God has not designed our eschatological life such that at some unknown future that life suddenly might become subject to his wrath, for what God already has done for us through Jesus Messiah sets the stage for, and signifies the truth of, what he will do for us in the future.

In 1 Thess 1:10, Paul repeated the early confessional, "Jesus, the one who delivers us from the wrath to come." This affirmation is spoken to those who "turned to God from idols" (1 Thess 1:9). Paul said in Rom 5:8–10 that the accomplished reconciliation now experienced by those who once were enemies to God signifies the future deliverance from wrath. This salvation is "in his life" (5:10). Already in 2:7 and 2:8, we have seen how "life" (ζωή, *zōē*) and "wrath" (ὀργή, *orgē*) are polarities of eschatological destiny in Paul. Thus, Rom 5:8–10 is what Paul said in 1 Thess 5:9–10.

---

[90] Derived independently from Barrett, *Romans*, 108; similarly, later, Moo, *Romans*, 309–11 (but not referencing Barrett). Moo, however, makes no observation and no comment on the missing "from the wrath" element in 5:10, so misses a point.

[91] Str-B 3:223–26.

Parallel Expressions

Rom 5:8b–9	Rom 5:10
while we were sinners	while we were enemies
Messiah died for us	through death of his Son
much more then	much more
justified in his blood	reconciled
we shall be saved	we shall be saved
through him	in his life
from the wrath	...

FIGURE 6.3. Parallel Expressions in Rom 5:8–10.

Note in the table in figure 6.3 above that the last element in 5:8b–9, "from the wrath," is absent in its counterpart in 5:10. This construction is intentional and an important signal. Paul's purpose for the discussion that immediately follows in 5:12–21—Adam and Christ—is to provide theological exegesis of the missing counterpart that should parallel "wrath" in 5:9. The polarities of eschatological destiny are the two foci of the discussion in 5:12–21. The "death" (θάνατος, *thanatos*) that Paul says reigns transcends physical death: this death the eschatological destiny of wrath (*orgē*).[92] In Paul's discussion of Adam and Christ, he is building upon what he said about the revelatory power of wrath in 1:18–32. In Paul's conclusion in 5:21, the eschatological life in Jesus Christ is set forth as the reign of grace: "As sin reigned in death, even

---

[92] Not emphasized by Cranfield, *Romans*, 1:279–81, who can be used as an example. Cranfield focused on physical death. Physical death is involved, because some sins inherently are deadly, but Pauline eschatological polarities are evident too. The complex interactions of these polarities, missed on occasion by commentators as in the case of Cranfield, is precisely the difference between Paul and the many Jewish traditions about Adam's sin producing physical death that Cranfield documents from various sources in his notes. For example, in the Apoc. of Mos. 14, physical death is the wrath of God. Alternately, at Qumran (Z 10:4–10), senility is the wrath of God. Paul's approach, however, is quite distinct from these Jewish traditions. Paul carefully has nuanced a complex interaction of historical, spiritual, and eschatological features. Thus, without Paul's integrated eschatological nuance—coming directly out of his vision of God's resurrected Son (Gal 1:12, 15–16; Rom 1:4)—Cranfield's interpretation of 5:13–14 is weak.

so grace might reign through righteousness unto eternal life through Jesus Christ our Lord." The law was not a matter for boasting because all the law did was to show definitively the seriousness of sin as transgression against God that God must condemn but law cannot solve. However, the reign of grace is proper cause for exultation in God (5:2, 11).

Nygren's label of 5:1–21 as "Free from the Wrath of God" is only partially correct.[93] In Romans 5, Paul does begin to expand the last part in the theme statement in 1:17, "shall live." However, Nygren's outline as a whole fails because he demotes Romans 9–11. He treats Romans 9–11 as without essential connection to the theme. Viewing Romans 9–11 this way is a traditional approach but exegetically myopic. One misses the significance of the "to all" as the concluding part of the phrase in 11:32 that summarizes the entire development of Romans 1–11. That is to say, Nygren's "shall live" focus from the theme statement surely applies to Israel as much as any group of humans on the planet. If Israel's eschatological destiny fails, and Israel does not "live" as raised from the dead specifically to fulfill that destiny (Rom 11:15), pagans have nothing to boast if they put their trust in that God.

One facet of eschatological life in Christ for Paul was freedom from the wrath of God. After this introductory section in 5:1–11, the term *orgē* disappears from the rest of the presentation of the reign of grace (6:1—8:39).[94] Confidence in this freedom from wrath is underscored in the concluding verses of Romans 5–8 in 8:35–39. In these verses, Paul declared nothing would separate the believer from the love of God in Christ Jesus, which, though unmentioned in the Romans litany of elements, includes future wrath (1 Thess 1:10).

ROMANS 9:22

Paul said in 8:16–17 that the indwelling Spirit was the mark of the eschatological "now" of salvation and of believers' rights as heirs. In this brief reference to heirs, Paul renewed the theme surfacing explicitly in 4:18–17, but already alluded to implicitly in the covenant language of "beloved of God" in the opening verses of Romans (1:7). In chapter 4,

---

[93] *Romans*, 191.

[94] Implicit divine wrath contexts with the use of "death" (*thanatos*) in both Rom 7:24 and 8:1.

Paul only touched on the promise to Abraham to be heir of the world. Already in 4:1–17, then, we have an exegetical hint that the motif of the promise to Abraham guides what Paul had to say about the law and the wrath of God.

Paul finally is ready to expand the theme of the promise to Abraham in Romans 9–11. These chapters are the climax of Paul's entire presentation beginning with the theme in 1:16–17.[95] In the theme, Paul said the gospel was "to the Jew first." Practical mission experience indicated that the Jew generally rejected the gospel. This present anomaly Paul reconciled in a salvation-historical interpretation of the promise to Abraham. From this promise, Paul derived the universal scope of salvation and the continuity between the old and the new. In this climactic part of the epistle, Paul exposed his heart and the ground of his mission to the nations of the world.[96]

In 9:6–13, Paul reviewed patriarchal history to demonstrate that God's prevenient grace meant that Israel was constituted as God chose before merit existed. Sovereign choice was the essence of the promise to Abraham. Therefore, "Israel" was up to God to define. However, the sovereignty of God was not capricious (9:14–18). God acted with purpose. Pharaoh was a case in point. God hardened Pharaoh's heart, but the divine power was demonstrated and the divine Name was proclaimed thereby.[97]

Did the divine sovereignty then destroy all human responsibility (9:19–21)? Paul considered the question pretentious. God the creator did not answer to a creature. Paul pressed home his rejection of the question with the illustration of the potter and his vessel.[98] Paul's purpose was to crush pretentiousness or any sense of privilege on the part

---

[95] Whether Romans 9–11 is assumed integral to Paul's argument in Romans 1–8 is the litmus test of Romans interpreters. This section can be assumed just an appendix, sidetrack, footnote, or an otherwise too sentimental Paul getting his head clouded with personal feelings for his Jewish heritage, so destroying his logic and confusing his theology—often according to gentile interpreters, of course.

[96] In Romans 9–11, the language of wrath generally is mitigated or its harshness highlighted. A determinism that seems to underlie the passages involved is difficult to handle. Barrett advised that the interplay of God's decree and Israel's responsibility is not to be obscured by a simplistic reduction of either (*Romans*, 196).

[97] Proclamation of the divine Name, as in the case of Pharaoh, is a significant motif in the following verses of Paul's argument.

[98] Cf. Isa 29:16; 45:9; 64:8–9; Jer 18:6; Wis 15:7.

of anyone, including the elect, with the exclusive sovereignty of God, a sovereignty expressed as the absolute autonomy of the divine will.[99]

A significant break occurs at 9:22. Paul left the diatribe style. Two elements signal the shift. First, a conditional sentence appears in which the apodosis is missing. Paul ran ahead of himself in thought. Second, the personal and relative pronoun combination, "even us whom" (Οὓς καὶ . . . ἡμᾶς, *Ous kai . . . hēmas*) in 9:24 shows that Paul brought the argument out of the abstract and into the concrete of the immediate present. The significance of the break is that in 9:20–21 Paul rejected the accusation that divine sovereignty destroyed human responsibility. Then Paul proceeded to give an answer to that same charge. In effect, Paul said an answer did not have to be given, but he gave one anyway.

The imagery of the potter and his vessel spills over into the language of wrath in 9:22–23.

> What if God, though[100] willing to demonstrate the wrath and make known his power, endured in great forbearance vessels of wrath having been prepared for destruction? Even that he might make known the riches of his glory upon vessels of mercy, which he prepared beforehand for glory?

That the language of divine wrath entered Paul's argument at this point is no surprise. Study of the Hebrew Scripture showed that the language of divine wrath was correlative to the language of divine sovereignty.[101] Further, divine sovereignty was shown as behind the revelation of wrath in 1:18–32. So, the general logic of Paul's potter's analogy is not incompatible with the previous argument about divine wrath.

Perhaps, however, Paul is more historically focused than generally allowed. A concept of "general forbearance" actually is strange at the historical level, since God has *not* passed over sins. Paul said the opposite. He presented a dual apocalypse of wrath that already has been released into history, one by the revealed creator (1:18), the other by the revealed lawgiver (3:9). So, God clearly has expressed his wrath.

---

[99] So Meyer, *Romans*, 395.

[100] The participle may be purposive, "willing" (Jewett, *Romans*, 595), causative, "because he wished" (Tasker, *Wrath of God*, 22; Barrett, *Romans*, 189–90; Cranfield, *Romans*, 2:494), or concessive, "although he wanted" (Sanday and Headlam, *Romans* 261). The concessive helps to contrast the following "in great forbearance" (cf. Fitzmyer, *Romans*, 569), but may diminish the parallelism between vv. 22 and 23.

[101] This correlation was demonstrated in discussion at 1:18–32.

FIGURE 6.4. Roman Potter's Wheel. Replica of a Roman potter's wheel as one would find in typical production shops with multiple artisans. Rotary motion was the key principle to the symmetrical shape of curved objects. A vertical axle connected the smaller diameter disk at the top holding the clay to a larger diameter disk at the bottom. Wet clay would be placed in an amorphous lump on the top surface of the smaller disk to be shaped with the hands and with wooden mold forms (hanging on nails at the top). The potter sat on the angled bench seat and rotated the larger disk at the bottom with his feet. The larger disk was heavier, sometimes having added weight, to utilize a flywheel principle to conserve rotational energy to counterbalance the weight of the clay the potter was manipulating on the top wheel. Animal fat was applied on the axle to reduce the high friction co-efficient for smoother spinning (HMM).

FIGURE 6.5. Roman Pottery Drinking Cup. An exquisite example of first-century Roman pottery found in ancient Corinth with ingenious applique of grape vine and grape clusters in high relief and accurate detail surrounding the body of this wine drinking vessel with curved handle evoking a branch. A beautiful piece of consummate artistic skill on the part of this pottery craftsman (AMAC).

FIGURE 6.6. Roman Pottery Storage Vessel. A typical example of a storage jar for various purposes that did not require an enclosed top or lid for the contents. This vessel was turned on a potter's wheel to create the grooved edges in the side and has fairly consistent shape. The decoration on the side, however, lacks the requisite symmetry and is rather simple and rudimentary (BMB).

Earlier Paul had argued that gospel events demonstrated the righteousness of God by serving to clarify the forbearance of God "passing over" sins committed beforehand (3:25).[102] Commentators commonly understand this "passing over" of sins generally to be of all sins before the Christ-event.[103] In a similar vein of thought, Jewett assumed this idea referred to any general time God delays justice purposefully for repentance, and other commentators agree with this approach.[104]

However, the fundamental flaw with all such proposals is they lack coherence with what Paul explicitly already has said and what is known from Scripture. The idea that "forbearance" should be interpreted as generally ignoring sins committed before the coming of the gospel does not appreciate the historical and personal dimension of the wrath of God described as "is being revealed." Further, a survey of the language of divine wrath in Hebrew Scripture indicates numerous examples, both of individuals and of entire nations, of God expressing his wrath, both toward pagan nations and toward his own people, as in Pharaoh enduring plagues on his kingdom, or Nebuchadnezzar going temporarily insane, eating grass like an ox (Dan 4:24–26). Further, with his own people, God most certainly did not "pass over" the sins of the northern and southern kingdoms. He expressed his wrath in total destruction of the northern kingdom of Israel by Assyria in 722 BC and a costly exile for the southern kingdom of Judah in 586 BC by Babylon. The "passing over" of sins contextually has to be something else.

Paul had a more concrete issue in mind. Note that already in 2:4, Paul highlighted God's present action as the riches of God's forbearance from wrath. For the theme of divine "forbearance," then, to have pertinence in historical context, a possibility not much considered is that Paul—both with the "passing over" of sins in 3:25 and with the "vessels of wrath" in 9:22—specifically is focused on obstinate Israel since the exile and in Paul's own missionary context. Though God not

---

[102] Against the idea of pretermission, the "passing over" (πάρεσις, *paresis*) here has been equated with "forgiveness (ἀφέσις, *aphesis*). So Käsemann, *Romans*, 98; Bultmann, *TDNT*, s.v. "ἀφίημι," 1:511.

[103] E.g., Barrett, *Romans*, 80; Cranfield, *Romans*, 1:212; Dodd, *Romans*, 60; Leenhardt, *Romans*, 107; Meyer, *Romans*, 138; Nygren, *Romans*, 159; Dunn, *Romans 1–8*, 181, and so forth.

[104] Jewett, *Romans*, 596; cf. Longenecker, *Romans*, 435.

yet has exhausted his forbearance with postexilic Israel, Israel's obstinate rejection of Messiah has exacerbated this situation acutely as Paul writes Romans. If history is any lesson at all, menacing thunderclouds are forming on the national horizon. Consistent rejection of the gospel is proof of Israel's hardness of heart, and that impiety will have its day.

Both by allusion and by reference, Paul showed himself steeped in the message of the ancient prophets. That prophetic heritage included the proclamation of the wrath of God to come upon a disobedient and sinful nation. The prophets issued the call for repentance before the hour of judgment overtook the nation. During the period of this forbearance, the preaching of repentance was a measure of the mercy of God. As Hosea said, even in the last moment Yahweh could turn his wrath (4:1–4). Eventually, the divine sovereignty was vindicated in the wrath of exile. When Ezekiel rehearsed the history of God's dealings with Israel, he said that Yahweh continually subordinated divine wrath to the proclamation of the divine Name among the nations. But when the divine wrath came, the humbling of Israel was also the humbling of the divine Name associated with Israel. For this reason, proclamation of the divine Name to reestablish God's reputation and glory was to characterize the regathered Israel.[105] Unfortunately, the message of Malachi shows that even the postexilic community defiled Yahweh's Name among the gentiles (1:6–14). How could the righteous God continue to associate his Name with Israel? Paul's answer was by forbearance until such a time as he could demonstrate to the world his righteousness for associating with Israel since the exile.

Paul seems to have extended up to his own time this motif of the longsuffering of Yahweh to establish the proclamation of the divine Name after the exile. God had been longsuffering with Israel prior to the exile. For Paul, God also had been longsuffering with Israel after the exile up to Paul's day. Thus, the "forbearance" of God in 9:22 concerning the vessels of wrath may be related to the "passing over" action of God in 3:25.[106] Paul had in mind Israel's postexilic history.

"But now," Paul proclaimed in 3:21, "apart from the law," the righteousness of God has been revealed in Christ Jesus, whom God

---

[105] Cf. Ezek 20:1–44.

[106] As well as the "forbearance" of God in 2:4.

presented (3:25).[107] The Gentile refusal to glorify God (1:21), also true of Israel (3:23), God reversed in Jesus Christ; at the same time, he was faithful to his promises to Israel.[108] God proclaimed his Name among the nations through Messiah who was of the stock of Israel (cf. 9:5). Positive response to Paul's gospel in the Greco-Roman world was proof that Paul in his mission was contributing to glorifying the divine Name among the nations. The Christ-event has vindicated God's continued association with Israel since the exile and consummated the purpose of postexilic divine forbearance.

While the inbreaking of the gospel demonstrated the righteousness of God, that inbreaking simultaneously was the harbinger of eschatological judgment. For this reason, the period of forbearance since the exile has its climax in the preaching of the gospel. After the divinely appointed time for this fateful forbearance, the future eschatological wrath of judgment could be expected (cf. 1 Thess 2:16). In 9:24, Paul included himself among the vessels of God's mercy. For Paul, vessels of wrath, who presently were experiencing the patience of God, as did he during his time of persecuting followers of Jesus, were prepared for eschatological destruction if their impiety persisted.

Actually, what Paul is saying here in Romans has a close analog to the 1 Thess 2:15b–16 passage some are of a mind to dismiss as an interpolation:

> They are not pleasing to God, but hostile to all men, hindering us from speaking to the gentiles that they might be saved, with the result that they always fill up the measure of their sins. But wrath has come upon them decisively.

In that context, while the translation of εἰς τέλος (*eis telos*) is debated ("at last," "decisively"), the phrase clearly points to eschatological destruction. The imminence of the parousia of Jesus informed Paul's proclamation to the Thessalonians that opposition to the gospel would be overwhelmed in a flood of eschatological judgment. The imminence of judgment is a motif in Romans too (Rom 13:11–12).

---

[107] Translating "presented" (προέθετο, *proetheto*) is difficult. "Put forward" (ESV) and "displayed publicly" (NASB) are other options.

[108] Rom 15:8–9a: "For I say Christ became a minister of the circumcision for the truthfulness of God, in order that the promises to the fathers might be confirmed and that the nations might glorify God for (his) mercy."

For Paul, the issue of eschatological destiny was determined by response to the gospel. Paul was certain that response to the gospel determined destiny, and this certainty is behind the perfect passive participle, "having been prepared" (κατητισμένα, *katērtismena*), in 9:22. The aorist tense of "endured" (ἤνεγκεν, *ēnegken*) results from the nature of the conditional sentence itself. Little is to be gained in distinguishing between the perfect, "having been prepared," and the aorist, "prepared beforehand" used of the vessels of wrath and of the vessels of mercy respectively. The change from passive to active voice is not a removal of God from the action concerning the vessels of wrath, as the earlier reference to the divine hardening of Pharaoh's heart shows (9:18). God has endured the vessels of wrath so that the riches of his glory might be known among those responding to the gospel. The motif in the Pharaoh story of the proclamation of the divine Name among the nations ties the present context to the former. God prepared vessels of wrath, as he hardened Pharaoh's heart, for a divine purpose: to show the riches of his glory to vessels of mercy, to proclaim his Name.

Paul in 9:25 correlated his argument with the message of Hosea. Hosea's message similarly was about Yahweh's longsuffering. God's action was grounded in the divine will (i.e., "prepared beforehand"). Paul used the prophet Isaiah (Isa 10:22–23), to substantiate his claim that the present situation was part of God's plan. This action of God in relation to vessels of wrath and vessels of mercy could not have been otherwise, for only in this way could the promise to Abraham not have been destroyed as completely as were Sodom and Gomorrah.[109]

Paul assigned Israel's failure since the exile to the pursuit of a law of righteousness outside of faith (9:31–32).[110] In such a misguided pursuit, Israel stumbled over the stone set for stumbling—Jesus Messiah, the righteousness of faith—an event Paul in 9:33 found illuminated by Isa 28:16. Though misguided, this pursuit that Paul assigned to Israel did not reduce the force of the emphasis upon the divine sovereignty in 9:19–24. Paul did not resolve the tension between divine sovereign-

---

[109] Rom 9:29; cf. Isa 1:9.

[110] Cf. Philo, *Heir* 94 [Colson]: "For nothing is so just or righteous as to put in God alone a trust which is pure and unalloyed."

ty and human responsibility.[111] He showed God's action as grounded in mercy, but he did not resolve the tension.[112] Paul simply eliminated any charge of injustice with God.[113]

ROMANS 12:19

The thought expressed in Rom 12:17–18 augments an understanding of "the wrath" that is mentioned in the next verse. In 12:17, Paul said that one never should pay back evil for evil. This call was not a maxim for non-retaliation, as Paul's secondary statement shows: Paul said that one should respect what is right in the sight of everyone. In other words, submit any particular case to the common consensus of what is right; do not exercise an arbitrary, personal vendetta.

In Rom 12:19, the principle of restraint from a personal vendetta was extended into matters that properly belonged to God. Emphatic pronouns convey the meaning. "Never *you yourselves* render vengeance, beloved, but give place to the wrath, for it is written, 'Vengeance is mine, *I myself* will repay,' says the Lord" (Rom 12:19). Paul here reproduced a quote of Deut 32:35 (cf. Lev. 19:18) that does not agree exactly with either the Hebrew or the Septuagint. Readings in the Targums agree more closely.[114] The Deuteronomy passage was used also in Heb 10:30. Both uses in Hebrews and in Romans correspond closely to the reading in *Onkelos*.[115]

To what wrath did Paul refer in 12:19, human, divine, or otherwise? Murray summarized four suggestions.[116] The two most viable options are that "the wrath" in 12:19 refers to the wrath of God, or else

---

[111] Cf. Homer, *Il.* 3.386; while action could be prompted by a god, the human still was held responsible.

[112] From Qumran, cf. ET 2. The mercy of God is in tension with the determinism of the divine lot marked out for each human.

[113] Again, from Qumran, cf. H 12:20–32; molded clay cannot understand God's ways, nor answer his charge, nor stand against his anger; yet God is ever righteous.

[114] *Onkelos* (Etheridge, 2:550); *Jonathan* (Etheridge, 2:668); *Jerusalem* (Etheridge, 2:668).

[115] The question of literary dependence is hard to answer. Perhaps the saying was a proverbial formula of warning current at the time and influencing the rendering in the Targum paraphrase; so Meyer, *Romans*, 480–81. With the idea in Rom 12:19, cf. Sir 28:1 (LXX), "The one who avenges will discover vengeance from the Lord."

[116] Murray, *Romans*, 2:140–41.

the wrath that will be mentioned a few verses later in 13:4–5, which is the agency of the state. In favor of the divine wrath is the supporting scriptural quotation from Deuteronomy that Paul adduced. In that quote, divine vengeance is explicit. Further, Paul's use of "wrath" in the absolute, as here in 12:19, is a construction that regularly means the wrath of God.[117] However, in favor of the wrath to be mentioned in 13:4, 5 (the sentence executed by the civil magistrate) is the closeness of the context. Further, later in 13:1–5, both vengeance and wrath are coordinated in 13:4.

An either-or decision for these last two options is unnecessary. In 13:4, the expression "a minister of God," applied to the civil magistrate, subordinates the civil office to the divine will. The civil magistrate's wrath in 13:4–5 may be the more fully developed idea of the divine wrath to give place to in 12:19.[118]

Yet, if "the wrath" in 12:19 is divine, is that wrath eschatological? Käsemann presumed that in this passage believers were warned not to anticipate the last judgment, God's wrath and retribution being at hand.[119] That for Paul the eschatological denouement was at hand is evident from 13:11–12. But no evidence was adduced to support the idea that believers generally presumed the divine judiciary function of the last judgment. Only the Pauline judgment pronouncements such as the anathemas in 1 Cor 16:22 and Gal 1:8–9 are comparable, and these are spoken out of Paul's special apostolic office, associated with the imminence of the parousia. Still, one could infer that the use of Deut 32:35 in 12:19 infuses this verse with eschatological overtones. For support, one could point to: (1) the eschatological function of the passage from Deuteronomy as used in Heb 10:30, (2) the Samaritan eschatology of the "Day of Vengeance" derived from Deut 32:35, (3) the eschatological nuance explicit in the reference to retribution in 2 Thess 1:8, and (4) the possible eschatological nuance for the tribulation mentioned in 12:12, and the persecution mentioned in 12:14.

However, a non-eschatological idea in 12:19 still may be present. The idea could be illustrated by material from various other Jewish writings. In the background study, passages from Josephus and 4 Mac-

---

[117] E.g., Rom 2:5, 8; 3:5; 5:9; 9:22; 1 Thess 1:10; 2:16; 5:9.

[118] Cf. Leenhardt, *Romans*, 319.

[119] Käsemann, *Romans*, 349.

cabees illustrated the non-eschatological use of divine retribution for justice in human affairs. Such use reflected the Greek idea that divine wrath preserved the proper order of government and religion. Further, another consideration that militates against affirming the eschatological sense in 12:19 is the context of the immediately following verses (13:1–5). In these verses, the divine wrath is operative in the civil sphere. The two contexts are juxtaposed, which is hard to ignore.

Why did Paul say that individuals never should take their own revenge? James issued his own warning to be slow to anger (Jas 1:19b–20). Being slow to wrath (*orgē*) was wise since human wrath often did not accomplish the righteousness of God. This idea of being slow to anger is met elsewhere in the New Testament, where human anger is to be eschewed.[120] Perhaps behind such thoughts was the idea that human judgment was impaired by anger.[121] Further, because human life is complicated by the aberration of sin, human anger cannot be free from impure motives. Submission to anger would be exposure to sin. In contrast, God judges righteously. Thus, Paul said that one should give place to the wrath of God. Do not usurp the divine prerogative of judgment. In other words, "no private person is at liberty to assume that his own vengeful feelings will carry out the divine sentence."[122]

From this perspective, the opening admonition in 12:17 to respect what is right in the sight of everyone has its parallel in the divine sphere. The admonition in 12:19 to "give place to the wrath" was grounded in the scriptural admonition to respect the divine prerogative of vengeance. In the first case, individuals should not take into their own hands what rightly should be a corporate judgment. In the second case, humans should not take into their own hands what rightly should be a divinely ordained judgment. The Greek mindset is illustrated when the Spartan king Archidamus II was going to war against Plataea in 429 BC. He first sought the gods' approval for his action as a matter of justice for long-standing grievances.[123]

---

[120] Cf. Eph 4:31 (though note 4:26); Col 3:8; 1 Tim 2:8. In Gal 5:20, Paul classifies "anger" (*thumos*) as a work of the flesh.

[121] Common in nonbiblical Greek. See Lycurgus, *Ag. Leoc.* 159.22; Menander, *Sam.* 155; Menander, *Min. Frag.* 574K, 629K; Plutarch, *Mor.* 441D, 450C; Diogenes Laertius, *Lives* 7.110.

[122] Barrett, *Romans*, 242.

[123] Thucydides, *War* 2.74.

ROMANS 13:4, 5

Paul in 13:1-6 said that the basis of subjection to ruling authorities[124] was their establishment under divine providence. To resist authority was to resist the divine counsel (13:1-2). The ruler stood as a cause for fear, not for the one who did good, but for the one who did evil.[125] In 12:19, Paul indicated that one should give place to the divine vengeance. Paul now expanded the thought in 13:3b-6.[126]

> Since you wish not to fear the authority, do the good, and you will have praise from the same; for [authority] is a servant of God for the good. But if you do the evil, (you should) fear; for [authority] does not bear the sword in vain; for [authority] is a minister of God, an avenger unto punishment [ὀρὴν, *orgēn*] to the one who practices evil. Therefore, to be in subjection is necessary, not only because of punishment [ὀρὴν, *orgēn*] but also because of conscience. For this reason also pay taxes; for they are servants of God engaged unto this very thing.

In the quote from Deuteronomy found in 12:19, God declared that vengeance was his responsibility; he would repay. According to 13:1-6, one way God repays is through the retribution of the civil magistrate. The life setting of the passage only can be speculated, but we can set out broad considerations.[127] First, Paul's comments are quite general. They contain no historical details of any kind or any special words that offer insight. Still, in general, Jewish communities both inside and outside Judea had regular problems

FIGURE 6.7. Denarius of Tiberius. Jesus was shown a Roman denarius with the image of the emperor in Matt 22:15-22, who would have been Tiberius (AD14-37), the successor to Augustus (BML).

---

[124] Not "angelic authorities," *contra* Cullmann, *Christ and Time*, 191-210. Note Barrett, *Romans*, 248-49.

[125] As Menander wryly observed, "The person who does no wrong needs no law" (*Min. Frag.* 845K [Allinson]).

[126] Cf. Stählin, *TDNT* s.v. "ὀργή," 5:440, n403.

[127] The discussion in Sanday and Headlam, *Romans*, 369-71, still holds.

with foreign taxation. Some wanted to make paying taxes a litmus test of Jewish patriotism. Jesus was challenged on this very issue, and Jewish revolutionaries revolted over taxes.[128] Second, Nero was the emperor at the time of Romans, but the infamous Nero of the later reign of the fire of Rome and the persecution of Jesus's followers not yet had surfaced. Nero's reign had two distinct phases.[129] The early reign was good under the tutelage of Seneca and Burrus, and Romans was written during Nero's early reign. Nero did institute some unpopular taxation policies, against Seneca's advice, but how much this local issue affected believers in Rome is unknown. Third, during his mission work Paul had had positive experiences with Roman magistrates,

FIGURE 6.8. Bust of Nero. Romans is written in the first period of Nero's reign, which was good (AMAC).

so his view of the Roman government was that of order and restraint. Sergius Paulus, the proconsul on the island of Cyprus (Acts 13:7), had responded positively to Paul's message, and Gallio, the proconsul in Corinth and brother of the famous Seneca in Rome, who was Nero's tutor, summarily dismissed the Jewish case against Paul (Acts 18:12).[130] Fourth, while his remarks are general, Paul would not be absent information about the local situation in Rome due to close associates of his mission such as Prisca and Aquila now leading a house church in Rome (Rom 16:3).

Thus, we probably can assume some action of Nero may have impressed believers in Rome just as negatively as the general Roman population. Whatever the exact circumstances, Paul obviously felt the question of paying taxes did not merit publicly leaving the impression

---

[128] Matt 22:18; Luke 20:22; cf. Judas, Theudas, and Eleazar (Josephus, *Ant.* 18.1.1; 20.5.1; *J.W.* 7.8.6).

[129] Aurelius Victor, *Caes.* 5.1–2; but cf. Thorton, Thorton, *Julio-Claudian*, 100.

[130] Later, the procurator Festus honored Paul's appeal to Caesar (Acts 25:12), and the centurion Julius showed kindness to Paul on the journey to Rome (Acts 27:3), and Paul had opportunity for visitors as soon as he arrived in Rome (Acts 28:16–17).

by resistance that followers of Jesus were revolutionaries desiring to destabilize or even overthrow the Roman government. His appeal in this specific context is for law, order, and civic responsibility. Penalties for not paying taxes potentially could be severe, depending on the exact circumstances, as "bearing the sword" in Rom 13:4 spoke to the power of execution in the judicial sphere of government.[131] This power of a Roman magistrate both to punish and to execute was represented by a special symbol called a "fasces" used in carved reliefs and on coins of a bound bundle (*fascis*) of wooden rods, often with an axe head showing in the middle. The symbol continues in use today, as in the Mercury dime coin of the United States mint on the reverse side of the coin, as well as behind the podium of the United States House of Representatives.

FIGURE 6.9. Roman Swords. The *gladius* was the main battle sword used for slashing and stabbing. The *pugio* short-blade sidearm had unknown auxiliary purposes.

FIGURE 6.10. Nero Coin with Fasces Symbol.

---

[131] Tacitus, *Hist.* 3.68; Cassius Dio, *Hist.* 42.27. Cf. Let. Aris. 254. Again, cf. Menander, "A law observed is nothing more than merely Law; when broken it is law and executioner" (*Min. Frag.* 700K [Allinson]).

Delling pointed out that Paul was using the vocabulary of Hellenistic administration.[132] Deissmann also drew connections with the legal and political realm.[133] From such vocabulary and associations, Käsemann concluded that "good" and "well" in the passage meant political good conduct, and this seems to be correct.[134] In the background study on Greek tragedy, divine wrath was shown to function to maintain the established order. This function had a parallel in Greek government. The Greek ruler was to preserve order, to avenge injustice. The term *orgē* in this context came to mean "punishment," and the expression of wrath could be righteous. Paul's use in 13:4–5 seems to be thoroughly in line with this Greek background. To translate *orgē* as "punishment" would be acceptable in 13:4–5. Paul ascribed to ruling authority the divine commission of executing wrath as a matter of retributive justice. Citizen subjection was proper, then, both because of "punishment" and for the sake of civil conscience (13:5).[135] Inasmuch as rulers fulfilled their function, taxes in their support should be accepted (3:6).

Käsemann said the passage in 13:1–6 was not eschatological, and he probably is correct. However, Käsemann added that the passage represented a one-sided argument motivated by a feared enthusiasm that needed to be curbed. In support, Käsemann mentioned the dominant place of derivatives of the ταγ- (*tag-*) stem in the verses, also noted by Cranfield.[136] For Käsemann, these derivatives have an antienthusiastic function elsewhere in the Pauline Epistles.[137] The point is moot, however, since Käsemann made no attempt to demonstrate that the situation at Corinth was the same at Rome.

Because Käsemann gave an eschatological meaning to 12:19 may suggest why he did not entertain an association between 12:19 and the demonstrably non-eschatological 13:4. The two passages could not be associated very well if one were eschatological and the other were not.

---

[132] Delling, *TDNT*, s.v. "τάσσω," 8:29–30.

[133] Deissmann, *Light*, 86–87.

[134] Käsemann, *Romans*, 353.

[135] Cf. Let. of Aris. 254. Cranfield noted that the verb "to be subordinated" (ὑποτάσσεσθαι, *hypotassesthai*) does not refer to "obedience" as much as to recognition that one is placed below another by God, that the other person is the representative of Christ to someone, "Some Observations on Romans XIII:1–7," 241–49.

[136] Cranfield, *Romans*, 2:69–70.

[137] As in Rom 12:3; 1 Cor 7:24; Käsemann, *Romans*, 351, 359.

However, if the eschatological interpretation of 12:19 is removed, a connection to 13:4 becomes not only possible, but probable, especially in light of the mutually complementary roles the two passages then exhibit as they function to interpret one another. The present chapter division may disguise the connection. The comments in 13:1–6, therefore, probably should be understood as an expansion of 12:17–21.[138]

SUMMARY

Romans 1:18

In Rom 1:18–4:25, Paul set out to demonstrate the universal disobedience of humans. In Rom 1:18–32, Paul set forth the present revelation of God's wrath. Divine wrath impounded humans in their disobedience to the revealed creator. Although Paul used the language of Jewish-Hellenistic apologetics, he inverted the logic to produce an accusation against humankind's suppression of the knowledge of God in unrighteousness. Paul focused the meaning of the revelation of God's wrath in the expression, "God delivered them over." God's deliverance was a transfer of lordship. God transferred humans over to the lordship of lust. Humans were allowed to choose their own perverted lust to take the rightful place of God. The divine verdict upon this choice of lust was "guilty," which Paul expressed with the potent thought, "disapproved mind." Paul's word play in Rom 1:28 was that as humans did not "approve" to have God's mind, God correspondingly "disapproved" this thinking pattern of the human mind. The vice list Paul produced illustrated the divine deliverance over to the lordship of lust. In the unrighteous lordship of lust, humans were called to account before God. The content of God's revelation of wrath was that the "disapproved mind" would lead to the ultimate destiny of eschatological death. Spiritual death, then, was God's "sentence" on the "disapproved mind."

This exegesis demonstrates that Dodd misrepresented Paul on the nature and function of the wrath of God, joined by others uncomfortable with a "God of love" also being a "God of wrath." While Paul does not present God as in a fit of uncontrollable emotion, Paul still understood and taught that God expressed his wrath. This expression

---

[138] Kallas's assertion that Rom 13:1–7 is a later non-Pauline interpolation has no support in the Greek manuscripts ("Romans XIII:1–7; an Interpolation," 365–74).

was revelation. Revelation basically means humans learned something they otherwise would not know so that they might repent and have life. Wrath is not simply the impersonal nexus of cause and effect. Even Greek philosophers were wise to that simple observation. Wrath, understood in a Pauline sense, is God at his best when humans are at their worst as God continues even to the last moment to try to save.

Many have noted the intertextuality of Romans 1. The most common motifs mentioned are Adam and Israel. Seeing the Genesis account of Adam behind Romans 1 is enticing, especially since the Adam motif will become explicit in Romans 5. The weakness of the theory is the inability to account for the present tenses of the verbs in Romans 1. However, as a means of dismantling the arbitrary division of humankind into Jew and gentile social categories, the allusions have rhetorical purpose.

The other intertextuality feature of Romans 1 actually is a feature of all of Romans. The bottom line to exegesis of Romans is that Romans is all about Israel. The history of Israel and Aaron's golden calf at the base of Mount Sinai before Moses can come down with the law God has for Israel is written all over Rom 1:23. Israel's story is the story of God's wrath. The conundrum of that story is how Isaiah's vision of Israel's destiny to call the nations to God will be fulfilled.

Romans 2:5, 8

In Rom 2:1–10, the theme of the universal guilt Paul began to apply more directly to Jewish humanity. The similarity of Paul's language to synagogue worship traditions reflected in Targum readings implicitly shows that he was addressing the Jew in this section, although the Jew specifically is not mentioned until 2:17. Thus, the "forbearance" of God in Rom 2:4 in context is related to God's present action concerning Jews who are disobedient to the gospel (cf. 2:8). In a later section, Paul charged that Jewish confidence in the law obscured the law's revelation of wrath through the curse (4:15). In the second chapter, Paul related the Jewish behavior concerning the revealed law to the pagan behavior concerning the revealed creator—disobedience. If persisted in without repentance and positive response to the gospel, such behavior was simply storing up wrath for the day of wrath.

Romans 3:5

In Rom 3:5, Paul insisted that God was not unrighteous to inflict his wrath, even though human unrighteousness demonstrated the righteousness of God. Romans is about Israel, and the allusion here is to the exile. This circumstance was not an excuse for humans to increase unrighteous behavior to further the display of the righteousness of God. In Rom 3:9, Paul included Jewish humanity into that humanity characterized as unrighteous in 1:18–32. Pagans had been disobedient to a revealed creator, but this theme of human disobedience to God was universal because the Jews, in reality, had been disobedient to God's revealed law. God inflicted the exile, and was absolutely just to do so. Indeed, not to annihilate the nation from the face of the earth was a move of pure mercy on God's part for the sake of his Name.

Romans 4:15

After Paul showed that all had been shut up by God in disobedience in Rom 1:18–4:25, he moved on to outline how God was able to show mercy to all through grace in the obedience of faith brought about in Jesus Christ. For his presentation of the grace in Jesus Christ, Paul reinterpreted the promise to Abraham that he would be heir of the world. The promise could not be realized through the law because of the wrath of the curse (4:15). The promise to Abraham was fulfilled in Jesus Messiah in the obedience of faith. Abraham's heirs were those of the faith of Abraham, a promise realized in Jesus.

Romans 5:9

In Rom 5:9, the reign of grace in Jesus Messiah inaugurates freedom from the wrath of God. This freedom includes deliverance from final wrath and its destiny of death. The truth of eschatological deliverance into the new aeon of the Messiah Paul expounded in the Adam and Christ typology following this reference to divine wrath in 5:12–21. The typological development takes the discussion all the way back to a creator God and the root cause of universal human disobedience. The opening discussion of the revelation of God's wrath in Rom 1:18–32 now comes to fruition. Paul integrates wrath and grace into his gospel. Theologically, grace cannot have its most potent effect for salvation absent the reality of the divine wrath. Otherwise, any less serious concept of God's holiness and righteousness turns so-called "grace" in reality into God's complicity with evil by indulging sin, even worse than Zeus indulging Athena over Achilles.

Romans 9:22

In Romans 9–11, Paul returned to the motif of the promise to Abraham in order to relate his preaching of the gospel to the nations of the world to the salvation of Israel. In Rom 9:22, "vessels of wrath" was an expression related to those who rejected the gospel. God's forbearance with the "vessels of wrath" was the consummation of a continuing forbearance with Israel since the exile. The wrath that God expressed in Israel's exile was subordinated to the proclamation of the divine Name among the nations. Israel was not destroyed utterly, which would have been just, but would not have accomplished God's purposes. Israel was preserved as a remnant through whom God could glorify his Name as associated with Israel. God vindicated the profanation of his divine Name in Israel's disobedience to him during the days of kingship in Israel through the coming true king, the Messiah. Through Jesus, who came out of the stock of Israel, Israel's task of the proclamation of the divine Name among the nations now was being accomplished. The response of the nations to the preaching of the gospel was proof of the honoring of the divine Name among the nations. Paul's preaching of the gospel to the nations was his participation in the honoring of the divine Name among the nations that was the task of the Israel of God. As apostle of the gospel of God, Paul considered himself faithful in the deepest sense to his Jewish heritage and Israel's mission. Paul included himself among the "vessels of mercy" that had responded positively to the gospel. Paul himself was an example that Israel's hardening to the gospel was only partial. The mystery of the partial hardening of Israel was, in the profound wisdom of God, part of the divine plan for the salvation of all Israel. However, in the context of the Christ-event and the preaching of the gospel, Paul felt God's present forbearance with the "vessels of wrath" was critical to assess and absorb. The coming of the gospel was the harbinger of eschatological judgment.

Romans 12:19; 13:4–5

A non-eschatological meaning for divine wrath is present in Rom 12:19 and 13:4–5. In Rom 12:19, Paul admonished Roman believers to give place to the wrath of retributive justice, and not to take the matter of retribution into one's own hands. God's business of divine retribution is not a matter for any one person's individual judgment.

In Rom 13:1–6, Paul expanded this exhortation in Rom 12:19. He turned attention to civil obedience. In the context of the government with which he dealt in the first part of Nero's reign, which was good due to the presence of court advisors Seneca and Burrus, Paul explained that the retribution of the civil magistrate accomplished divine retribution, since the function of ruling authorities was a divine ordination. The "punishment" administered by the civil magistrate discussed in Rom 13:4–5 reflects the typical Greek idea that proper rulers properly avenge injustice in society.

7

Pauline: Other Contexts
Prison Epistles and Implicit Contexts

THE LANGUAGE OF DIVINE WRATH Paul uses in Romans is so distinctive as almost to beg the claim of being unique in the ancient world. Unfortunately, his subtlety often has been missed and the power of his hermeneutic lost to the detriment of Pauline theology. Yet, Paul also can invoke uses of divine wrath in Romans that are right down the line literary motifs his audience would find familiar.

PRISON EPISTLES

Two remaining letters to consider with explicit references to the wrath of God are Ephesians and Colossians. Pauline authorship of these epistles has been the object of debate since the Tübingen style of criticism inaugurated by F. C. Baur. In general, Ephesians is less trusted as Pauline than Colossians, but often the reasons given are faulty, such as complaining that the impersonal tone and absence of knowledge of the recipients does not correspond with Paul's three years of mission work in that city. Yet, this complaint assumes what the original Greek manuscripts do not support: that the document originally was composed specifically for Ephesus.[1] In these and other ways, adequate re-

---

[1] "In Ephesus" in Eph 1:1 is missing in the earliest and best manuscripts; cf. Metzger, *Textual Commentary*, 601.

sponse in defense of Pauline authorship of these letters has been made and is assumed in this study.[2]

Another issue is the close literary relationship between Ephesians and Colossians.[3] While this issue needs adequate explanation, the following discussion will show that the matter becomes a moot point for the purposes of this study. The mother lode of what Paul has to say about divine wrath already is provided in the undisputed letters of 1 Thessalonians and Romans, so the matter of authorship and literary relationship, while important considerations, will not weigh adversely against the results already established in this survey of Pauline language of divine wrath. On the other hand, even if these documents are written by a disciple of Paul or in a later generation of Pauline communities, the usage simply confirms that the basic lines drawn by Paul on divine wrath are maintained in later generations with little modification.

Ephesians 2:3

The Hebraism "children of wrath [ὀργῆς, *orgēs*] by nature" occurs in 2:3. Probably the idea behind this expression is "deserving of wrath." The "by nature" in this context means "naturally."[4] The idea is of being marked out for wrath, as in Cain's description as a "son of wrath" in *Apoc Mos*. 3.

The two expressions "childen of disobedience" and "children of wrath by nature" are complementary. Disobedience and wrath are associated through these expressions in this passage. The association between disobedience and wrath leads to the observation of parallels between this passage in Ephesians and Paul's presentation in Romans. The universal disobedience of humans presented in Rom 1:18—3:20 is reflected in the expression "children of disobedience." The present revelation of divine wrath in Rom 1:18–32 is reflected in the expression "were children of wrath by nature." The basic instrumentality of human lust effecting immorality in Rom 1:24 surfaces again here in Eph 2:3.

---

[2] Achtemeier, Green, and Thompson, *Introducing the New Testament*, 378–80; 418–20; Marshall, Travis, and Paul, *Exploring the New Testament*, 2:223–27; deSilva, *Introduction*, 685–89; 696–701; 716–23; Carson and Moo, *Introduction*, 337–50.

[3] Marshall, Travis, and Paul, *Exploring the New Testament*, 169–72.

[4] Abbott, *Ephesians and Colossians*, 44–45. Lincoln, *Ephesians*, 99. Bruce, *Colossians, Ephesians, Philemon*, 284–85. The expression occurs in Sib. Or. 3:309.

Further, in Eph 2:3 lust is coordinated with errant human "reasoning," reflecting the "disapproved mind" of Rom 1:28. The presentation of divine wrath in Romans led to the presentation of the universal reign of grace in Rom 3:21—8:39. This logical flow is paralleled in the present passage in Ephesians, since reference to the "children of wrath" is followed by reference to the gift of salvation through faith grounded in grace (2:5-8). Thus, in a theologically concentrated form, the essence of Rom 1:18—8:39 is given in Eph 2:1-10.

Ephesians 5:6

In 5:1-20, judgment is understood as a reality for the church.[5] Constructions using imperatives convey the exhortations. The believer is exhorted to "walk" in love, purity, and integrity (5:2-4). The one who was immoral, impure, covetous, or an idolater had no inheritance in the kingdom of Messiah and God, "For because of these things the wrath of God [ἡ ὀργὴ τοῦ θεοῦ, *hē orgē tou theou*] comes upon the children of disobedience" (5:6).[6]

The following admonition to the church functioned as a warning: "Be not fellow partakers with them" (5:7). The similar expression in 5:11 seems to indicate the avoidance of the deeds of darkness. The problem seems to have been the possibility of relapse into sin. The warning was that divine wrath would not discriminate between pagan immorality and immorality in the church. In 5:1-14, disobedience and disinheritance were applied to the church itself through the language of divine wrath.[7] This warning parallels that of the warning that olive branches could be pruned off in Rom 11:20-24. Although one might wonder if the wrath here is the revealed wrath that works through history in real time, as in Rom 1:18 and 3:9, the context in Ephesians seems to be eschatological, as in Rom 2:5. Expressions such as "he also raised us up with him" (Eph 2:6) and "in the coming ages" (Eph 2:7) give this passage an air of consummation and final judgment.

---

[5] Cf. Ps 38:1 (LXX).

[6] Cf. Rom 14:17; 1 Cor 6:9-11; 15:50; Gal 5:21; 2 Thess 1:5. The Tannaitic baptismal catechism included the depiction of a former life of sin contrasted to the present life of righteousness, followed by rehearsal of penalties; Daube, *The New Testament and Rabbinic Judaism*, 132-33. For the idea that the wrath of God "comes," see 1 Thess 1:10; Matt 3:7; Luke 3:7; cf. Rev 6:17; 11:18.

[7] Barth, *Ephesians*, 564, 592-98.

198 DIVINE WRATH IN PAUL: AN EXEGETICAL STUDY

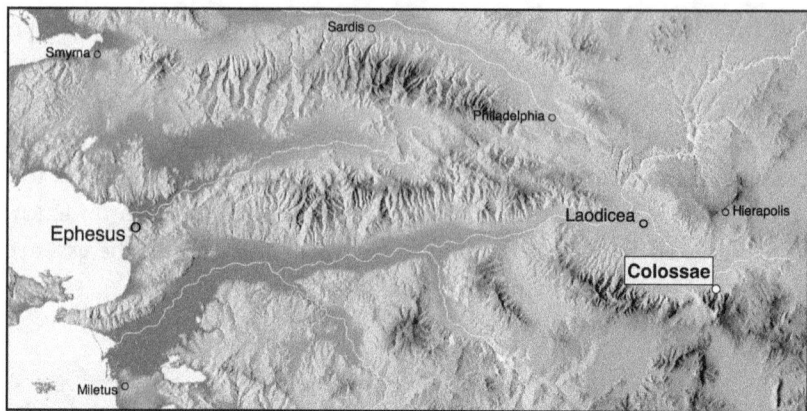

FIGURE 7.1. Map of Ancient Colossae. Colossae was part of a tri-city complex in the Lycus River valley along with Laodicea and Hierapolis, about 128 miles inland from Ephesus on the coast. Epaphras, one of Paul's associates on the Ephesian campaign, likely established the church at Colossae (cf. Col 1:7; 4:12; Phlm 23).

FIGURE 7.2. Colossae Tel. At the foot of Mount Cadmus, the tel of Colossae lies unexcavated. Laodicea nearby was destroyed by a powerful earthquake about AD 61, but rebuilt with its own wealth (Tacitus, *Ann.* 14.27). Colossae presumably did not survive.

Colossians 3:6

One distinctive idea in Colossians is "your life hidden in Messiah in God" (Col 3:3). This life hidden in Messiah was the consequence of a divine deliverance, "For He delivered [ἐρρύσατο, *errysato*] us from the authority of darkness and transferred us to the kingdom of his beloved Son" (1:13). The use of the verb "deliver" (ῥύομαι, *hryomai*), in an eschatological context of kingdom language is reminiscent of the formula in 1 Thess 1:10 and the expression in Rom 7:24.

The imperative "put to death" in 3:5 is expanded by three associated imperatives of what to do to fulfill this exhortation in "put away" (3:8), "do not live" (3:9), and "put off" (3:9). These imperatives are the negative side. Positively, the imperative "put on" is given in 3:10.[8] In the context of the negative imperatives, two vice lists of five elements each are produced (2:5, 8).[9] After the first vice list comes the warning, "For on account of these things comes the wrath of God [ἡ ὀργὴ τοῦ θεοῦ, hē orgē tou theou]" (3:6).[10] The meaning of the present tense here could be either predictive future or a statement of present reality. The future perspective seems to conform to the spirit of 3:6 as a warning admonition.[11] In Rom 1:18–32, God's wrath governs the growth of immorality (the idea of the "greenhouse of God's wrath"). In Eph 5:6 and Col 3:6, God's wrath falls on immorality. The two perspectives on divine wrath are thoroughly compatible. The wrath here is described with a verb such as "comes" implies that divine wrath is understood as an instrumentality of God more than an emotion. The believer is delivered from the terror of that dark time of reckoning that has to bear the divine wrath (1:13), which is a paraphrase of 1 Thess 1:10.

In short, explicit references to divine wrath in both Ephesians and Colossians are thoroughly compatible with statements in other undisputed Pauline letters. Indeed, they comprise concise restatements with similar nuances, particularly representing the Pauline view when the focus is eschatological. References in the Prison Epistles do not emend or altar results from a study of other occurrences in Paul.[12]

---

[8] Cf. Lohse, *Colossians and Philemon*, 136.

[9] In Col 3:12, a five-member virtue list accompanies the positive imperative.

[10] On the textual variant, "upon the children of disobedience," consult UBS[5] and NA[28] Greek texts. The variant has strong attestation, and the sense both allows and calls for the reading. The "you also" in 3:7 seems to indicate an assumed contrasting group of unbelieving gentiles. If the variant were original, its omission would have been accidental. At the same time, the parallel in Ephesians renders credible an early interpolation. Note Abbott, *Ephesians and Colossians*, 281–82; Metzger, *Textual Commentary*, 624–25.

[11] Cf. 1 Thess 1:10; 4:6; 5:9; Rom 2:5–6.

[12] Thus, as far as the language of divine wrath is concerned, explicit references to divine wrath in the Prison Epistles offer no challenge to Pauline authorship.

IMPLICIT CONTEXTS

Selected passages are examined for the language of divine wrath in those Pauline contexts in which the primary terms (ὀργή, θυμός, *orgē, thymos*) do not occur but the context involves related issues of judgment, eschatology, punishment, and so forth. The treatment does not need to be exhaustive to illustrate Pauline profiles. For this purpose, the approach is topical, arranged according to eschatological and non-eschatological contexts. The passage 2 Thess 1:5–10 receives closer attention because of its thematic expansions of comments in 1 Thessalonians.

Eschatological Contexts

Eschatological Destruction

Used only by Paul in the New Testament, the term "destruction" (ὄλεθρος, *olethros*) occurs in 1 Cor 5:5; 1 Thess 5:3; 2 Thess 1:9; and 1 Tim 6:9. All contexts are eschatological, except 1 Tim 6:9. In the Septuagint, we have the extremely rare expression, "eternal destruction" (ὄλεθρον αἰώνιον, *olethron aiōnion*), found only at 4 Macc 10:15. In 1 Thess 5:3, *olethros* stands in contrast with "salvation" (σωτηρία, *sōtēria*) in 5:9.

The background of the Septuagint is germane.[13] In the Septuagint, *olethros* often referred to supernatural intervention in the form of the judgment of God upon the heathens, or, less frequently, upon Israel.[14] Both Jer 31:8 and Obad 12:13 illustrate the synonymous connotations of *olethros* and *apōleia* (ἀπώλεια). In Ezek 6:12–14, reference to the desolation (*olethros*) of the land parallels the statement, "and I will consummate my anger against them."[15] Note that the language of divine wrath is incorporated into this context of *olethros*. Ezekiel 6:12–14 is important because the war, sword, siege, famine, pestilence, and desolation of the land were prophesied against Israel itself.

---

[13] Frame, *Thessalonians*, 187, said the figure in 1 Thess 5:8 was natural to Paul. Yet, similarity to Isa 59:17 might suggest that in 5:1–11, Paul's thought was moving along the lines of Hebrew Scripture. Thus, the context of the LXX may help to explain Paul's expressions at various points; e.g., cf. 2 Thess 1:8, 9 and 1 Cor 10:22.

[14] E.g., Jer 28:55; 31:3, 8, 32; Ezek 6:14; 14:16; Obad 13.

[15] Ezek 6:12. (LXX): καὶ συντελέσω τὴν ὀργήν μου ἐπ᾽ αὐτούς *(kai suntelesō tēn orgēn mou ep autous)*.

As in the Septuagint, Paul also used *olethros* with the meaning of destruction. Another Pauline word used for destruction was ἀπώλεια (*apōleia*) and its cognates, usually occurring in eschatological contexts and contrasted to "salvation" (σωτηρία, *sōtēria*).[16] Paul also contrasted *sōtēria* with θάνατος (*thanatos*) in 2 Cor 7:10.

By taking note of Paul's use and the Septuagint background, the question arises whether the elements of the triad *olethros-apōleia-thanatos* function as theological equivalents in Paul for the operation of divine wrath. This equivalency is suggested in that these words are set by Paul into eschatological contexts standing opposite in meaning to "salvation." Thus, the function of each member of the triad appears to be compatible to the operation of "the wrath of God" (ἡ ὀργὴ θεοῦ, *hē orgē theou*).[17] In Paul, the triad augmented the theological meaning of "wrath" (ὀργή, *orgē*) as the opposite of "salvation" (σωτηρία, *sōtēria*), an idea explicit in 1 Thess 5:3, 9.

Eschatological Retribution

Jesus is portrayed in 2 Thess 1:5–10 in a judgment theophany.[18] His appearance is described with the word "revelation" (ἀποκάλυψις, *apokalypsis*, 1:7).[19] The *apokalypsis* itself is given further description through three prepositional phrases in 1:7b–8a: (1) "from heaven," (2) "with his powerful angels," and (3) "in fiery flame."

The first prepositional phrase, "from heaven," makes sense, as heaven was the present sphere of Messiah's hidden life, in Paul's thought, at the right hand of God.[20] The concept of "from heaven" also suggests both the cosmic significance and the inescapability of the event.[21]

---

[16] 2 Thess 2:10; 1 Cor 1:18; 2 Cor 2:15; Phil 1:28.

[17] Cf. the function of τέλος (*telos*) in 1 Thess 2:16.

[18] The Pauline authorship of 2 Thessalonians is in dispute. The issue of pseudepigraphy already was discussed in the context of Ephesians and Colossians. This passage is included to demonstrate Pauline verisimilitude in terms of the language of divine wrath.

[19] Use of the term in a religious context was foreign to Greek thought; cf. Trench, *Synonyms*, 354; Oepke, *TDNT*, s.v. "καλύπτω," 3:571. Paul's use seems to emphasize the divine initiative in the eschatological crisis and the supernatural directive of the events.

[20] Cf. Rom 8:34; 1 Thess 1:10; 4:16.

[21] Cf. Rom 1:18, but the Romans context is a historical revelation in the present lives of rebellious creatures, whereas 2 Thess 1:7 is eschatological. Even so, these two revelations are interrelated theologically. The historical anticipates the eschatological.

FIGURE 7.3. Signorelli's Judgment Angels. Signorelli's fresco masterpiece (1499–1502) depicting scenes of the Apocalypse in the chapel of the Madonna di San Brizio in Orvieto, Italy. This scene is over the doorway exiting the chapel nave back into the main auditorium of the Orvieto Cathedral. Tour guides point out the "death rays" of the angels of divine judgment, apparently under the spell of one too many Star Trek movies. Signorelli's images and scenes, while a Renaissance masterpiece, reveal the serious problem in art and in theology in trying to understand the operation of the judgment of God. The matter becomes acute in preconceived ideas of any age that unthinkingly and automatically are imported into reading the Bible.

The second prepositional phrase, "with his powerful angels," has an apocalyptic background. In non-canonical literature, the presence of angels heightened the supernatural character of judgment or they participated themselves in the final retribution.²² Gaster said these traditions used Zech 14:5, in which the "holy ones" (קְדֹשִׁים, *qdšym*) accompany the Lord in a judgment theophany.²³ What was the function of the angels in 2 Thess 1:7? Some apocalyptic texts have them participating in the judgment as agents of retribution. Grammar, however, indicates the participle translated "inflicts" is in the singular, that is, is in concord with the singular "Lord Jesus," not with the angels.²⁴ Thus, Jesus alone performs the action in this context. The angels are secondary. They serve to heighten the supernatural character of the revelation, but not to participate in the retribution.

The third prepositional phrase, "in fiery flame," is awkward, because literally the expression, "in a flame of fire," is logically backwards; the meaning is clear, but the grammatical form confusing.²⁵ Scribes altered the phrase to the more natural "in a flame of fire."²⁶ The construction in the text is rare but is found in Exod 3:2 (LXX).²⁷ Perhaps the most influential text in terms of the wording of "fiery flame" in an eschatological context is Isa 66:4, 15, in which God metes out punishment as an avenger to those afflicting his people.²⁸ The move is classic Pauline hermeneutic. The original text is referring to God as the Lord and those not obeying him. Paul has subsumed Jesus Messiah under the rubric of "Lord" and the gospel as the issue of the disobedience.²⁹

---

[22] 1 En. 1:8–9 (cf. Jude 14–15); 53:3; 63:1; 91:5, 14; T. Levi 2:11; 3:3; 2 Bar. 51:11; at Qumran, H 3:34–36; 10:35; W 1:1–7; 15:14; Ex 1.1.5–15; LJ 12:15.

[23] Gaster, *Dead Sea Scriptures*, 249, n11.

[24] I.e., "when he inflicts" (διδόντος, *didontos*). Note the near absence of angels cooperating in the judgment in rabbinic thought; cf. Str-B 1:672–73; Grundmann, von Rad, and Kittel, *TDNT*, s.v. "ἄγγελος," 1:84.

[25] The Greek is ἐν πυρὶ φλογός (*en pyri phlogos*). All "flame" inherently is "fire," so adding as a descriptor "of fire" to "flame" seems superfluous.

[26] Greek: ἐν φλογὶ πυρός, *en phlogi pyros* (B, D, G, et al.).

[27] Also Sir 8:10; Pss. Sol. 12:5; Acts 7:30 (A, C, E). Use of fire in theophanic revelations was common in the Hebrew Scripture (Exod 13:21; 19:18; Deut 5:4; Judg 6:21; Ezek 1:4; 8:2; Dan 7:9). The element of fire could represent the destructive nature of judgment (e.g., Isa 29:6; 66:15); cf. 2 Pet 3:10.

[28] Bruce, *1 and 2 Thessalonians*, 151; Fee, *First and Second Thessalonians*, 256–57. Some, however, dissent with the view of the influence of Isaiah 66, pointing out that the peculiar form of the phrase itself disallows the influence of Isa 66:15 (LXX). Rather, the odd phrasing itself suggests more the influence of Exod 13:1 (LXX); cf. Blass-Debrunner, *Grammar*, 92.

[29] Fee, *First and Second Thessalonians*, 257.

The "fiery flame" phrase in 2 Thess 1:8a could be interpreted as the judgment of retribution in 1:8b.[30] However, several observations indicate that the fire in 2 Thess 1:8 is not the destructive fire of judgment. First, as noted already, the angels in 1:7 do not participate in the judgment as agents of the divine retribution. This observation decreases the element of destruction that might appear to be present on a first reading. Second, commentators in general, as well as critical editors of the Greek New Testament, are agreed that the phrase "in a fire of flame" should be broken with a comma and related to the previous thought in 1:7, and not to the thought of the retribution in 1:8.[31]

While the fire in 1 Thess 1:7 should be understood as the fire of theophany[32] rather than the destructive fire of judgment, the thought should be expanded. Besides theophany and judgment, fire also was a sign of heavenly glory.[33] The idea of heavenly glory is allied to the idea of a theophany. But heavenly glory goes beyond the basic idea of divine presence. The heavenly glory is a revelation of the power and majesty of the divine presence. Several considerations support the view that "in a fire of flame" as intended in the context is meant to describe the "glory" character of the revelation as of the divine, not the nature of the retributive punishment, which actually is described otherwise here.

First, the use of fire and its brilliance as a motif of heavenly glory and divine majesty was common in the intertestamental literature.[34] So, the language is traditional and establishes a conventional context for understanding the passage. Second, the structure of 2 Thess 1:7–9 shows that the origin of the divine "glory" is the divine power asso-

---

[30] As the revelation itself, see Frame, *Thessalonians*, 232; Best, *Thessalonians*, 259; Morris, *Thessalonians*, 118. As the eschatological fire of judgment, see Lang, *TDNT*, s.v. "πῦρ," 6:944. Lightfoot maintained both aspects of the majesty of the revelation and the instrument of divine judgment, *Notes on the Epistles of St Paul*, 102.

[31] The noun "flame" (φλογός, *phlogos*) is genitive feminine singular.

[32] Or, more specifically, a Christophany in this Pauline context.

[33] Cf. Rev 1:14–15; 2:18; 19:12; note also heavenly beings in Rev 4:5; 10:1. Lang (*TDNT* s.v. " πῦρ," 6:946–47), noted this category but did not apply this perspective to the present passage in Thessalonians.

[34] In 2 En. 29:3, God created the angels out of fire, and their weapons and raiment also are represented as fire; cf. 2 Bar. 21:6. Rabbinic teaching was that the angels were created of fire (Str-B 3:678); cf. the Targum on Gen 1:26. Descriptions of angels included fire and radiance motifs: faces shining like the sun, eyes as burning lights, fire from the lips, the flaming hosts; see 2 Esd 7:97; 2 En. 1:5; 19:1; 2 Bar. 59:11.

ciated with Jesus (1:9).³⁵ In the context of 1:7–9, this glory that derived from the divine power is illustrated through the angelic retinue attending Jesus. The angels marked the appearing of Jesus as "from heaven." The angels in a "fire of flame" give substance to the event as a revelation. For Paul, until the parousia, the divine glory of Jesus is apparent only to the church. "In that day," however, the glory of Jesus openly will be revealed to the world through the blazing glory of the heavenly hosts.³⁶ Third, the actual penalty of the "retribution" Paul delineated explicitly in the context. In 1:9, the penalty of eternal destruction was not destruction by fire; rather, this destruction was exclusion from "the glory of his strength."³⁷ This "glory of his strength" in 1:9 in part will be manifest in the "angels of his power," a heavenly host that would appear "in a fire of flame," reflecting the splendor of the divine "glory." Paul anticipated a similar future transformation of believers that will reflect the divine glory.³⁸ Schoeps pointed to 2 Bar. 51:5, 12.³⁹ Especially note the lines in 2 Bar. 51:10:

> For in the heights of that world shall they dwell,
> And they shall be made like unto the angels,
> And be made equal to the stars,
> And they shall be changed into every form they desire,
> From beauty into loveliness,
> And from light into the splendor of glory.

Fourth, one may refer to the statement in 2:14: "And for this reason he called you through our gospel in order that you might obtain the glory of our Lord Jesus Christ." This statement in 2:14 seems coordinated with that already made in the previous letter in 1 Thess 5:9. In that passage, the negative content of salvation was deliverance from wrath. In the present passage in 2:14, the positive content is endowment with

---

³⁵ Taking "strength" (ἰσκύως, *ischyōs*) as genitive of origin. The coming of Messiah is the manifestation of exaltation power, Grundmann, *TDNT*, s.v. "δύναμαι," 2:305.

³⁶ Oepke, *TDNT* s.v. "καλύπτω,"3:583. On the multifarious roles given to angels in apocalyptic literature, see Russell, *The Method and Message of Jewish Apocalyptic*, 235–62.

³⁷ Probably adopted from Isa 2:10, 19, 21, (LXX), which contains the refrains of a judgment theophany; the Lord alone would be exalted "in that day" (Isa 2:11, 17).

³⁸ In 1 Cor 15:51–53 at the sound of the trumpet, similar to 1 Thess 4:16.

³⁹ Schoeps, *Paul*, 105, n1.

the divine "glory" (δόξα, *doxa*).[40] For this striking difference in Paul's approach, contrast the harsh language of eschatological destruction as in 2 En. 10:1–6. Paul spoke of judgment over unbelievers not as obsessively absorbed in conjuring lurid images of their ruin. Rather he did so to warn, instruct, or nurture the church.[41] As Towner noted, Paul's use of the language of divine retribution compares to that in the book of Daniel in terms of an absence of focus on gory details.[42] Hanson in his study on the development of apocalyptic literature in Jewish life pointed out that Isaiah 66 is representative of that prophetic focus not on the fate of those punished but on the deliverance for God's people: "the rather extended section of comfort and salvation in verses 7–14 is necessary, in that the latter clarifies the ultimate purpose behind Yahweh's mighty demonstration of power, namely, the final deliverance of the oppressed community."[43] Further illustrating the Jewish background, Jewish expressions are involved in the language of the might of divine glory that undergirds life for the believer.[44] One is reminded of the subordination of the language of retribution to the purpose of comforting afflicted believers in the book of Revelation.

A comparison of two verses in the two Thessalonian letters is instructive. They demonstrate theologically compatible ideas between the two letters when the incompatibility of their eschatology so often is emphasized. Note the striking parallel structure and eschatological frame:

- 1 Thess 5:9b:
"unto obtaining salvation through our Lord Jesus Messiah"
εἰς περιποίησιν σωτηρίας διὰ τοῦ κυρίου ἡμῶν Ἰησοῦ Χριστοῦ
eis peripoiēsin sōtērias dia tou kyriou hēmōn Iēsou Christou

- 2 Thess 2:14b:
"unto obtaining the glory of our Lord Jesus Messiah"
εἰς περιποίησιν δόξης τοῦ κυρίου ἡμῶν Ἰησοῦ Χριστοῦ
eis peripoiēsin doxēs tou kyriou hēmōn Iēsou Christou

---

[40] See Foerster and Fohrer, *TDNT*, s.v. "σῴζω," 7:993.
[41] Similarly, Roetzel, *Judgment*, 93.
[42] Towner, "Retributional Theology in the Apocalyptic Setting," 203–14.
[43] Hanson, *The Dawn of Apocalyptic*, 163.
[44] Lohse, *Colossians and Philemon*, 30, especially the notes.

Finally, the function of the angels from heaven as revealing the divine glory of Jesus has its earthly counterpart. When Jesus is to come, he would come "to be glorified in his saints on that day."⁴⁵

Therefore, the "retribution" in 2 Thess 1:8 Paul considered the task of Jesus and described this action as "eternal destruction" (1:9). However, Paul did not describe this "destruction" as by fire. The "destruction" was banishment, not burning. Paul explained that the "destruction" would be exclusion "from the presence of the Lord and from the glory of his strength."⁴⁶ The contrast Paul outlined was that the *doxa* from which unbelievers were separated was the *doxa* that the believers shared.⁴⁷ For Paul, these two opposing eschatological destinies centered upon the Lord Jesus Messiah. One destiny was life "with the Lord" (1 Thess 4:17); the other was "destruction" through exclusion "from the presence of the Lord" (2 Thess 1:9). To distinguish two different groups in 2 Thess 1:8 is unnecessary. That is, the "ones not knowing God" and the "ones not obeying the gospel of our Lord Jesus" are equivalent. The operation of the implicit divine wrath in this context is not described as a divine emotive reaction. The implicit wrath is described in terms of a presence denied ("from the presence of the Lord") and of a quality of existence subsequently lost ("from the glory of his strength").⁴⁸

Finally, we must note that the function of the Lord as "avenger" is not limited to unbelievers exclusively. In 1 Thess 4:6, Paul reminded Thessalonian believers that the Lord was an avenger among believers in their relationships with one another in the matters he was discussing. Admittedly, since the following passage in 5:1–11 on the "times and the seasons" and the parousia is eschatological, the question can be asked whether the intervention of the Lord as avenger in the preceding passage in 4:6 is in present history or at the parousia. The answer is not entirely clear, particularly in the light of a sense of imminence.⁴⁹

---

⁴⁵ 2 Thess 1:10; cf. Eph 1:12; Col 3:4.

⁴⁶ The proposition, "from" (ἀπό, *apo*) is a preposition after an implied verb of separation; cf. Frame, *Thessalonians*, 234; Lightfoot, *Notes on the Epistles of St Paul*, 103. For other translations, cf. Best, *Thessalonians*, 263; but, contrast Lohse, *TDNT*, s.v. "πρόσωπον," 6:777.

⁴⁷ See von Rad and Kittel, *TDNT*, s.v. "δοκέω," 2:254–55.

⁴⁸ A similar idea occurs in Jer 52:3.

⁴⁹ Note Schrenk, *TDNT*, s.v. "ἐκδικέω," 2:445.

Eschatological Anathema

Something that was "anathema" (ἀνάθεμα, *anathema*) fundamentally was a votive offering devoted to a god or goddess, as in gifts dedicated to God in the Jerusalem temple (2 Macc 2:13; Luke 21:50). The flip side of consecration to a god was being accused by a god. Curse is the typical meaning in the New Testament. Those plotting against Paul put themselves under a curse until fulfillment of their scheme (Acts 23:12, 14, 21). In a dramatic moment, Paul said he could wish himself accursed on behalf of his Jewish kinsfolk, which he defined as being "cut off" from Messiah (Rom 9:3). Ecstatic speech in the church could become excessive with the declaration, "Jesus is cursed" (1 Cor 12:3). Or, one could utter a curse as profanity (Mark 14:71). On occasion, this curse of anathema seems to have eschatological nuance.

1 Corinthians 16:22. Paul's anathema in 1 Cor 16:22 was an eschatological judgment pronouncement to the Corinthian congregation, as the juxtaposed "Our Lord, come!" (μαράνα θά, *marana tha*) demonstrates.[50] Käsemann categorized 1 Cor 16:22 as one of the pre-Pauline "sentences of holy law" delivered by charismatic prophets in the early church.[51] For Paul, the power of eschatological curse overtook those who contributed to the fragmentation of the body of Christ. While the curse was spoken in present time, the full force of the curse awaited the coming of Jesus to consummate its judgment. Invoking an eschatological curse that awaits its full enforcement in the future has a parallel in 1 En. 5:6j, 7c. Similarly at Qumran, the Levites were called upon to invoke an eschatological curse upon all who cast their lot with Belial (M 1:16—2:18). Such a curse was invoking the judgment wrath of God. Paul's anathema here has this eschatological nuance via the appeal to the coming of Jesus and assumes a function of the wrath of God.

Galatians 1:8-9. Paul's anathema curse is delivered twice in Gal 1:8-9. The first curse is spoken against heavenly functionaries, such as angels (Gal 1:8). The second curse is spoken against earthly functionaries, those preaching a false gospel (Gal 1:9). This doublet curse, then, subsumes the entire universe of both spiritual and physical worlds.

---

[50] Taken as an Aramaic prayer ("Our Lord, come!"), as demonstrated by Fitzmyer, "The Aramaic Language and the Study of the New Testament," 13.

[51] That is, *Sätze heiligen Rechtes*; Käsemann, *New Testament Questions of Today*, 66-81. Challenged by Berger, "Zu den sogenannten Sätzen heiligen Rechtes," 10-40.

The curse rhetorically indicates Paul does not consider the situation a "minor disagreement." Thus, distortion of the gospel has disastrous consequences for the lives of human beings and their eternal destiny. The judgment pronouncement in Gal 1:8–9 seems designed to jar the Galatians into realizing their perilous position. The anathema effectively activates exposure to the wrath of God. Desertion of Christ Jesus, in the context of the anathemas pronounced by Paul, would incur divine wrath. In this context, the curse is delimited to the one preaching the false gospel, not to the Galatians themselves. The one disturbing the Galatians would bear personal judgment (Gal 5:10). Paul entertained the hope that he could cause a return to Christ among the Galatians. At the same time, an element of contingency to his conviction seems expressed. Paul's warning placed a deserter into the same camp as the false preacher.[52]

Eschatological Disobedience

The contour of thought in Eph 4:17–19 is a silhouette of Rom 1:18–32. The wrath of God implicit within the context of Eph 4:17–19 becomes explicit in Eph 5:1–6. The degradation of pagan existence and God's judgment upon that degradation served as a warning for the church in the manner of its "walk."[53] This warning is reemphasized in the concluding statement, "Therefore, be careful how you walk" (5:15).

The wrath of God that can be inferred in 4:18 was not presented so much as a passion of God than as a predicament of humans. The reality of the wrath of God is "being separated from the life [ζωῆς, zōēs]

---

[52] Cf. Gal 4:11; 5:4. Roetzel equated the action in 1 Cor 5:3–5 with the anathema in 1 Cor 16:22 but classified the anathema a "milder form" of judgment that could be altered by repentance (*Judgment*, 122–23, 162). However, the two cannot be the same. Anathema curse did not intend the salvation of an individual, but was a grave warning of ultimate judgment. As Behm cautioned about a spoken anathema, "We can hardly think of an act of Church discipline," (*TDNT*, s.v. "ἀνατίθημι," 1:354). This evaluation is confirmed in Kleinknecht, Baumgärtel, Bieder, Sjoberg, and Schweizer, *TDNT*, s.v. "πνεῦμα," 6:435–36. Admittedly, the expression "destruction of the flesh that the spirit may be saved" in 1 Cor 5:3–5 is obscure and difficult to understand, but that does not negate that the end result is salvation. Donfried argued that "spirit" in this verse referred to the possible loss of the presence of the Holy Spirit as the divine gift to the church ("Justification and Last Judgment in Paul," 150–51), but that seems unlikely. For extended discussion of the exegesis of this difficult passage, cf. Fee, *First Epistle to the Corinthians*, 210–14.

[53] Cf. Eph 4:20–22; 5:7.

of God." If the "life of God" (ζωῆς τοῦ θεοῦ, *zōēs tou theou*) is equated with the idea of "eternal life" (ζωὴ αἰώνιος, *zōē aiōnios*), then the statement in Eph 4:18 (in the light of Eph 5:6) functions as the functional and theological equivalent to the statement in John 3:36. Functionally, in John 3:36 the wrath of God is said to abide on the one who does not obey the Son; in Eph 5:6 the wrath of God comes upon the sons of disobedience.[54] Theologically, in Eph 4:18, the condemnation is characterized as exclusion from the life of God. In John 3:36 the condemnation is that one "shall not see life [ζωήν, *zōēn*]" (cf. Jer 52:3). Further, the condition of wrath in both statements in John 3:36 and Eph 5:6 is a present experience, as the present tense verbs in each passage indicate. The thought is parallel, but literary dependence not likely.

Non-Eschatological Contexts

Law's Curse (Gal 3:1–14)

Paul's argument in Gal 3:1–14 is striking for its lack of application of the wrath of God in the passage. The curse had clear associations with the wrath of God in the ancient Hebrew mode of thought, and, as has been demonstrated, was a major part of prophetic speech leading into exile. The law was the theological foundation of blessing and cursing of the nation for faithfulness or unfaithfulness to Yahweh. The golden calf episode at the foot of Sinai was a straw in the wind of where the covenant experience of Israel eventually would land. Thus, law, curse, wrath, exile was a sequence already carved in stone, so to speak, from the beginning. Yet Paul never made such explicit association with the language of divine wrath in this context of speaking of the curse of the law where such language was right to hand, and almost required from a Jewish point of view.

Paul did have some explicit comments on the law and the wrath of God, such as, "the law works wrath" (Rom 4:15). In those contexts, to be clear, however, Paul never said explicitly that God's wrath was upon Messiah. Yet, in Gal 3:13, Paul did say of Messiah, "by becoming a curse for us" (γενόμενος ὑπὲρ ἡμῶν κατάρα, *genomenos hyper hēmōn katara*), but what does this mean? One could argue this assertion is simple historical observation: Jesus hung on a tree. Now, a Jew who

---

[54] On the motif of wrath and disobedience, cf. Barth, *Ephesians 4–6*, 25.

knew the law, as did Saul of Tarsus, knew that the Law said someone hanging on a tree had broken the Law and so, obviously, had been cursed (Deut 21:23). Jesus, however, broke no Law. Jesus's innocence offers quite the enigma to a Jew for interpreting the death of Jesus. If Jesus was totally innocent, then how did he come to hang on a tree? The biblical answer is that he hung on a tree because wicked leaders put him there. So, wicked leaders *treated* Jesus as a lawbreaker ("he blasphemes!" Matt 26:65), but he was not. So, we should be careful about assuming that Paul said the wrath of God was on Jesus, because Paul never actually said that explicitly. The Reformers, of course, made this logical deduction from this implicit context, and from there the tradition has propagated throughout Protestant exegesis of Paul.[55]

Handling the statement in Gal 3:13 as referring to how Jesus was treated and not to the reality of his person actually is parallel to the typical exegesis of 1 John 1:10. In the 1 John passage in referring to God, humans are said to "make him a liar" (ψεύστην ποιοῦμεν αὐτὸν, *pseustēn poioumen auton*). No one interprets that remark to mean God in his fundamental nature transforms into a liar. God is *treated* as if a liar, but he is not a liar. Jesus was *treated* as if a blasphemer, but he was not a blasphemer. So, Jesus did hang on a tree, like God being called a liar. However, Jesus did not hang on the cross because he suddenly was sinful. He hung on the cross because he was perfectly innocent, a spotless lamb sacrificed. Otherwise the sacrifice had no efficacy. Thus, Paul will say, indeed, "Messiah died for us" (Rom 5:8), and he will add that this death was "for our sins" (1 Cor 15:3), but nowhere can Paul ever be quoted as saying, "The wrath of God was on Messiah."[56]

Wilderness Wrath (1 Cor 10:1–12)

The exhortation in 1 Cor 10:1–12 was written as a warning against idolatry. Instances of wilderness wrath upon the Israelites provided allusions as argumentative support.[57] The first is the destruction of the generation released from Egyptian bondage who murmured against

---

[55] Cf. Calvin, *The Epistles of Paul the Apostle to the Galatians, Ephesians, Philippians and Colossians*, 55; Luther, *Galatians*, 279.

[56] That interpretation of Gal 3:13 is complex is understood. The caution here is that assumptions about the nature of the rhetoric too easily are made.

[57] Cf. use of the wilderness wrath motif in Heb 3:7–11, 15–19 (cf. 4:3).

Yahweh in 1 Cor 10:5 (Num 14:26–30). The second is the whoredom with the daughters of Moab that caused a plague of death in 1 Cor 10:8 (Num. 25:1–9). The third is the fiery serpents sent against complaints about the rough journey in 1 Cor 10:9. The fourth is the Korah rebellion in 1 Cor 10:10 (Num 16:19–50).

The first allusion to the murmurings against the divine manna provided the context for Paul's thought in his application of the warning in 1 Cor 10:14–33.[58] That application he capsulized in 1 Cor 10:22. The Corinthian Christian must not partake of the table of the Lord and also participate in pagan sacrificial meals. Otherwise, judgment would fall, as upon the Israelites who despised the manna. The Corinthian behavior would be spiritual harlotry, the parallel that likely called forth Paul's second example using the Moabite whoredom.

In the second example of wilderness wrath, Moabite whoredom, the Septuagint context might help to explain the only occurrence in the New Testament of the possibility of "provoking" (παραζηλόω, *parazēloō*) the Lord that appears in 1 Cor 10:22.[59] The issue was eating at what Paul considered the table of demons as if non-consequential. Paul asked, "Do we provoke to jealousy [παραζηλοῦμεν, *parazēloumen*] the Lord? Are we stronger than he is?" In Num 25:11 (LXX), the Lord told Moses, "Phineas the son of Eleazar the son of Aaron the priest has caused my wrath [θυμόν μου, *thymon mou*] to cease from the children of Israel, when I was exceedingly zealous in my jealousy [ἐν τῷ ζηλῶσαι μου τὸν ζῆλον, *en tōi zēlōsai mou ton zēlon*], and I did not consume the children of Israel in my jealousy [ζήλῳ μου, *zēlōi mou*]." Paul's question to the Corinthians in 1 Cor 10:22 may reflect the use of the Septuagint context of the Moabite whoredom. Just as the Israelites in the wilderness could not avoid divine judgment, neither could the Corinthians withstand God if they continued to dishonor the Lord's table.[60] A matter of fundamental allegiance was at stake. This application here stands in contrast to 1 Cor 11:32. The later context did not involve the eschatological wrath of God, because behavioral correction by

---

[58] In Pauline writings, "murmur" (γογγύζω, *gongyzw*) is used only here; the verb possibly reflects the use of the LXX, as in the apparent parallel in Jude 16. Thus, the Pauline use of "murmur" in 10:10 may hint at common traditions in the early church informed by the wilderness wrath motif.

[59] Cf. similar ideas, but different vocabulary, in Heb 3:8, 15; 4:16.

[60] Cf. Moule, "Judgment Theme in the Sacraments," 472.

divine discipline probably was in mind. The matter of fundamental allegiance to God was not at stake as in the earlier passage.⁶¹

Divine Severity (Rom 11:19–22)

Paul perhaps suspected that his analogy of the grafting in of wild olive branches (Romans 11) could engender dangerous pride among gentile converts (Rom 11:19). Paul showed how the analogy not only was an example but also served as a warning as well. Natural branches were broken off because of unbelief, and the gentiles were grafted in by faith. A grafting analogy should have functioned to warn gentile believers that their unbelief would cause them to be cut off. Gentiles would not be spared, just as Israel was not spared.⁶² Paul concluded in 11:22, "Behold the kindness and severity [ἀποτομίαν, *apotomian*] of God; upon the ones who fell, severity, but to you God's kindness, if you remain in the [his] kindness; otherwise even you will be cut off."⁶³ Juxtaposition of both God's goodness and severity was a prominent theme in Jewish wisdom. The admonition Paul gave in

FIGURE 7.4. Ancient Olive Tree. Across the Kidron Valley from Jerusalem is the Mount of Olives, in ancient times having olive groves. Olive oil was a major part of the Judean economy. On the slopes today is this olive tree several centuries old.

---

⁶¹ *Contra* Roetzel, *Judgment*, 139.

⁶² Cf. Moody, "Romans," 244.

⁶³ The noun "severity" [ἀποτομίαν, *apotomian*] occurs only here in biblical Greek. The cognate noun, ἀπότομος (*apotomos*), occurs only five times (Wis 5:20; 6:5; 11:10; 12:9; 18:15), and the cognate noun, ἀποτόμως (*apotomōs*), occurs just once (Wis 5:22). Note that all cognate occurrences are in the Wisdom of Solomon.

Rom 11:20 followed wisdom style, and Paul's warning probably followed a Jewish wisdom theme.[64] In Jewish wisdom, the profound kindness of God usually is contrasted with the forensic severity of God. Paul may have considered the severity of God here as a divine attribute corresponding to the activity of divine wrath.[65] If so, divine wrath is implicit in the thought expressed by Paul in Rom 11:22. The severity in mind seems to echo the language of wrath concerning vessels of wrath in Rom 9:22–23. That the fate here in Rom 11:22 does not have to be considered permanent is integral to the argument in both metaphors of Romans 9 and 11. In Romans 9, vessels of wrath can become vessels of mercy. In Romans 11, as the natural branches, even though cut off, can be engrafted again, so also presumably the wild branches.

SUMMARY

Prison Epistles

After investigating the premier texts in 1 Thessalonians and Romans, the explicit language of divine wrath is found in the Prison Epistles. The usage showed typical Pauline contours already established. For example, the discussion in Eph 2:1–10 is closely analogous to Paul's earlier presentation in Rom 1:18–8:39. Then, in both Eph 5:6 and Col 3:6, the language of divine wrath functions as a warning and exhortation to the church itself, on a practical pattern evocative of Rom 12:19 and 13:4–5. Such use of the language of wrath also will be seen to be parallel to use in implicit contexts of the motif of wilderness wrath to warn Corinthian believers in 1 Corinthians 10.

Eschatological Implicit Contexts

Eschatological Destruction

Implicit contexts of divine wrath in Paul are more general and topical. Basically, they fall out, as one might expect, into eschatological and non-eschatological categories, that is, similar to the explicit cases. One example of a general category in the eschatological dimension is eschatological "destruction." Paul used a triad of terms, two rare terms

---

[64] Köster, *TDNT*, s.v. "τέμνω," 8:108. Cf. Wis 5:20; 6:5.
[65] So Barrett, *Romans*, 218.

for destruction and one for death. These terms characteristically and distinctively are tied to the operation of eschatological wrath.

Eschatological Retribution

Another category is eschatological "retribution," a standout example of which is 2 Thess 1:5–10. The study revealed that this passage, though couched in apocalyptic rhetoric, does not contradict what Paul said in explicit contexts about divine retribution. Divine retribution in 2 Thess 1:5–10, that is, is not the language of burning in the fires of Gehenna. Retribution, rather, quite radically is described as the reality of a presence denied and a quality of existence subsequently lost, all centered on the divine glory of Jesus Messiah. Paul, that is, in comparison with the world around him, was quite restrained, measured and calculated in how he presented and worded the nature of God's retribution. A tendency to recoil from the language of divine wrath may be a matter more of not actually reading Paul and simply assuming Homer.

Eschatological Anathema

Another general eschatological category is the anathema curse. Although rare in Paul, the anathema curse was a serious act of prophetic judgment on behalf of God that anticipated God's final judgment. In 1 Cor 16:22 and Gal 1:8–9, Paul used the anathema curse as a means of conveying the reality of eschatological judgment. His pronouncement here has a foreboding finality to its expression, as if destiny were in the balance.

Eschatological Disobedience

Finally, a disobedience motif is another implicit use of divine wrath in an eschatological context. The thought in Eph 4:17–19 is an example. A study of this passage shows a compatibility with Pauline language in explicit contexts. The "children of disobedience" in the Ephesians passage, for example, have the same characterization and destiny as the "vessels of wrath" of Romans 9. More interestingly, though, Eph 4:17–19 turns out to be the functional and theological equivalent in the Pauline universe of thought to the explicit use of wrath in John 3:36.

Non-Eschatological Implicit Contexts

Curse of the Law

The rhetoric of the curse of the law in Gal 3:13 is a non-eschatological implicit context that assumes the reality of the wrath of God. The curse of the law, of course, historically is consummated in the exile. Paul, however, is not explaining the exile in Gal 3:13. Rather, he is providing a hermeneutic on the death of Jesus in terms of the law's pronouncement that anyone who hangs on a tree is cursed of God. While the theological discussion is complex, Paul probably should not be interpreted to mean that he understood God's wrath to be upon Jesus. More likely, Paul meant simply that wicked humans treated Jesus as cursed because they hung him on a tree. God however, overturned that verdict with the resurrection, meaning that Jesus was not cursed; in fact, he was innocent entirely of any sin. Thus, the law's declaration in this case has to be understood within the reality of Messiah.

Wilderness Wrath

Wilderness motifs provide other examples of implicit divine wrath in in non-eschatological contexts. In 1 Corinthians 10, Paul used multiple examples of wilderness wrath to warn Corinthians about the gravity of participation in pagan sacrificial meals. Whatever judgment is presumed to take place would happen in current time, as for the Israelites in their wilderness journeys.

Divine Severity

The severity of God is another implicit context that is non-eschatological. In Rom 11:12, Paul used the Jewish wisdom theme of the paradox of the kindness and severity of God to warn gentile believers that their grafting into the stock of Israel was not unconditional. Through the same severity of God that had cut off branches of unbelieving Israel, gentile unbelief could invoke a like consequence. Paul's analogy of the grafting in of wild olive branches was not to be the basis of gentile boasting.

8

Conclusion

Divine Wrath as Pauline Theology

PAUL'S EXCLUSIVE USE OF THE PRIMARY terms for divine wrath may have been in line with a literary trend whose incipient forms in Jewish thought could be represented in the translational features of the Septuagint. The Septuagint translators knew Homeric terms for wrath, but they seemed to avoid them intentionally in contexts of Yahweh's wrath. Epicurean and Stoic philosophers already had criticized uncontrolled and harsh outbursts of anger by the gods in Greek myth. However, the Homeric language of wrath continued to be a popular understanding. Prayers to the gods for help and propitiation of the gods against harm continued to remain important to common people.

The impact of Greek ideas on Hebrew thought is evident in works such as 4 Maccabees and the Letter of Aristeas, and in writers such as Philo. While the wrath of Yahweh could be described in graphic images and using frequent anthropomorphisms by ancient Hebrew writers, the concern of Septuagint translators may have been to eliminate a too facile identification of the wrath of Yahweh with that of the Greek gods. The Hebrew idea of Yahweh's wrath, though pictured with vivid imagery, was bound by convictions of Yahweh's holiness and his consistently righteous action. Further, Yahweh was understood to be gracious and merciful and by nature slow to wrath. His relationship with his people was characterized by his lovingkindness. This relationship between Yahweh and his people was signified in his covenant. Yahweh's wrath was an aggressiveness to preserve his holiness and the integrity of his covenant. Yahweh's wrath demonstrated his personal zeal, his power to judge, and his sovereignty over Israel. However, Yahweh's wrath was subordinated to the proclamation of the divine Name. Yahweh judged Israel, but not so as utterly to destroy. In this way, Yahweh's wrath was personal and purposeful, but incomparable to the often capricious and vicious rage of the gods of Greek myth. In writers who were communicating Hebrew thought to a Greco-Roman world—Septuagint translators, Philo, Josephus—a preference for the primary terms over the Homeric terms for divine wrath might be evidence for a Jewish literary trend with which the New Testament writers including Paul were in sympathy.

However, caution needs to be exercised in making the above observation. Though not a Homeric term in particular, *orgē* had been in use as far back as Hesiod, and Greek inscriptions show the cultic use of *orgē*. Thus, the use of *orgē* in particular has ancient lineage even if not found in Homer. Writers such as Aristotle provide clear evidence that *orgē* could be equated with the Homeric terms for divine wrath. Further, this equation can be confirmed in the first centuries AD in writers such as Pausanias and in papyri evidence. Still, one might be justified in concluding that the *exclusive* use of the primary terms for divine wrath by Paul (*orgē*, *thumos*) when other terms were available in the semantic domain may have served at least to reduce associations with the undesirable connotations of Homeric terms for divine wrath.

Paul's language of wrath was not the language of an abstract principle. Paul did not think of God's wrath as simply a situation in which humans were left to themselves in a world where evil brought its own moral retribution. Though Paul did not speak of God's wrath as a passion of God, Paul's language of wrath still was personal. The language of divine wrath for Paul was a powerful way to describe the human predicament. Humans as created beings had made themselves enemies to their own creator by choosing the illegitimate lordship of their own lust. By rejecting the creator, humans had severed themselves from the very source of life, having embraced in reality a destiny of death. Creatures who had spurned the creator to worship idols and other items of their own making could understand Paul's language of wrath. The exchange of lordship on humanity's part was expression of a broken relationship between creator and creature. The function of the vice list in Rom 1:29–31 was not to demonstrate a principle of sin and retribution. Paul used the vice list to demonstrate a crucial exchange of lordship for which any human was responsible. All were culpable for disobedience to the creator. Even the nexus of sin and guilt in the context of the revealed law for Jewish humanity was not an impersonal process. Sin was sin against God. Divine wrath was the aggressiveness of divine zeal to preserve the integrity of personal relationship in the covenant to which Israel had bound itself as a nation through Moses.

Paul's eschatological language of wrath was personal because any theology grounded in the Christ-event would be, *de facto*, personal. The original disciples experienced the reality of Jesus as personal if anything else, and that personal reality is what threw Saul off his horse on the Damascus Road: "I am Jesus, whom you are persecuting" (Acts 9:5; Gal 1:12). That heavenly revelation that changed Saul's life plays into revelation language used of the wrath of God as presently "being revealed from heaven" (Rom 1:18). The language of wrath as related to the rejection of the gospel (e.g., 1 Thess 2:16) was not the language of impersonal retribution. By contrast, Paul described the retribution of Jesus in 2 Thess 1:5–10 in the personal terms of a presence denied and a quality of existence subsequently lost. To receive the gospel was to change personal reality to the new aeon "in Christ" (Rom 3:21) and to share a quality of existence of incomparable glory (Eph 2:1–7). Thus, Paul's language of wrath was the language of disrupted fellowship between God and humans that God was working to restore. Like the historian Polybius, Paul's use of the language of divine wrath, while not frequent, was judicious. Paul used the language of wrath to communicate carefully the human predicament in disobedience to God. Disobedience is not without serious consequence, whether now or in the final judgment, whether in the world or in the church. Quite unlike the gods and goddesses of Olympus, God expressed his wrath in order to try to save. God's wrath underscored his grace. God's wrath magnified God's grace. Therefore, a gospel supposedly exalting in the grace of God cannot be known nor appreciated for its inestimable value and eternal consequence without a proper theology of divine wrath.

A common feature in both Jewish and non-Jewish writers was the association of divine wrath with "impiety" or "godlessness." Thus, Paul's equation in Rom 1:18 of wrath against "godlessness" would have been quite familiar to his Greco-Roman readers. What those readers would not have evaluated properly was just what was "ungodly." That was up to a particular god or goddess to say. Paul made clear exactly what God the creator thought ungodly: creatures worshipping idols made with their own hands, not the creator, and thereby losing their way in proper behavior among themselves, most certainly not as beasts of the field with no image of God stamped on their creation. Jewish monotheism and creation theology are written all over Paul's theology of the wrath of God in Romans 1.

Uncommon to the Greco-Roman world was Paul's presentation of divine wrath as a divine "revelation." God does not create and walk away. God speaks. He communicates. He enjoins fellowship. He strives for consummating the purposes of creation. One of the ways God communicates is through his wrath. Paul insisted that the "revelation" through which God communicated presently was taking place and signified in the action "God delivered them over." The instrumentality of God's action was the lust of the human heart. The content of the revelation was that a mind turned away from the creator was a mind "disapproved" by God. The sentence of the divine verdict of living according to that mind was "death." Paul's language of wrath in Rom 1:18–32 was strategically different from that in apocalyptic contexts such as 1 Enoch or the Dead Sea Scrolls at the very point of the nature and purpose of the divine wrath. Paul said that the revelation of God's wrath was part of God's continuing efforts to save humanity. God through his wrath revealed the destiny of human disobedience in an effort to warn of impending doom. The reality of the revelation of wrath in Rom 1:18–32 made clear that the destiny of death was a self-induced consequence of one's own decisions, unlike the destiny produced by the wrath of the Homeric gods or the *fatum* of *ira deum* for Roman historians. Similarly, Paul inverted the logic of Jewish–Hellenistic apologetics by his presentation of the knowledge of God as a knowledge that condemned, not a knowledge that represented the highest ascent of the reason toward apprehension of the divine.

At the same time, the distinctiveness of the Pauline language of wrath in Rom 1:18–32 should not obscure how Paul elsewhere could incorporate Greek and Roman ideas without basic alteration. One example is the language of divine retribution in Rom 12:19 and 13:4, 5. Paul here has incorporated typical Greek expectations related to the exercise of divine wrath with little modification.

Study of the creedal formula that Paul worked into his introduction to 1 Thessalonians at 1:10 demonstrated the possibility that Paul's language of divine wrath took its essential form from the traditions of the primitive church in missionary preaching to the gentiles. Had Paul's language of divine wrath been rabbinic, its formulation probably would have been closer to that of Matthew, who seemed to relate the wrath of God to the concept of Gehenna. Paul, instead, coordinated his thought with the early preaching of the church on the death, burial, and resurrection of Jesus, which included a note of final judgment. Precisely on that note of final judgment Paul parked his thoughts on the nature and purpose of divine wrath, both now and future.

The centrality of the Christ-event also was crucial to Paul's understanding of the gospel and the gospel's relationship to eschatological issues. Jesus was the "one who delivers us from the coming wrath" (1 Thess 1:10). To be "in Christ" was to know freedom from the wrath of God (1 Thess 5:9; Rom 5:9). Eschatological life could be characterized as "with him" (1 Thess 4:17; 5:10; Eph 2:6; cf. 1 Thess 5:9; 2 Thess 1:9; Rom 8:35–39). In contrast, to be outside of Christ was to be exposed to divine wrath. The crux of the gospel for the language of wrath was that one's response to Jesus discriminated the issue of eschatological destiny. Similarly, obstruction of the preaching of the gospel was an eschatological sign pointing toward a person's final destiny in the disposition of divine wrath (1 Thess 2:6; Rom 9:22).

The theme of judgment is a common denominator in Paul's various uses of the language of wrath. Yet, complexity of application and emphasis on judgment marks Paul's language of wrath. At one point, Paul could incorporate the language of wrath from an early creed to summarize the theme of an epistle (1 Thess 1:10); at another point, Paul could use the language of wrath with a distinctively Pauline meaning to introduce another letter (Rom 1:18). Paul could use the language of wrath to comfort persecuted believers (2 Thess 1:5–10) and to inspire confidence in the hope of salvation in anxious believers (1 Thess 5:9). Still, Paul also could use the language of wrath as an exhortation of grave warning both to believers (1 Cor 16:22; Gal 1:8–9; Eph 5:6; Col 3:6; 1 Corinthians 10; Rom 11:12) and to nonbelievers (Rom 2:5–8). Paul's language of wrath could be non-eschatological, that is, anticipating an expression in contemporary history (Rom 1:18; 3:5; 4:15; 12:19; 13:4, 5) or eschatological, that is, fundamentally not consummated until the judgment (1 Thess 1:10; 5:9; Rom 2:5, 8; 5:9). Paul could speak of human responsibility (Rom 1:18–32) but later in the same letter could speak of "vessels of wrath" that had been "prepared" to show the riches of God's glory upon "vessels of mercy" (Rom 9:22). In these terms, tomorrow's destiny was revealed by today's choices.

The basis for this noetic flexibility seems to have been a semantic universe of general conceptual categories. One can establish connections between selected Pauline terms, such as "destruction," as trigger words for general eschatological categories orbiting around the language of wrath. Paul's eschatological terms were general terms. He could apply them as the particular circumstance and need directed. Paul's use of the language of wrath even could have an apocalyptic resonance (2 Thess 1:5–10) without typical apocalyptic nuances on the wrath of God. This apocalyptic profile can mislead readers expecting images of the death rays of God's angels wiping out humanity. Paul's own contextualization needs to be followed carefully to capture his literary distancing when he expresses himself with an apocalyptic seasoning to his sauce. One may compare the use of the language of wrath to comfort persecuted believers in the book of Revelation, which, likewise, often is so easily misread. The call by Jesus's disciples for fire from heaven to destroy a Samaritan village (Luke 9:54) is another example that may be contrasted to the overall statement in 2 Thess 1:8. Modern readers of Paul need to be careful not to read Paul like these disciples of Jesus mistakenly were trying to read Jesus.

Paul used scriptural judgment motifs in typical general categories (1 Corinthians 10; Rom 9:29), as with other New Testament writers (cf. Heb 3:11; 4:3; 10:25–39). Luke 21:23 provides a comparison of a general eschatological category of "coming wrath" (3:7) rendered with specificity and concreteness in terms of judgment of individuals in the book of Acts.

The Prison Epistles evidence Paul still anticipated the soon consummation of all things in an imminent parousia of Jesus. This expectation must be factored into his language of divine wrath. While the imminence factor may have diminished later in Christian thought, the Gospel of John, likely finalized in its canonical form toward the end of the first century, shows that the language of divine wrath continued to be preserved in later communities of believers. In light of this Johannine theology, a study of Eph 4:17–19 suggested a close analog both functionally and theologically to John 3:36. The analog in John 3:36 could be even more significant when set into the context of Eph 2:1–

10 in the same epistle. This passage was shown to preserve the essence of Rom 1:18–8:39 in a theologically concentrated form. One might speculate that the Pauline tradition concerning the language of divine wrath survived at Ephesus, and that John 3:36 is evidence for this continuing tradition, but that speculation historically is not demonstrable. The significance of John 3:36, if in any way reflecting Pauline traditions at Ephesus, would be that though the Pauline language of wrath may have been reformulated to accommodate a distinctive Johannine theology, particularly in its realized eschatology, the general categories of Pauline language of divine wrath were preserved.

Paul's language of wrath found its main orientation in the prophetic traditions of ancient Israel and the eschatological perspective characteristic of the early church as controlled by the events surrounding the story of Jesus the Messiah. In this context, Paul's language of wrath emphasized:

- God's decisive action in Christ—one's destiny as based on one's response to the gospel (1 Thess 2:16; 1 Cor 16:22; Gal 1:8, 9)

- God's revelation—his continuing efforts to save recalcitrant humans (Rom 1:18–32); the negative result of his revealed law, both as an instrument of "storing up" eschatological wrath in the day of God's judgment (Rom 2:5, 8), and as a misunderstood means of fulfilling the promise to Abraham (Rom 4:15)

- God's sovereignty—the sentence of "death" on the "disapproved mind" (Rom 1:18–32; Eph 2:3; 4:17–24); the severity with Israel (Rom 9:22; 11:22); the judgment of the church itself (1 Cor 10:22; Rom 11:22; Eph 5:6; Col 3:6)

- God's righteousness—in any expression of his judgment historically (Rom 3:5) or eschatologically in salvation history (Rom 9:22; 11:22)

- God's power—to use all means possible, whether conceived as negative or positive, to complete the work of salvation (1 Thess 1:10; 5:9; Rom 5:9) or to preserve his own (2 Thess 1:5–10)

- God's ordination of ruling authority—as one of the instruments of divine retribution in church and in society (Rom 12:19; 13:4, 5)

Thus, the revelation of the wrath of God in Paul's understanding operated in both historical and eschatological dimensions, and surfaced in his letters in both explicit and implicit contexts. Historically, divine wrath is revealed to disobedient creatures in God's greenhouse of wrath that forces the maturation of sin's deadly consequences in the attempt to enlighten darkened minds. Divine wrath also historically is revealed to a nation unfaithful in covenant obligations to a holy God through loss of land and nationhood. Divine wrath also historically is revealed in God the avenger acting on his own to bring justice into human experience, as well as by providing government as a divine avenger against those breaking the law, since humanity's basic curse is chronic disobedience, whatever the source of the law. God would not be God to allow violence and anarchy to reign endlessly among his creatures. Historical instances of divine wrath can be used to exhort the church. Eschatologically, divine wrath will be revealed at the last judgment. The last judgment will be the final destination of all the pebbles of divine wrath rolling down the hill of history to gather at the bottom into one pile before the inevitable finality of God's will.

Bibliography

Abbott, T. K. *A Critical and Exegetical Commentary on the Epistles to the Ephesians and to the Colossians*, ICC (Edinburgh: T& T Clark, 1897).

'*Abodah Zarah*. Translated by A. Mishcon and A. Cohen. In *The Babylonian Talmud*, Isidore Epstein, trans. and ed., 2 vols. London: Soncino Press, 1935.

Accordance, Version 13. OakTree Software Specialists, Altamonte Springs, Fla., 2013.

Achtemeier, Paul J., Joel B. Green, and Marianne Meye Thompson. *Introducing the New Testament: Its Literature and Theology*. Interpretation. Grand Rapids, Cambridge: Eerdmans, 2001.

Aeschylus. Translated by Herbert Weir Smyth. LCL. London: William Heinemann; New York: G. P. Putnam's Sons, 1922-26.

Aland, Barbara, Kurt Aland, Johannes Karavidopoulos, Carlo M. Martini, and Bruce M. Metzger, eds. *The Greek New Testament*. 5th Rev. ed. Stuttgart: United Bible Societies, 2014.

Aland, Barbara, Kurt Aland, Johannes Karavidopoulos, Carlo M. Martini, and Bruce M. Metzger, eds. *Novum Testamentum Graece*. 28th ed. Stuttgart: German Bible Society, 2012.

Ancient Near Eastern Texts Relating to the Old Testament. Edited by James B. Pritchard. 2d ed. Princeton: Princeton University Press, 1955

Apocalypses Apocryphae. Edited by Konstantin von Tischendorf. Hildescheim: Georg Olms Verlagsbuchhandlung, 1966.

Apocalypsis Baruchi Graece. Edited by J.-C. Picard. *Testamentum Iobi*. Edited by S. P. Brock. Pseudepigrapha Veteris Testamenti Graece, no. 2. Edited by A. M. Denis and M. De Jonge. Leiden: Brill, 1967.

Apocalypsis Henochi Graece. Edited by M. Black. *Fragmenta Pseudepigraphorum Quae Supersunt Graeca*. Edited by Albert-Marie Denis. Pseudepigrapha Veteris Testamenti Graece, no. 4. Edited by A. M. Denis and M. De Jonge. Leiden: Brill, 1970.

The Apocrypha of the Old Testament. Revised Standard Version. Edited by Bruce M. Metzger. New York: Oxford University Press, 1965.

The Apocrypha and Pseudepigrapha of the Old Testament in English; with Introductions and Critical and Explanatory Notes to the Several Books. Edited by R. H. Charles. 2 vols. Oxford: Clarendon Press, 1913; reprint ed., 1977.

Aristeas to Philocrates (Letter of Aristeas). Edited and translated by Moses Hadas. In *Jewish Apocryphal Literature, Dropsie College Edition*, Solomon Zeitlin, ed. New York: KTAV, 1973.

Aristides, Aelius. *The Complete Works: Orations 1–16*. Leiden, The Netherlands: Brill, 1997.

Aristotle. *The Art of Rhetoric*. Translated by John Henry Freese. LCL. London: William Heinemann; Cambridge: Harvard University Press, 1959.

Arndt, W. F., and F. W. Gingrich, trans. and eds. *A Greek-English Lexicon of the New Testament and Other Early Christian Literature*. 2d ed. rev. and augmented by F. W. Gingrich and F. W. Danker from Walter Bauer's 5th ed., 1958. Chicago: University of Chicago Press, 1979.

Aune, David Edward. *The Cultic Setting of Realized Eschatology in Early Christianity*. Supplements to Novum Testamentum, no. 28. Leiden: Brill, 1972.

Aurelius, Marcus. *The Communings with Himself of Marcus Aurelius Antoninus, Emperor of Rome, Together with His Speeches and Sayings*. Translated and revised by Charles Reginald Haines. LCL. London: William Heinemann; New York: G. P. Putnam's Sons, 1930.

Aurelius Victor: De Caesaribus. Translated with an Introduction and Commentary by H. W. Bird. Translated Texts for Historians LUP (Book 17). Liverpool: Liverpool University Press, 1994.

Aus, Roger David. "Comfort in Judgment: The Use of Day of the Lord and Theophany Traditions in Second Thessalonians 1." PhD thesis, Yale University, 1971.

_____. "God's Plan and God's Power: Isaiah 66 and the Restraining Factors of 2 Thess. 2:6–7." JBL 96 (1977): 537–53.

The Babylonian Talmud. Edited and trans. by Isidore Epstein, 2 vols. London: Soncino Press, 1935.

Barrett, C. K. *A Commentary on the Epistle to the Romans*. BNTC. New York, Evanston, London: Harper and Row, 1957.

_____. *From First Adam to Last: A Study in Pauline Theology*. London: Adam and Charles Black, 1962.

Barrett, C. K., ed. *The New Testament Background: Selected Documents*. New York: Harper and Row; Harper Torchbooks/The Cloister Library, 1961.

Barrois, G. A. "Jehoshaphat, Valley of," IDB 2:816.

Barth, Karl. *A Shorter Commentary on Romans*. Translated by D. H. van Daalen. London: SCM, 1959.

Barth, Markus. *Ephesians*. AB, Vols. 34, 34A. Garden City, NY: Doubleday, 1974.

_____. "Speaking of Sin; Some Interpretive Notes on Romans 1:18–3:20." SJT 8 (1955): 288–96.

Barton, William Eleazar. *The Samaritan Pentateuch: The Story of a Survival among the Sects*. Oberlin, OH: Bibliotheca Sacra Co., 1903.

Beare, Francis W. "The Epistle to the Ephesians: Introduction and Exegesis." IB. New York: Abingdon, 1953.

Becker, Jürgen. *Paul: Apostle to the Gentiles*. Trans. by O. C. Dean, Jr. Foreword by Marion L. Soards, Louisville: Westminster John Knox, 1993.

Beker, J. Christiaan. *Paul the Apostle: The Triumph of God in Life and Thought*. Philadelphia: Fortress, 1980.

Behm, Johannes. "ἀνατίθημι," TDNT 1:353–56.

Berger, Klaus. "Zu den sogenannten Sätzen heiligen Rechtes." NTS 17 (1970): 10–40.

Bergman, Jan and Elsie Johnson. "אַף," TDOT 1:348–60.

Best, Ernest. *A Commentary on the First and Second Epistles to the Thessalonians*, BNTC. London: Oliphants; Marshall, Morgan, and Scott, Ltd., 1971.

Biblia Hebraica. Edited by Rudolf Kittel. Stuttgart: Wurttembergische Bibelandstalt, 1937.

Blackwell, Ben C., John K. Goodrich, and Jason Maston, eds. *Reading Romans in Context: Paul and Second Temple Judaism*. Grand Rapids: Zondervan, 2015.

Blass, F., and A. Debrunner. *A Greek Grammar of the New Testament and Other Early Christian Literature*. Chicago: University of Chicago Press, 1961.

Bloch, Joshua. *On the Apocalyptic in Judaism*. JQRMS, no. 2. Edited by Abraham A. Neuman and Solomon Zeitlin. Philadelphia: Dropsie College for Hebrew and Cognate Learning, 1952.

Boers, Hendrikus. "Form Critical Study of Paul's Letters: 1 Thessalonians as a Case Study." NTS 22 (1976): 140–58.

Bornkamm, Günther. "Die Offenbarung des Zornes Gottes, Rom 1–3." BET 16 (1952): 9–33.

_____. *Jesus of Nazareth*. Translated by Irene McLuskey, Fraser McLuskey, and James M. Robinson. New York: Harper and Row, 1960.

_____. *Early Christian Experience*. Translated by Paul L. Hammer. New York: Harper and Row, 1969.

Bowman, John. *The Samaritan Problem: Studies in the Relationships of Samaritanism, Judaism, and Early Christianity*. Franz Delitzch Lectures 1959. Translated by Alfred M. Johnson, Jr. Pittsburgh: Pickwick, 1975.

Brown, Francis, S. R. Driver, and Charles A. Briggs, eds. *A Hebrew and English Lexicon of the Old Testament*. Oxford: Clarendon Press, reprint ed., 1974.

Bruce, F. F. *The Epistle of Paul to the Romans: An Introduction and Commentary*. TNNC. Grand Rapids: Eerdmans, 1963.

_____. *1 and 2 Thessalonians*. WBC. Waco, TX: Word Books, 1982.

_____. *The Epistles to the Colossians, to Philemon, and to the Ephesians*. NICNT. Grand Rapids: Eerdmans, 1984.

_____. *The Book of Acts: Revised Edition*. NICNT. Grand Rapids: Eerdmans, 1988.

Buck, Carl Darling. *A Dictionary of Selected Synonyms in the Principal Indo-European Languages: A Contribution to the History of Ideas*. Chicago: University of Chicago Press, 1949.

Büchsel, Friedrich. "θυμός," TDNT 3:167–72.

Bultmann, Rudolf. *History of the Synoptic Tradition*. Translated by John Marsh. Rev. ed. New York: Harper and Row, 1963.

_____. *Theologie des Neuen Testaments*. Tübingen: Mohr, 1984.

_____. *Theology of the New Testament*. With a New Introduction by Robert Morgan. Waco: Baylor Press, 2007.

_____. "ἀφίημι," TDNT 1:509–12.

Calvin, John. *The Epistles of Paul the Apostle to the Galatians, Ephesians, Philippians and Colossians*. Translated by T. H. L. Parker. Grand Rapids: Eerdmans, 1965.

_____. *The Epistles of Paul the Apostle to the Romans and Thessalonians*. Translated by Ross McKenzie. Grand Rapids: Eerdmans, 1960.

_____. *The Deliverance of God: An Apocalyptic Rereading of Justification in Paul*. Grand Rapids: William B. Eerdmans, 2009.

Campbell, William S. "Romans 3 as a Key to the Structure and Thought of Romans," 252–64. *The Romans Debate: Revised and Expanded Edition*. Ed. by Karl P. Donfried. Edinburgh: T & T Clark, 1991.

Campenhausen, Hans von. *The Formation of the Christian Bible*. Translated by J. A. Baker. Philadelphia: Fortress, 1972.

Carson, D. A. and Douglas J. Moo. *An Introduction to the New Testament*. 2nd ed. Grand Rapids: Zondervan Academic, 2005.

Cassius Dio, Cocceianus. *Dio's Roman History*. Translated by Ernest Carey. LCL. London: William Heinemann; New York: G. P. Putnam's Sons, 1914–1927.

Charles, R. H. *A Critical History of the Doctrine of the Future Life in Judaism, and in Early Christianity, or Hebrew, Jewish and Christian Eschatology from Pre-prophetic Times til the Close of the New Testament Canon*. London: Adam and Charles Black, 1913.

_____. *A Critical and Exegetical Commentary on the Revelation of St. John*. ICC. Edinburgh: T&T Clark, 1920; reprint ed., 1970.

Charlesworth, James H., ed. *The Messiah: Developments in Earliest Judaism and Christianity*. Minneapolis: Fortress, 1992.

Chilton, Bruce. *Rabbi Paul: An Intellectual Biography*. New York: Doubleday, 2004.

Christiansen, Ellen Juhl. *The Covenant in Judaism and Paul: A Study of Ritual Boundaries as Identity Markers*. Leiden: Brill, 1995.

Ciampa, Roy E. and Brian S. Rosner. *The First Letter to the Corinthians*. PNTC. Grand Rapids: Eerdmans, 2010.

Cicero, M. Tullius. *De Natura Deorum, Academica*. Translated by H. Rackham. LCL. London: William Heinemann; Cambridge: Harvard University Press, 1933.

_____. *De Officiis*. Translated by Walter Millar. LCL. London: William Heinemann; Cambridge: Harvard University Press, 1913.

_____. *De Re Publica, De Legibus*. Translated by Clinton Walker Keyes. LCL. London: William Heinemann; Cambridge: Harvard University Press, 1928.

_____. *The Speeches*. Translated by John Henry Freese, R. Gardner, and N. H. Watts. LCL. London: William Heinemann; Cambridge: Harvard University Press, 1931.

_____. *Tusculan Disputations*. Translated by J. E. King. LCL 141. Cambridge, Mass.: Harvard University Press, 1927.

Coffey, David M. "Natural Knowledge of God; Reflections on Romans 1:18–32." TS 31 (1970): 674–91.

Collins, John J. "Jewish Apocalyptic Against Its Hellenistic Near Eastern Environment." ASOR 220 (1975): 27–36.

_____. *The Sibylline Oracles of Egyptian Judaism*. SBL Dissertation Series, no. 13. Missoula, MT: Society of Biblical Literature, 1972.

Cooper, Mark Dwain. "The Intertextual Link between Parazēloō and Leimma in Rom 11:1–15." Unpublished PhD dissertation, New Orleans Baptist Theological Seminary, 2018.

Cranfield, C. E. B. *The Gospel According to Saint Mark*. CGTC. Cambridge: Cambridge University Press, 1959.

_____. *The Epistle to the Romans*. ICC, 2 Vols. Edinburgh: T&T Clark, 1979.

Cullmann, Oscar. *Christ and Time: The Primitive Christian Conception of Time and History*. 3d ed. Eugene, OR: Wipf and Stock, 2018.

Curtius, Georg. *Principles of Greek Etymology*. Translated by Augustus S. Wilkens and Edwin B. England. 5th ed. London: John Murray, 1886.

Dahlberg, B. T. "Wrath of God," *IDB* 4:903-08.

Danker, Frederick W. *A Greek-English Lexicon of the New Testament and Other Early Christian Literature* (BDAG), 3rd ed, rev. and ed. by Frederick William Danker. Based on the 6th ed. of Walter Bauer's *Griechisch-Deutsches Worterbuch*. Chicago and London: University of Chicago Press, 2000.

Daube, David. *The New Testament and Rabbinic Judaism*. Jordan Lectures in Comparative Religion, no. 2 (1952). London: Athlon Press, 1956.

_____. *The Sudden in the Scriptures*. Leiden: Brill, 1964.

Davies, J. G. "Genesis of Belief in an Imminent Parousia." JTS 14 (1963): 104–07.

Davies, W. D. *The Sermon on the Mount*. Nashville: Abingdon, 1966.

_____. *Paul and Rabbinic Judaism: Some Rabbinic Elements in Pauline Theology*. 2nd ed. London: SPCK, 1962.

_____. "Apocalyptic and Pharisaism." ET 59 (1948): 233–37.

The Dead Sea Scriptures. An English translation with Introduction and Notes by Theodor H. Gaster. 3d ed. rev. and enlarged. Garden City, N.Y.: Anchor Press, Doubleday, 1976.

Deissmann, Adolf. *Light from the Ancient East: The New Testament Illustrated by Recently Discovered Texts of the Graeco Roman World*. Lionel R. M. Strachan, trans. Eugene, OR: Wipf and Stock, 2004.

De Jonge, Henk Jan. "Notes on Testament of Levi II–VII." In *Studies on the Testaments of the Twelve Patriarchs, Text and Interpretation*. Edited by M. De Jonge. Studia in Vetris Testamenti Pseudepigrapha, no. 3. A. M. Denis and M. De Jonge, eds. Leiden: Brill, 1975, 247–60.

_____. "Die Patriarchentestamente von Roger Bacon bis Richard Simon, mit einen Namenregister." In *Studies on the Testaments of the Twelve Patriarchs, Text and Interpretation*. Edited by M. De Jonge. Studia in Vetris Testamenti Pseudepigrapha, no. 3. A. M. Denis and M. De Jonge, eds. Leiden: Brill, 1975, 3–42.

DelRio, Delio. *Paul and the Synagogue: Romans and the Isaiah Targum*. Eugene, OR: Wipf and Stock, 2013.

Delling, Gerhard. "τάσσω," *TDNT* 8:27–48.

Demosthenes. Translated by C. A. Vince, J. H. Vince, Norman W. DeWitt, and Norman J. DeWitt. LCL. London: William Heinemann; Cambridge: Harvard University Press, 1953–1962.

deSilva, David A. *An Introduction to the New Testament: Contexts, Methods and Ministry Formation*. Downers Grove: InterVarsity, 2004.

Dio Chrysostomus. Translated by J. W. Cohoon and H. Lamar Crosby. LCL. London: William Heinemann; Cambridge: Harvard University Press, 1932–1951.

Diogenes Laertius. *Lives of Eminent Philosophers*. Translated by R. D. Hicks. LCL. London: William Heinemann; Cambridge: Harvard University Press, 1925.

Dittenberger, Wilhelmus. *Orientis Graecae Inscriptiones Selectae, Supplementum Sylloges inscriptionum graecarum*. Lipsiae: S. Hirzel, 1903.

Dodd, Charles H. *The Apostolic Preaching and Its Development*. New York: Harper-Collins, 1936.

_____. *The Epistle of Paul to the Romans*. MNTC. London: Hodder and Stoughton, 1936.

Donaldson, John W. *The New Cratylus*. 3rd ed. London: John W. Parker and Son, 1859.

Donfried, Karl P. "Justification and Last Judgment in Paul." *Interpretation* 30 (1976): 140–52.

Doty, William G. *Letters in Primitive Christianity*. Guides to Biblical Scholarship, New Testament Series. Edited by Dan O. Via, Jr. Philadelphia: Fortress, 1973.

Dunn, James D. G. *Romans*. WBC, Vols. 38a, 38b. Dallas: Word, 1988.

———. *The Theology of Paul the Apostle*. Grand Rapids, Cambridge: Eerdmans, 1998.

Ebeling, Gerhard. "The Ground of Christian Theology." JTC 6 (1969): 47–68.

Eichrodt, Walter. *Theology of the Old Testament*. Translated by J. A. Baker. OTL. Philadelphia: Westminster, 1961 and 1967.

Ellingworth, Paul, and Eugene A. Nida. *Translator's Handbook on Paul's Letters to the Thessalonians*. Helps for Translators Series. New York: United Bible Societies, 1976.

Epictetus. *The Discourses as Reported by Arrian, the Manual and Fragments*. Vol. 2. Translated by W. A. Oldfather. LCL 218. 1926–1928. Cambridge, Mass.: Harvard University Press, 1969.

Epicurus. *Letters, Principle Doctrines, and Vatican Sayings*. Translated with an Introduction and Notes by Russel M. Geer. In *Library of Liberal Arts*. Indianapolis: Bobbs-Merrill Co., 1964.

Euripides. Translated by Arthur S. Way. LCL. London: William Heinemann; Cambridge: Harvard University Press, 1950.

Fee, Gordon D. *The First and Second Letters to the Thessalonians*. NICNT. Grand Rapids: Eerdmans, 2009.

———. *The First Epistle to the Corinthians*. NICNT. Rev. ed. Grand Rapids: Eerdmans, 2014.

Ferguson, Everett. *Backgrounds of Early Christianity*. Third Edition. Grand Rapids: Eerdmans, 2003.

Fitzmyer, Joseph A. *Romans: A New Translation with Introduction and Commentary*. AB 33. New York: Doubleday, 1993.

———. "The Aramaic Language and the Study of the New Testament." JBL 99 (1980): 5–21.

Flesher, Paul V. M. and Bruce Chilton. *The Targums: A Critical Introduction*. Waco, TX: Baylor University Press, 2011.

Foerster, Werner. "σέβομαι," *TDNT* 7:168–96.

Foerster, Werner and Georg Fohrer. "σῴζω," *TDNT* 7:965–1024.

Frame, James E. *A Critical and Exegetical Commentary on the Epistles of St. Paul to the Thessalonians*. ICC. Edinburgh: T&T Clark, 1912; reprint ed., 1970.

France, R. T. *The Gospel of Mark*. NIGTC. Grand Rapids: Eerdmans, 2002.

Freedman, David Noel. "The Flowering of Apocalyptic." JTC 6 (1969): 166–74.

Fritsch, Charles T. *The Anti-Anthropomorphisms of the Greek Pentateuch*. Princeton: Princeton University Press, 1943.

Fuchs, Ernst. "On the Task of a Christian Theology." JTC 6 (1969): 69–98.

Gager, John G. "Functional Diversity in Paul's Use of End-Time Language." JBL 89 (1970): 325–37.

Garlington, Don B. "The Obedience of Faith in the Letter of Romans—Part II: The Obedience of Faith and Judgment by Works." WTJ 53 (1991): 47–72.

Gaster, Theodor H. *Festivals of the Jewish Year: A Modern Interpretation and Guide*. New York: William Morrow, 1952, 1953.

———. "Gehenna," *IDB* 2:361–62.

Gaston, Lloyd. *Paul and the Torah*. Vancouver, BC: University of British Columbia Press, 1987.

Gathercole, Simon J. *Where Is Boasting? Early Jewish Soteriology and Paul's Response in Romans 1-5.* Grand Rapids, Cambridge: Eerdmans, 2002.
Godet, Frederic. *Commentary on St. Paul's Epistle to the Romans.* Translated by A. Cusin. Rev. and edited with an Introduction and Appendix by Talbot W. Chambers. 2nd ed. New York: Funk and Wagnalls, 1885.
Grundmann, Walter. "δόκιμος," *TDNT* 2:255-60.
_____. "δύναμαι," *TDNT* 2:284-317.
_____. "σύν-μετά with the Genitive," *TDNT* 7:766-97.
Grundmann, Walter, Gerhard von Rad, and Gerhard Kittel. "ἄγγελος," *TDNT* 1:74-88.
Guelich, Robert A. *Mark.* WBC. Vols. 34A, 34B. Grand Rapids: Zondervan Academic, 2017.
Guthrie, Donald. *New Testament Introduction.* 3rd ed. rev. Downers Grove, IL: InterVarsity Press, 1970.
Haney, Herbert M. *The Wrath of God in the Former Prophets.* New York: Vantage, 1960.
Hanse, Hermann. "ἔχω," *TDNT* 2:816-32.
Hanson, Anthony T. *The Wrath of the Lamb.* London: SPCK, 1957.
Hanson, Paul D. *The Dawn of Apocalyptic: The Historical and Sociological Roots of Jewish Apocalyptic Eschatology.* Rev. ed. Philadelphia: Fortress, 1979.
_____. "Apocalypticism," *IDB* 5:28-34.
Hatch, Edwin, and Henry A. Redpath. *A Concordance to the Septuagint and the Other Greek Versions of the Old Testament.* Oxford: Clarendon Press, 1897 and 1906.
Heider, George C. "Molech." *AYDB* 4:897-98.
Heilig, Christoph, Thomas Hewitt, and Michael F. Bird, eds. *God and the Faithfulness of Paul: A Critical Examination of the Pauline Theology of N. T. Wright.* Minneapolis: Fortress, 2017.
Hengel, Martin. *Judaism and Hellenism: Studies in Their Encounter in Palestine in the Early Hellenistic Period.* Trans. John Bowden, 2 vols. Minneapolis: Fortress, 1981.
_____. *The Son of God: The Origins of Christology and the History of Jewish-Hellenistic Religion.* Translated by John Bowden. Philadelphia: Fortress Press, 1976.
Hengel, Martin and Anna Maria Schwemer. *Paul between Damascus and Antioch: The Unknown Years.* Trans. by John Bowden. Louisville: Westminster John Knox, 1997.
Hennecke, Edgar and Wilhelm Schneemelcher, eds. *New Testament Apocrypha.* Edited and translated by R. McL. Wilson. 2 vols. Philadelphia: Westminster Press, 1959 and 1964.
Herodotus. *The Persian Wars.* Translated by A. D. Godley. LCL. Cambridge: Harvard University Press, 1921-1925.
Heschel, Abraham J. *The Prophets.* New York: Harper and Row, 1962.
Hesiod. *The Homeric Hymns and Homerica.* Translated by Hugh G. Evelyn-White. LCL. London: William Heinemann; Cambridge: Harvard University Press, 1954.
Hofmann, J. B. *Etymologisches Wörterbuch des Griechischen.* Munich: R. Oldenbourg, 1950.
Homer. *The Iliad.* Translated by A. T. Murray. LCL. London: William Heinemann; Cambridge: Harvard University Press, 1924-1925.
_____. *The Odyssey.* Translated by A. T. Murray. LCL. London: William Heinemann; Cambridge: Harvard University Press, 1919.
Hooker, Morna D. "Adam in Romans I," *NTS* 6 (1959-60): 297-307.
_____. "Further Notes on Romans I," *NTS* 13 (1967): 181-83.

Hultgren, Arland J. *Paul's Letter to the Romans: A Commentary*. Grand Rapids: Eerdmans, 2011.
Hunter, Archibald M. *The Epistle to the Romans*. TBC. London: SCM Press, 1955.
_____. *Interpreting the Parables*. Philadelphia: Westminster, 1960.
_____. *Paul and His Predecessors*. Rev. ed. London: SCM, 1961.
Hyldahl, Niels. "Reminiscence of the Old Testament at Romans 1:23," NTS 2 (May 1956): 285-88.
Index Volume to the Soncino Talmud. Compiled by Judah J. Slotki. Foreword by Israel Brodie. In *The Babylonian Talmud*, Isidore Epstein, trans. and ed., 2 vols. London: Soncino Press, 1952.
Jeffers, James S. *The Greco-Roman World of the New Testament Era: Exploring the Background of Early Christianity*. Downers Grove: InterVarsity, 1999.
Jeremias, Joachim. *The Parables of Jesus*. Translated by S. H. Hooke. Rev. ed. New York: Charles Scribner's Sons, 1963.
_____. "γέεννα," *TDNT* 1:657-58.
The Jerusalem Talmud: A Translation and Commentary on CD. Edited by Jacob Neusner. Trans. by Jacob Neusner and Tzvee Zahavy. Peabody, Mass.: Hendrickson, 2010.
Jewett, Robert. *A Chronology of Paul's Life*. Philadelphia: Fortress, 1979.
_____. *Romans: A Commentary*. Hermeneia. Minneapolis: Fortress, 2007.
Josephus, Flavius. Translated by H. St. J. Thackeray et al. LCL. Cambridge: Harvard University Press, 1926-1965; reprint 1968.
Kallas, James. "Romans XIII:1-7; an Interpolation." NTS 11 (July 1965), 365-74.
Käsemann, Ernst. *New Testament Questions of Today*. Translated by W. J. Montague. Philadelphia: Fortress Press, 1969.
_____. "The Beginnings of Christian Theology." JTC 6 (1969): 17-46.
_____. "'The Righteousness of God' in Paul." *New Testament Questions of Today*. London: SCM-Canterbury Press Ltd, 1969, 168-82.
_____. *Perspectives on Paul*. Translated by Margaret Kohl. NTL. London: SCM, 1971.
_____. "The Faith of Abraham in Romans 4." *Perspectives on Paul*. Translated by Margaret Kohl. NTL. London: SCM, 1971, 79-101.
_____. *Commentary on Romans*. Translated and edited by Geoffrey W. Bromiley. Grand Rapids: Eerdmans, 1980.
Kaiser, Otto. *Isaiah 13-39, a Commentary*. Translated by R. A. Wilson. OTL. Philadelphia: Westminster, 1974.
Kasch, Wilhelm. "ῥύομαι," *TDNT* 6:998-1003.
Kaye, Bruce N. "Eschatology and Ethics in 1 and 2 Thessalonians." NT 17 (1975): 47-57.
Kim, Seyoon. *Paul and the New Perspective: Second Thoughts on the Origin of Paul's Gospel*. Grand Rapids, Cambridge: Eerdmans, 2002.
Klein, William, Craig Blomberg, and Robert Hubbard. *Introduction to Biblical Interpretation*. Rev. ed. Downers Grove: InterVarsity, 2004.
Kleinknecht, Hermann, Friedrich Baumgärtel, Werner Bieder, Erik Sjöberg, and Eduard Schweizer. "πνεῦμα," *TDNT* 6:332-455.
Kleinknecht, Hermann, Oskar Grether, Johannes Fichtner, Erik Sjöberg, Gustav Stählin, and Otto Procksch. "ὀργή," *TDNT* 5:382-447.

Koch, Klaus. *The Rediscovery of Apocalyptic: A Polemical Work on a Neglected Area of Biblical Studies and Its Damaging Effects on Theology and Philosophy.* Translated by Margaret Kohl. London: SCM, 1972.

Köster, Helmut. "τέμνω," *TDNT* 8:106–12.

_____. *Introduction to the New Testament. Volume 1: History, Culture, and Religion of the Hellenistic Age*, 2d ed. 2 Vols. New York: Walter de Gruyter, 1995.

Kruse, Colin G. *Paul's Letter to the Romans.* PNTC. Grand Rapids, Cambridge: Eerdmans, 2012.

Kümmel, Werner Georg. *Introduction to the New Testament.* Translated by Howard Clark Kee. Rev. ed. Nashville: Abingdon, 1975.

Lake, Kirsopp. *The Earlier Epistles of St. Paul, Their Motive and Origin.* 2nd ed. London: Rivingtons, 1914.

Lane, William L. *The Gospel of Mark.* Second rev. ed. Grand Rapids: Eerdmans, 1974.

Lang, Friedrich. "πῦρ," *TDNT* 6:928–52.

Leenhardt, Franz J. *The Epistle to the Romans.* London: Lutterworth, 1961.

Levi, Israel, ed. *The Hebrew Text of the Book of Ecclesiasticus.* Semitic Study Series, no. 3. Edited by Richard J. H. Gottheil and Morris Jastrow, Jr. Leiden: Brill, 1904.

Liao, Paul Shang-hsin. "The Place of Covenant in the Theology of the Apostle Paul." PhD thesis, Hartford Seminary Foundation, 1973.

Licht, Jacob. "Taxo, or the Apocalyptic Doctrine of Vengeance." *JJS* 12 (1961): 95–103.

Lightfoot, J. B. *Notes on the Epistles of St Paul (I and II Thessalonians, I Corinthians 1–7, Romans 1–7, Ephesians 1:1–14), Based on the Greek Text from Previously Unpublished Commentaries.* Grand Rapids: Zondervan, 1957.

Lincoln, Andrew T. *Ephesians.* WBC 42. Grand Rapids: Zondervan Academic, 2014.

Linebaugh, Jonathan A. "Wisdom of Solomon and Romans 1:18—2:5: God's Wrath against All." In *Reading Romans in Context: Paul and Second Temple Judaism.* Edited by Ben C. Blackwell, John K. Goodrich, and Jason Maston. Grand Rapids: Zondervan, 2015, 38–45.

Livius, Titus. *Ab urbe condita (History of Rome).* Translated by B. O. Foster, F. G. Moore, Evan T. Sage, A. C. Schlesinger, and R. M. Geer. LCL. London: William Heinemann; Cambridge: Harvard University Press, 1919–1959; reprint 1965.

Ljungmen, Henrik. *Pistis: A Study of Its Presuppositions and Its Meaning in Pauline Use.* Lund: C. W. K. Gleerup, 1964.

Lohse, Eduard. *The New Testament Environment.* Translated by John E. Steely. Nashville: Abingdon, 1976.

_____. *Colossians and Philemon.* Hermeneia. Philadelphia: Fortress, 1971; Minneapolis: Fortress, 1988.

_____. "πρόσωπον," *TDNT* 6:768–80.

Longenecker, Richard N. *The Epistle to the Romans: A Commentary on the Greek Text.* NIGTC. Grand Rapids: Eerdmans, 2016.

Lucretius Carus, Titus. *De Rerum Natura.* Translated by W. H. D. Rouse. LCL. London: William Heinemann; Cambridge: Harvard University Press, 1924–1937.

Luther, Martin. *A Commentary on St Paul's Epistle to the Galatians, Based on Lectures Delivered by Martin Luther.* London: James Clarke, 1953.

Lycurgas. *Minor Attic Orators.* Translated by K. J. Maidment and J. O. Burtt. LCL. London: William Heinemann; Cambridge: Harvard University Press, 1953–1954.

Lysias. Translated by Walter Rangely Maitland Lamb. LCL. William Heinemann; New York: G. P. Putnam's Sons, 1930.

Macdonald, John. *The Theology of the Samaritans*. NTL. London: SCM, 1964.

Mann, Jacob. *The Bible as Read and Preached in the Old Synagogue: A Study in the Cycles of the Readings from Torah and Prophets, as well as from Psalms, and in the Structure of the Midrashic Homilies*. Vol 1: The Palestinian Triennial Cycle: Genesis and Exodus. Prolegomenon by Ben Zion Wacholder. LBS. New York: KTAV, 1971.

Marshall, I. Howard, Stephen Travis, and Ian Paul. *Exploring the New Testament: A Guide to the Letters and Revelation*. Vol. 2. Downers Grove, IL: InterVarsity, 2002.

Martin, D. Michael. *1, 2 Thessalonians: An Exegetical and Theological Exposition of Holy Scripture*. NAC. Nashville: Holman, 1995.

Mattill, A. J., Jr. "The Way of Tribulation." JBL 98 (1979): 535–39.

McCarthy, Dennis J. "The Wrath of Yahweh and the Structural Unity of the Deuteronomistic History." In Essays in Old Testament Ethics (J. Philip Hyatt, *In Memoriam*). Edited by James L. Crenshaw and John T. Willis. New York: KTAV, 1974, 97–110.

Memar Marqah: The Teaching of Marqah, 2 vols. Trans. and edited by John MacDonald. Beihefte zur Zeitschrift für die altertestamentliche Wissenschaft, no. 84, Georg Fohrer, ed. Berlin: Verlag Alfred Töpelmann, 1963.

Menander, The Principal Fragments. Translated by Francis G. Allinson. LCL. London: William Heinemann; Cambridge: Harvard University Press, 1930.

Meyer, Heinrich A. W. *Critical and Exegetical Hand-Book to the Epistle to the Romans*. Translated by John C. Moore and Edwin Johnson. Revised and edited by William P. Dickson. Preface and Supplementary Notes to the American Edition by Timothy Dwight. New York: Funk and Wagnalls, 1884.

Minucius Felix, Marcus. *Minucius Felix*. Translated by Gerald R. Rendall based on an unfinished version by W. C. A. Kerr. LCL. London: William Heinemann; Cambridge: Harvard University Press, 1931.

Metzger, Bruce M. *A Textual Commentary on the Greek New Testament: A Companion Volume to the United Bible Societies' Greek New Testament (Fourth Revised Edition)*. 2nd ed. Stuttgart: German Bible Society, 1994.

Meyer, Heinrich August Wilhelm. *Critical and Exegetical Commentary to the Epistle to the Romans*, 2 vols. CECNT. London: T&T Clark, 1881.

The Mishnah. Translated by Herbert Danby. Oxford: Oxford University Press, 1933; reprint ed. 1977.

Montgomery, James Alan. *The Samaritans, The Earliest Jewish Sect: Their History, Theology and Literature*. Introduction by Abraham S. Halkin. New York: KTAV, 1968.

Moo, Douglas J. *The Epistle to the Romans*. Grand Rapids, Cambridge: Eerdmans, 1996.

Moody, Dale. "Romans." BBC. Nashville: Broadman, 1970.

Morford, Mark P. O. and Robert J. Lenardon. *Classical Mythology*. New York: David McKay, 1971.

Morris, Leon *1 and 2 Thessalonians*. TNTC. Grand Rapids: Eerdmans, 1956; Downers Grove, IL: InterVarsity, 1984.

_____. *The Gospel According to Matthew*. PNTC. Grand Rapids: Eerdmans, 1992.

Morrish, George. *A Concordance of the Septuagint*. Grand Rapids: Zondervan, 1976.

Moule, C. F. D. "The Influence of Circumstances on the Use of Eschatological Terms." JTS, n.s. 15 (1964): 1–15.

_____. "The Judgment Theme in the Sacraments." In *The Background of the New Testament and Its Eschatology*. Edited by W. D. Davies and D. Daube. Cambridge: Cambridge University Press, 1956, 464–81.

Moule, H. C. G. *The Epistle of Paul the Apostle to the Romans, with Introduction and Notes*. CBSC. Cambridge: Cambridge University Press, 1952.
Moulton, James Hope, and George Milligan. *The Vocabulary of the Greek Testament, Illustrated from the Papyri and Other Non-Literary Sources*. Grand Rapids: Eerdmans, 1930; reprint ed., 1976.
Mounce, Robert H. *The Book of Revelation* NICNT. Grand Rapids: Eerdmans, 1997.
Munck, Johannes. *Paulus und die Heilsgeschichte*. Acta Jutlandica 26:1; Tellogisk serie 6. Aarhus: Aarhus University Press, 1954.
_____. *Paul and the Salvation of Mankind*. Translated by Frank Clarke. Atlanta: John Knox, 1959; paperback, 1997.
_____. "I Thess. i.9-10 and the Missionary Preaching of Paul; Textual Exegesis and Hermeneutical Reflexions." NTS 9 (1963): 95-110.
Murray, John. *The Epistle to the Romans: The English Text with Introduction, Exposition and Notes*. NICNT. Grand Rapids: Eerdmans, 1959, 1965, 1968.
Nanos, Mark D. and Magnus Zetterholm. *Paul within Judaism: Restoring the First-Century Context to the Apostle*. Minneapolis: Fortress, 2015.
Nedarim. Translated by H. Freedman. In *The Babylonian Talmud*. Edited by Isidore Epstein. London: Soncino Press, 1936.
The New American Standard Bible. Study ed. Philadelphia: A. J. Holman Co., 1975.
Nickelsburg, George W. E. "The Apocalyptic Message of 1 Enoch 92-105." CBQ 39 (1977): 309-28.
Neill, Stephen. *Jesus through Many Eyes: Introduction to the Theology of the New Testament*. Philadelphia: Fortress, 1976.
Nygren, Anders. *Commentary on Romans*. Trans. by Carl Rasmussen. Philadelphia: Fortress, 1949.
Oepke, Albrecht. "εἰς," *TDNT* 2:420-34.
_____. "καλύπτω," *TDNT* 3:556-92.
The Old Testament in Greek According to the Septuagint. Edited by Henry Barclay Swete. 4th ed. Cambridge: Cambridge University Press, 1912.
Orientis Graeci Inscriptiones Selectae. Edited by Wilhelmus Dittenberger. Lipsiae: S. Hirzel, 1903.
O'Rourke, J. J. "Romans 1:20 and Natural Revelation." CBQ 23 (1961): 301-6.
Osborne, Grant. *Romans*. IVP NTC. Downers Grove, IL: InterVarsity, 2004.
Otto, Rudolf. *The Idea of the Holy: An Inquiry into the Non-Rational Factor in the Idea of the Divine and Its Relation to the Rational*. Translated by John W. Harvey. Oxford: Oxford University Press, 1925.
The Oxyrhynchus Papyri. Edited with translations and notes by many scholars. In *Graeco-Roman Memoirs*. London: Egypt Exploration Society, 1898-1972.
Pannenberg, Wolfhart. *Theology and the Kingdom of God*. Philadelphia: Westminster, 1969.
Pao, David W. *Acts and the Isaianic New Exodus*. Grand Rapids: Baker Academic, 2002; reprint of J. C. B. Mohr, 2000.
Pausanias. *Description of Greece*. Translated by W. H. S. Jones. LCL. Companion volume arranged by R. E. Wycherley. London: William Heinemann; Cambridge: Harvard University Press, 1918-1935; rev. ed., 1955.
Ploger, Otto. *Theocracy and Eschatology*. Translated by S. Rudman. Oxford: Basil Blackwell, 1977.

Purvis, James D. *The Samaritan Pentateuch and the Origin of the Samaritan Sect*. Harvard Semitic Monographs, no. 2. Cambridge: Harvard University Press, 1968.
Pummer, Reinhard. *The Samaritans: A Profile*. Grand Rapids: Eerdmans, 2016.
Petronius, Arbiter. *Petronius*. Translated by W. H. D. Rouse and E. H. Warmington. LCL. Cambridge: Harvard University Press, 1913; updated by Michael Heseltine 1987.
Philo. *Philo*. Translated by F. H. Colson, LCL. London: William Heinemann Ltd.; Cambridge, MA: Harvard University Press, 1937.
Plato. *Laws*. Translated by R. G. Bury. LCL. London: William Heinemann; Cambridge: Harvard University Press, 1926.
Plutarch. *The Parallel Lives*. Translated by Bernadotte Perrin et al. LCL. Cambridge: Harvard University Press, 1914–1969.

———. *Moralia*. Translated by F. C. Babbitt et al. LCL. London: William Heinemann; Cambridge: Harvard University Press, 1927–1969.
Polybius. *The Histories*. Trans. W. R. Paton, LCL. Cambridge: Harvard University Press; London: William Heinemann, 1925; reprinted 1954.
Postell, Seth D. *Adam as Israel: Genesis 1–3 as the Introduction to the Torah and Tanakh*. Eugene, OR: Pickwick, 2011.
Pummer, Reinhard. *The Samaritans: A Profile*. Grand Rapids: Eerdmans, 2016.
Quell, Gottfried , Gerhard Kittel, and Rudolf Bultmann. "ἀλήθεια," *TDNT* 1:232–51.
Quell, Gottfried and Gottlob Schrenk. "δίκη," *TDNT* 2:174–225.
Rad, Gerhard von. *Old Testament Theology*. Translated by D. M. G. Stalker. New York: Harper and Row, 1962 and 1965.

———. *Wisdom in Israel*. Translated by James D. Martin. Nashville: Abingdon, 1972.
Rad, Gerhard von and Gerhard Kittel. "δοκέω," *TDNT* 2:232–55.
Räisänen, Heikki. *Paul and the Law*. Philadelphia: Fortress, 1983.
Ringgren, Helmer. *Sacrifice in the Bible*. Word Christian Books, no. 42. 2d series. New York: Association Press, 1962.
Roetzel, Calvin J. "The Judgment Form in Paul's Letters." JBL 88 (1969): 305–12.

———. *Judgment in the Community: A Study of the Relationship between Es-chatology and Ecclesiology in Paul*. Leiden: Brill, 1972.

———. *The Letters of Paul: Conversations in Context*. Louisville: Westminster/John Knox, 1991.
Rollins, Wayne G. "New Testament and Apocalyptic." NTS 17 (1971): 454–76.
Rowley, H. H. *The Relevance of Apocalyptic: A Study of Jewish and Christian Apocalypses from Daniel to the Revelation*. 2d ed. London: Lutterworth, 1963.
Russell, D. S. *The Method and Message of Jewish Apocalyptic, 200 BC–AD 100*. OTL. Philadelphia: Westminster, 1964.
Rylaarsdam, J. Coert. "Exodus: Introduction." IB. New York: Abingdon, 1957.
Safrai, Shmuel. "The Synagogue." In *The Jewish People in the First Century: Historical Geography, Political History, Social, Cultural and Religious Life and Institutions*. Edited by Shmuel Safrai and M. Stern. Vol 2. CRINT. Assen/Maastricht: Van Gorcum; Philadelphia: Fortress, 1974, 1987, 908–44.
Safrai, Shmuel and M. Stern, eds. *The Jewish People in the First Century: Historical Geography, Political History, Social, Cultural and Religious Life and Institutions*. 2 Vols. CRINT. Assen/Maastricht: Van Gorcum; Philadelphia: Fortress, 1974, 1987.
The Samaritan Chronicle No. II (or: Sepher Ha-Yamim), From Joshua to Nebuchadnezzar. Edited and translated by John Macdonald. Beihefte zur Zeitschrift für die

alttestamentliche Wissenschaft, no. 107. Edited by Georg Fohrer. Berlin: Walter de Gruyter, 1969.

Sanday, William and Arthur C. Headlam. *A Critical and Exegetical Commentary on the Epistle to the Romans*. Fifth Edition. ICC. Edinburgh: T&T Clark, 1902.

Sanders, E. P. *Judaism: Practice and Belief, 63 BCE–66 C*. London: SCM; Philadelphia: Trinity Press International, 1992.

_____. *Paul and Palestinian Judaism: A Comparison of Patterns of Religion*. Minneapolis: Fortress, 1977.

Sanhedrin. Translated by H. Freedman. In *The Babylonian Talmud*. Edited and trans. by Isidore Epstein, 2 vols. London: Soncino Press, 1935.

Saphir, Athialy Philip. "The Mysterious Wrath of Yahweh: An Inquiry into the Old Testament Concept of the Suprarational Factor in Divine Anger." ThD dissertation, Princeton Theological Seminary, 1965.

Schilier, Heinrich. "θλίβω," *TDNT* 3:139–48.

Schlatter, Adolf. *Gottes Gerechtigkeit: Ein Kommentar zum Römerbrief*. 2nd ed. Stuttgart: Calwer Verlag, 1952.

_____. *Romans: The Righteousness of God*. Trans. by Siegfried S. Schatzmann. Foreward by Peter Stuhlmacher. Peabody, MA.: Hendrickson, 1995.

Schmithals, Walter. *The Apocalyptic Movement: Introduction and Interpretation*. Translated by John E. Steely. Nashville: Abingdon, 1975.

Schneemelcher, Wilhelm. "Apocalyptic Prophecy of the Early Church: Introduction." Translated by David Hill. In *New Testament Apocrypha*. Edited by Edgar Hennecke and Wilhelm Schneemelcher. English translation edited by R. McL. Wilson. 2 vols. Philadelphia: Westminster, 1959 and 1964, 2:684–89.

Schoeps, H. J. *Paul, the Theology of the Apostle in the Light of Jewish-Religious History*. Translated by Harold Knight. Philadelphia: Westminster, 1961.

Schonweiss, H. and H. C. Hahn. "Anger, Wrath," NIDNTT 1:105–13.

Schreiner, Thomas R. *The Law and Its Fulfillment: A Pauline Theology of the Law*. Grand Rapids: Baker, 1993.

_____. *Romans*. BECNT. Ed. by Moises Silva. Grand Rapids: Baker, 1998.

_____. *1, 2 Peter, Jude*, The New American Commentary. Gen. ed. E. Ray Clendenen. Nashville: Broadman and Holman, 2003.

Schrenk, Gottlob. "ἐκδικέω," *TDNT* 2:442–46.

Scott, R. B. Y. "The Book of Isaiah: Introduction and Exegesis." IB. New York: Abingdon, 1956.

Select Papyri. Translated by A. S. Hunt and C. C. Edgar. LCL. London: William Heinemann; New York: G. P. Putnam's Sons, 1932.

Seneca, Lucius Annaeus. *Epistolae morales ad Lucilium*. Translated by Tichard M. Gummere. LCL. Cambridge, Mass.: Harvard University Press, 1920.

The Septuagint Version of the Old Testament, with an English Translation. Grand Rapids: Zondervan Publishing House, 1970.

Sevenster, J. N. *Paul and Seneca*. Supplements to Novum Testamentum, no. 4. Leiden: Brill, 1961.

Shabbath. Translated by H. Freedman. In *The Babylonian Talmud*. Isidore Epstein, trans. and ed. 2 vols. London: Soncino Press, 1938.

Sifre: A Tannaitic Commentary on the Book of Deuteronomy, Translated from the Hebrew with Introduction and Notes by Reuven Hammer, Yale Judaica Series, Ed.

Leon Nemoy, Vol. XXIV: Sifre on Deuteronomy. London: Yale University Press, 1986.

Simpson, William Henry. "Divine Wrath in the Eighth Century Prophets." PhD dissertation, Boston University Graduate School, 1968.

Skinner, John. *The Book of the Prophet Isaiah, Chapters XL–LXVI in the Revised Standard Version with Introduction and Notes.* Cambridge: Cambridge University Press, 1954.

Skipper, Ben. "Echoes of Eden: An Intertextual Analysis of Edenic Language in Romans 1:18–32." Unpublished PhD dissertation. New Orleans Baptist Theological Seminary, 2017.

Smith, Taylor Clarence. "The Meaning of ὀργὴ θεοῦ [sic] in the Pauline Epistles." Unpublished ThD thesis, Southern Baptist Theological Seminary, 1944.

Sophocles. Translated by F. Storr. LCL. London: William Heinemann; Cambridge: Harvard University Press, 1912–1913.

Stanley, Christopher D. *Paul and the Language of Scripture: Citation Technique in the Pauline Epistles and Contemporary Literature.* SNTS 74. Cambridge: Cambridge University Press, 1992.

———. *Arguing with Scripture: The Rhetoric of Quotation in the Letters of Paul.* New York, London: T&T Clark, 2004.

Stendahl, Krister. *Paul Among Jews and Gentiles.* Philadelphia: Fortress, 1976.

Stevens, Gerald L. "The Literary Background and Theological Significance of ΟΡΓΗ ΘΕΟΥ in the Pauline Epistles." Unpublished PhD dissertation. New Orleans Baptist Theological Seminary, 1981.

———. *Revelation: The Past and Future of John's Apocalypse.* Eugene, OR: Pickwick Publications, 2014.

———. *Acts: A New Vision of the People of God.* Second Edition. Eugene, OR: Pickwick Publications, 2019.

———. *Romans: The Gospel of God.* Eugene, OR: Pickwick Publications. Forthcoming.

Stewart, James S. *A Man in Christ: The Vital Elements of St. Paul's Religion.* Grand Rapids: Baker, 1975.

Stoicorum Veterum Fragmenta. Edited by Hans F. A. von Arnim. Stuttgart: B. G. Teubner Verlagsgesellschaft, 1964.

Strack, Hermann L., and Paul Billerbeck. *Kommentar zum Neuen Testament aus Talmud and Midrasch.* 6 vols. Munich: C. H. Becksche Verlagsbuchhandlung, Oskar Beck, 1924.

Strong, L. Thomas III. "The Significance of the 'Knowledge of God' in the Epistles of Paul." Unpublished PhD dissertation, New Orleans Baptist Theological Seminary, 1992.

Suetonius, Tranquillus, C. *Lives of the Twelve Caesars.* Translated by J. C. Rolfe. LCL. Cambridge: Harvard University Press, 1914; rev. ed., 1951; reprint, 1965.

Summers, Ray. *Worthy Is the Lamb, an Interpretation of Revelation.* Nashville: Broadman, 1951.

Sylloge Inscriptionum Graecarum. Edited by Wilhelmus Dittenberger. Lipsiae: S. Hirzel, 1898.

Tacitus, Cornelius. *The Annals.* Translated by John Jackson. LCL. London: William Heinemann; Cambridge: Harvard University Press, 1925–1937.

———. *The Histories.* Translated by Clifford H. Moore. LCL. London: William Heinemann; Cambridge: Harvard University Press, 1925–1937.

The Targums of Onkelos and Jonathan Ben Uzziel on the Pentateuch, with the Fragments of the Jerusalem Targum, from the Chaldee. Translated by J. W. Etheridge. 2 vols. in 1. New York: KTAV, 1968.

Tasker, R. V. G. *The Biblical Doctrine of the Wrath of God.* London: Tyndale, 1951.

Teeple, Howard M. *The Mosaic Eschatological Prophet.* JBLMS. Philadelphia: Society of Biblical Literature, 1957.

Testamenta XII Patriarcharum, Edited According to Cambridge University Library MS Ff 1.24 fol. 203a-262b. With short notes by M. De Jonge. Pseudepigrapha Veteris Testamenti Graece, no. 1, A. M. Denis and M. De Jonge, eds. Leiden: Brill, 1964.

Testamentum Iobi. Edited by S. P. Brock. Pseudepigrapha Veteris Testamenti Graece, no. 2. Edited by A. M. Denis and M. De Jonge. Leiden: Brill, 1967.

Thayer, Joseph Henry. *A Greek-English Lexicon of the New Testament.* Trans., rev., and enlarged 4th ed. New York: American Book Co.; Harper and Bros. Publishers, 1889.

Thielman, Frank. *Paul and the Law: A Contextual Approach.* Downers Grove, IL: InterVarsity, 1994.

Thomas, R. L. "Imprecatory Prayers of the Apocalypse." BS 126 (1969): 123–31.

Thompson, Alden Lloyd. *Responsibility for Evil in the Theodicy of IV Ezra: A Study Illustrating the Significance of Form and Structure for the Meaning of the Book.* SBLDS. Missoula, MT: Scholars Press, 1977.

Thornton, M. K. and R. L. Thornton, *Julio-Claudian Building Programs: A Quantitative Study in Political Management.* Mundelein, IL: Bolchazy-Carducci, 1989.

Thucydides. *History of the Peloponnesian War.* Trans. Charles Forster Smith, LCL, Vol. 1. Cambridge: Harvard University Press, 1923, rev. and reprinted 1935.

Tomson, Peter J. *Paul and the Jewish Law: Halakha in the Letters of the Apostle to the Gentiles.* CRINT. Section 3: Jewish Traditions in Early Christian Literature. Assen/Maastricht: Van Gorcum; Minneapolis: Fortress, 1990.

Towner, W. S. "Retributional Theology in the Apocalyptic Setting." USQR 26 (1971): 203–14.

Trench, Richard C. *Synonymns of the New Testament.* 9th ed. improved. London: Macmillan, 1880.

VanHorn, Nathan W. "Arguing from Abraham: Remembrance as Rhetorical Warrant in Romans 1–4." Unpublished PhD dissertation, New Orleans Baptist Theological Seminary, 2016.

Vergilius Maro, Publius. *Virgil.* Translated by H. Rushton Fairclough. LCL. Cambridge: Harvard University Press, 1916, rev. ed., 1934.

Vielhauer, Philip. "Apocalyptic in Early Christianity: Introduction." Translated by David Hill. In *New Testament Apocrypha.* Edited by Edgar Hennecke and Wilhelm Schneemelcher. English translation edited by R. McL. Wilson. 2 vols. Philadelphia: Westminster, 1959 and 1964, 2:608–42.

———. "Apocalypses and Related Subjects: Introduction." Translated by David Hill. In *New Testament Apocrypha.* Edited by Edgar Hennecke and Wilhelm Schneemelcher. English translation edited by R. McL. Wilson. 2 vols. Philadelphia: Westminster, 1959 and 1964, 2:582–600.

Vos, Geerhardus. *The Pauline Eschatology.* Grand Rapids: Eerdmans, 1953.

Vriezen, Th. C. *An Outline of Old Testament Theology.* Newton Centre, MA.: Charles T. Branford, 1966.

Wedderburn, Alexander J. M. "Adam in Paul's Letter to the Romans." JSNTSup 3 (1980): 413–30.
_____. *The Reasons for Romans*. Minneapolis: Fortress, 1991.
Westerholm, Stephen. *Israel's Law and the Church's Faith: Paul and His Recent Interpreters*. Grand Rapids: Eerdmans, 1988.
_____. *Perspectives Old and New on Paul: The "Lutheran" Paul and His Critics*. Grand Rapids, Cambridge: Eerdmans, 2004.
Westermann, Claus. *Isaiah 40–66, a Commentary*. Translated by David M. G. Stalker. OTL. Philadelphia: Westminster, 1969.
Wharton, Edward Ross. *Etymological Lexicon of Classical Greek: Etyma Graeca*. Chicago: Ares Publishers, 1924.
Whiteley, D. E. H. *Thessalonians in the Revised Standard Version with Introduction and Commentary*. NCB. Oxford: Oxford University Press, 1969.
Wiens, Devon Harvey. "Holy War Theology in the New Testament and Its Relationship to the Eschatological Day of the Lord Tradition." Unpublished ThD thesis, University of Southern California, 1967.
Wise, Michael O. *The First Messiah: Investigating the Savior Before Christ*. New York: HarperSanFrancisco, 1999.
Wolff, Hans Walter. *Anthropology of the Old Testament*. Philadelphia: Fortress, 1974.
Wright, Nicholas Thomas. *The Climax of the Covenant: Christ and the Law in Pauline Theology*. Minneapolis: Fortress, 1991.
_____. *Paul and the Faithfulness of God*. Christian Origins and the Faithfulness of God, Vol. 4. Minneapolis: Fortress, 2013.
_____. *Paul and His Recent Interpreters*. Minneapolis: Fortress, 2015.
_____. *The Paul Debate: Critical Questions for Understanding the Apostle*. Waco, TX: Baylor University Press, 2015.
Young, Edward J. *The Prophecy of Daniel, a Commentary*. Grand Rapids: Eerdmans, 1953.
Zebabim. Translated by H. Freedman. In *The Babylonian Talmud*. Isidore Epstein, trans. and ed. 2 vols. London: Soncino Press, 1948.

Scripture Index

OLD TESTAMENT

Genesis
1:26	204n34
2:17	151
6–9	60n35
15:16	125n29
18:20—19:29	60n35
18:30	6n19
18:32	6n19
19:24	102
32	55n5
32:30	55n8
40:6	5
49:7	69

Exodus
3:2	203
3:5	57n22
5:21	61n36
4:14	60n31, 69n70
4:24–25	55n8
4:24	55n5
9:16	68n60
12:23–32	68n66
13:1	203n28
13:21	203n27
14:11	61n36
15:21	141n6
15:24	61n36
16:2	61n36
17:2–3	61n36
19:9–25	55n6, 55n8
19:10–13	57n22
19:18	203n27
19:21–25	57n22
20:5	57n20
20:18–21	55n8
22:24	52n16, 69n69
24:15–18	158
32	59
32:1–5	157
32:1	61n36
32:6–9	157
32:1	61n36
32:9–14	55n11
32:10–12	157
32:10	69n70, 157
32:11	69n70
32:12	5, 69n71
33:7	58
33:14	58n23
33:20	55n8
33:21	58
34:4–7	58
34:7	57n20
34:29–35	57n22
39:30	57n22

Leviticus
10:1–6	56n15
10:1–2	56n16
18:21	78n107
19:18	182
20:2	78n107
20:3	78n107
20:4	78n107
20:5	78n107
22:3	58n23

Numbers
1:52–53	55n8
1:53	58, 70n79
6:25	58n23
11:1	61n36, 69n70
11:4	61n36
11:10	6n22, 69n70
12:1–15	60n31
12:1	61n36
12:9	69n71
14:2	61n36
14:11–12	61n37
14:13–21	68n61
14:22–23	61n37
14:26–38	61n37
14:26–30	212
14:34	69n71
16	61n38
16:19–50	212
16:22	56n15
16:28–35	57n18
17:13	58
18:5	58
21	96
21:4–9	61n38
22:22	6n21, 55n5, 60n31, 69n69
23:7–8	60n30
25:1–11	56n15

25:1–9	212	32:35	82, 86	16:33	70n76, 70n77
25:3	69n69			19:10	125n29
25:4	69n71	**Judges**		20:20	70n76
25:11	55n14, 212	2:12	59	20:22	70n76, 70n77
32:10	69n69	2:13	70n76	21:17–22	57n18
32:13	69n69	2:14	69n69	22:20–21	55n8
32:14	69n71	2:20	69n69	22:54	70n76
		3:8	59n28, 69n69		
Deuteronomy		6:21	203n27	**2 Kings**	
1:34–35	97	9:30	69n68	1:9–16	105
1:37	70n75	10:7	59n28, 69n68,	1:18	69n70
4:21	70n75		69n69	3:27	6n19
4:25	70n76	13:22	55n6, 55n8	13:3	6n22, 59n29,
4:26	53n2	14:19	69n68		69n69
5:4	203n27			16:3	78n107
6:15	6n22, 68,	**1 Samuel**		17	59n27
	69n69	6:19	55n6, 55n8	17:5	164
7:4	69n69	12:22	68n61	17:11	70n76
7:6	57n22	26:19	55n8	17:17	70n76
9:8	70n75	28:18	6n22, 60n31,	17:18	70n75
9:19	70n72		69n71	17:36	53
10:16–17	160			18:4–6	59n29
11:17	69n68, 69n70	**2 Samuel**		21:6	59n29, 78n107
11:26	59	5:17–25	60n35	22:13	59n29, 60n30
11:29	59	6:7	6n22, 55n6,	23:10	78n107
13:17	69n71		55n8, 69n70	23:26	69n71, 70n77
18:18	83	12:1–14	57n18		
21:1–9	57	12:1–6	110	**1 Chronicles**	
21:23	211	22:8–9	6n22	13:10	6n22, 69n70
29:19–20	60n30	22:8	70n75	21:1	7n24
29:23	60n30, 70n72	24:1	7n24, 55n5		
29:24–28	59n27			**2 Chronicles**	
29:24	69n71	**1 Kings**		12:2–7	59n28
29:26–27	60n30	8:42–43	68n60	19:2	60n31
29:27	69n69	9:3	68n60	24:18	59n27
29:28	53n2, 70n72	11:7	78n107	28:9–11	59n28
30:1	59	11:9	59n29, 70n74	28:11	69n71
31:17–18	58n23	12:26–30	63f3.2	28:13	69n71
31:17	69n69	14:9	59n29	28:25	70n76
31:25–29	61n39	14:15	53n2	29:8	69n68
31:29	70n76	15:30	5, 70n76,	29:10	59n29, 69n71
32:1–43	67		70n77	30:8	59n29, 69n71
32:19	77	16:2	59n29, 70n76	32:24–25	60n31
32:20	58n23	16:7	70n76	32:26	60n31
32:24	70n78	16:13	70n76	33:15–17	71n85
32:32	60n30	16:26	70n76	33:19	71n85

34:21	59n29	24:1	68	95	105n39
35:19	69n69, 69n71, 70n77	25:11	68n61	95:6–8	97
		30:5	58	95:10–11	59n27
36:13–21	61n40	30:6	58n25	95:11	96, 97
36:15–16	158	37:1	70n73	96:13	68n63
36:16	6n22, 65	38:1	60n32, 197n5	97:5	57n22
		38:4	60n30	98:9	68n63

Ezra

		38:11	55n11	101:10	70n72
5:12	61n40, 70n76	44:14–15	66	102:8–9	161n70
7:23	67	51:11	58n23	102:9	69, 70n74
9:14	59n27	58:4	70n78	102:10	60n32
10:14	6n21, 66, 69n71	59:1	70n74	103:8	58n24
		59:11–13	6n20	104:11	164
		68:2	57n22	105:20	144

Nehemiah

		68:25	69n71	105:23	70n71
9:17	58n24	69:9	104n28	105:40	69n69
13:8	66	69:22–28	68n63	106	158
		69:24	6n22	106:8	68n60

Job

		74:1–8	66n52, 170n87	106:20	158
6:4	70n78	76:7	6n20	106:39–40	62n47
12:6	70n76	77:9	55n11	106:40	6n22
14:1–4	55n5	77:38	70n73	106:43–45	59
16:9	55n11	77:40	70n76	109:21	68n61
20:23	6n22	77:49	69n71, 70n73	110:5	60n34
21:20	6n21, 6n22	78:5	70n74	114:7	57n22
29:11	55n11	78:31	6n21	145:5–6	141n6
40–41	55n9	78:38	61n40	145:8	58n24
42:7	6n22, 60n31, 70n79	78:49	6n22	148	141n6
		79:4	70n74		
		79:5	55n14, 58n26		

Proverbs

Psalms

		79:6	60n34	15:1	70n73
2:1	99	79:7	68n61	19:11	77n101
2:5	60n34, 70n73	80:4	58n26	21:14	70n73
2:12	70n74	84:3	69n69	24:24	60n30
6:1	55n11, 70n73	84:5	70n74	27;4	70n73
7:12	77n102, 161n70	85:1–4	61n40		

Ecclesiastes

		85:4–6	66n52, 170n87	5:5	70n74
8:1	68n60, 141n6	85:5	58n26	5:6	60n31
8:9	68n60, 141n6	88:7	60n32	5;16	69
9:8	68n63	88:15	55n11	7:9	77n101
16:11	58n23	89:7	69n71		
17:7	70n74	89:11–12	70n73		

Isaiah

17:8	70	89:46	6n22	1:4	70n76
17:15	70	90:9	170n87, 60	1:9–10	60n35
19	141n5	90:11	6n20	1:9	181n109
21:9	60n34	93:11	149n37		

2:10	205n37	29:16	174n98	64:5	70n74		
2:11	205n37	30:27–30	6n22	64:7	149n36		
2:12	68n64	30:27	70n71	64:8–9	174n98		
2:17	205n37	30:30	70n72	64:9	58n25, 66n52, 70n74, 170n87		
2:19	98, 205n37	30:33	6n22				
2:21	205n37	32:35	78n107	66	203n28, 206		
3:9	60n35	34:1–10	68n64	66:4	203		
5:16–25	65n50	34:8–9	102	66:14	67n54, 70n80		
5:16	68n63	34:2	70n73	66:15	203, 203n27, 203n28		
5:18–19	61n42, 170n88	37:29	70n75				
5:21	150n40	38:19	141n6				
5:25	6n22, 69n68, 69n70, 70n72	40:1–3	68	**Jeremiah**			
		40:1–2	65	2:1–3	61n44		
7:4	70n71	40:18–20	147n28	2:5	144, 164		
9:12	59n28	42:13	67n56	2:11	158		
9:19	70n71	42:25	61n40, 70n71	2:13	61n44		
10:1–6	65n49	44:18	149n37	2:31–32	61n44		
10:4	69n68	45:9	174n98	3:1–2	61n44		
10:5–15	67n58	47:6	61n40	3:2	69		
10:5–6	59n28	48:9–11	67n56	3:12	58n25		
10:5	60n30, 70n72	48:9	68n62	3:19–20	61n44		
10:22–23	181	50:11	6n22	4:4	61n44, 160		
10:22	68n63	51:17	6n22, 61n40	4:22	61n44		
11	158	51:22	6n22	4:26	70n71		
11:10	11, 11n40, 157	52:5	165	5:7–9	61n44		
12	141n6	54:7–8	58	5:9	163n73		
12:1	70n74	54:8	61n40	6:11	61n44		
13:9–11	68n64	54:9	60n35, 70n75	6:22	61n44		
13:9	60n35	55:8–9	55n9	6:26	61n44		
13:13	68n64, 70n71	57:6	70n74	7:4	61n42, 170n88		
13:19	70n72	57:15	57n22	7:14–15	68n60		
14:4–6	67n58	57:16	58n25, 70n74	7:18	70n76		
16:6–7	67n58	57:17	70n79	7:20	61n44, 70n72		
24:1–23	68n64	58:6	92	7:28–29	65n49		
26:9	68n63	59:8	67n54	7:29	61n44		
26:19–21	68n64	59:11	132n54	7:32	78n109		
26:20–22	123	59:17	67n56, 200n13	8:26	61n44		
26:20–21	68	59:19	70n72	10:10	60n30		
26:20	5	59:20–21	159	10:14	150n40		
27:4	5	60:10	5, 61n40	10:24	55n11		
28:13	61n43	61:1–2	92	10:25	6n22, 69n68		
28:14–22	61n42, 170n88	63:1–6	6n22, 104	11:20	148		
28:16	181	63:3–6	67n54	12:7–13	62n46		
28:28	70n74	63:3	102	13:25	61n44		
28:21	60n35, 61n43	63:15	67n56	14:7	62		
29:6	203n27	64:5–7	149n36	14:22	141n5		

15:14	6n22	**Lamentations**		23:1–35	62n48
15:17	61n44	1:12	70n71	23:25	70n71
17:4	61n44	2:1–3	61n40	25:1–7	67n59
17:13	61n44	2:2	70n73	25:14	70n73
18:6	174n98	2:3	70n71	28:2	67n59
18:15	61n44	2:4	6n22	29:3	67n59
19:4	61n44	2:11	66	36:21–22	68n61
19:6	78n109	3:3	58n24		
20:9	61n44	3:31	58n25	**Daniel**	
21:5	70n72	4:6	60n35	4:24–36	178
23:2	163n73	4:11	69n68, 70n71	7:9	203n27
23:9	61n44	5:7	57n20	8:9	69n67
23:14	60n35	5:20	58n26	8:19	5
23:19–20	6n22, 61n44	5:22	61n40, 70n74	9:16	68n63, 70n72
23:39	58n23, 61n43			9:24–27	9n36
25:11	9n36	**Ezekiel**		11:36	5
25:12–16	101n17	1:4	203n27	12:13	125n29
25:15	6n22	5:13	6n22, 61n42,		
28:1–17	61n42, 170n88		70n72, 170n88	**Hosea**	
28:55	200n14	5:15	62n48	3:1	62n47
30:23–24	6n22	6:12–17	131	4:1–4	179
31:2–3	61n44	6:12–14	200	4:7–19	62n47
31:3	200n14	6:12	6n22, 62n48,	4:9	163n73
31:8	200, 200n14		200n15	5:1–7	62n47
31:9	61n44	6:14	200n14	5:10	6n22, 62n47
31:15–17	62n46	7:8	6n22, 62n48,	8:5	6n22
31:32	200n14		70n73	9:1	62n47
32:29–32	65n49	8:2	203n27	9:9	154
32:31	61n44	8:18	62n48	10:8	98
32:35	78n109	13:13	60n35, 70n73	11:7	70n75
32:37	61n40	14:16	200n14	11:8	60n35
36:7	61n44	14:19	6n22, 62n48	11:9	6n22, 70n71
36:10	9n36	16:26	70n76	13:9–11	59n29, 61n42,
37:23	70	16:38	61n42, 62n48,		170n88
37:24	70n71		170n88	13:11	70n73
39:31	70n73	16:42	62n47	14:1–4	65n49, 122n20
39:37	70n73	16:46–56	60n35		
43:7	70n72	20:1–44	179n105	**Joel**	
44:8	65n49	20:8	6n22, 62n48,	2:1–11	68n64
45:5	70n73		70n73	2:11	98
49:18	60n35	20:9	68n60	2:12	162
50:13	60n33	20:14	68n60	2:13	58n24
50:40	60n35	20:21	70n73	2:28–32	68n64
51:6	70n73	20:22	68n60	2:31	98
52:3	58, 207n48,	20:44	68n60	3:2	103n25
	210	22:31	70n73	3:9–16	68n64

3:12	103n25	3:8	70n74		
3:13	102			**APOCRYPHA**	
3:14	103n25	**Zephaniah**			
3:21	163n73	1:12	65n50	**Tobit**	
5:18	162	1:14–18	68, 123	14:6	119n5
		1:14	98		
Amos		1:15	98	**Judith**	
3:2	61n42, 170n88	1:18	5, 55n14	8:14	71n83, 72n88
3:10	162n71	2:2	61n42, 70n73, 170n88	8:18–19	71n86, 72n88
4:11	60n35			9:8–9	71n86
4:13	141n6	2:9	60n35	9:8	71n83
5:8	141n6	3:4	68n63	9:9	71n83
5:18–20	68n64	3:8	68n64, 70n71		
5:18	61n42, 170n88			**Wisdom**	
9:5–6	141n6	**Haggai**		1:16	152n49
9:10	65n50	1:5–11	66n52, 170n87	2:21	149n37
				2:23–24	156n60
Obadiah		**Zechariah**		5:17–23	72n91
12:13	200	1:2	61n40, 70n74	5:18	71n83, 73
13	200n14	1:3	66n52, 170n87	5:20	213n63, 214n64
		1:12	61n40, 70n80, 170n87	5:22	213n63
Jonah				6:5	213n63, 214n64
3:9	60n33, 70n71	1:14	67n55		
4:2	58n24	1:15	67, 70n74	11:9	72n88
		1:16–21	67n56	11:10	213n63
Micah		2:1–5	67n55	12:9	213n63
2:7	70n76	7:8–14	61n40	13:1—14:31	144
3:4	58n23	7:12	65n49	13:1	144
3:11	61n42, 170n88	8:2	67n55	13:10	147n28
5:15	60n33, 70n72	8:7	67n55	15:1–6	160
7:18	58n25	8:14	70n76	15:7	174n98
		14	94	16:5–7	75
Nahum		14:5	203	16:5–6	72n88
1:2–3	161n70			16:5	71n83, 72n87, 127n40
1:2	55n14, 163n73	**Malachi**			
1:3	58n24	1:4	67n57, 70n80	16:7	75
1:5	57n22	1:6–14	179	18:15	213n63
1:6	6n20, 6n22, 60n30, 70n71, 70n73, 99	1:7–12	68	18:20–25	75
		1:11	68	18:20	71n83
1:9	67n57	3:1–4	94	18:21	71n83
3:19	67n57			18:22	71n83
				19:1	71n83, 71n86, 72n88, 127n40
Habakkuk					
3:2	5, 55n11			19:4	125n29
3:12	60n33				

Scripture Index

Sirach (Ecclesiasticus)

5:6	71n82, 71n86, 72n88, 96n11
5:7	71n82, 71n86, 122n20
6:6	71n86
8:10	203n27
10:12–13	150n39
15:20	150
15:26–28	152n48
16:11	71n82
16:6	71n86
16:11	72n88
18:24	71n86
28:1	182n115
36:7	71n82, 71n86
36:8–9	72n91
36:11	73n94
36:23	71n86
36:39	71n86
39:23–30	72n91
39:23	71n82
44:17	72n87, 75
45:19	71n82, 72n87
47:20	72n87
48:9–10	75
48:10	72n91, 73n94

Baruch

1:13	71n83, 71n86
2:13	71n83, 71n86
2:20	71n83, 71n86
4:6	71n83, 71n86
4:7	71n83
4:9	71n83, 71n86
4:25	71n83, 71n86
6	147n28
6:53	141n5

1 Maccabees

1:64	71n83, 71n86
2:24	74
2:49	71n83, 71n86
3:8	71n83, 71n86, 72n88, 139

2 Maccabees

2:13	208
5:17-20	71n86
5:17	72n88
5:20	72n88
6:12–17	125n29
7:1–42	74
7:33	71n86, 72n88
7:38	71n86, 75

2 Esdras

4:30	156n60
6:59	9n36
7:36	79n110
7:97	204n34
8:30–35	73, 73n96
8:30	71n86
8:34–35	71n86
8:59–60	141n6, 152n48, 73

4 Maccabees

4:13	74
4:21	72n86, 74
9:32	71n84, 74
10:15	200

NEW TESTAMENT

Matthew

3:7	2n2, 7n27, 91, 92, 197n6
3:11–12	91
3:13	91
5:14	34f2.34
5:22	105n33
6:2	34f2.34
6:5	34f2.34
6:16	34f2.34
7:5	34f2.34
8:1–4	104n28
8:12	105n33
10:15	105n38
11:23–24	105n38
13:42	105n33
15:7	34f2.34
18:8–9	105n33
18:23–34	7n31, 87
18:34	2n2, 107
20:22	105n29
22:1–14	7n31, 88
22:7	2n2
22:13	105n33
22:15–22	185f6.7
22:18	34f2.34, 186n128
23:13–39	161
23:13	34f2.34
23:15	34f2.34
23:23	34f2.34
23:25	34f2.34
23:27	34f2.34
23:29–35	125n29
23:29	34f2.34
23:32	105n33
23:33	92
24:8	9n36
24:37–39	64f3.5, 105n37
24:51	34f2.34, 105n33
25:30	105n33
25:41	105n33
26:39	105n29
26:65	211

Mark

1:40–45	7n32, 89
1:41	2n2, 90
3:5	7n30, 89n3, 90, 104n28, 105n39, 107, 164
7:6	34f2.34
7:9–13	161
7:22	161
8:27	63f3.3
9:43–49	105n33
10:14	89n3
10:38–39	105n29
13	98
13:8	9n36

13:10	127	4:25	83n130, 95	20:17–35	23f2.17
14:36	105n29	4:26	95	20:33	123n22
14:71	208	4:35–38	102	23:3	105n35
		5:38	96n11	23:12	208
Luke		6:56	96n11	23:14	208
3:7	2n2, 7n27, 91, 92, 106, 197n6	7:23	1, 5, 50n88	23:21	208
		8:35	96n11	23:33	153
4:18–19	92, 106	9:1–2	170n89	25:12	186n130
5:12–16	104n28	9:3	105n32	26:1	18f2.10
6:42	34f2.34	9:39–41	105n32	27:3	186n130
9:51–56	105	12:46	96n11	28:16–17	186n130
9:54	222	14:10	96n11		
10:1–16	105n36	15:4–7	96n11	Romans	
10:2	102	15:9–10	96n11	1–11	12, 137, 159, 173
10:12	105n38	18:11	105n29		
12:56	34f2.34			1–8	174n95
13:1–5	105n32, 170n89	Acts		1–4	3, 12, 137, 141, 169n86
		1:15–20	105n35		
13:15	34f2.34	2:24	9n36	1	11, 110, 122, 139, 151, 151n44, 155, 156, 157, 158, 158n66, 190, 220
13:28	105n33	4:25–28	99		
14:16–24	7n27, 88	5:1–11	105n35		
14:21	2n2	7:30	203n27		
17:26–27	105n37	7:39–43	147n30		
17:29	105n38	7:43	78n107		
20:22	186n128	7:48	17f2.8	1:3	120
21:20–24	93	8	82	1:4	120, 172n92
21:20	93	8:20	105n35	1:5	11n40, 163
21:23	2n2, 7n27, 92, 93, 106, 222	9:5	219	1:7	173
		9:20	120n12	1:9	120
21:34–36	130	10:42	10n38	1:16–17	174
21:50	208	12:20–23	105n35	1:18—8:39	197, 214, 223
22:42	105n29	12:21–23	142n9	1:18—4:25	189, 191
23:28–30	98	13:7	186	1:18—3:20	196
		13:10–11	105n35	1:18–32	1, 146n25, 137, 152, 153, 158, 159, 189, 191, 196, 199, 209, 220, 221, 223
John		13:13	33f2.33		
2	94	14;17	141n5		
2:17	104n28	16:14–15	117f5.16		
3:16	95	16:15	117f5.16		
3:19–21	132n53	16:40	117f5.16	1:18–23	140
3:36	2n2, 7n26, 94, 95, 106, 210, 215, 222, 223	17	120n8	1:18	3, 7n26, 109n1, 140, 162, 197, 201n21, 219, 221
		17:2	123n22		
		17:22–23	21f2.13		
4	82, 94	17:29	17f2.8		
4:19	95	17:30–31	10n38	1:19–20	141n5
4:20	95	18:2	123n22	1:23	156, 158, 190
4:21–24	95	18:12	48f2.50, 186	1:24–32	147n29

Scripture Index

1:24	153, 196	5	173, 190	11:3	125n29	
1:28	189, 197	5:1–11	171, 173	11:12	216, 221	
1:29–31	218	5:5	171	11:15	173	
1:32	151n 46	5:6	119n5, 171	11:19–22	213	
2	159, 165, 169, 169n86	5:8–10	171, 172f6.3	11:19	213	
		5:8	119n5, 211	11:20–24	197	
2:1–10	190	5:9	7n27, 109n1, 183n117, 171, 191, 221, 223	11:20	214	
2:4–8	162			11:22	214, 223	
2:4	190			11:26–27	159	
2:5–11	111	5:12–21	159	11:26	119, 137	
2:5–8	221	5:13	156	11:32	137	
2:5–6	199n11	5:14	156	12:3	188n137	
2:5	7n27, 109n1, 159, 163, 183n117, 197, 221, 223	5:15–19	11n40	12:17–18	182	
		5:20	156	12:19	7n27, 109n1, 163n73, 182, 182n115, 193, 214, 220, 221, 223	
		6:1—8:39				
		6:21	128n43			
2:6	163	6:22	128n44			
2:8	7, 7n27, 109n1, 109n2, 159, 163, 183n117, 221, 223	7	156	13:1–7	189n138	
		7:11–13	155	13:1–6	110, 193	
		7:24	119, 173n94, 199	13:4–5	193, 214	
				13:4	7n27, 109n1, 185, 187, 220, 221,223	
2:9	163	8	120			
2:14–16	147n29	8:1	173n94			
2:16	163n76	8:3	120	13:5	7n27, 185, 220, 221, 223	
2:14–15	151	8:16–17	173			
2:24	165	8:29	125n28, 120	13:11–12	180	
2:26	157n64	8:32	120	13:11	126	
3:1–8	169	8:34	201n20	13:12–14	132n54	
3:5	7n27, 109n1, 183n117, 191, 221	8:35–39	173, 221	14:12	163n78	
		8:38	132n55	14:15	119n5	
		9–11	12, 111, 122, 137, 169, 173, 174, 174n95, 174n95, 192	14:17	197n6	
3:9	191, 197			15:8–9	180n108	
3:21—8:39	197			15:12	11, 11n40, 157	
3:21	219			16:3	186	
3:23	168	9	214, 215			
3:30	157n64	9:3	124, 208	## 1 Corinthians		
4	169	9:6–13	174			
4:1–17	174	9:14–18	174	1:8	127n40, 128n41, 131n51	
4:9	157n64	9:19–21	174			
4:15	7n27, 109n1, 169, 171, 210, 221, 223	9:22–23	214			
		9:22	7n27, 109n1, 183n117, 192, 221, 222, 223	1:9	120n11	
				1:13	119n5	
4:18–17	173			1:18	201n16	
4:25	153	9:29	181n109, 222	3:13	163n78	
5–8	12, 137, 169, 173	10:13–16	105n36	4:12	123n22	
		11	213, 214	5:3–5	209n52	

5:5	200	1:13	127n34	**Philippians**	
6:9–11	197n6	1:15–16	172n92	1:28	126, 201n16
6:9–10	146n26	1:16	161	3:6–8	161
7:18–19	157n64	2:1–9	157	3:18–21	10
7:24	188n137	2:20	119n5, 120n11	3:19	128n43
8:11	119n5	3:1–14	210	4:2	117f5.16
10	214, 216, 221, 222	3:13	210, 211, 213n56, 216	**Colossians**	
10:1–12	170, 211	3:17	133n56	1:7	198f7.1
10:5	212	4:9	119	1:13	198
10:8	212	5:10	209	3:3	198
10:9	212	5:19–21	146n26	3:4	207n45
10:10	212	5:20	109, 184n120	3:5	146n26
10:10	106n42	5:21	197n6	3:6	2n2, 7n26, 109n1, 119, 198, 199, 214, 221, 223
10:14–33	212	**Ephesians**			
10:22	104n28, 200n13, 212, 223	1:1	195n1		
		1:12	207n45	3:8	109n1, 109n2, 109n3, 146n26, 184n120
11:32	212	2:1–10	197, 214, 222		
12:3	208	2:1–7	219		
15:3	211	2:3	2n2, 7n27, 109n1, 196, 197, 223	3:12	199n9
15:28	120n11			4:12	198f7.1
15:50	197n6				
15:51–53	205n38	2:6	197, 221	**1 Thessalonians**	
16:22	183, 208, 209, 215, 221, 223	2:7	197	1:2–10	120
		4:17–24	223	1:2–5	120
2 Corinthians		4:17–19	209, 215, 222	1:2	133
1:13	127n40	4:18	209, 210	1:3	111, 133
1:18–19	120n11	4:20–22	209n53	1:4	133
2:15	201n16	4:26	184n120	1:6–9	120
3:16	119	4:31	109n1, 109n2, 109n3, 184n120	1:6	9n36
5:10	163n78			1:7	111, 204
5:14	119n5			1:9–10	119, 120, 121
7:10	201	5:1–20	197	1:9	111, 132n55, 171
11:15	128n43	5:1–14	197		
12:20	109n2	5:1–6	209	1:10	2, 2n2, 7n27, 9n34, 109n1, 111, 120, 121, 122, 125, 126, 131n50, 135, 136, 162, 171, 173, 183n117, 197n6, 199, 199n11, 201n20, 220, 221, 223
		5:2–4	197		
Galatians		5:6	2n2, 7n26, 109n1, 197, 199, 210, 214, 221, 223		
1:2	157				
1:8–9	183, 208, 209, 215, 221				
1:8	208, 223	5:7	197, 209n53		
1:9	208, 223	5:11	197		
1:12	172n92, 219	5:15	209		
1:13–14	161				

Ref	Pages
2:3–12	8, 123
2:6	221
2:7	171
2:8	171
2:12	131n51
2:13	123
2:14–16	124, 125n29
2:15–16	180
2:16	2n2, 7n27, 109n1, 123, 124, 125n28, 127, 128, 136, 180, 183n117, 201n17, 219, 223
2:17–18	8
2:19	9n34, 9n36, 131n50
3:1–7	8
3:2	111
3:6–10	111
3:10	134n61
3:11–13	133n59
3:11	8
3:13	9n34, 9n36, 131n50, 131n51,
4:3	131n51
4:6	131n51, 199n11, 207
4:7	131n51
4:11	123n22
4:13—5:11	130
4:13	134n61
4:14	10, 121
4:15	9n34, 9n36, 131n50
4:16	131n50, 201n20, 205n38
4:17	207, 221
5:1–11	130, 133, 171, 200n13, 207
5:1–10	136
5:2	9n34, 131n50
5:3	130, 131n50, 200, 201
5:4	132
5:5	132
5:8–10	171
5:8–9	133
5:8	132, 132f5.20, 134n60, 200n13
5:9–10	126, 126n31, 171
5:9	2n2, 7n27, 109n1, 128, 128n44, 129, 221, 223, 132, 136, 183n117, 199n11, 201, 205, 206, 221
5:10	133, 171, 221
5:22	131n51
5:23	9n34, 9n36, 131n50, 131n51, 133n59
5:24	133
5:27	133

2 Thessalonians

Ref	Pages
1:5–10	200, 201, 215, 219, 221, 222, 223
1:5–7	163
1:5	197n6
1:6–10	99
1:6	163
1:7–9	204
1:7–8	201
1:7	102, 163, 201n21, 203
1:8	164, 183, 200n13, 204, 207, 222
1:9	200, 200n13, 207, 221
1:10	207n45
2:1–2	126
2:10	201n16
2:11	150n40
2:14	134n63, 206
3:7	123n22

1 Timothy

1:13	127n34
2:8	109n1, 184n120
6:9	200

Philemon

23	198f7.1

Hebrews

3:6	127n40
3:7–11	105n39, 211n57
3:8	105n39, 212n59
3:10	105n39
3:11	2n2, 7n27, 96, 107, 222
3:14	127n40
3:15–19	211n57
3:15	105n39, 212n59
3:16	105n39
3:17	105n39
4:3	2n2, 7n27, 96, 107, 211n57, 222
4:11–13	97
4:16	212n59
6:11	127n40
10:25–39	106n41, 222
10:30	182, 183
11:7	105n37

James

1:19–20	184
3:6	122n18
4:12	106n41
5:8–9	106n41

1 Peter

1:17	106n41,

	163n78	2:13	17f2.9	14:6–13	101
3:20	105n37	2:18	204n33	14:8	3, 100, 101, 102
4:7	106n41	2:23	163n78	14:10–11	102
4:13	106n41	2:26	127n40	14:10	2n2, 7n26, 101
4:17	106n41	4–11	100	14:13	102
		4–5	97, 98	14:14–20	101, 102
2 Peter		4:5	204n33	14:15–17	102
2:4	105n40	5	104	14:18	101
2:5	105n37	5:6	99	14:19	2n2, 102
2:6	105n38	6–16	97, 98	14:20	102
3:7	105n33	6	98	15:1	2n2, 99
3:10	203n27	6:1	99	15:7	2n2, 99
		6:9–17	99	16:1	2n2, 100
1 John		6:10	98	16:19	2n2, 3, 7n25, 7n26, 100
1:10	211	6:11	98	17–20	97, 101
4:8	3	6:12–17	98	17	103
		6:16	2n2, 7n28, 98, 99	17:17	104
Jude		6:17	2n2, 7n29, 98, 197n6	18	103
6	105n40	9:11	22f2.16	19	103, 104
7	105n33, 105n38	10:1	204n33	19:12	204n33
14–15	203n22	11:17	99	19:15	2n2, 7n25, 7n26, 102, 102n19, 103, 104
14	106n41	11:18	2n2, 7n27, 101, 197n6		
15	106n41	12–20	100		
16	106, 212n58	12	101	19:20	103n24
17	106n41	12:11	99, 104	20:10	103n24
18	106n41	14	101	20:14	103n24
		14:1–5	101	20:15	103n24
Revelation		14:5	101		
1:14–15	204n33				
1:5	99				

Ancient Documents Index

Pseudepigrapha
Greek Apoc. of Ezra

15	73n96

Assumption of Moses

8:1	72n86
10:3–10	72n91
10:3	72n86

2 Baruch

2:13	72n88
4:9	72n88
11:1	101n17, 102n18
21:6	204n34
24:4	9n36
48:14–17	73n96
48:14–15	71n86
48:17	71n86
51:5	205
51:10	205
51:11	203n22
51:12	205
54:17–19	156n60
59:6	72n88, 161n70
59:10	79n110
59:11	204n34
64:4	71n86
85:13	79n110

1 Enoch

1:8–9	203n22
1:9	106n41
2:1—5:3	152n48
5:6	208
5:7	208
5:9	72n88
10:22	71n83, 72n86, 72n91
13:8	71n83, 73n95
18:16	73n95
27:1–3	79n110
53:1	103n25
53:3–5	73n95
53:3	203n22
55:3	72n91, 73n95
62:10–12	72n91
62:12	72n86
63:1	203n22
68:4	73n95
84:4–6	73n95
90:15	72n86, 72n91
90:18	72n86, 72n91
90:26	79n110
91:5	203n22
91:6–9	126n32
91:7–9	72n91, 73n93
91:7	72n86, 72n88
91:9	72n86
91:14	203n22
99:9	142n9, 145n21, 152n48
99:16	71n83, 72n86, 72n91
100:3	102
101:3	71n83, 72n86
106:5	71n83
106:15	72n87

2 Enoch

1:5	204n34
10:1–6	206
19:1	204n34
29:3	204n34

Life of Adam and Eve

1	156n60

Letter of Aristeas

254	187n131

Psalms of Solomon

4:25	71n86
7:4	71n86, 72n88
8:7–9	73, 71n86
12:5	203n27

Sibylline Oracles

3:309	72n89
3:51–56	72n86
3:309	196n4
3:545–61	72n91
3:556–61	121n14
3:796–812	72n91
4:130–39	74
4:159–60	72n86, 72n88
4:160–61	72n91
5:143–45	102n18
5:143	101n17
5:159	101n17
5:298–305	72n91
5:298	72n89
5:344–60	72n91
5:508	72n86, 72n91

Ancient Documents Index

Testament of Benjamin
5:3   132n53

Testament of Levi
2:11   203n22
3:3   203n22
3:10   72n86, 73
6:11   72n87, 124n23
19:1   132n53
106:15   71n83

Testament of Naphtali
2:7–10   132n53
3:3   142n9, 152n48
3:4   147n28

Testament of Reuben
4:4   71n83, 71n84

Jubilees
3:23   71n84
5:1–7   73n95
7:21   73n95
15:34   71n86, 72n88, 73n93, 126n32
24:28–33   72n90
24:30   71n86
36:10   71n86, 72n87, 72n90, 73n93

Other Ancient Sources

Aeschylus
Agamemnon
70   30n10, 30n14
215   30n14
221   30n10

Prometheus vinctus
190   30n10

Aristotle
Ethica nicomachea
4.5.14   40n38

Rhetorica
2.2.1   37n19
2.2.2   37n19
2.2.6   37n19
2.2.7   37n19
2.3.16   37n19
2.5.21   38n28

Aurelius Victor
De Caearibus
5.1–2   186n129

Cassius Dio
Historia Romana
40.51.2   38n27
42.27   187n131

Chrysippus
Minor Fragments
567   43n47

Cicero
Pro Murena
29   42n41

De natura Deorum
1.16   47n74
3.2   47n79
3.40   47n76

De officiis
3.102   47n76
3.116–20   47n74
3.29   154n56

Tusculanae disputat.
4.1   46n70
4.3.6   47n74
4.9   46n71
4.10   42n44
4.21   42n45
4.23   42n44
5.27.78   47n74

Dead Sea Scrolls

Epochs of Time
2   79n114, 81n122, 81n123, 182n112
3:4–8   80n120

Exhortation
1.1.5–15   203n22

The Book of Hymns
1:5–9   79n117
3:25–29   81n122, 81n123
3:34–36   203n22
10:35   203n22
12:20–32   182n113
12:25–32   79n117
14:15–20   81n122, 81n123
14:16   80n118
15:15–20   79n114, 79n116, 81n122
15:15   79n115
15:20   125n27

Habakkuk Com.
1:12–13   79n115
2:16   81
2:20   81n122, 81n124

Hosea Com.
2:8   79n115

Lamentation for Zion
1:2:1   80n119

Last Jubilee
12:15   203n22

Manual of Discipline
1:16–2:18   81n122, 81n123, 81n124, 208
1:9   132n53
1:10   132n53
3:13—4:26   79n114, 81, 81n122, 81n123, 81n124, 126n30
3:13   132n53
3:24   132n53

Ancient Documents Index 255

4:12	81	10:4–10	172n92	Epictetus	
5:7–20	80, 125n27, 125n28	13:20	79n115	*The Discourses*	
		14:18	79n115	1.16.15–21	141n6

Prayer for Intercession

		15:1—16:20	79n115	*Fragments*	
		16:11—17:15	80n120		
2	80n120, 81, 170n87	Demosthenes		363	45n63
		De Chersoneso		365	45n63
6	81, 170n87			366	45n63

Rout of Belial

		1	38n25	Epicurus	
5–6	80n119, 81n122	*De falsa legatione*		*Letter to Menoeceus*	
		7	38n23	123–24	40n40

War Sons Light/Dark

De Halonesso

				Euripides	
1:1–7	203n22	1	38n25	*Medea*	
1:1	132n53	*Pro Megalopolitanis*		130	30n13
1:3	132n53	19	38n25	1172	30n12, 30n14
1:7	132n53	6	38n25	*Hippolytus*	
1:10	132n53	*In Midiam*		43	30n12
1:16	132n53	147	38n25	438	30n14
3:1—6:6	81, 81n122	*Philippica iii*		*Bacchae*	
3:1–11	125n27	31	38n23	1348	37n15
3:6	132n53	*De Rhodiorum libertate*		1348	39n30
3:9	132n53	1	38n25	Hesiod	
3:1	132n53	*In Timocratem*		*Opera et dies*	
3:12—4:2	81n124, 125n27	118	38n22	302	4n13
6:4	81	Dio Chrysostum		Homer	
15:1–2	81n124	*Tarsica Prior*		*Ilias*	
15:14	203n22	33.50	45n65	1.82	37n19

Zadokite Document

Diogenes Laertius
Lives of Eminent Phil.

1:1—2:12	79n115			1.92–100	29n3
2:2–13	79n114, 81n124	7.110	42n44, 184n121	1.103	46
				1.356	37n19
2:14—3:12	80n119, 80n120, 127n40	1.111	42n42	2.66–67	29n3
		7.113	42n45	2.196	37n19
3:12	132n53	7.114	4n17	3.386	182n111
4:6–12	79n115	7.171	43n49	4.23–24	13n1
4:12—5:17	80n121, 125n28	7.173	43n49	5.177–78	29n3
		10.139	39n31, 40n39	5.34	13n1, 29n3
5:17—7:6	79n115			5.440–44	29n3
7:9—8:21	80n119, 81n122, 81n124, 125n28			5.762	13n1
				6.138–43	29n3
				8.1–27	13n1
9:2–8	80n119			8.397	13n1

8.407	13n1			43.13.1–2	49n87	
8.421	13n1	**Josephus**				
8.430	13n1	*Jewish Antiquities*		**Lucretius**		
8.449	13n1	1.20	75, 75n99	*De rerum natura*		
8.460–61	13n1	1.194–95	75n99	1.58–89	47n75	
9.98–99	38n22	3.321	75n98, 75n99	2.645–46	47n75	
9.534–40	29n3	4.130	75n98	2.651	47n75	
15.119–41	13n1	11.127	75n98, 75n99	5.1194–96	47n75	
15.184–99	13n1	11.141	75n98, 75n99	5.399–401	46n71	
15.212–17	13n1	12.221	75n98	6.51–53	47n75	
16.707–11	29n4	14.2.2	75n99, 142n9	6.70–72	47n75	
17.546	29n9	14.4.4	49n86	6.753–54	47n75	
17.626–27	29n9	17.168	75n99			
18.109	37n19	15.243	75, 75n99	**Lycurgus**		
18.367	29n3	15.299	75, 75n99	*Against Leocrates*		
19.112–34	13n1	15.376	75n99	159.22	39n33, 184n121	
21.136–47	29n3	15.7.7	75n99			
21.388–90	14n2	16.222	75n98	**Marcus Aurelius**		
22.208–13	29n5	16.2.3	49n86	*Communings/Himself*		
22.297–305	29n6	16.263	75n98	5.27–28	47n78	
24.134–37	29n3	16.7.2	75n99, 142n9	9.1	169n85	
24.54	37n19	17.168	75n99	10.30	47n78	
24.55	13n1	17.5.2	75n99	11.8	47n78	
24.479	13n1	18.1.1	186n128			
24.606	29n3	18.85–87	83n130	**Marcus Minucius Felix**		
		19.8.2	142n9	*Octavius*		
Odyssea		19.19	75n98	7	47n79	
1.60–62	29n7	20.5.1	186n128	7.2	49n86	
1.66–79	29n3	*The Jewish War*		**Menander**		
3.134–36	29n3	5.13.6	76	*Epitrepontes*		
3.141–47	29n3	7.11.4	76	872–79	39n36	
5.7–20	38n22	7.34	75, 75n99	*Eunuchus*		
5.145–47	29n3	7.332	75	187K	39n34	
5.146	13n1	7.8.6	186n128	190K	39n34	
7.308–10	38n29			*Heros*		
9.477	154n54	**Livy**		29–51	39n34	
9.553	39n32	*Ab urbe condita*		*Minor Fragments*		
11.71–73	29n3	1.9	46n72	574K	39n33, 184n121	
12.376–83	29n3	2.36	47n81, 49n85			
12.415–19	29n3	5.14	47n80	629K	39n33, 184n121	
13.139–45	29n3	8.8	47n80			
14.283–84	29n3	8.9	48n82	700K	170n89,	
19.409–10	29n7	9.29	47n80			
24.539–44	29n8	22.9	48, 47n80			
		25.6	48, 49n83			
		27.23	47n80			

Ancient Documents Index 257

	187n131
845K	185n125

Samia

155	39n33, 184n121
187–89	39n35

Pausanias
Graeciae descriptio

1.1.7	45n64
2.4	45n64
2.5	45n64
4.6	45n64
7.6	45n64
8.25.6	45n65
8.3–4	45n64
10.32.10–11	45n65
24.6	45n64

Petronias
Satyricon

126–41	46n73

Philo
On the Life of Abraham

202	76n100

On Dreams 1, 2

1.235	76n100
2.177–79	76n100
2.179	76

Who Is the Heir?

90	139n1
94	181n110
313–16	169n86

On the Life of Moses 1, 2

1.6	76n100
1.119	76n100

Sacrifices of Cain, Abel

95–96	76n100

That God Is Unchangeable

52–54	76n100
59–60	76n100

Plato
Leges

731D	39n37

Plutarch
Caesar

69.3	49n87

Cicero

1.2	49n87

Moralia

12.20	45n62
12.25	45n62
441C	42n44
441D	42n43, 184n121
446F	42n43
447B	45n62
450C	42n43, 184n121
454B–D	43n48

Pericles

39	45n62

Polybius
Histories

1.4	43n52, 49n84
1.48	43n53
1.35.2	43n52
1.58.1	43n52
1.81.5–9	154n55
2.7.1–2	43n52
2.27.6	43n52
2.35.5–6	43n52
2.58.15	43n51
2.70.4–8	43n53
3.3.3	43n51
3.4.8–9	44n54
3.7.2	43n51
3.62.8	44n58
3.111.10–11	44n58
3.112.8–9	44n58
3.118.6	43n52
3.118.8–9	44n55
4.4.7	43n51
4.26	49n87
4.29.7	43n51
4.33.3	44n58
4.62.3–4	44n56
4.81	49n87
6.1.9–10	44n55
7.9.1–3	44n58
9.16.2–4	44n55
10.2.7	44n55
11.23.8	44n56
12.23.3	44n56
15.5.11	43n51
15.9.4	43n52
15.33.10	43n51
16.1.2	43n51
16.2.5	44n55
16.2.9	44n55
18.54.11	44n56
23.10.2	43n52
27.8.4	44n58
30.6.6	43n52
32.15.14	44n56
36.17.15	44n57
38.18.10	43n51

Seneca
Epistulae m. ad Lucilim

10–12	47n77

Sophocles
Ajax

776	30n11, 30n14

Antigone

280	39n32
325–27	154n54
672	152n48
766	39n32
870–80	37n16
999–1033	37n20
1200	30n11

Oedipus tyrannus

404–07	37n18
523–24	37n17, 38n29, 39n32

Suetonius
Divus Augustus
92	49n87
93	49n85

Divus Claudius
46	49n87

Galba
18	49n87

Tacitus
Annales
1.39	47
3.61	46n71
4.1	48
12.43	49n87
13.17	49n87
14.22	47n81
14.27	198f7.2
16.16	47, 49n84

Historiae
2.38	47, 49n85
3.68	187n131
4.26	49n83
4.54	48

Talmud (Babylonian)
'Abodah Zarah
4b	77n102

Nedarim
32a	77n106

Šabbat
55a	105n31

Sanhedrin
105b	77n102
111b	77n105
113b	77n105

Zebaḥim
102a	77n104

Thucydides
His. Peloponnesian War
2.74	184n123
2.8	150n38

Virgil
Aeneid
1.2–4	49n84
5.784	49n84
7.285–316	46n71
8.50–58	49n84

Modern Authors Index

Abbott, T. K., 196n4, 199n10
Achtemeier, Paul J., 196n2
Aphrodisias, 31f2.29
Aune, David E., 121, 121n16
Aus, Roger D., 3, 3n6
Barrett, C. K., 11n42,
    148n33, 154n55,
    156n59, 171n90,
    172n96, 175n100,
    178n103, 184n122,
    185n124, 214n65
Barrois, G. A., 103n25
Barth, Karl, 142n11, 149n35
Barth, Markus, 142n9,
    197n7, 210n54
Barton, William E., 83n125
Berger, Klaus, 208n51
Best, Ernest, 119n4, 120n7,
    121n15, 124n26,
    127n36, 130, 130n45,
    204n30, 207n46
Boers, Hendrikus, 120n9
Bornkamm, G., 105n30, 123,
    123n21, 139n1, 142n8,
    143, 143n15, 144n18
Bowman, J., 82n125, 83n131
Bruce, F. F., 124n25, 148n33,
    196n4, 203n28
Bultmann, Rudolf, 11n36,
    88, 89n2, 167n84
Calvin, J., 142n10, 211n55
Campenhausen, H., 169n86
Carson, D. A, 196n2
Charles, R. H., 9n36, 73, 74,
    102, 102n20, 121n14,
    141n6
Coffey, David M., 147n25
Collins, John J., 121n14
Cooper, Mark D. 125n29
Cranfield, C. E. B., 105n30,
    141n5, 142n11, 146n26,
    148n33, 161, 161n70,
    169n86, 172n92,
    175n100, 178n103, 188,
    188n135, 188n136
Cullmann, Oscar, 185n124
Curtius, Georg, 4n15
Daube, D., 131n49, 197n6
Davies, J. G., 9n34
Davies, W. D., 9n35, 91n6
Deissmann, A., 9n36, 141n7,
    147n29, 188, 188n133
De Jonge, H., 71n83, 124n23,
    142n9, 147n28
deSilva, David A., 196n2
Dodd, Charles H., 2, 3,
    10n38, 152–155,
    152n50, 155n57,
    166n84, 178n103, 189
Donaldson, John W., 4n16
Donfried, Karl P., 131n51,
    209n52
Doty, William G., 143n17
Dunn, J., 140n3, 151n44,
    156n59, 164, 165n80,
    166n84, 167n84,
    169n86, 178n103
Eichrodt, W., 55n7, 55n14,
    56n17, 57n21
Fee, G. D., 124n26, 203n28,
    203n29, 209n52
Ferguson, Everett, 82n125
Fitzmyer, J. A., 140n3,
    151n43, 166n84,
    175n100
Frame, J. E., 122n20, 127,
    127n36, 127n39,
    200n13, 204n30,
    207n46
France, R. T., 89n4
Fritsch, Charles T., 70n80
Gager, John G., 122n19
Garlington, Don B., 156n59,
    156n62
Gaster, J. G., 54n4, 79n112,
    79n113, 79n114, 203,
    203n23
Gaston, Lloyd, 140n3
Gathercole, Simon J., 166n81
Godet, Frederic, 140n4, 144,
    144n20, 148n33
Green, Joel B., 196n2
Guelich, Robert A., 89n4
Haney, Herbert M., 55n9
Hanson, A. T., 88n1, 103,
    103n22, 122n18,
    166n84, 206, 206n43
Hengel, Martin, 66n53, 120,
    120n12
Heschel, Abraham, 62n46
Hooker, M. D., 156, 156n58
Hultgren, A. J., 140n3,

Modern Authors Index

158n65, 158n66
Hunter, A. M., 10n39, 88n1
Hyldahl, Niels, 156, 156n58
Jeremias, J., 79n112, 88n1, 92, 92n7, 131n49
Jewett, Robert, 8n33, 139n2, 140n3, 151n43, 166n84, 175n100, 178, 178n104
Kallas, James, 189n138
Käsemann, Ernst, 11n42, 139n1, 140n3, 140n4, 143, 143n14, 147n29, 148, 148n32, 159n68, 166n84, 169n86, 178n102, 183, 183n119, 188, 188n134, 188n137, 208, 208n51
Kaiser, Otto, 68n65
Kaye, Bruce N., 133n57
Lake, Kirsopp, 9n35
Lane, William L., 89n4
Leenhardt, Franz J., 148n33, 183n118
Liao, Paul S., 166n82
Licht, Jacob, 74, 74n97
Lightfoot, J. B., 204n30, 207n46
Lincoln, Andrew T., 196n4
Linebaugh, J. A., 144n19
Ljungmen, Henrik, 166n82
Lohse, E., 147n29, 199n8, 206n44, 207n46
Longenecker, R. N., 139n1, 140n3, 141n5, 142n11, 144n19, 166n84, 178n104
Luther, Martin, 211n55
Macdonald, John, 82n125, 82n126, 82n127, 83n131, 83n132
Marshall, I. H., 196n2, 196n3
Martin, D. Michael, 133n57

Mattill, A. J., Jr., 9n36
McCarthy, Dennis J., 53n3
Metzger, Bruce M., 89n3, 195n1, 199n10
Meyer, Heinrich, 140n4, 143, 143n12, 143n16, 149n35, 164, 164n79, 175n99, 178n103, 182n115
Montgomery, J. A., 82n125
Moo, D. J., 171n90, 196n2
Moody, D., 148n33, 213n62
Morford, Mark P. O., 46n71
Morris, Leon, 91n6, 204n30
Moule, C., 9n35, 10n39, 122n19, 131n51, 212n60
Moule, H., 152n47, 155n57
Mounce, Robert H., 103n25
Munck, J., 12n42, 119n5
Murray, J., 148n33, 182, 182n116
Nickelsburg, G. W. E., 72n92
Neill, Stephen, 119n6, 120n8
Nygren, Anders, 142n10, 173, 178n103
O'Rourke, J. J., 141n5
Otto, Rudolf, 2, 2n4, 55n12
Pannenberg, W., 163n72
Purvis, J. D., 82n125, 83n131
Postell, Seth D., 158n67
Pummer, Reinhard, 82n125
Rad, G. von, 57n19, 57n21
Räisänen, H., 140n3, 169n86
Ringgren, Helmer, 57n20
Roetzel, Calvin J., 78n108, 127n33, 143n17, 206n41, 209n52, 213n61
Russell, D. S., 205n36
Rylaarsdam, J. Coert, 53n1
Sanday, Headlam, 166n84, 175n100, 185n127
Sanders, E. P., 9n35, 169n86

Saphir, A. P., 55n10, 55n12, 55n13, 59, 60n30
Schlatter, Adolf, 139n1, 142n11, 147n30, 150n41, 156n61
Schoeps, H. J., 10n39, 205, 205n39
Schreiner, Thomas R., 169n86
Scott, R. B. Y., 65n51
Sevenster, J. N., 147n29
Simpson, William H., 61n41
Skinner, John, 104n26
Smith, T. C., 2, 2n3, 2n4, 2n5, 166n84
Stevens, G. L., 82n125, 94n9, 97n12, 101n14, 101n15, 102n18, 102n21, 104n27, 156n63
Stewart, James S., 147n27
Strong, L. Thomas III, 152n48
Tasker, R. V. G., 88n1, 175n100
Teeple, Howard M., 83n129
Thielman, Frank, 169n86
Thompson, Alden L., 73n95
Thompson, M. M., 196n2
Towner, W. S., 206n42
VanHorn, N., 12n42, 169n86
Vos, Geerhardus, 9n37
Vriezen, Th. C., 68n63
Westerholm, S., 169n86
Westermann, Claus, 57n21
Whiteley, D. E. H., 135n64
Wiens, Devon H., 132n54
Wise, Michael O., 160n69
Wolff, Hans Walter, 141n6
Wright, N. T., 166n82, 169n86
Young, Edward J., 69n67
Zanker, Paul, 561n41

Subject Index

Abraham(ic), 11, 11n42, 12, 168, 169, 169n86, 170, 174, 181, 191, 223
Achilles, 14f2.1, 14f2.2, 21f2.14, 29, 138, 192
Adam(ic), 151n44, 156, 158, 159, 168, 172, 172n92, 190, 191
Adriatic, 8f1.1
Agrippa, 18f2.10, 105n35, 124
Ahab, 63f3.2
Alexander, 21f2.14, 25f2.22
anathema, 183, 208, 209, 209n52, 215
angel(ic), 55, 68n66, 74, 82, 99, 100, 101, 105, 185n124, 201, 202, 202f7.3, 203, 203n24, 204, 204n34, 205, 205n36, 207, 208, 222
Angel of Destruction, 77, 86, 110
Aphrodite, 64f3.4
apocalyp(se)(tic), 2 72, 81, 86, 97, 98, 99, 101, 132n94, 147n29, 148, 155, 175, 202, 202f7.3, 203, 205n36, 206, 215, 220, 222
Apollo, 22f2.15, 22f2.16, 23f2.17, 29
Apollonius, 74, 85
Areopagus, 17f2.8

Aris, 64f3.4
Artemis, 30, 64f3.4
Asklepios, 23f2.18, 23f2.19, 64f3.4
Aspendos, 33f2.33
Athena, 14f2.2, 18f2.10, 19f2.11, 20f2.12, 21f2.13, 21f2.14, 30, 64f3.4, 138, 192
Athen(s)(ian), 13, 14f2.2, 17f2.8, 21f2.13, 21f2.14, 35f2.37, 38, 40f2.40, 41f2.41, 41f2.42, 150n38
Augustus, 10f1.2, 11n40, 45, 49n87, 64f3.4, 113f5.4, 114f5.7, 114f5.8, 132f5.20, 185f6.7
Burrus, 186, 193
Caesar, 38, 48f2.50, 63f3.3, 186n130
Caesarea, 63f3.3, 64f3.4, 124, 153
Caesarea Philippi, 63f3.3, 64f3.4
Cassander, 112f5.1
Cerberus, 27f2.25
Chrysippus, 42
Claudius, 38, 46, 124
cognate, 5, 7, 13, 46, 50n88, 69, 75, 149n36, 164, 201, 213n63
Colossae, 198f7.1, 198f7.2
Corinth(ians), 8, 21f2.14,

36f2.38, 47, 48f2.50, 111, 170, 171, 177f6.5, 186, 188, 208, 212, 214, 216
covenant, 6, 54, 56, 57, 59, 60, 62, 65, 84, 88, 90, 97, 111, 122, 126n32, 157, 165, 166, 166n82, 167, 168, 173, 210, 217, 219, 224
cult(ic), 11, 44, 45, 47, 47n79, 48, 49, 51, 57, 63f3.2, 74, 82, 97, 106, 109, 116f5.12, 116f5.14, 121, 139n1, 141n7, 160, 218
curse, 36f2.38, 55, 59, 60, 62, 78, 166, 167, 169n86, 170, 190, 191, 208, 209, 209n52, 210, 211, 215, 216, 224
Day of the Lord, 9n36, 68, 84, 98, 122, 127, 128, 131, 132, 133, 136, 162
Day of Vengeance, 82, 83, 86, 92, 93, 94, 95, 104, 183
death, 10, 14f2,1, 14f2.2, 15f2.4, 36f2.38, 41f2.42, 48, 49, 55, 57, 68n66, 73, 74, 92, 103, 105n35, 106, 108, 119, 124, 128, 129, 130, 133, 142n9, 150, 151, 151n43, 152, 155, 159, 162, 172, 172n92, 173n94, 189, 191, 199, 202f7.3, 211,

Subject Index

212, 215, 216, 218, 220, 221, 222, 223
Demeter, 25f2.21, 26f2.24
Demetrios, 118f5.18, 129
denarius, 185f6.7
destiny, 11, 11n40, 29, 49, 50, 51, 67, 93, 105, 110, 111, 122, 126, 127, 135, 136, 140, 141n6, 147, 150, 152, 155, 157, 158, 159, 171, 172, 173, 181, 189, 190, 191, 207, 209, 215, 218, 220, 221, 222, 223
destruction, 9n37, 16f2.7, 47, 54, 60, 66, 76, 79, 81, 92, 93, 95, 98, 102n18, 106, 121, 125, 128, 128n43, 130, 130n47, 131, 146, 149, 150n41, 151n42, 162, 175, 178, 180, 200, 201, 204, 205, 206, 207, 209n52, 211, 214, 215, 222
Diana, 22f2.15
Dionysus, 18f2.10, 28f2.26, 35f2.36, 35f2.37, 36f2.39, 64f3.4, 115f5.10
disapproved, 148, 149, 150, 161, 168, 189, 197, 220, 223
disobedience, 11, 12, 96, 137, 138, 139, 152, 152n48, 161, 164, 165, 166, 168, 169, 189, 190, 191, 192, 196, 197, 199n10, 203, 209, 210, 210n54, 215, 219, 220, 224
Domitian, 22f2.16
doxology, 12, 144, 159
Dyrrachium, 8f1.1
Eleazar, 186n128, 212
emotion, 2, 4, 6, 34f2.34, 38, 39, 40, 42, 43, 50, 51, 58, 104, 110, 189, 199
eschatolog(y)(ical), 2, 3, 8, 9,

9n35, 9n37, 11, 11n40, 68, 69, 72, 73, 74, 79, 81, 82, 83, 83n129, 84, 85, 86, 92, 93, 94, 95, 96, 98, 102, 103, 105n36, 106, 111, 119, 120, 121, 121n16, 122, 122n20, 123, 124n23, 125, 126, 126n32, 127, 128, 130, 130n47, 131, 132n54, 133, 133n57, 134, 135, 136, 144, 151n42, 156, 157, 158, 162, 166, 166n81, 166n84, 167, 169, 169n86, 171, 172, 172n92, 173, 180, 181, 183, 184, 188, 189, 191, 192, 193, 197, 199, 200, 201, 201n19, 201n21, 203, 204n30, 206, 207, 208, 209, 210, 212, 214, 215, 216, 219, 221, 222, 223, 224
Eleusinian, 25f2.21, 26f2.24
Epicurean, 41f2.42, 46, 47, 51, 110, 217
Eumenes II, 17f2.9
exile, 53, 59, 60, 61, 62, 64f3.4, 65, 66, 67, 68, 69n67, 71, 78, 84, 100, 107, 156, 158, 159, 162, 168, 169n86, 170, 178, 179, 180, 181, 191, 192, 210, 216
explicit, 2, 3, 11n40, 38, 58, 68n63, 73, 87, 96, 97, 104, 104n28, 105n36, 106, 108, 124, 124n24, 135, 140, 150, 157, 160, 165, 168, 173, 178, 183, 190, 195, 199, 199n12, 201, 205, 209, 210, 211, 214, 215, 224
fasc(is)(es), 187, 187f6.10
fatum, 49, 51, 220
Festus, 186n130

forbearance, 161, 175, 178, 179, 179n106, 180, 190, 192
forensic, 3, 75, 153, 214
Galen, 23f2.19
Galerius, 112f5.2
Gallikos River, 8f1.1
Gallio, 48f2.50, 186
Gehenna, 78, 78n108, 79, 86, 92, 107, 122, 122n18, 136, 141n6, 215, 221
gentile, 11, 11n40, 119, 119n5, 123, 124, 136, 140, 141n6, 142n9, 147n29, 156, 157, 158, 158n65, 164, 165, 168, 174n95, 179, 180, 190, 199n10, 213, 216, 221
Gerizim, Mount, 83, 86, 94, 95
golden calf, 59, 63f3.2, 66, 157, 158, 164, 190, 210
gospel, 10, 11, 92, 104, 120, 125, 126, 127, 127n34, 129, 135, 136, 138, 139, 142, 143, 143n13, 145n23, 163, 164, 165, 170, 174, 178, 179, 180, 181, 190, 191, 192, 203, 205, 207, 208, 209, 219, 221, 223
government, 37, 47, 51, 110, 184, 186, 188, 193, 224
grace, 11, 30, 58, 152, 169, 170, 171, 172, 173, 174, 191, 192, 197, 219
Hades, 26f2.24, 27f2.25, 103
Hector, 14f2.1, 14f2.2, 15f2.3, 15f2.4, 15f2.5, 29
Helios, 22f2.16
Hera, 64f3.4
Hercules, 25f2.22
Hermes, 18f2.10, 46
Herod, 34f2.34, 63f3.3, 64f3.4, 75, 105n35, 124, 142n9
Hinnom, 78, 78f3.6
hol(y)(iness), 2, 2n4, 55,

Subject Index   263

55n12, 57, 58, 68, 83n130, 88, 90, 131, 132n54, 140, 158, 162, 171, 192, 203, 208, 209n52, 217, 224

Hygieia, 23f2.19

impersonal, 2, 55, 84, 130, 155, 190, 195, 219

immoral(ity), 38, 101, 102, 147, 155, 196, 197, 199

immutable, 3, 43, 69, 85, 110

implicit, 2, 3, 7, 61n41, 78n107, 87, 97, 104, 105, 108, 110, 130n47, 151n42, 173, 173n94, 190, 195, 200, 207, 209, 211, 214, 215, 216, 224

ira deum, 46, 47, 49, 51, 93, 106, 220

irrational(ity), 37, 38, 39, 42, 44, 46, 51, 54, 55, 55n9, 84, 109, 110

Isis, 27f2.25, 116f5.12

Israel(ites), 11, 12, 53, 54, 56f3.1, 58, 59, 61, 62, 63f3.2, 64f3.5, 65, 66, 67, 68, 72, 77, 81, 82, 84, 91, 93, 96, 105n39, 106, 107, 111, 137, 139, 144, 144n19, 155, 156–159, 158n65, 160, 162, 164, 167, 168, 170, 173, 174, 174n96, 178, 179, 180, 181, 190, 191, 192, 200, 210, 211, 212, 213, 216, 218, 219, 223

Jeroboam, 63f3.2

Jerusalem, 11, 53, 54, 62, 63f3.2, 64f3.5, 65, 66, 67, 74, 76, 78, 78f3.6, 92, 93, 94, 95, 98, 99, 103n25, 106, 108, 131, 160, 163, 208, 213f7.4

John the Baptist, 91–94, 91n6, 91f4.1, 106, 107, 122

Judas, 105n35, 139, 186n128

judgment, 10, 38, 39, 40, 42–44, 53, 54, 57, 58, 61, 62, 65, 68, 73, 75, 78–80, 83–86, 91, 91n6, 92–100, 100f4.4, 101– 107, 111, 119, 122, 124n24, 125, 127, 128, 132, 135, 136, 141, 153, 154, 156, 159, 161–164, 166, 168, 169, 179, 180, 183, 184, 192, 193, 197, 200–202, 202f7.3, 203, 203n24, 203n27, 204, 204n30, 205n37, 206, 208, 209, 209n52, 212, 215, 216, 219, 221–224

Julius, 48f2.50, 186n130

Jupiter, 88

Lydia, 117f5.16

Macedonia, 8f1.1, 21f2.14, 44, 117f5.16, 129f5.19

mask, 30f2.27, 31f2.28, 31f2.29, 32f2.30, 32f2.31, 34f2.34, 34f2.35, 35f2.36, 35f2.37

Medea, 36f2.38

Messiah, 9n36, 93, 94, 101, 103, 123, 126, 135, 136, 159, 169, 171, 179, 180, 181, 191, 192, 197, 198, 201, 203, 206, 207, 208, 210, 211, 215, 216, 223

Metropolis, 28f2.26

Minerva, 10f1.2, 19f2.11

mission(ary), 8, 9, 10, 11, 11n40, 55, 113f5.5, 120, 121, 123, 125, 127, 131, 134, 139, 168, 174, 178, 180, 186, 192, 195, 221

moral, 39, 41f2.41, 76, 147, 153, 160, 218

muse, 31f2.28, 31f2.29, 32f2.31, 35f2.36

mytholog(y)(ical), 2, 13, 16f2.6, 31f2.29, 46,

46n71, 158,158n66

nations, 11, 11n40, 62, 66, 67, 68, 99, 100, 101, 111, 122, 137, 138, 141n5, 144, 156, 157, 158, 163, 168, 174, 178, 179, 180, 180n108, 181, 190, 192

Nebuchadnezzar, 54, 178

Neopythagorean, 42f2.43

Nero, 46, 47, 186, 186f6.8, 187f6.10, 193

nexus, 2, 166, 167, 170, 190, 219

Odysseus, 28, 29, 154

Olymp(us)(ian), 14, 14f2.2, 17f2.9, 18f2.10, 25f2.22, 28, 40, 88, 90, 109, 110, 131, 138, 139, 140, 219

Ostia, 14f2.1, 32f.2.30

Pan, 30, 35f2.37, 63f3.3, 64f3.4

Panias, 63f3.3, 64f3.4

Papposilenus, 36f2.39

Parthenon, 21f2.13

parousia, 9, 9n36, 119, 120, 125, 127, 128n41, 130, 131, 132, 133, 134, 134n60, 136, 180, 183, 205, 207, 222

passion, 3, 4, 7, 40, 42, 43, 45, 47, 76, 97, 101, 101n16, 102, 146, 149, 150, 153, 154n55, 209, 218

Pergamum, 17f2.9, 23f2.18, 23f2.19, 28f2.26, 32f2.31

Perge, 33f2.33

Pericles, 21f2.13

Persephone, 26f2.24, 27f2.25

personal, 29, 49n87, 55, 56, 59, 76, 84, 106, 11, 127n34, 134, 150n41, 151n46, 159, 160, 161, 174n95, 175, 178, 182, 209, 217, 218, 219

philosoph(y)(er), 1, 2, 3, 6,

37, 39, 40, 40f2.40, 41f2.41, 41f2.42, 42, 42f2.43, 45, 46, 47, 47n74, 51, 70, 76, 77, 85, 110, 141n5, 143, 150n40, 160, 169n86, 190, 217
Pluto, 30, 37, 27f2.25
Pompey, 38
pontifex maximus, 49
Poseidon, 17f2.8, 24f2.20, 25f2.21, 26f2.23, 28, 29, 115f5.11
postexil(e)(ic), 5, 6, 65, 66, 67, 68, 94, 167, 179, 180
potter, 174, 175, 176f6.4, 177f6.5, 177f6.6
primary terms, 1n1, 200, 217, 218
punishment, 38, 51, 66, 73n95, 75, 79, 86, 89, 105n35, 110, 116f5.14, 163, 185, 188, 193, 200, 204
Qumran, 80f3.7, 125n27, 125n28, 126, 126n30, 127n40, 132n53, 155, 172n92, 182n112, 182n113, 203n22, 208
rational(ity), 39, 42, 50, 51, 54, 56, 60, 77, 141n5
resurrection, 10, 83, 90, 94, 120, 126, 129, 153, 216, 221
retribution, 2, 38, 75, 85, 86, 94, 104, 108, 153, 155, 155n57, 183, 184, 185, 193, 201, 203, 204, 205, 206, 206n42, 207, 215, 218, 219, 220, 223
Rome, 10, 11, 11n40, 13, 14f2.1, 27f2.25, 32f2.30, 33f2.33, 36f2.38, 36f2.39, 44, 46, 48f2.50, 49, 76, 88, 93, 101, 102, 102n18, 103, 108, 111, 124, 138, 146n25, 159,

186, 186n130, 188
sarcophagus, 14f2.1, 30f2.27, 36f2.38
Satan, 7, 17f2.9, 90n5
satyr, 36f2.39
Sepphoris, 34f2.34
Septuagint, 4, 69, 70, 71n81, 85, 110, 164, 182, 200, 201, 212, 217, 218
Serapis, 27f2.25
Sergius Paulus, 186
sin(ner), 2, 57, 58, 59, 61, 65, 68, 70, 72, 73, 77, 84, 90, 102, 105, 111, 124, 125, 125n28, 126, 126n32, 127, 139, 140, 144, 146, 147, 148, 149n36, 150, 150n39, 151, 154, 155, 155n57, 162, 166, 167, 168, 170, 172, 172n92, 173, 175, 178, 179, 180, 184, 192, 197, 197n6, 211, 216, 218, 219, 224
Sinai, 54, 58, 59, 66, 156, 157, 158, 164, 190, 210
slave, 34f2.35, 35f2.37, 36f2.38, 88, 118f5.17, 129f5.19
Smyrna, 35f2.36
Solomon, 63, 72n87, 144
soul, 42, 43, 45, 51, 121n14, 129, 154
sovereign(ty), 53, 60, 61, 66, 67, 79, 84, 97, 98, 125n27, 128, 138, 141, 141n7, 143, 144, 155, 157, 158, 162, 174, 175, 179, 181, 218, 223
Spain, 10
spirit, 4, 36f2.39, 39, 48, 50, 74, 81, 126, 142n9, 199, 209n52
Spirit, Holy, 92, 95, 171, 173, 209n52
spiritual, 90, 107, 130, 132,

147, 150, 155, 172n92, 208, 212
Stoic(ism), 42, 42n41, 43, 45, 47, 51, 74, 76, 85, 110, 141n6, 143, 147, 217
synagogue, 92, 123n22, 163, 165, 166n82, 190
Syracuse, 33f2.32
Taheb, 83, 86, 94, 95, 111
Targum, 163, 182, 182n115, 190, 204n34
Taxo, 74, 85, 99
theater, 28f2.26, 30, 30f2.27, 31f2.28, 31f2.29, 32f2.30, 32f2.31, 33f2.32, 33f2.33, 34f.2.34, 34f2.35, 35f2.36, 35f2.37, 112f5.3, 114f5.6
theology, 6, 11, 46, 57, 82, 86, 87, 93 96, 97, 109, 120, 121, 122, 129, 130, 130n47, 134, 137, 138, 139, 141n5, 144, 149, 152, 153, 154, 155, 163, 167, 172, 174n95, 191, 195, 197, 201, 201n21, 202f7.3, 206, 210, 215, 216, 217, 219, 220, 222, 223
theophany, 158, 201, 203, 203n27, 204, 205n37
Thessalonica, 8, 9, 23f2.19, 111, 112, 12f5.2, 112f5.3, 113f5.4, 113f5.5, 114f5.6, 114f5.7, 114f5.8, 115f5.10, 115f5.11, 116f5.12, 116f5.13, 117f5.15, 117f5.16, 118f5.18, 123, 125, 129, 129f5.19, 131, 134, 136
Theudas, 124, 186n128
Tiberius, 185f6.7
Timothy, 8, 111
Troy, 14f2.2, 15f2.4, 16f2.6,

16f2.7, 21f2.14, 29
ungodl(y)(iness), 50, 72n88,
79, 86, 139, 139n1, 140,
142, 144, 150, 154, 159,
169, 169n85, 171, 219, 220

Vespasian, 76
Vesuvius, Mount, 74
Via Egnatia, 8, 8f1.1, 112f5.2
zealot, 75
Zeus, 14, 14f2.2, 17f2.8, 17f2.9,

18f2.10, 20f2.12, 23f2.19,
25f2.22, 28, 28f2.26, 29,
30, 31f2.29, 45, 50,
64f3.4, 88, 115f5.11,
146, 192

www.ingramcontent.com/pod-product-compliance
Lightning Source LLC
Chambersburg PA
CBHW071241230426
43668CB00011B/1535